Common Goods

Governance in Europe
Series Editor: Gary Marks

Common Goods

Reinventing European and International Governance

EDITED BY ADRIENNE HÉRITIER

ROWMAN & LITTLEFIELD PUBLISHERS, INC.
Lanham • Boulder • New York • Oxford

ROWMAN & LITTLEFIELD PUBLISHERS, INC.

Published in the United States of America
by Rowman & Littlefield Publishers, Inc.
4720 Boston Way, Lanham, Maryland 20706
www.rowmanlittlefield.com

12 Hid's Copse Road, Cumnor Hill, Oxford OX2 9JJ, England

British Library Cataloguing in Publication Information Available

Library of Congress Cataloging-in-Publication Data

Common goods : reinventing European and international governance / edited by
Adrienne Héritier.
    p. cm. — (Governance in Europe)
  Includes bibliographical references and index.
  ISBN 0-7425-1700-4 (alk. paper) — ISBN 0-7425-1701-2 (pbk. : alk. paper)
    1. Welfare economics. 2. Public goods. 3. International cooperation. 4.
  International economic relations. 5. Europe—Economic integration. I. Windhoff-
  Héritier, Adrienne. II. Series.

HB846.5 .C66 2002
330.12'6—dc21

                                                                          2002017705

Printed in the United States of America

⊖™ The paper used in this publication meets the minimum requirements of American
National Standard for Information Sciences—Permanence of Paper for Printed Library
Materials, ANSI/NISO Z39.48-1992.

Contents

European Level

National Level

Privatizing Governance in the Financial Markets

Preface and Acknowledgments

The provision of common goods, defined by accessibility and (non)-rival consumption, has significantly changed with the dramatic increase in interaction across boundaries in the contemporary world. New institutional means of providing such goods, which extend across boundaries, have been developed in a variety of forms by a multiplicity of actors. These means of providing goods require highly coordinated activities among individual corporate actors who are pursuing similar and conflicting interests. In coordinating activities across boundaries—be they national boundaries or public/private boundaries—hierarchical means of intervention cannot be resorted to. Rather, the means have to be negotiated among relatively autonomous public and private actors. The plethora of new institutional means for providing common goods across boundaries is at the center of this volume. It constitutes the core research program of the political scientists at the Max Planck Project Group "Common Goods: Law, Politics and Economics" and has been subject to intensive discussions in the Project Group's discussion circles, workshops, and at conferences organized at the Project Group. This book is the result of these discussions.

I am indebted to many people who have lent important support in the production of this volume. The Max Planck Society has generously funded workshops and conferences as well as the research staff of the Project Group working on this topic. The participants of these conferences and workshops have made important critical comments on the manuscripts in this volume. The anonymous reviewing process has been a source of criticism and encouragement. Viola Stark-Woldring, together with Darrell Arnold, who has lent great support in copyediting the volume, was responsible for the editorial production of the book. Gabi Scherer has very efficiently helped organize the workshops and conferences in which the topic was discussed. I owe all of them a special debt of gratitude.

Introduction

Adrienne Héritier

The nature of collective-action problems that have to be solved in order to provide common goods changes as the interdependence of problems increases, both in Europe and worldwide. The institutional provision of common goods increasingly has to be organized across national boundaries, across levels of government, across sectors, and in collaboration of public and private actors.

This calls for new institutional and instrumental arrangements which challenge existing modes of governance and require the involvement of new actors in the provision of common goods. This means that hierarchical means of guidance, like those that can be applied within the classical nation-state, are harder to employ here, while negotiation and self-regulation that rely heavily on the interaction of independent public and private actors increase in importance. In turn, the new modes of governance have repercussions on the more traditional forms of governing within the nation-state, rendering some functions obsolete, transforming old ones, and requiring that new ones be adopted. The changes in governance also give rise to normative questions of political accountability and democratic legitimation.

The above issues are at the center of this volume: that is, questions related to the institutional provision of common goods under conditions of problem interdependence in a multi-arena context; questions related to the increasing involvement of private actors in governance; and questions related to the implications of these new modes of governance for nation-states. Common goods may be defined in two ways: on the one hand, economic analysis defines them in terms of objective properties (Samuelson 1954; Cornes and Sandler 1996). On the other hand, they may be defined in reference to institutions and political processes. In the first instance, common goods are viewed as goods by virtue of properties inherent in the good as such, namely, accessibility, and the non-rivalry of consumption. Accessibility means that the good is available to everyone; non-rivalry means that the consumption of the good by one individual does not reduce the possibilities for consumption by other individuals. There are three types of common goods, depending on which of these properties they have: (1) goods characterized by accessibility and non-rivalry are called "public goods"; (2) goods characterized by accessibility and rival consumption, where the consumption by one individual implies that others will have less at their disposal, are called "common pool resources" (Ostrom 1990); and finally (3) goods to which access can be limited and consumption is rival are called "club goods" or "toll goods" (Ostrom 1990). In accord with the economic analysis, the term "common good" applies to all three types of goods: public goods, common pool resources, and club/toll goods.

The institutional and political perspective, on the other hand, questions whether the properties of accessibility and non-rivalry are inherent properties of a good as such. Proponents of this perspective point out that accessibility may depend on political and normative options, and the existence and socially embedded use of a technology. In the first case, common goods are understood as such because the accessibility to them and the non-rival consumption of them are considered desirable from a political and legal perspective. So, things such as health services or general education are considered common goods. In the second case, free access is linked to physical attributes of the good or the lack of a technology that would make exclusion possible; in other words, there is free access because property rights cannot be assigned (Malkin and Wildavsky 1991, 355ff.).

But regardless of whether common goods are defined in terms of their inherent characteristics or in terms of institutional and political goals, in each case we are confronted with problems of generating incentives to produce and provide these goods in institutions. If access to the good cannot be controlled, there are no motives for individuals to produce and provide the good on the market. This being the case, it was traditionally considered necessary that the state should produce and provide these goods; or if the goods are provided by nature, it was viewed as necessary that the government should protect them from depletion with specific institutional arrangements. However, more recently it has been convincingly argued that it is not necessary for the state to secure the provision of common goods; they can also be provided by communal organizations and private actors, without centralized government (Ostrom 1990).

Under the specific conditions of problem interdependence across political boundaries, the institutional provision of common goods is faced with new challenges.[1] The origin and scope of the impact of a particular problem do not coincide with the boundaries of a political unit. Rather, the source of a problem lies in one political unit (say, political unit A), whereas the impact of the problem is felt in another political unit (say, political unit B). Hence, in order to deal with this type of interdependent problem, the cooperation between the two political units is necessary: if B is not to bear the burden of the negative impacts of the problem caused by A, then A and B must cooperate. With the enormous increase in international communication, trade, and mobility, rendered possible by modern technologies and the worldwide liberalization of economies, problems of interdependence have multiplied and fundamentally changed. In order to tackle these problems and to provide for common goods under conditions of internationalization, the provision of common goods has to be reconsidered. The question now to be asked is which institutional arrangements are appropriate for providing the common goods under these conditions. In other words, which modes of multilevel and multi-arena government and governance have emerged to deal with the provision of common goods in this changed context of cross-boundary problem interdependence?

Multilevel government refers to the interaction of public actors vertically across multiple levels of government. The interaction is needed in order to come to a political decision (joint decision-making—Scharpf 2000). Thus member states in the European Council of Ministers have to accept draft legislation on the basis of unanimity or a qualified majority if such proposed legislation is to become law. They then have to implement it. Multi-arena government—in the horizontal dimension—refers to the fact that the collaboration between different decision-making arenas may be necessary to arrive at a decision: examples of this include the co-decision procedure of the Council of Ministers and the European Parliament.

As opposed to a wider notion of governance, which consists of all conceivable notions of government (see Knill and Lehmkuhl in this volume), a stricter notion of governance implies that private actors are involved in decision-making in order to provide common goods and that nonhierarchical means of guidance are employed (Mayntz in this volume). Government, by contrast, indicates that only public actors are involved and that hierarchical steering can be used. Where there is governance, private actors may be independently engaged in self-regulation, or a regulatory task may have been delegated to them by a public authority, or they may be regulating jointly with a public actor. This interaction may occur across levels (vertically) or across arenas (horizontally).

The interaction between actors at different levels and across arenas reveals different decision-making styles (Scharpf 2000). In the case of spontaneous coordination/mutual adjustment, no institutionalized interaction takes place, but the individual actors anticipate the reaction of the other involved actors, and they adjust their behavior accordingly. In the case of joint decision-making, all the independent actors involved from different levels and arenas engage in negotiation processes, and they have to come to a consensual decision. In a more deeply institutionalized setting, such as the Council of Ministers in the European Union, the possibility of reaching a majority decision may be provided for.

If private actors are engaged in cross-level and cross-arena decision-making to provide common goods under conditions of problem interdependence, the decision styles applied depend on the particular actor setting. If private actors are engaged in self-regulation, they will negotiate agreements among independent private actors. If private actors are engaged in co-regulation with public actors, the shadow of hierarchy always looms. Formally, public actors cannot negotiate on an equal standing with private actors. In practice, however, in view of the resources available to private actors, regulatory agreements are frequently negotiated between public and private actors. In this, however, the ultimate possibility for hierarchical intervention by public actors is one of their important resources.

The involvement of private actors is discussed here in connection with policy formulation, rather than in connection with the policy-making phase of implementation. Precisely because policy-making has traditionally been the exclusive role of public actors, the role of private actors here is particularly interesting and surprising. By contrast, private actors—besides administrative actors—have always played an important role in policy implementation. One important argument for involving private actors in policy formulation is that if they have a role in shaping policy targets and instruments, they will have increased incentives to engage in implementation.

If it is true that providing common goods across political, administrative, and sectoral boundaries in order to deal with interdependent problems has become more frequent, then the following question arises: namely, what are the implications for the more traditional forms of governing at the national and the supranational European levels? There are many indications that the tasks traditionally performed by nation-states and European bodies will not become completely obsolete as state functions, but will very likely be transformed, instead. In other words, new governance is not a zero-sum game; rather, it is a positive-sum game that may be compared to two connecting pipes. The water rises in both arms of the pipes: the private and the public. Why would that be so? Many modes for providing common goods need a framework in which to operate; and these frameworks are established by public decision-making bodies. Frequently public actors delegate tasks to private actors, but maintain the possibility of stepping in and taking over the functions should private actors not perform well. Further, the new modes of operation may be challenged, not for their problem-solving capacity, but for the possibility of holding private actors accountable for their actions and for related problems of legal certainty and democratic legitimation.

The contributions in this volume all deal with the problems of providing common goods across boundaries and the problems related to the involvement of private actors. But they approach these problems from different angles and accentuate different aspects of them. The first section discusses the notion of common goods or collective goods and links specific properties of goods to the interest constellations of actors engaged in the institutional provision of goods (Mayntz, Ostrom, Holzinger). The second section focuses on the role of private actors in the provision of common goods on an international scale and the implications of this for public actors (Knill and Lehmkuhl, Farrell, Cutler, Börzel). The third section investigates the role of private actors in providing common goods in the European context and scrutinizes the consequences for nation-states and the implications for policies (Héritier, Moral Soriano). The fourth section looks into the typical features of national regulatory regimes which are responsible for controlling the private actors who are engaged in providing common goods; it discusses their particular role in the newly altered administrative procedures and discusses the normative/legal implications of private actors who are engaged in policy-making (Böllhoff, Peters). Finally, the fifth section analyzes a particular aspect of private actors' governance, namely, the role of rating agencies in the financial markets (Sinclair, Kerwer, Strulik).

In the first section, where the concept of common goods is linked to particular institutional provision and underlying interest constellations of the involved actors, Renate Mayntz shows that the notion of common goods can be situated in the debate on general welfare or the *bonum commune*, which is based on different theoretical traditions. In the utilitarian tradition, the notion of public welfare is the aggregation of individual utilities; in the tradition of systems theory (Parsons 1951), it emphasizes the well-being of society in its entirety, that is, the viability of the system as such; and finally, in a view prevalent in some more recent research, there is the notion of common goods—that is, public goods, common pool resources, and club/toll goods—based on a distinction between public and private goods and defined in terms of accessibility and the rivalry of consumption. Mayntz argues that the last notion of common goods— as opposed to the general welfare notion and the viable system theoretic notion—is interaction- and policy-oriented. Thereby it immediately links up with questions of governance, defined by Mayntz as a "type of regulation typical of the cooperative state, where state and non-state actors participate in mixed public/private policy networks" (21) and differing from hierarchy. This points to the need for more information about the conditions under which horizontal forms of coordination succeed in problem solving. Actor-centered institutionalism (Mayntz and Scharpf 1995), which calls attention to actor constellations, with their particular distribution of resources and interest constellations (prisoner's dilemma, battle of the sexes), and actors' orientations, with their normative beliefs and particular interaction-orientation (cooperative, competitive, hostile), may account for the outcome of collective-action attempts. Additionally, by analytically distinguishing between problem generation, problem impact, and problem coping, it is possible to clarify the differing scopes of the respective activities which then play an important role in dealing with collective-action problems under conditions of problem interdependence on a global scale and across multiple arenas.

Among the possible concepts of the *bonum commune*, Elinor Ostrom focuses on public goods, that is, those collective-action problems where consumption by one person does not reduce the amount of the good available to others, and common pool resources, where, by contrast, there is rival consumption. Both have difficulties in excluding those who do not contribute to providing a collective benefit. And for both, particular aspects of the production and appropriation functions raise specific collective-action problems. In the production of a collective good, "acceleration" or "deceleration" affect the contribution to the collective good. When there is deceleration, the marginal benefits decrease as more individuals contribute, whereas when there is acceleration, they increase as more individuals contribute. Similarly, "step levels" may play a crucial role in bringing about an output; until this level is reached, it is not possible to take advantage of the contributions of others by free riding. Institutional solutions in the form of "sharing formulas" can ensure that the input is sufficient to reach this point. With respect to the allocation of benefits, in the case of a nondivisible, universal public good, such as peace and stability, each individual benefits in a similar way without reducing the benefits to others. In the case of common pool resources, with accessibility and rival consumption, Ostrom shows that there is a huge variety of allocation possibilities: in accord with the value of assets held, the seniority of claims, the spatial or temporal formula, and other factors. Hence, raising the question about the nature of common goods is tantamount to raising the question about their institutional provision.

Using the same economic concept of common goods, Katharina Holzinger focuses on the specific properties of goods and the social context in which they are provided. The properties of a good, and in many cases the attributes of a social situation in which a good is provided, influence the incentive structure of the actors involved. They will determine whether actors find themselves in a dilemma situation or in a different type of strategic constellation. The interest constellation, in turn, influences the type of institutional solution found for the problem at hand. Holzinger applies her theoretical argument to the case of European transboundary emission regulation in environmental policy, investigating the conditions under which a race to the bottom or a race to the top will ensue. By applying a series of matrix games and varying the conditions of homogenous or heterogenous preferences, as well as the type of standard used, and the prevailing trade regime, she concludes that the variation of the factors leads to four different strategic constellations: a prisoner's dilemma, an assurance game, a weak harmony game, and a pure harmony game. Each implies different opportunities for institutional solutions to the problem of providing common goods.

While the contributions of Renate Mayntz, Elinor Ostrom, and Katharina Holzinger place a particular emphasis on the nature of common goods and the implications of this for the institutional mode used to provide these goods, the following contributions shift the emphasis to the nature of the actors participating in making the institutional arrangements for the provision of common goods. First, this question is treated in reference to issues at the international level (Knill and Lehmkuhl, Farrell, Cutler, Börzel). Knill and Lehmkuhl start out by stressing that governance capacity in general hinges upon three factors: the congruence of the scope of the problem and the scope of the regulatory structure; the problem type (coordination problems, agreement/ redistribution problems and defection/free riding problems), which gives rise to specific interest constellations; and finally the institutional context. Each of these has different effects: a congruence of scope enhances governance capacity and defection problems invite free riding by public and private actors alike. From an institutional perspective, the public actors' potential for regulatory adjustment to new challenges in providing common goods depends on the existing formal and factual veto points in the decision-making process; for private actors, their organizational structure and the rules in their relevant decision-making arenas determine their capacity to adjust. Depending on the relative governance capacity—defined by the congruence of the problem scope and regulatory scope, the type of problem, and the institutional context—they derive four ideal types of governance involving different forms of interaction between public and private actors: (1) interventionist regulation, where public actors strongly intervene to provide common goods; (2) regulated self-regulation, where public and private actors both have a strong governance capacity, but public authorities remain ultimately responsible for providing the good in question; (3) private self-regulation, where public actors can no longer intervene in private self-regulation; and finally, they propose an additional type of public intervention, characterized as (4) "interfering intervention." In this form, neither public nor private actors have a high governance capacity: private actors are not interested in being regulated in the first place, and public actors' interference is restricted to "pin-pricks" that disturb private activities without being able to steer them. Discussing various forms of Internet regulation, the authors show that internationalization gives rise to different paths of transition from one type of public-private regulation to another. In the regulation of domain names, they identify a transition from interventionist to regulated self-regulation; in the protection of copyrights, they see a change from interventionist regulation to private self-regulation; and finally, in Internet content regulation, they note a transformation from interventionist regulation to interfering regulation.

In his contribution, Henry Farrell analyzes a novel mode of "regulated private self-regulation" (in Knill and Lehmkuhl's terms), which was developed to solve a problem of international problem interdependence, namely, data protection on the Internet. He shows that globalization problems that spill over state borders can be solved by negotiating new solutions. Focusing on the political process in which the institutional solution was developed, he investigates the bargaining process between the European Union (EU) and the United States in what is known as the "Safe Harbor" arrangement on data protection and privacy. He accounts for the outcome of the agreement by conceptualizing the negotiations in terms of three interlinked games between the European Commission (hereafter, the Commission), the European Parliament, the member states, the data protection commissioners, the U.S. administration, businesses in the United States, and consumer organizations in the United States. In the first game, the United States and the EU were headed for collision in a "chicken game." The collision was avoided by a complex process of compromise building in which the EU had a structural advantage—already having legislation in place that required an adequate standard for third countries. It additionally drew bargaining strengths from the pressure of the member states within the EU. The EU-U.S. negotiations, in turn, had an important impact upon the second game, the U.S. domestic game. It helped U.S. privacy advocates push business to acquiesce to a self-regulatory proposal. The third decision-making game, within the EU, was also connected with the other two decision-making arenas. Institutional requirements of the existing data protection directive strengthened the Commission's position in dealing with the United States. And vice versa: the negotiated result with the United States helped the Commission to defend its stance in the European Parliament. The analysis shows that linked bargaining arenas under conditions of problem interdependence may lead to a level of regulation in providing a common good which runs counter to the expectation of a "race to the bottom."

The political implications of private self-regulation in the provision of common goods are investigated in Claire Cutler's article, too. She, however, focuses on the distributional outcomes and the problems of the political accountability and democratic legitimacy of private self-regulation in the case of the modern law merchant. She identifies the general increase in the significance of private governance, and of juridification; she also looks into the pluralism of the regulatory forms of the political economy. In discussing the developments of the modern law merchant in relation to the universalistic private system of law, she argues that creating law and resolving disputes have long been governed by pluralist public/private institutions and that public authorities have offered wide discretion to private international commercial arbitrators. She argues that contemporary private governance structures do not constitute a reversion to the medieval period when merchants regulated international private law privately through merchant associations and guilds; rather, the present private government structures are uniquely embedded in the global political economy and are responsive to its transformations: the replacement of the welfare state by the "competition state," the transnationalization of capital, and the advent of flexible accumulation relying on soft, ad hoc law. The problems of political accountability and the democratic legitimation of the private modes of governance are thereby magnified.

While most of the contributions to this governance discussion focus on the aspects of policy formulation that are at play in drawing up institutional solutions to the problems of providing common goods at the international level, Tanja Börzel looks at questions of policy implementation. She raises the question of the role of state and non-state actors in complying with international agreements. She questions the widespread claim that nation-states are dwindling in importance as global governance increases in importance. She defines compliance as the "rule-consistent behavior of those actors, to whom a rule is formally addressed and whose behavior is targeted by the rule" (160). She also distinguishes between the outputs, outcomes, and impacts by which compliance can be measured. In order to study the behavior of private actors in complying with rules, she distinguishes between for-profit economic actors, on the one hand, and not-for-profit societal actors, on the other. Against the background of various theories that distinguish between the level of analysis and three underlying logics of action (the logic of consequentialism versus logic of appropriateness and a linking of the two), she arrives at a range of hypotheses accounting for compliance. Assuming a mismatch between existing national policies and the requirements of international treaties, Börzel claims that state compliance with international rules is more likely if a hegemonic state provides incentives for compliance, if monitoring mechanisms are elaborated, and if there are autonomous international institutions involved in settling disputes; compliance is also more likely if there is a low number of domestic veto players, if transnational networks mobilize pressure, and if the required rules are considered part of the general legal system. Similarly, compliance will be facilitated if addressees and target actors participate in the formulation of the rules, if the relevant rules are institutionalized at an international level, if norm-violators are implicated in a reasoned discourse about the (in)appropriateness of their behavior, and if the state has the resources to ensure compliance, or has access to outside resources. Most of the formulated hypotheses are complementary to each other, and only a few are mutually exclusive. Only empirical testing can determine which ones are most powerful.

In the next section, the focus shifts from the international to the European context, emphasizing new modes of governance within the European Union. I investigate two new modes of governance that have been strongly advocated in recent years: "benchmarking" and "voluntary accords." Both seek to avoid legislation, which is viewed as a cumbersome policy-making path, and they rely upon private actors in policy formulation. I develop the underlying rationale, pointing out the advantages of these new modes of governance: they are considered to allow speedier decision-making and to cause less political opposition, particularly when compared to the multilevel governmental decision processes of public actors, which are linked with a strong need for consensus; they are also regarded as more flexible, as having ready access to expertise and practical implementation knowledge; and because the implementers also participate in the formulation of the policy, those implementers are thought to be committed to carrying it out. In short, the political-institutional and instrumental capacities of these forms of governance are considered to be superior to the capacities of legislation. A high political-institutional capacity exists when those who bear the costs of regulation are very willing to participate in the decision-making process and to support politically the development of such modes of governance; high instrumental capacity exists when the actors involved have strong incentives to implement a decision on a new mode of governance and the instrument used has the capacity to contribute to solving the problem at hand. In the empirical analysis, I investigate European policy measures over the last fifteen-month period to identify the quantitative importance and nature of the new type of governance and then to validate the claims about institutional and instrumental capacity. The results show that not many measures can be classified as new modes of governance as described above and that most of the new modes that do exist are to be found in environmental and social policy. With respect to institutional capacity, the research shows that while measures proposed by new modes of governance are faster than measures decided via legislation, the political decision-making process is lengthier and more contested than expected: member states and private actors often engage in long negotiations before they can agree on targets. Further, the new modes of governance often need an element of "hierarchy" in order to come about in the first place: that is, they are initiated by the Commission; or when private actors lag behind in decision-making, a legislative procedure is invoked. With respect to instrumental capacity, the new modes are linked to "hierarchy" too; that is, they are backed up by the threat of legislation or public intervention when they perform unsatisfactorily.

Another form of new governance is at the center of the two contributions that examine the implications of the liberalization of the formerly state-owned network industries that provide common goods in the form of utilities. Leonor Moral Soriano addresses the normative-legal implications of this new mode of governance, raising the question of the role of public missions in the provision of the network infrastructure and services. What role has the European Court of Justice (ECJ) played by taking issue with the question of the public mission of network utilities under conditions of liberalization? Can equal access, affordable prices, and the security of these services be guaranteed under conditions of liberalization? Moral Soriano argues that there is a conflict of interest between the Commission, which seeks to abolish public monopolies, viewing them as an impediment to European free trade and competition rules, and member states, which wish to maintain their discretionary powers to intervene in their national economies to secure public-interest services. Hence she scrutinizes how the ECJ deals with the conflict between free competition and the free movement of goods and services and the public mission assigned to public monopolies and privileged undertakings. She elaborates the tension enshrined in Article 86, which establishes a delicate balance between the presumption that public monopolies and privileged undertakings are legal because they provide for a common good, on the one hand, and the presumption that monopolies are illegal because they restrict competition, on the other. The outcome of the balance is that the Court backs the discretionary powers of member states to grant special or exclusive rights to undertakings that provide common goods, and it backs the quasi-legislative powers of the Commission (Article 86[3]) in competition policy. The messages of the Court in various cases (Höfner, ERT, Merci, Corbeau, Almelo, Gas and Electricity Monopoly Case) are that public monopolies and privileged undertakings are prima facie contrary to European competition rules, unless they can be justified as providing a service in the public interest.

In the next section, moving to the national level of liberalized network industries, Dominik Böllhoff analyzes the formation of new regulatory regimes, which have been created to regulate the newly liberalized industries with two purposes: namely, to create and maintain markets; and to correct the negative external effects of markets. These regulatory functions can be provided in the context of various institutional arrangements: through regulation by ministries, through administrative agencies, through competition authorities, through the self-regulation of the industry, or through independent regulatory agencies. The question addressed by Böllhoff is why one country opts for one specific institutional design and another for a different one. The author bases his argument on diffusion theory and historical institutionalism, and proceeds to account for the generation of particular regulatory structures in the telecommunications branch in both Great Britain and Germany. He argues that at the macro-organizational level, in the overall regulatory structures, diffusion prevails, while at the micro-organizational—internal, administrative—level, there is institutional path-dependency.

Guy Peters's contribution focuses on a specific form of intraorganizational reform for private actors: contracting out public services to private actors as a mode of reform for the public sector. A political motive for contracting services out to the private sector has been to make the state "look smaller." However, he points out that the process may work the other way around: that is, by co-opting a significant number of private actors, the latter are induced to shape their services to the availability of public funds. He also shows that shaping contracts between public and private actors in such a way as to preserve the advantages of the flexibility of private actors while at the same time preventing their "shirking" is very difficult. Likewise, different policy areas are more or less amenable to contracting. He concludes that it is necessary to examine closely the conditions in which a contract is made and to shape the contract to those conditions.

In the last section of the book, the analysis turns to a sector characterized by a particularly powerful dynamics of internationalization, the financial services. It deals with the role of private actors in offering information on activities in this sector, thereby providing a common good. Specifically, private actors strive to increase transparency and to reduce risk in the application of financial instruments. Timothy Sinclair analyzes how private institutions acquired the right to legitimately provide common goods, and he argues that the new global finance, epitomized by the major American bond rating agencies, provides a significant example of this development. He considers how specialized forms of intelligence-gathering and judgment-determination seem increasingly important as sources of governance in this era of financial market volatility. As embedded knowledge networks, rating agencies fundamentally alter the balance of public and private influence on policy. From a systemic-risk perspective Torsten Strulik argues that credit rating agencies, based on expertise and reputation, contribute to coordinating the cooperative work of economic actors and to supporting the efficiency of markets. The supervisory-legal application of rating underlies the relevance of mixed public-private regulatory regimes, which increasingly make use of the market actors' expertise and proximity to problems. He also argues that rating institutions' activities can best be understood as management of and by complexity, giving rise to inevitable new uncertainties themselves. Dieter Kerwer focuses on the accountability problematic of rating agencies. Within the context of the transformation of global governance structures brought about by the global integration of financial markets, the commercial credit rating agencies have established themselves as influential gatekeepers of the international credit market. One problem with this form of intermediation is that when there are errors, rating agencies can do considerable damage to borrowers and investors alike. Still, it is very difficult to hold rating agencies accountable. The standards of creditworthiness established by the rating agencies are difficult to challenge because, on the one hand, they are based on neutral expertise, yet, on the other, they are subject to mandatory enforcement by financial market regulation. The resulting compliance without the complementary right to complain substantially reduces the possibilities for learning. Hence the preconditions and institutional remedies for accountability problems in the case of global governance by private intermediary organizations are preeminent.

Note

1. Of course, there are many common goods which are provided within the boundaries of a political entity, that is, where the scope of problem source and regulatory competencies are congruent. Then there is no need for large-scale provision across boundaries. Providing them in smaller units may be much more preferable (Low et al. 2001).

12   *Adrienne Héritier*

References

Cornes, R., and T. Sandler. 1996. *The Theory of Externalities, Public Goods, and Club Goods*. 2d ed. Cambridge: Cambridge University Press.
Low, B., E. Ostrom, C. Simon, and J. Wilson. 2001. Redundancy: How Does It Influence the Management of Natural Resources? In Navigating Nature's Dynamics: Responding to Change in Socio-Ecological Systems, ed. F. Berkes, C. Folke, and J. Colding. Cambridge: Cambridge University Press.
Malkin, J., and A. Wildavsky. 1991. Why the Traditional Distinction between Public and Private Goods Should Be Abandoned. Journal of Theoretical Politics 3 (4): 355-78.
Mayntz, R., and F. W. Scharpf. 1995. Steuerung und Selbstorganisation in staatsnahen Sektoren. In Gesellschaftliche Selbtsregulierung und politische Steuerung, ed. R. Mayntz, and F. W. Scharpf. Frankfurt am Main: Campus.
Ostrom, E. 1990. Governing the Commons: The Evolution of Institutions for Collective Action. Cambridge: Cambridge University Press.
Parsons, T. 1951. *The Social System*. Glencoe, Ill.: Free Press.
Samuelson, P. A. 1954. The Pure Theory of Public Expenditure. *Review of Economics and Statistics* 36: 387-89.
Scharpf, F. W. 2000. Notes toward a Theory of Multilevel Governing in Europe. MPIfG Discussion Paper 2000/5.

Part 1

Common Goods

1

Common Goods and Governance

Renate Mayntz

All of the major social sciences share an interest in the preconditions of reaching a socially relevant end or goal-state: in economics it may be wealth, in macrosociology social integration, and in political science it is public welfare or *Gemeinwohl*, the *bonum commune* of old. These various dependent variables are not identical. Moreover, each discipline pays attention to a different set of factors or independent variables. Governance is one such variable; it plays a focal role in political science approaches dealing with the production of public welfare or *Gemeinwohl*. This is the causal nexus I shall take as the starting point for the following analytical considerations.

In everyday parlance, public welfare or *Gemeinwohl* is a very diffuse concept needing specification before questions relating to its preconditions can be precisely formulated. I shall argue that there are at least three distinct theoretical traditions which lead to three different, if partly interrelated, definitions of the *bonum commune*. One of these is connected with the concept of common goods. This line of thinking is today popular in political science, though it goes back to the arguments of economists trying to specify which goods can be supplied by the market, and which goods it is unlikely to supply. In present-day welfare economics, we find a second, formal definition of public welfare as the (quantitatively measurable) sum of utilities achieved—or received—by the individual members of a "public." This definition of the *bonum commune* is in turn to be distinguished from a sociological definition of welfare that refers not to individuals but to the social system as such; here the criterion is system viability (system survival, ultrastability). The well-being of the system members ultimately rests on the viability of the system, but what serves the latter does not eo ipso maximize aggregate individual utility.

These three different versions of what "public welfare" or the *bonum commune* might refer to—the achievement of "common goods," the maximization of aggregate individual utility, or system viability—have common roots in classical social philosophy. It was only later, when the substance of the *bonum commune* was no longer felt to be self-evident and hence not in need of definition, that social scientists of different disciplinary orientations made conscious efforts to spell it out and define it more stringently. In the social philosophy of Plato, the philosopher king knows what is just and lies in the public interest.[1] Aristotle's good monarch also knows what lies in the public interest, and he acts so as to serve it; the tyrant, in contrast, only seeks his own advantage. Plato as well as Aristotle distinguished between the (selfish) orientation towards one's own and the orientation towards the interest of the community. However, they and later political theorists following the classical tradition envisaged no contradiction between individual interest and public interest, because the well-being of the social whole, the polis, was identified with the well-being of its citizens. It was, as Kaufmann points out, the liberal critique of the absolutist state that first led to define public welfare and individual welfare in different terms. The well-being of the polity was seen to rest on the achievement of inner order and external security, characteristics that clearly refer to the whole, the system. External security and inner order provided the framework for the individual pursuit of happiness, but are not identical with the satisfaction of individual needs. In spite of this incipient conceptual differentiation, no contradiction was seen between the maximization of individual happiness and the public interest (Kaufmann 1994, 358). In the economic theory of Adam Smith, they were even seen to be positively linked by an invisible hand, the assumption being that public well-being, defined as a nation's wealth, resulted automatically from the individual pursuit of selfish goals. This is still the assumption underlying the public welfare concept of modern welfare economics. Modern political discourse, in contrast, became framed in terms of the functions that need to be fulfilled in the interest of the nation-state (*Staatsfunktionen*). In sociological systems theory, which similarly adopts a "holistic" approach to the definition of public welfare, the state functions of political theory became the function of the political subsystem and thus one, if only one, of the functional prerequisites of system viability.

Today we are faced with the widespread conviction that the common interest is an elusive construct. What "public welfare" means in concrete terms cannot be established objectively, so the argument goes, but depends on variable (contextualized) historical processes of (subjective) definition—mere social conventions whose substance changes with the procedures regulating the process of opinion formation. Quite in contrast to this conviction, both welfare economics and sociological systems theory claim to offer substantive and objective definitions of the *bonum commune*, the welfare of all and/or of the whole. The notion of common goods is less sweeping, referring to a plurality of different goods to be sought, but it still claims to be based on objective criteria. I shall briefly outline these three "objectivizing" approaches, emphasizing the differences between them rather than what sets all of them off from the constructivist conviction.

Public welfare as originally defined in welfare economics consists of the sum total of the utilities achieved, or received, by the individual members of the public in question—the aggregate utility for short. There are several difficulties with such a conception, which have been variously addressed. Utility is necessarily a one-dimensional concept, otherwise individual utilities could not be added up. Now it would be easy if utility could be defined in terms of money, but obviously not all individually cherished values can be measured in terms of money. This also speaks against the operationalization of public welfare as the sum of all monetary transactions, i.e., GNP (Albert 1998). But even if it were possible to assign a fixed abstract utility to different kinds of goods, the aggregation of individual utilities to form a measurable public welfare would still face the problem that individual preference orders differ, and hence also the relative value a given good has for different individuals. Even money, and hence the subjective value of a given amount of it, does not have the same utility for all individuals. This problem stimulated attempts in the theory of social choice to develop an algorithm that takes different preferences into account (Albert 1998, 13), but apparently an algorithm transforming different individual preferences into a logically consistent collective preference order cannot be defined (Scharpf 1994, 385-86). Another problem with the concept of public welfare as aggregate utility lies in its disregard for the distributive dimension, i.e., the equal or unequal distribution of the sum total of realized utilities among the members of the "public." To take the distributive dimension into account, Amartya Sen has developed a measure of poverty to enter into the calculation of aggregate utility, by which irrespective of subjective preferences, goods given to the poor produce a higher utility than goods given to the rich (Gaertner 1998).

But a just distribution of valued goods is not all there is to public welfare. Even John Rawls has recognized that a "viable human community" requires more than distributive justice, mentioning for instance coordination, efficiency, and stability (Rawls 1972, 6). This observation points to what is probably the crucial weakness of this particular way of defining public welfare: by taking individual preferences as reference point, it neglects the social value, the systemic functionality or disfunctionality of given preferences. Reckless driving, drug consumption, and child abuse can be strong individual satisfactions, but they surely detract from, rather than add to, what commonly passes as public welfare. If the external effects of individual need satisfaction were taken into account, this would even hold for public welfare as the sum of individual satisfactions. The different social value of individual satisfactions calls for different yardsticks to measure individual and collective utility, respectively. What links individual interests and public welfare is a causal relationship, not an algorithm aggregating the former to the latter.

To counter this critique, individual preferences are sometimes taken to refer not to the satisfaction of needs that individuals presently feel, but to their "enlightened self-interest"—their long-term, rationally considered interests. In this way the possibility of a conflict between individual interests and public welfare is ruled out—by definition, as it were. But individual interests that are already disciplined by taking the long-term collective consequences of their possible satisfaction into account are mere theoretical attributions. It is only in normative conceptions of a rational societal discourse à la Rawls or Habermas that this version of Kant's categorical imperative can be assumed to guide observable behavior.

If the welfare economics approach to defining public welfare neglects the system level in so doing and concentrates on the individual, the reverse is true of system theoretic approaches. The most impressive attempt to conceptualize what might be called the well-being of the social whole, or systems rationality, in contrast to individual rationality, can probably be found in the work of Talcott Parsons (1951; 1956). Starting from the identification of various ways leading to the dissolution and ultimate disappearance of a social system (i.e., biological death or total apathy of its members, the war of all against all, or absorption into another system), Parsons developed his theory of the functional prerequisites of system stability, or the survival of a social system as a functioning whole. Having identified four basic problems any social system—or action system in his own terminology—must solve, Parsons specified four functions that must be fulfilled to this end: adaptation, goal attainment, integration, and latent pattern maintenance. It might seem possible to use this scheme of system imperatives as a measuring device of system viability, asking whether and to what extent the four functions are fulfilled by the institutions of a given society. This, however, is impossible because we can neither measure directly different degrees of adaptation, integration, etc., nor can we infer the fulfillment of system functions from the existence of observable social institutions. Because of the fact of widespread equi-functionality, there exists no fixed relationship between social form and function, so that we cannot infer the fulfillment (or nonfulfillment) of a given function from the existence (or nonexistence) of a given institution, or structural characteristic of a social system. Nor does Parsons offer operationalizations, and hence measuring sticks for the four system functions, making it impossible to differentiate directly between varying degrees of fulfillment. Short of observable processes of system disintegration, it is thus impossible in the framework of Parsonian theory to conclude that a given society is less viable than another one.

According to Parsons's view of social evolution, societal subsystems arise in the process of historical development and specialize in the fulfillment of one of the system functions, leading to higher overall efficiency. The economy, for instance, serves the function of adaptation, and the political subsystem, the function of goal attainment. Parsons did not believe in the empirical existence of a tendency inherent in all social systems to fulfill the four functional imperatives, but he was interested in the conditions under which this would be true. For Parsons the crucial precondition rests in the integration of the personality system (of system members) with the values and norms of the society's cultural system. The values and norms of the cultural system shape the social roles which system members learn to adopt in the process of socialization. If socialization is successful, role norms become internalized, which means that they are transformed into subjective need dispositions. Where this does not succeed completely, social control comes in as a supplementary mechanism that guarantees conformity by rewarding compliance with, and sanctioning deviation from, normative expectations. If the values and norms of the cultural system embody the requirements of system viability, and if socialization is successful, the individual members of a social system consequently have no needs that would conflict with the needs of system viability; the pursuit of presumably private goals unwittingly serves the fulfillment of system needs. Socialization plus social control is Parsons version of Adam Smith's "invisible hand"—a version that is less rationalistic, but otherwise curiously similar to the "enlightened self-interest" solution used in welfare economics to avoid the problem of potentially conflicting private and public interests.

The attempts of welfare economics and of systems theory to establish what constitutes public welfare are both one-dimensional in that they neglect the qualitative difference and hence the possibility of a conflict between individual (private) and collective (public) interests. The two approaches differ only insofar as in welfare economics, the satisfaction of individual desires is identified with the satisfaction of system needs, while in Parsonian systems theory individual needs are derived from, and therefore in accord with, system needs. And yet conflicts between the satisfaction of individual and of system needs obviously do exist; for instance, a high innovation rate may be needed to secure long-term system viability, but this may demand that sacrifices in the maximization of short-term individual utilities are made. Both of the approaches treated so far thus define away a major practical and theoretical question, i.e., how private and public interests are interrelated, how they interact, and how it is possible to solve conflicts between them. In contrast, the third approach to the definition of public welfare via the concept of common goods allows such questions to be tackled because it starts from the distinction between private and public interests. Another advantage is that common goods are defined at a lower level of generality than a comprehensive concept of "public welfare" which refers to a systemwide end-state. Of course public welfare implies the achievement of common goods, and it could in fact even be so defined, i.e., as a system state in which all important common goods are being supplied. But it is conceptually much easier to identify (and measure the achievement of) a single concrete "good" than an overall state of public welfare defined at the system level.

Though often treated as a synonym of "public goods," the term "common goods" is also used in a wider sense as including two distinct types of collective problem solutions, namely, the solution of common pool resource problems in addition to the provision of formally defined public goods.[2] This is the way in which I shall be using the term here. Based on definitional attempts by Musgrave and Samuelson, public goods are formally defined as goods characterized by non-rivalry of consumption, and non-excludability from consumption (Ostrom, this volume). Public goods are contrasted to private goods, which are characterized by both rivalry of, and excludability from, consumption. Private goods are typically provided by the market economy. But it is not in the individual interest to produce goods which, once produced, are available to all and thus invite free riding. At least initially it therefore appeared that public goods must be provided by the state; in fact the "public" character of a good served to legitimate state intervention to ensure its supply. Common pool resource problems, like the famous tragedy of the commons, exist where there is rivalry in the consumption of a scarce resource, coupled with non-exclusion from consumption.[3] This typically leads to overutilization and hence the exhaustion (destruction, erosion) of the resource. The starting point is a conflict between the short-term individual interest in maximal consumption, and the long-term collective interest in maintaining future consumption chances. Elinor Ostrom has intensively studied common pool resource problems and the conditions of their solu-

tion (Ostrom 1990). The big question is whether a central (hierarchical) authority is needed to solve common pool resource problems, or whether such problems can also be solved through horizontal coordination.

Though both can be called collective problem solutions, there is an important difference among the two types of common goods. In the case of formally
defined public goods, the problem is the production of a certain good. It is not
available unless produced, and if produced, scarcity is no problem—which is
already implied in the characteristic of non-rivalry. In the case of common pool
resources, we are typically dealing with "goods" that are naturally available,
such as water or fish, but which are scarce resources. Here the basic problem is
therefore sustainable utilization, and it is solved by establishing rules regulating
consumption. Scarcity, of course, is a variable; arable land or clean water can be
abundant for a small population in a given area, but can become scarce as the
population grows and demand rises. There is therefore no fixed boundary between the two types of common goods. Nevertheless, the solution of the two
collective problems requires different strategies. Whereas the solution of a
common pool resource problem requires regulation, i.e., setting up and enforcing rules for resource utilization, the provision of a public good such as national
defense or general education needs much more than rules of access, namely, to
set up a public production structure, complete with armies or with schools,
teachers, etc., respectively.

Common goods are generally considered a component of public welfare,
though the exact relationship between their provision and public welfare in the
sense of system viability (or quality) is unclear. System stability or survival may
require the provision of some, but it is not equal to the provision of all imagin-
able public goods. The production of a public good such as national security can
be called the solution of a system problem, but certainly not all kinds of products
that the market will not supply because they are characterized by non-rivalry and
non-excludability would eo ipso be a condition of system viability. Similarly,
system viability will require the regulation of the utilization of crucial, but presumably not of all, common pool resources. On the other hand it is open to debate whether all system problems, all social "bads," fall either into the category
"failure to provide a public good" or into the category "failure to solve a common pool resource problem." Efforts at risk avoidance (e.g., in the fields of
nuclear energy production or climate change) can be formulated in terms of
common goods provision, and so can market regulation, since productive market
exchanges presuppose institutional frameworks within which such exchanges
can take place. But would it also be meaningful to define the fulfillment of
functional imperatives which are not recognized as such, and hence not desired,
as "common goods"? The functionality of interethnic tolerance, for instance,
may well be denied by the ethnic groups involved where ethnic cultures clash,
group identification is strong, and conflicts are violent. Nor is it generally recognized that it contributes to social integration if we define persons unable to
play their roles effectively as "ill" because this obviates the need to subject them
to sanctions. In systems theory, the fulfillment of functional imperatives often

happens behind the backs, as it were, of the system members; it is to a large extent the unrecognized latent functions upon which system maintenance rests.

In contrast, common goods typically refer to recognized collective action problems. It is in fact a distinct characteristic of the common goods approach to public welfare to be action oriented, or even specifically policy oriented. The action orientation of the common goods perspective quite naturally directs attention to the actor constellations and action orientations conducive to their achievement. In this way governance becomes a focal factor, and the form of governance which is most conducive to their achievement plays a major role in the discussion about common goods. But the term "governance," like the term "public welfare" previously, can mean different things and it therefore needs specification.

Before it became the hallmark of modern political theory, the English term governance had been equated with governing, the process aspect of government. Governance thus complemented the institutional perspective of government studies. Today, the term governance is most often used to indicate a mode of governing that is distinct from the hierarchical control model characterizing the interventionist state. Governance is the type of regulation typical of the cooperative state, where state and non-state actors participate in mixed public/private policy networks. As an alternative to strict hierarchical control the term governance has been applied to processes of policy-making at the national and at the European level (e.g., Kooiman 1993; Rhodes 1997). Most particularly, however, we find this meaning of the term in the literature on "global governance." Driven by economic globalization and the international networks of transport and communication, we appear to be approaching an age in which problems transcending national boundaries increasingly call for international and transnational forms of regulation, which, lacking an inclusive world government, takes place in the form of "governance without government" (Rosenau and Czempiel 1992). In fact, the use of the term in the study of international and transnational relations has probably been the main reason for identifying governance with nonhierarchical forms of coordination and rule setting.[4]

This presently dominant meaning of the term governance has pushed into the background, if not supplanted, another conceptual tradition that started with Oliver Williamson's analysis of market and hierarchy as alternative forms of economic organization (Williamson 1979). Williamson's typology was quickly extended to include other forms of social coordination such as clans, associations, and—most importantly—networks (Hollingsworth and Lindberg 1985; Powell 1990). In this way, the meaning of governance was gradually extended to become a summary term for all basic forms of social order. Among these forms, the market is an important subcategory. But where governance is mainly used to distinguish horizontal (network) coordination from hierarchy, markets are no longer considered, and the main substantive issue becomes the problem solving potential of horizontal forms of coordination. Sometimes it is asked specifically whether self-regulation (or horizontal coordination) can produce problem solutions of the same or even superior quality as hierarchical coordination (e.g., Scharpf 1993). This discussion complements, as it were, the earlier discussion revolving around the comparative advantages and disadvantages of state (hierarchical) and market solutions that led, among other things, to the distinction between public and private goods and continues today in debates about the pros and cons of deregulation and privatization.

In principle, these two strands of scientific debate—hierarchy versus network, and hierarchy versus market—could be integrated in a theory of governance if this concept were used in its widest possible sense. In a discussion of the conditions facilitating the production of common goods, however, the "market" form of governance plays no role—at least no positive role. Market coordination is assumed to contribute to public welfare in the sense of aggregate utility, among other things, because where preferences differ as a consequence of the division of labor, market exchanges permit a higher degree of aggregate individual satisfaction. At the same time, however, the theory of market failure states that where market principles dominate, no "public goods" will be produced. Nor is spontaneously arising market exchange able to solve common pool resource problems; the possible use of market principles to this end presupposes the political creation of a market, as when a scarce resource is divided authoritatively into limited shares and offered for sale. The debate therefore concentrates on hierarchy and networks as those governance forms that can be positively related to common goods. A minor role is also played by clans/solidarity. In sociological theory, solidarity is widely considered important for system integration; it is thus linked especially to conceptions of system viability. Solidarity and small group size clearly also facilitate the solution of common pool resource problems. Especially in connection with horizontal coordination, solidarity (possibly in the shape of trust and the norm of reciprocity) is considered important for the production of common goods.

The common goods discussion in fact concentrates on the conditions under which horizontal coordination can succeed. Two reasons may play a role in this selective attention. One reason is that much of the present discussion about common goods starts from the observation that state powers (i.e., hierarchy) are either insufficient for the solution of many problems, or totally absent, i.e., if we move to the global level. Hence the question becomes how much problem solution is possible without having recourse to hierarchy. The second reason is a general normative preference for horizontal over hierarchical forms of coordination, even where the latter might be more effective. Again this gives priority to the question of how we can get problems solved without having recourse to hierarchy.

It cannot be the purpose of these remarks to summarize the results of the various empirical and theoretical inquiries into the preconditions of successful horizontal coordination for the production of common goods. Ostrom (1999), for instance, discusses four "blocks" of variables affecting the chance of reaching a problem solution via horizontal coordination. Aside from certain characteristics of the resource in question, these are the action orientation of individuals, attributes of group structure (particularly size), and the rules-in-use in a given collective action situation. The framework of actor-centered institutionalism (Mayntz and Scharpf 1995; Scharpf 1997) similarly calls attention to actor constellations and action orientations. The actor constellation refers to the type and number of actors involved in a given problem situation, the distribution of resources among them, and the interest structure (e.g., prisoner's dilemma or battle of the sexes) underlying the situation. The individual actors also have normative beliefs, they have—false or correct—perceptions (of the problem in question, of available solutions), and they have cooperative, competitive, or downright hostile action orientations. The chances of cooperative problem solution depend on the specifics of given constellations.

The perspective just sketched is undoubtedly fruitful for policy research, and it fits well with the dominant action (or policy) orientation of the common goods approach. However, it remains a selective perspective insofar as in analyzing the causal nexus between governance and common goods, the emphasis is generally on the potential of a given constellation to solve a recognized problem. A more comprehensive approach might want to distinguish between three aspects: problem generation (who causes a given problem by what kind of behavior), problem impact (who suffers what kind of negative effects) and problem solution (who engages in what kind of coping behavior). The genetic, impact, and coping structures correspond to stages in a process that are linked in a causal way. Set in the framework of a common goods analysis, we have initially a population of rational actors in pursuit of their personal interests: to produce only goods that can be sold on a market, or to consume as much as possible of a scarce resource. This initial interest structure motivates behavior which gives rise to a problem, here the nonavailability of a desired public good, or the erosion of a scarce resource, i.e., the destruction of an available good. The impact of the problem creates a new interest structure, defined by the perceived need to arrive at a problem solution—to stay the erosion of the resource or to provide the desired public good. The coping efforts which ensue will be shaped by cost-benefit considerations; actors suffering from the erosion of a vital resource or the absence of a public good will weigh the benefits of a problem solution against the costs this imposes on them, directly (i.e., as taxpayers) or in terms of the foregone immediate benefits of noncooperative behavior. For a comprehensive case analysis it is important to consider not only the coping structure, but all three structures and their interrelation. The genetic structure in particular must be known because it shows why and how the problem arises and what, therefore, must be changed if it is to be avoided or solved. The impact structure is important because it shows who has an interest in arriving at a problem solution. This in turn is an important precondition for the emergence of a coping structure.

A dimension of utmost importance for the dynamics of the process of problem creation and problem solution is the scope of the genetic, impact, and coping structures, i.e., the answer to the question of which actors exactly each structure is composed.[5] Where we deal with problems of the tragedy of the commons type, the scope of the genetic, impact, and coping structures is identical, i.e., they include typically the same group of actors: the problem is produced by the behavior of the group members; they are themselves affected by the negative long-term consequences of this behavior, and they also have the chance to agree upon rules of utilization which avoid the exhaustion/destruction of the resource. While this is less explicit, the same kind of congruence appears to underlie cases where a perceived market failure motivates efforts to produce a public good. For Mancur Olson, the provision of a public good is efficient only if its users are the same as those who pay for, and those who mandate, its production (see Holzinger 2000, 5). But it is in fact a very special type of situation where those creating a problem in the first place are also those who suffer from its long-term effects, and where the cooperation of the latter is both a necessary and sufficient cause for the solution of the problem. Many public "bads" are negative external effects visited upon those who have no share in their production, and many problems cannot be solved by those whom they afflict. In such cases it makes sense to separately describe the genetic, impact, and coping structures, specifying where they overlap (in social and possibly geographic terms) and where they involve different parts of a population instead.

A more realistic analysis would also have to take into account that none of the three structures is composed of uniform elements. There are differences in the extent to which different actors contribute to the production of a problem; some, for instance, use up more, some less of a common resource. Similarly, there are differences within an affected population in the intensity of suffering from the erosion of a given resource, and there can be differences in the benefits derived from the provision of a public good, as for instance the construction of dikes. Such differences result in different cost-benefit balances when it comes to coping. Finally, there are also differences in coping potential. Effective coping can only be expected from actors able to affect the emergence of the problem at hand, either directly by changing their own (problem producing) behavior, by sanctioning those who produce the problem, or by making arrangements for the production of a public good. But the potentially effective actors, i.e., those who dispose of the relevant direct and/or indirect problem solving capacities, are not necessarily motivated to join the coping effort spontaneously. Under such circumstances, the formation of an effective coping structure becomes a challenge of its own.

This point can be well illustrated by a practical case I recently had to deal with: the local implementation of a federal German program of urban melioration that goes under the name "Die soziale Stadt" (Schader-Stiftung 2001). The problem in this case is the physical deterioration and social disintegration of urban quarters where problem groups (unemployed, relief recipients, single parent households, drug peddlers and users, criminals of various kinds) concentrate. To stop the growing degradation in such areas (neighborhoods), the program envisages the creation of area networks set up and coordinated by an area network manager, who is typically not a city official. The melioration program set up by such a network is to receive financial aid from program funds, and practical support by city officials of different departments. A comparison of cases where this program was or was not at least partially successful shows that the gravest obstacle to the solution of this problem, which is largely created by the external effects of a host of different economic and social processes at the societal level, does not primarily depend on the willingness of local actors (actors in the impact structure) to engage in positive coordination, but on the sheer availability of actors disposing of a certain problem solving power among those who could be recruited into the area network. In areas where the houses belong to a variety of private absentee owners there was less of a chance of this than where a single owner was responsible for the upkeep of most of the dwellings. In areas with a variety of smaller shops and firms with local employment, the chances to mobilize resourceful actors into the coping structure were infinitely better than where these lack.

If "governance" refers specifically to a coping structure, the problem solving capacity of the given actor constellation depends on the availability of actors who, if they become part of the constellation, might jointly produce a problem solution because they are able to manipulate the factors causing the problem, or at least possess resources necessary to compensate for its negative effects. This fact is easily overlooked where only the already existing constellation of actors engaged in a problem solving effort is considered, as in many formal analyses of actor constellations and their problem solving capacity. Where, on the other hand, the multilevel character of political systems is the focus of analysis, differences between the genetic, impact, and coping structures of a problem are a familiar topic—at least in the reduced form of a recognized discrepancy between problem scope and the scope of institutions available for problem solving. In the optimal case, the coping structure (or political jurisdiction) would be co-extensive with the problem generation and the problem impact structures, because such congruence provides a strong incentive to cooperate. But where problems are of supranational or even global scope, there is typically no such congruence. Especially in the literature on European integration and on global governance, the difference between the sociogeographical scope of collective problems, on the one hand, and the nation-state as the dominant coping structure, on the other hand, is held to generate pressure for the growth of new coping structures at a higher (regional, international) level—whether these are political institutions proper, international regimes, or sectoral networks of non-governmental organizations. If, as I have argued, the common-goods-and-governance perspective is indeed the preferred approach where we deal with problems falling outside of the jurisdiction of existing (national and sub-national) political institutions, the analytical potential of this perspective might be enhanced by the systematic inclusion of the distinction between the problem generating, the impact, and the problem solving structures.

Notes

1. Here a fourth theoretical tradition in defining a socially desirable end or goal-state comes in, i.e., justice as a reference point of legal theory. This strand of thinking will not be systematically considered here, though it becomes relevant also for the development of a formal definition of public welfare as aggregate utility.

2. Elinor Ostrom (1999, 4) similarly names public goods and common pool resources as the major subtypes of collective action problems.

3. A third type of common goods mentioned by Héritier in the introduction to this volume, i.e., club goods, is not considered here, since by definition club goods are for the

use of limited groups only. From a global perspective, however, the population of a given nation-state may be considered a "club." This calls attention to the fact that the social reference of "common" or "public" is a matter of definition.

4. In the March 1999 issue of the *International Social Science Journal*, which is entirely devoted to governance in the sense of nonhierarchical modes of coordination, this very meaning of the concept is traced to an international source, namely a 1989 World Bank report (UNESCO 1998).

5. The genetic and impact structures are often collapsed into the dimension "problem scope," which is then related to the regulatory (= coping) structure; see Knill and Lehmkuhl in this volume.

References

Albert, H. 1998. Bemerkungen zur Wertproblematik. Von der Bewertung des Sozialprodukts zur Analyse der sozialen Ordnung. Lectiones Jenenses, Heft 15, Jena: MPI zur Erforschung von Wirtschaftssystemen.

Gaertner, W. 1998. Armut und Verteilungsgerechtigkeit. *Spektrum der Wissenschaft*: 30-34.

Hollingsworth, J. R., and L. N. Lindberg. 1985. The Governance of the American Economy: The Role of Markets, Clans, Hierarchies, and Associate Behavior. In *Private Interest Government: Beyond Market and State*, ed. W. Streeck and P. Schmitter, 221-54. London: Sage.

Holzinger, K. 2000. Optimale Regulierungseinheiten für Europa. Flexible Kooperation territorialer und funktionaler Jurisdiktionen. Vortragsmanuskript, Bonn: Max-Planck-Projektgruppe. Recht der Gemeinschaftsgüter.

Kaufmann, F.-X. 1994. Staat und Wohlfahrtsproduktion. In *Systemrationalität und Partialinteresse*, ed. H.-U. Derlin, U. Gerhardt, and F. W. Scharpf, 357-80. Baden-Baden: Nomos.

Kooiman, J., ed. 1993. *Modern Governance: New Government—Society Interaction*. London: Sage.

Mayntz, R., and F. W. Scharpf, eds. 1995. *Gesellschaftliche Selbstregelung und politische Steuerung*. Frankfurt am Main: Campus.

Ostrom, E. 1990. *Governing the Commons: The Evolution of Institutions for Collective Action*. New York: Cambridge University Press.

———. 1999. *Context and Collective Action: Four Interactive Building Blocks for a Family of Explanatory Theories*. Indiana University: Workshop in Political Theory and Policy Analysis (manuscript).

Parsons, T. 1951. *The Social System*. Glencoe, Ill.: Free Press.

Parsons, T., and N. J. Smelser. 1956. *Economy and Society*. New York: Free Press.

Powell, W. W. 1990. Neither Market nor Hierarchy: Network Forms of Organization. *Research in Organizational Behavior* 12: 295-336.

Rawls, J. A. 1972. *Theory of Justice*. Oxford: Clarendon Press.

Rhodes, R. W. A. 1997. *Understanding Governance: Policy Networks, Reflexivity, and Accountability*. Buckingham, Pa.: Open University Press.

Rosenau, J. N., and E.-O. Czempiel, eds. 1992. *Governance without Government: Order and Change in World Politics*. Cambridge: Cambridge University Press.

Schader-Stiftung, ed. 2001. *Politische Steuerung der Stadtentwicklung. Das Programm "Die soziale Stadt" in der Diskussion*. Darmstadt: Schader-Stiftung.

Scharpf, F. W. 1993. Coordination in Hierarchies and Networks. In *Games in Hierarchies and Networks: Analytical and Empirical Approaches to the Study of Governance Institutions*, ed. F. W. Scharpf, 125-65. Frankfurt am Main: Campus.

————. 1994. Politiknetzwerke als Steuerungssubjekte. In *Systemrationalität und Partialinteresse*, ed. H.-U. Derlien, U. Gerhardt, and F. W. Scharpf, 381-402. Baden-Baden: Nomos.

————. 1997. *Games Real Actors Play: Actor-Centered Institutionalism in Policy Research*. Boulder, Colo.: Westview Press.

UNESCO. 1998. Governance. *International Social Science Journal*.

Williamson, O. E. 1979. Transaction-Cost Economics: The Governance of Contractual Relations. *Journal of Law and Economics* 22: 233-61.

2

Property-Rights Regimes and Common Goods: A Complex Link

Elinor Ostrom

The Concept of Public Goods in the Theory of Collective Action

By centering his theory of collective action on the concept of a "public good," Mancur Olson (1965) built his edifice on a presupposition that the type of problem(s) that individuals attempt to solve affects the responses that they make to these problems. This is by no means a unique presupposition, as shown by several chapters in this volume (in particular, see Héritier and Holzinger). Once this position is accepted, however, the knotty problem remains as to *which* attributes of goods are most important in dividing the problems that humans face into as parsimonious a set as possible. An endless number of attributes could be posited.

A major debate over this issue was brewing when Olson wrote *The Logic of Collective Action* (1965). The debate was initiated in 1954 by Paul Samuelson when he used one attribute—jointness of consumption—to divide the world into two classes: private consumption goods and public consumption goods. Samuelson assumed that private consumption goods could be divided and allocated to different consumers but that collective consumption goods are those that "all enjoy in common in the sense that each individual's consumption of such a good leads to no subtraction from any other individual's consumption of that good" (Samuelson 1954, 387). While market catallactics would allow rational egoists to pursue narrow self-interest and yet produce socially optimal provision of private consumption goods, Samuelson argued that decentralized spontaneous solutions could not work to provide an optimal level of collective consumption goods. In 1959, Richard Musgrave argued that a different attribute of goods—whether or not someone can be excluded from benefitting once the good is produced—is more important than jointness of consumption. Musgrave asserted that the exclusion principle can be used by itself to divide the world into private and public goods. The classification debate was associated with major policy issues over the role of government in allocating resources.

Figure 2.1.   Samuelson's and Musgrave's Classification of Goods

	Samuelson's Classification	
Musgrave's Classification	One person's consumption subtracts from total available to others	One person's consumption does not subtract from total available to others
Exclusion Is Feasible	Cell A	Cell B
Exclusion Is Not Feasible	Cell C	Cell D

Both Samuelson and Musgrave were interested in the same question. They attempted to find a single criterion that would enable them to predict when market institutions would perform optimally and when markets would fail. The difference in their approach can be illustrated in figure 2.1. Samuelson uses his classification to argue that all of the left-hand column, and none of the right-hand column, includes goods that can be effectively allocated through market mechanisms. Musgrave uses his classification to argue that all of the top row and none of the bottom row includes goods that are best allocated through the market. Changing the assumption regarding the *impossibility* of exclusion to a *high cost* of exclusion, the definition of common goods used by Héritier in the introduction, refers to all of the cells except Cell A.

Olson explicitly adopted Musgrave's definition. Using this one-dimensional criterion, Olson then tried to establish a *general theory* for all goods meeting Musgrave's definition. It was a grand vision, but overly ambitious. Multiple scholars have shown that several of Olson's propositions do not hold for all goods meeting the Musgrave definition even though these same propositions do hold for a subset of goods for which exclusion is costly or difficult (Chamberlin 1974; R. Hardin 1982; V. and E. Ostrom 1977). Obviously, Olson shared both Samuelson and Musgrave's hope of developing as general a theory as possible.

Multiple Types of Collective Action Problems

Exclusion as the Key Attribute

Olson had a profound insight when he adopted Musgrave's criterion as the defining attribute for collective action problems. The name he used to characterize these problems—public goods—has appropriately come to be used for a subset of collective action problems. Public goods are those collective action problems identified as Cell D of figure 2.1 where consumption by one person does not reduce the amount available to others (see Holzinger, this volume). Cell C has come to be known as representing a set of collective action problems known as common-pool resources (E. Ostrom and V. Ostrom 1977; E. Ostrom, Gardner, and Walker 1994). While Musgrave and Olson tended to assume that exclusion was impossible for a subset of all goods, more recent theoretical work has understood that the capacity to exclude potential beneficiaries depends both on the technology of physical exclusion devices, such as barbed-wire fences and electronic-sensing devices, as well as the existence and enforcement of various bundles of property rights (Cornes and Sandler 1994; E. Ostrom, Gardner, and Walker 1994). Thus, as discussed below, many people facing collective action problems in the field have changed the structure of the problem they face by building walls (the walled cities of medieval times were, after all, a way of excluding outsiders from the defenses of the city) or creating property rights (inshore fishers have long used customary law to enforce locally devised rules as to who was allowed to fish).

Consequently, all collective action problems share an initial characteristic that excluding those who do not contribute to providing a collective benefit is nontrivial. Collective action problems differ in regard to how costly or difficult it is to devise physical or institutional means to exclude others. Some of these differences stem from the biophysical world itself. It will always be more difficult to exclude users from an ocean than from a farmer's pond. Other differences stem from the constitutional order in which the problem is located. In some legal codes, for example, it is illegal to exclude anyone from using water for domestic purposes.

Subtractability

The next conundrum to be resolved is whether one theory can explain all patterns and outcomes for collective action problems as Olson, Samuelson, and Musgrave had hoped, or whether a family of closely related theories is needed. After half a century of unsuccessful efforts to build one explanatory theory for all collective action problems, and multiple insightful critiques of these efforts, further efforts to build a single general theory are counterproductive.

Olson actually started this task. He himself classified what he called public goods into two subsets: exclusive public goods and inclusive public goods. Olson made radically different predictions for these two subclasses. His "exclusive public good" is Cell C in figure 2.1. Here, Olson expected groups to try to keep their size as small as possible, to try to get 100 percent participation since "even one non-participant can usually take all of the benefits brought about by the action of [others] for himself" (Olson 1965, 41). Inclusive groups, on the other hand, will try to increase members. The more members in an inclusive group, the more individuals who will share the costs of providing a good to all beneficiaries. Olson also predicts that bargaining and strategic interactions will be less intense in an inclusive group than in an exclusive one.

Instead of calling these two types of goods "exclusive" and "inclusive," scholars have come to refer to one of them as "public goods." Public goods are characterized by difficulties of exclusion and joint consumption (e.g., one person's use does not subtract from the benefits available to others). The second type of good is referred to as a common-pool resource. Common-pool resource problems share with public goods the problems of free riding, but they also include the problems of overharvesting and overcrowding. The concept of common goods that is addressed by all chapters in this volume includes Cells B, C, and D of figure 2.1.

In the field, groups using a common-pool resource (exclusive public goods) who have found ways to reduce overappropriation almost always try to limit members, as Olson predicted, through clear and enforced boundary rules specifying exactly who can use the resource (E. Ostrom 1990). Not all of the differences predicted by Olson have been tested, but laboratory experiments provide clear evidence that common-pool resources and public goods are different subclasses of collective action problems. In a public-goods setting, noncooperative actions by one individual do not make a dramatic difference for others. In this setting, increasing the number of participants frequently brings additional resources that could be drawn on to provide a benefit that will be jointly enjoyed by all. It is because of the additional resources available in a larger group and the nonsubtractability characteristic of public goods, that Marwell and Oliver (1993, 45) conclude that when "a good has pure jointness of supply, group size has a *positive* effect on the probability that it will be provided." For example, the level of resources provided to support public radio is greater when a larger population can be called upon than for a smaller population. Thus, whether the dilemma is a public good or a common-pool appropriation problem affects how other variables impact on rates of cooperation.

In a common-pool resource situation, one person's aggressive withdrawals can generate very high costs for everyone else. In finitely repeated public-goods experiments, the typical pattern is for subjects to contribute about 50 percent of the optimal level in the first round and then follow a pulsing decay pattern toward, but never reaching, the symmetric Nash equilibrium in the last rounds (as shown in figure 2.2). In common-pool resource problems, on the other hand, the typical pattern is just the opposite. In the initial rounds, subjects do much *worse* than Nash and then pulse upward toward the symmetric Nash equilibrium from below as shown in figure 2.3.

In addition to differences among collective action problems in regard to whether consumption is joint or subtractive, other characteristics affect the types of problems that people face in the field. In regard to common-pool resources, for example, Schlager, Blomquist, and Tang (1994) identify whether the products to be appropriated are mobile like fish or stationary like trees. Such attributes affect the costs of learning about the yield of a resource. Similarly, whether there is storage in the system affects the predictability of resource unit availability. When conducting field research, these attributes have strong impacts on the likelihood of successful collective action and the form that collective action takes (see Tang 1992; Lam 1998; Schlager 1994; Blomquist 1992). Instead of trying to identify the myriad of specific factors that are potenti-

Figure 2.2. Contributions to Public Goods: 10, 40, and 60 Round Horizons
Source: Adapted from Isaac, Walker, and Williams (1994, 29).

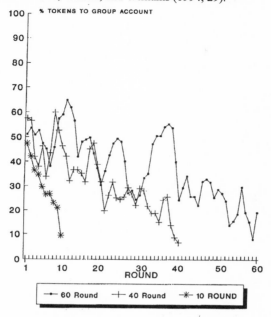

Figure 2.3. The Effect of Increasing Investment Endowment (25-token design)

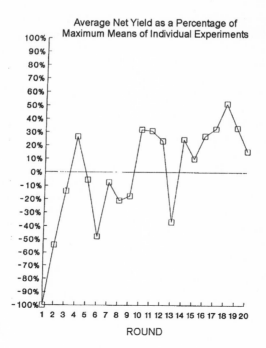

ally important in the context of any well-designed fieldwork, however, I will first discuss two abstract forms of representing some of these important differences—the shape of the production and appropriation functions that characterize a particular problem. In a later section, I will focus on how further attributes of a common-pool resource may affect the feasibility of diverse types of property regimes.

Production Functions

It is well understood that the production function to produce private goods takes on many shapes and forms that affect the expected efficiency of the firms in a particular industry. The same is true of public goods and common-pool resources. The most frequently assumed production function is linear. In a linear public-goods game, there are N identical players who are each assigned an endowment, E. Each player i must then decide between keeping the endowment or contributing some part of the endowment xi_i to the production of a public good G. A production function that determines the total amount of the public good, TG, is:

$$TG = P \left(\Sigma x_i \right) \tag{1}$$

In the linear public-goods game, P is referred to as the Marginal Per Capita Return (MPCR) and is defined as the value of switching one unit from private consumption to the production of the good (Isaac and Walker 1988). If the MPCR is .25, for example, each person who contributes $1.00 generates a public good of $.25 for everyone in the game. If four people contribute $1.00 each, the total return just equals the total cost. In this instance, the minimum number of individuals contributing $1.00, where benefits exceed costs, or k, would be five.

In addition to MPCR and k, social psychologists have identified several aspects of the payoff function of a particular type of collective action problem—a Prisoner's Dilemma (PD) game—that are posited to affect behavior. In the two-person PD game, Rapoport and Chammah (1965) called attention to the relationships among the payoffs that are called *Cooperator's Gain* (the difference between both cooperating and both defecting), *Greed* (the payoff for one player in defecting as contrasted to both cooperating), and *Fear* (the loss for one player in cooperating versus both defecting).

The production function that relates individual actions to group outcomes may take any of a wide diversity of forms, as shown in figure 2.4. The yield functions for common-pool resources have been represented since the seminal article of Scott Gordon (1954) as a quadratic function (see figure 2.4d). Too many "contributions," rather than too few, is the problem to overcome in a common-pool resource dilemma. Marwell and Oliver (1993) focus on several other nonlinear production functions including general third-order functions (4c), decelerating (4e), and accelerating (4f), that are characteristic of different types of public interest activities.

Figure 2.4.   General Types of Production Functions

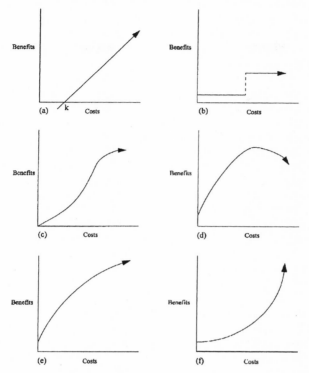

Functions: (a) linear, (b) step function, (c) general third order, (d) quadratic, (e) decelerating, (f) accelerating.

Source: Modified from Marwell and Oliver (1993, 59).

Marwell and Oliver analyzed a variety of monotonically increasing, non-linear production functions relating individual contributions and the total benefits produced. They distinguish between production functions that are decelerating and those that are accelerating. In the decelerating case, while every contribution increases the total benefits that a group receives, marginal returns decrease as more and more individuals contribute.[1] When contributions are made sequentially, the initial contributions have far greater impact than later contributions. With an accelerating production function, initial contributions make small increments and later contributions yield progressively greater benefits. "Accelerating production functions are characterized by *positive interdependence*: each contribution makes the next one more worthwhile and, thus, more likely" (Marwell and Oliver 1993, 63). Settings where mass actions are needed in order to gain a positive response involve accelerating functions.[2]

Marwell and Oliver's (1993) theoretical predictions concerning the success of collective action depend sensitively on the particular shape of the production function, on heterogeneity of wealth, on the sequence in which individuals contribute, and on the information generated by each action. Thus, they do not depend only on the type of production function to predict behavior and outcomes. Rather, they analyze how a configuration of variables operates together—or how the effect of one set of variables depends upon other variables.

Step-level functions (figure 2.4, 4b) have also been of considerable interest to scholars of collective action.[3] Discussing the findings related to step-level production functions helps us to understand how a very subtle difference in just the production function of a collective good can make an immense difference in behavior and outcomes. In a step-level production function, actions by up to k participants make no difference in the outcomes obtained, but actions by k or more participants discontinuously shift the benefit upward.[4] Russell Hardin (1976) was among the first to argue that when the shape of the production function for a public good was a step function, solving social dilemmas could be facilitated since no good would be provided if participants did not gain sufficient inputs to equal or exceed the provision point (k). Until the benefit is actually produced, it is not possible to "free ride" on the contributions of others. In these settings, individuals may assume that their participation is critical to the provision of the good. This type of production function creates an "assurance problem" rather than a strict social dilemma. For those who perceive their contribution as critical, not contributing is no longer the unique Nash equilibrium.

Sharing formulas can also make each person of a group, or a designated minimal contributing group, feel that their contribution is critical (van de Kragt, Orbell, and Dawes 1983). By agreeing that each person will contribute a set proportion of what is believed to be the total cost of obtaining a good, the individuals in such a minimal contributing set face a choice between not contributing and receiving nothing or contributing and receiving the benefit (assuming others in the minimal contributing set also contribute). The game has been transformed from a social dilemma to an assurance game.

An early communication experiment was conducted by van de Kragt, Orbell, and Dawes (1983) in a one-shot, provision-point public-goods game described more fully below. In all twelve communication experiments, subjects used the opportunity for discussion to decide exactly who would or would not be expected to contribute to the public good (van de Kragt, Orbell, and Dawes 1983). They used lotteries, overt volunteering, and in one case, the need of several subjects for the additional $5.00 associated with noncontribution. In ten of these twelve experiments, the discussion led to a decision designating the optimal number of participants. In all ten cases, those designated did contribute even though their decision was independently and privately made. In the other two experiments, the discussion led to the identification of a group of contributors larger than necessary.[5] The authors attribute the high level of success in these communication experiments to the sense of criticalness that participants gained when a minimal contributing set was actually designated through their discussion period.

In a series of public-goods experiments, Robin Dawes, John Orbell, and colleagues created a public good provision problem with a discrete provision point (or a step-level function). All of these experiments had seven participants who were given a promissory note for $5.00 at the beginning of the experiment. Subjects were told that if a minimal contributing set (or as defined above, k)— either three or five—contributed their promissory note, all subjects would receive $10.00 including those who had not contributed. With less than the required number of contributions, no good would be provided. In a series of baseline experiments, subjects were not allowed to communicate and were told only the size of the minimal contributing set needed to obtain the public good. In one of these baseline experiments, subjects were asked to estimate three probabilities prior to their own and others' decisions: (1) the probability of their action being futile if they were to contribute, (2) the probability of their action being critical to the achievement of the public good, and (3) the probability of their action being superfluous. The level of cooperation in these one-shot games without communication is quite high. The public good is provided in seven out of ten of the experiments where the minimal contributing set equaled three (50 percent of the individuals contributed) and in four out of ten of the experiments with a minimal contributing set of five (64 percent of the individuals contributed). On the other hand, the experiments where subjects were asked to estimate the probabilities of their own contribution being futile, critical, or superfluous, none of the five experiments achieved the minimal contributing set that had been set at five (23 percent contributed).

The Allocation Function

In addition to the function that transforms contributions into a collective benefit, a second function, A, assigns individuals a share of the total benefits obtained. This function can initially be used to represent the "natural" allocation in a base game or the changed allocation rules used to transform the base game by an organized group or by external authorities. In a nondivisible good, each person would receive TG. For universal public goods, such as peace and stability, each individual benefits in a similar manner without subtraction from the existence of these states of affairs. In linear public-goods experiments, A is frequently operationalized as $1/N$. (Thus, if the MPCR is .25 as mentioned above, everyone receives the public good of $.25 for everyone who contributes, whether or not they contributed themselves.) In a common-pool resource game, A can be operationalized as $x_i/\Sigma x_i$ or as a proportionate share of the total. These are three simple allocation functions, but a host of allocation functions is actually found in field settings including allocation according to (1) the value of assets held (the function that Olson used); (2) seniority of claims; and (3) spatial or temporal formula.

Thus, the initial specification of a collective action problem is one where once a collective benefit is produced, exclusion is nontrivial. Within this very broad definition of a collective action problem, a very large number of different situations exist depending on whether consumption is subtractive or not and on other variables that affect the shape of production and allocation functions. It is this variety of situations in the world—as contrasted to the overly simplified models of the world used in much of contemporary policy analysis—that is the foundation for considerable policy debate. There are several key confusions, besides those related to the core definitions of what is a public good and what is a common-pool resource, that have made policy debates more difficult to understand.

The Confusion between a Resource System and a Property Regime

The term "common-property resource" is frequently used to describe the type of economic good that has been defined above as a "common-pool resource." Recognizing a class of goods that shares these two attributes enables scholars to identify the core theoretical problems facing all individuals or groups who wish to utilize such resources for an extended period of time. Using "property" in the context used to refer to a type of good reinforces the impression that goods sharing these attributes tend everywhere to share the same property regime.

Common-pool resources share with public goods the difficulty of developing physical or institutional means of excluding beneficiaries. Unless means are devised to keep nonauthorized users from benefiting, the strong temptation to free ride on the efforts of others will lead to a suboptimal investment in improving the resource, monitoring use, and sanctioning rule-breaking behavior. Second, the products or resource units from common-pool resources share with private goods the attribute that one person's consumption subtracts from the quantity available to others. Thus, common-pool resources are subject to problems of congestion, overuse, and potential destruction unless harvesting or use limits are devised and enforced. In addition to sharing these two attributes, particular common-pool resources differ on many other attributes that affect their economic usefulness, including their size, shape, and productivity, and the value, timing, and regularity of the resource units produced.

Common-pool resources may be owned by national, regional, or local governments; by communal groups; by private individuals or corporations; or used as open-access resources by whomever can gain access. Each of the broad types of property regimes has different sets of advantages and disadvantages, but at times may rely upon similar operational rules regarding access and use of a resource (see Mayntz, this volume; Feeny et al. 1990). Examples exist of both successful and unsuccessful efforts to govern and manage common-pool resources by governments, communal groups, cooperatives, voluntary associations, and private individuals or firms (Bromley et al. 1992; Singh 1994; Singh and Ballabh 1996). Thus, as discussed below, there is no automatic association of common-pool resources with common-property regimes—*or, with any other particular type of property regime.*

The Confusion between the Resource and the Flow of Resource Units

Common-pool resources are composed of resource systems and a flow of resource units or benefits from these systems (Blomquist and Ostrom 1985). The resource system (or alternatively, the stock or the facility) is what generates a flow of resource units or benefits over time. Examples of typical common-pool resource systems include lakes, rivers, irrigation systems, groundwater basins, forests, fishery stocks, and grazing areas. Common-pool resources may also be facilities that are constructed for joint use, such as mainframe computers and the Internet. The resource units or benefits from a common-pool resource include water, timber, medicinal plants, fish, fodder, central processing units, and connection time. Devising property regimes that effectively allow sustainable use of a common-pool resource requires rules that limit access to the resource system and other rules that limit the amount, timing, and technology used to withdraw diverse resource units from the resource system.

Property as Bundles of Rights

A property right is an enforceable authority to undertake particular actions in a specific domain (Commons 1968). Property rights define actions that individuals can take in relation to other individuals regarding some "thing." If one individual has a right, someone else has a commensurate duty to observe that right. Schlager and Ostrom (1992) identify five property rights that are most relevant for the use of common-pool resources, including access, withdrawal, management, exclusion, and alienation. These are defined as:

Access:	The right to enter a defined physical area and enjoy nonsubtractive benefits (e.g., hike, canoe, sit in the sun).
Withdrawal:	The right to obtain resource units or products of a resource system (e.g., catch fish, divert water).
Management:	The right to regulate internal use patterns and transform the resource by making improvements.
Exclusion:	The right to determine who will have an access right, and how that right may be transferred.
Alienation:	The right to sell or lease management and exclusion rights (Schlager and Ostrom 1992).

In much of the economics literature, private property is defined as equivalent to alienation. Property-rights systems that do not contain the right of alienation are considered to be ill defined. Further, they are presumed to lead to inefficiency since property-rights holders cannot trade their interest in an improved resource system for other resources, nor can someone who has a more efficient use of a resource system purchase that system in whole or in part (Demsetz 1967). Consequently, it is assumed that property-rights systems that include the right to alienation will be transferred to their highest valued use. Larson and Bromley (1990) challenge this commonly held view and show that much more information must be known about the specific values of a large number of parameters before judgments can be made concerning the efficiency of a particular type of property right.

Instead of focusing on one right, it is more useful to define five classes of property-rights holders as shown in table 2.1. In this view, individuals or collectivities may hold well-defined property rights that include or do not include all five of the rights defined above. This approach separates the question of whether a particular right is well-defined from the question of the effect of having a particular set of rights. "Authorized entrants" include most recreational users of national parks who purchase an operational right to enter and enjoy the natural beauty of the park, but do not have a right to harvest forest products. Those who have both entry and withdrawal use-right units are "authorized users." The presence or absence of constraints upon the timing, technology used, purpose of use, and quantity of resource units harvested are determined by operational rules devised by those holding the collective-choice rights (or authority) of management and exclusion. The operational rights of entry and use may be finely divided into quite specific "tenure niches" (Bruce 1995) that vary by season, by use, by technology, and by space. Tenure niches may overlap when one set of users owns the right to harvest fruits from trees, another set of users owns the right to the timber in these trees, and the trees may be located on land owned by still others (Bruce, Fortmann, and Nhira 1993). Operational rules may allow authorized users to transfer access and withdrawal rights either temporarily through a rental agreement, or permanently when these rights are assigned or sold to others (see Adasiak 1979, for a description of the rights of authorized users of the Alaskan salmon and herring fisheries).

"Claimants" possess the operational rights of access and withdrawal plus a collective-choice right of managing a resource that includes decisions concerning the construction and maintenance of facilities and the authority to devise limits on withdrawal rights. The net fishers of Jambudwip, India, for example, annually regulate the positioning of nets so as to avoid interference, but do not have the right to determine who may fish along the coast (Raychaudhuri 1980). Farmers on large-scale government irrigation systems

frequently devise rotation schemes for allocating water on a branch canal (Benjamin et al. 1994).

"Proprietors" hold the same rights as claimants with the addition of the right to determine who may access and harvest from a resource. Many of the property systems that are called "common-property" regimes involve participants who are proprietors and have four of the above rights, but do not possess the right to sell their management and exclusion rights even though they most frequently

Table 2.1.   Bundles of Rights Associated with Positions

	Owner	Proprietor	Authorized Claimant	Authorized User	Authorized Entrant
Access	X	X	X	X	X
Withdrawal	X	X	X	X	
Management	X	X	X		
Exclusion	X	X			
Alienation	X				

Source: E. Ostrom and Schlager (1996, 133).

have the right to bequeath it to members of their family (see Berkes 1989; Bromley et al. 1992; K. Martin 1979; McCay and Acheson 1987).

Empirical studies have found that some proprietors have sufficient rights to make decisions that promote long-term investment and harvesting from a resource. Place and Hazell (1993) conducted surveys in Ghana, Kenya, and Rwanda to ascertain if indigenous land-right systems were a constraint on agricultural productivity. They found that having the rights of a proprietor as contrasted to an owner in these settings did not affect investment decisions and productivity. Other studies conducted in Africa (Migot-Adholla et al. 1991; Bruce and Migot-Adholla 1994) also found little difference in productivity, investment levels, or access to credit. In densely settled regions, however, proprietorship over agricultural land may not be sufficient (Feder et al. 1988; Feder and Feeny 1991). In a series of studies of inshore fisheries, self-organized irrigation systems, forest user groups, and groundwater institutions, proprietors tended to develop strict boundary rules to exclude noncontributors; established authority rules to allocate withdrawal rights; devised methods for monitoring conformance; and used graduated sanctions against those who did not conform to these rules (Agrawal 1994; Blomquist 1992; Schlager 1994; Tang 1994; Lam 1998).

"Owners" possess the right of alienation—the right to transfer a good in any way the owner wishes that does not harm the physical attributes or uses of other owners—in addition to the bundle of rights held by a proprietor. An individual, a private corporation, a government, or a communal group may possess full ownership rights to any kind of good including a common-pool resource (Montias 1976; Dahl and Lindblom 1963). The rights of owners, however, are never absolute. Even private owners have responsibilities not to generate particular kinds of harms for others (Demsetz 1967).

What should be obvious by now is that the world of property rights is far more complex than simply government, private, and common property. These terms better reflect the status and organization of the holder of a particular right than the bundle of property rights held. All of the above rights can be held by single individuals or by collectivities. Some communal fishing systems grant their members all five of the above rights, including the right of alienation (Miller 1989). Members in these communal fishing systems have full ownership rights. Similarly, farmer-managed irrigation systems in Nepal, the Philippines, and Spain have established transferable shares to some of these systems. Access, withdrawal, voting, and maintenance responsibilities are allocated by the amount of shares owned (E. Martin and Yoder 1983a, 1983b, and 1983c; E. Martin 1986; Siy 1982; Maass and Anderson 1986). On the other hand, some proposals to "privatize" inshore fisheries through the devise of an Individual Transferable Quota (ITQ), allocate transferable use rights to authorized fishers but do not allocate rights related to the management of the fisheries, the determination of who is a participant, nor the transfer of management and exclusion rights. Thus, proposals to establish ITQ systems, which are frequently referred to as forms of "privatization," do not involve full ownership.

The next two sections are devoted to a discussion of the attributes of common-pool resources that are conducive to communal proprietorship or communal ownership as contrasted with individual ownership. Groups of individuals are considered to share communal property rights when they have formed an organization that exercises at least the collective-choice rights of management and exclusion in relationship to some defined resource system and the resource units produced by that system. In other words, all communal groups have established some means of governing themselves in relationship to a resource (E. Ostrom 1990). Where communal groups are full owners, members of the group have the further right to sell their access, use, exclusion, and management rights to others, subject in many systems to the approval of the other members of the group. Some communal proprietorships are formally organized and recognized by legal authorities as having a corporate existence that entails the right to sue and be sued, the right to hold financial assets in a common bank account, and to make decisions that are binding on members. Other communal proprietorships are less formally organized and may exercise de facto property rights that may or may not be supported by legal authorities if challenged by nonmembers. Obviously, such groups hold fewer well-defined bundles of property rights than those who are secure in their de jure rights even though the latter may not hold the complete set of property rights defined as full ownership. In other words, well-defined and secure property rights may not involve the right to alienation.

Attributes of Common-Pool Resources Conducive to the Use of Communal Proprietorship or Ownership

Even though all common-pool resources share the difficulty of devising methods to achieve exclusion and the subtractability of resource units, the variability of common-pool resources is immense, as briefly mentioned above, in regard to other attributes that affect the incentives of resource users and the likelihood of achieving outcomes that approach optimality. Further, whether it is difficult or costly to develop physical or institutional means to exclude nonbeneficiaries depends both on the availability and cost of technical and institutional solutions to the problem of exclusion and the relationship of the cost of these solutions to the expected benefits of achieving exclusion from a particular resource.

Let us start initially with a discussion of land as a resource system. Where population density is extremely low, land is abundant, and land generates a rich diversity of plant and animal products without much husbandry, the expected costs of establishing and defending boundaries to a parcel of land of any size may be greater than the expected benefits of enclosure (Demsetz 1967; Feeny 1993). Settlers moving into a new terrain characterized by high risk due to danger from others, from a harsh environment, or from lack of appropriate knowledge, may decide to develop one large, common parcel prior to any divisions into smaller parcels (Ellickson 1993). Once land becomes scarce, conflict over who has the rights to invest in improvements and reap the results of their efforts can lead individuals to want to enclose land through fencing or institutional means to protect their investments. There are trade-offs in costs to be considered, however. The more land included within one enclosure, the lower the costs of defending all the boundaries, but the higher the costs of regulating the use of the enclosed parcel.

The decision to enclose need not be taken in one step from an open-access terrain to a series of private plots owned exclusively by single families (Field 1984, 1985, 1989; Ellickson 1993). The benefits of enclosing land depend on the scale of productive activity involved. For some agricultural activities, as discussed below, there may be considerable benefits associated with smaller parcels fully owned by a family enterprise. For other activities, the benefits may not be substantial. Moving all the way to private plots is an efficient move when the expected marginal returns from enclosing numerous plots exceed the expected marginal costs of defending a much more extended system of boundaries and the reduced transaction costs of making decisions about use patterns (Nugent and Sanchez 1995).

In a classic study of the diversity of property-rights systems used for many centuries by Swiss peasants, Robert Netting (1976, 1981) observed that the same individuals fully divided their agricultural land into separate family-owned parcels, but that grazing lands located on the Alpine hillsides were organized into communal property systems. In these mountain valleys, the *same* individuals used different property-rights systems side by side for multiple centuries. Each local community had considerable autonomy to change local rules, so there was no problem of someone else imposing an inefficient set of rules on them. Netting argued that attributes of the resource affected which property-rights systems were most likely for diverse purposes. Netting identified five attributes that he considered to be most conducive to the development of communal property rights:

1. low value of production per unit of area,
2. high variance in the availability of resource units on any one parcel,
3. low returns from intensification of investment,

4.   substantial economies of scale by utilizing a large area, and
5.   substantial economies of scale in building infrastructures to utilize the large area.

Steep land where rainfall is scattered may not be suitable for most agricultural purposes, but can be excellent land for pasture and forests if aggregated into sufficiently large parcels. By developing communal property rights to large parcels of such land, those who are members of the community are able to share environmental risks due to the unpredictability of rain-induced growth of grasses within any smaller region. Further, herding and processing of milk products is subject to substantial economies of scale. If individual families develop means to share these reduced costs, all can save substantially. Building the appropriate roads, retaining walls, and processing facilities may also be done more economically if these efforts are shared.

While the Swiss peasants were able to devote these harsh lands to productive activities, they had to invest time and effort in the development of rules that would reduce the incentives to overgraze and would ensure that investments in shared infrastructure were maintained over time. In many Swiss villages, rights to common pasturage were distributed according to the number of cows that could be carried over the winter using hay supplies produced on the owners' private parcels. In all cases, the village determined which farmers would be allowed to use, the specific access and withdrawal rights to be used, how investment and maintenance costs were to be shared, and how the annual returns from common processing activities were to be shared. All of these systems included at least village proprietorship rights, but some Swiss villages developed full ownership rights by incorporating and authorizing the buying and selling of shares (usually with the approval of the village). Netting's findings are strongly supported by studies of mountain villages in Japan, where thousands of rural villages have held communal property rights to extensive forests and grazing areas located in the steep mountainous regions located above their private agricultural plots (McKean 1982, 1992). Similar systems have existed in Norway for centuries (Sandberg 1993; Örebech 1993).

The importance of sharing risk is stressed in other theoretical and empirical studies of communal proprietorships (Nugent and Sanchez 1993; Gupta 1986; Antilla and Torp 1996). Unpredictability and risk are increased in systems where resource units are mobile and where storage facilities, such as dams, do not exist (Schlager, Blomquist, and Tang 1994). Institutional facilities for sharing risk, such as formal insurance systems or institutionalized mechanisms for reciprocal obligations in times of plenty, also affect the kinds of property-rights systems that individuals can devise. When no physical or institutional mechanisms exist for sharing risk, communal property arrangements may enable individuals to adopt productive activities not feasible under individual property rights. A recent study has demonstrated that the variance in the productivity of land over space—due largely to the variance in rainfall from year to year—is strongly associated with the size of communally held parcels allocated to grazing in the Sudan (Nugent and Sanchez 1995). Ellickson (1993) compares the types of environmental and personal security risks faced by new settlers in New England, in Bermuda, and in Utah to explain the variance in the speed of converting jointly held land to individually held land in each of these settlements.

A consistent finding across many studies of communal property-rights systems is that these systems do not exist in isolation and are usually used in conjunction with individual ownership. In most irrigation systems that are built and managed by the farmers themselves, for example, each farmer owns his or her own plot(s) while participating as a joint proprietor or owner in a communally organized irrigation system (Tang 1992; Sengupta 1991, 1993; Vincent 1995; Wade 1992; Coward 1980). Water is allocated to individual participants using a variety of individually tailored rules, but those irrigation systems that have survived for long periods of time tend to allocate water and responsibilities for joint costs using a similar metric—frequently the amount of land owned by a farmer (E. Ostrom 1992). In other words, benefits are roughly proportional to the costs of investing and maintaining the system itself.

Further, formally recognized communal systems are usually nested into a series of governance units that complement the organizational skills and knowledge of those involved in making collective-choice decisions in smaller units (Johnson 1972). Since the Middle Ages, most of the Alpine systems in both Switzerland and Italy have been nested in a series of self-governing communities that respectively governed villages, valleys, and federations of valleys (Merlo 1989). In modern times, cantonal authorities in Switzerland have assumed an added responsibility to make periodic, careful monitoring visits to each alp on a rotating basis and to provide professional assessments and recommendations to local villages, thereby greatly enhancing the quality of knowledge and information about the sustainability of these resources (Glaser 1987).

Contrary to the expectation that communal property systems lacking the right to alienate ownership shares are markedly less efficient than property-rights systems involving full ownership, substantial evidence exists that many communal proprietorships effectively solve a wide diversity of local problems with relatively low transaction costs (Hanna and Munasinghe 1995a, 1995b; Wilson 1995; Sandberg 1993, 1996a, 1996b; Gaffney 1992; Chakravarty-Kaul 1996). Obtaining valid and reliable measures of outputs and costs for a large number of property-rights systems covering similar activities in matched environmental settings is extremely difficult. In regard to irrigation, a series of careful studies of the performance of communal proprietorship systems, as contrasted with government-owned and managed systems, clearly demonstrates the higher productivity of the communal systems controlling for relevant variables (Tang 1992; Benjamin et al. 1994; E. Ostrom 1996; Lam 1998). Schlager's (1990) studies of inshore fisheries demonstrate that fishers who have clearly defined proprietorship are able to solve difficult assignment problems and assign the use of space and technology so as to increase both the efficiency and equity of their systems. Wilson's (1995) studies also demonstrate that communal proprietorship systems are more efficient than frequently thought.

Performances of communal property-rights systems vary substantially, however, as do the performances of all property-rights systems. Some communal systems fail or limp along at the margin of effectiveness just as private firms fail or barely hang on to profitability over long periods of time. In addition to the environmental variables discussed above that are conducive in the first place to the use of communal proprietorship or ownership, the following variables related to the attributes of participants are conducive to their selection of norms, rules, and property rights that enhance the performance of communal property-rights systems (E. Ostrom 1993):

1. Accurate information about the condition of the resource and expected flow of benefits and costs is available at low cost to the participants (Blomquist 1992; Gilles and Jamtgaard 1981).

2. Participants share a common understanding about the potential benefits and risks associated with the continuance of the status quo as contrasted with changes in norms and rules that they could feasibly adopt (E. Ostrom 1990; Sethi and Somanathan 1996).

3. Participants share generalized norms of reciprocity and trust that can be used as initial social capital (Cordell and McKean 1992).

4. The group using the resource is relatively stable (Seabright 1993).

5. Participants plan to live and work in the same area for a long time (and in some cases, expect their offspring to live there as well) and, thus, do not heavily discount the future (Grima and Berkes 1989).

6. Participants use collective-choice rules that fall between the extremes of unanimity or control by a few (or even bare majority) and, thus, avoid high transaction or high deprivation costs (E. Ostrom 1990).

7. Participants can develop relatively accurate and low-cost monitoring and sanctioning arrangements (Berkes 1992).

Many of these variables are, in turn, affected by the type of larger regime in which users are embedded. If the larger regime recognizes the legitimacy of communal systems, and is facilitative of local self-organization by providing accurate information about natural resource systems, providing arenas in which participants can engage in discovery and conflict-resolution processes, and providing mechanisms to back up local monitoring and sanctioning efforts, the probability of participants adapting more effective rules over time is higher than in regimes that ignore resource problems or presume that all decisions about governance and management need to be made by central authorities.

Two additional variables—the size of a group and its homogeneity—have been noted as conducive to the initial organization of communal resources and to their successful performance over time (E. Ostrom 1992; Libecap 1989a, 1989b; Kanbur 1991). As more research has been conducted, however, it is obvious that much more theoretical and empirical work is needed since both variables appear to have complex effects. Changing the size of a group, for example, always involves changing some of the other variables likely to affect the performance of a system. Increasing the size of a group is likely to be associated with at least the following changes: (1) an increase in the transaction costs of reaching agreements; (2) a reduction of the burden borne by each participant for meeting joint costs such as guarding a system, and maintenance; and (3) an increase in the amount of assets held by the group that could be used in times of emergency. Libecap (1995) found that it was particularly hard to get agreements to oil unitization with groups greater than four. Blomquist (1992), on the other hand, documents processes conducted in the shadow of an equity court that involved up to 750 participants in agreeing to common rules to allocate rights to withdraw water from groundwater basins in southern California. The processes took a relatively long period of time, but they have now also survived with little administrative costs for half a century. Agrawal (2000) has shown that communal forestry institutions in India that are moderate in size are more likely to reduce overharvesting than are smaller groups because they are able to mobilize more resources for guarding than smaller groups.

Group heterogeneity is also multifaceted in its basic causal processes and effects. Groups can differ along many dimensions including their assets, their information, their valuation of final products, their production technologies, their time horizons, their exposure to risk (e.g., headenders versus tailenders on irrigation systems), as well as their cultural belief systems. Libecap's (1989b) research on inshore fisheries has shown that when fishers have distinctively different production technologies and skills, all potential rules for sharing withdrawal rights have substantial distributional consequences and are the source of conflict that may not easily be overcome. Libecap and Wiggins's (1984) studies of the prorationing of crude oil production reveal an interesting relationship between the levels and type of information available to participants and the likelihood of agreement at various stages in a bargaining process. In the early stages of negotiation, all oil producers share a relatively equal level of ignorance about the relative claims that each might be able to make under private-property arrangements. This is the most likely time for oil unitization agreements to be reached successfully. If agreement is not reached early, each participant gains asymmetric information about their own claims as more and more investment is made in private information. Agreements are unlikely at this stage. If producers then aggressively pump from a common oil pool, all tend to be harmed by the overproduction and are willingly late in the process to recognize their joint interests.

Libecap's (1995) study of marketing agreements among orange growers also shows a strong negative impact of heterogeneity. The theoretical work of Mancur Olson (1965) on privileged groups, on the other hand, predicts that when some participants have substantial assets and whose interests are aligned with achieving an agreement, such groups are more likely to be organized. The empirical support for this proposition comes more from studies of global commons (Mitchell 1995; Oye and Maxwell 1995).

Attributes of Common-Pool Resources Conducive to Use of Individual Rights to Withdrawal, Management, Exclusion, and Alienation

The advantage of individual ownership of strictly private goods—where the cost of exclusion is relatively low and one person's consumption is subtractive from what is available to others—is so well established that it does not merit attention here. Industrial and agricultural commodities clearly fit the definition of private goods. Individual rights to exclusion and to transferring control over these goods generate incentives that lead to higher levels of productivity than other forms of property arrangements.

It has frequently been assumed that land also is always a private good and therefore best allocated using market mechanisms based on individual ownership rights. Agricultural land in densely settled regions is usually best allocated by a system of individual property rights. Gaining formal title to land, however, may or may not increase efficiency. Feder et al. (1988) conducted an important econometric study that showed that agricultural land in Thailand without a formal title was worth only one-half to two-thirds of land with a formal title. Further, increasing the security of private-property rights also led to an increased value of the crops produced (between one-tenth and one-fourth higher than those without secure title). More secure titling also provided better access to credit and led to greater investments in improved land productivity (see also Feder and Feeny 1991).

Title insurance is another mechanism used to reduce the risk of successful challenges to ownership of land. Registering brands is still another technique used to increase the security of ownership over resource units in the form of cattle that may range freely over a large area until there is a communal effort to undertake a roundup. Gaining formal titles is, however, costly. In societies that do not yet have high population densities and where customary rights are still commonly understood and accepted, formal titling may be an expensive method of increasing the security of a title that is not associated with a sufficiently higher return to be worth the economic investment (see Migot-Adholla et al. 1991). In addition, it should now be clear that the cost of fencing land by physical and/or institutional means is nontrivial and that there are types of land and land uses that may be more efficiently governed by groups of individuals rather than single individuals.

A commonly recommended solution to problems associated with the governance and management of mobile resource units, such as water and fish, is their "privatization" (Christy 1973; Clark 1980). What private ownership usually means in regard to mobile resource units, however, is individual ownership of withdrawal rights. Water rights are normally associated with the allocation of a particular quantity of water per unit of time or the allocation of a right to take water for a particular period of time or at a particular location. Fishing rights are similarly associated with quantity, time, or location. These rights are typically "withdrawal" rights that are tied to resource units and not to a resource system. In addition to the individual water rights that farmers hold in an irrigation system, they may also jointly own—and, therefore, govern and manage—the irrigation facilities themselves (Tang 1992). In addition to the quotas or "fishing units" that individual fishers may own, no one owns the fishing stock and governmental units may exercise various types of management rights in relationship to these stocks (Schlager 1990). In groundwater basins that have been successfully litigated, individual pumpers own a defined quantity of water that they can produce, rent, or sell, but the groundwater basins themselves may be managed by a combination of general-purpose and special-purpose governmental units and private associations (Blomquist 1992).

Implementing operational and efficient individual withdrawal rights to mobile resources is far more difficult in practice than demonstrating the economic efficiency of hypothetical systems. Simply gaining valid and accurate measurements of "sustainable yield" is a scientifically difficult task. In systems where resource units are stored naturally or by constructing facilities such as a dam, the availability of a defined quantity of the resource units can be ascertained with considerable accuracy, and buying, selling, and leasing rights to known quantities is relatively easy to effectuate in practice. Many mobile resource systems do not have natural or constructed storage facilities, and gaining accurate information about the stock and reproduction rates is very costly and involves considerable uncertainty (Allen and McGlade 1987; Wilson et al. 1991). Further, as Copes (1986) has clearly articulated, appropriators from such resources can engage in a wide diversity of evasive strategies that can destabilize the efforts of government agencies trying to manage these systems. Further, once such systems have allocated individual withdrawal rights, efforts to further regulate patterns of withdrawal may be very difficult and involve expensive buyback schemes (Örebech 1982). Experience with these individual withdrawal-rights systems has varied greatly in practice (see Pinkerton 1992, 1994; McCay 1992; McCay et al. 1996; Wilson and Dickie 1995).

Exactly which attributes of both physical and social systems are most important to the success of individual withdrawal rights from common-pool resources is not as well established as the attributes of common-pool resource systems conducive to group proprietorship or ownership. On the physical side, gaining accurate measurements of the key variables (quantity, space, technology) that are to be involved in management efforts is essential. Resource systems that are naturally well bounded facilitate measurement as well as ease of observing appropriation behavior. Storage also facilitates measurement. Where resource units move over vast terrain, the cost of measurement is higher than when they are contained (e.g., it is easier to develop effective withdrawal-rights systems for lobsters than for whales).

Considerable recent research has also stressed the importance of involving participants in the design and implementation of such property-rights systems. When participants do not look upon such rules as legitimate, effective, and fair, the capacity to invent evasive strategies is substantial (Seabright 1993; Wilson 1995). The size of the group involved and the heterogeneity of participants also affect the costs of maintaining withdrawal-rights systems (Edwards 1994). And, the very process of allocating quantitative and transferable rights to resource units may undo some of the common understandings and norms that allowed communal ownership systems to operate at lower day-to-day administrative costs.

Common-Property Regimes in the Twenty-First Century

Much of this chapter has focused on natural resources. Many of the lessons learned from the operation of common-property regimes in these sectors, however, are quite relevant for a wide diversity of similar property regimes that are currently in wide use and likely to have a substantial presence in the next century. A very large number of housing developments—both apartment houses and individual family dwellings—involve individual property to the housing unit itself combined with common property to the grounds, recreational facilities, and other joint facilities. While individuals can buy and sell their individual housing units, at the time of purchase they assume a set of duties in respect to the closely related communal properties. Monthly assessments for the repair and maintenance of these common facilities are not unlike the assessments made by a community of irrigators on themselves for the maintenance of their own system. Further, purchase and sales frequently require the permission of other members of the group. Similarly, many sports clubs allocate use quotas to members and assess members' regular fees for the maintenance of the commonly owned facilities.

As Cutler (this volume) shows, private governance is frequently related to common-pool resources. The modern corporation is frequently thought of as the epitome of private property. While buying and selling shares of corporate stock is a clear example of the rights of alienation at work, relationships within a firm are far from being "individual" ownership rights. Since the income that will be shared among stockholders, management, and employees is itself a common pool to be shared, all of the incentives leading to free riding (shirking) and overuse (padding the budget) are found within the structure of a modern corporation (Putterman 1995; Seabright 1993; Ghoshal and Moran 1996). Thus, where many individuals will work, live, and play in the next century will be governed and managed by mixed systems of common property and individual property rights. Hopefully, the complexity of the goods, of the users, and of the property-rights systems linking users with goods will also be recognized in future work. Otherwise, we will face another half century of searching for the holy grail of the single attribute that clearly identifies the optimal property-rights system for all goods.

Notes

The support by the National Science Foundation (Grant #SBR 9521918) and the Bradley Foundation is gratefully acknowledged. Comments by participants at the conference held in Bonn, Germany, in July 2000, were extremely useful—particularly those of Adrienne Héritier and Christoph Engel. Patty Zielinski's superb editing skills are once again deeply appreciated.
 1. The example they use to illustrate such a production function is calling about a pothole in a neighborhood where a city administration is sensitive to citizen support (Marwell and Oliver 1993, 62). The first call brings the pothole to the attention of city officials and puts it on the list of things to be repaired (raising the probability of repair from zero to perhaps .4 or higher). The second call increases the probability of repair still further, but not as much as the first call. Later calls continue to increase the probability but with a smaller and smaller increment.
 2. A strike involving only a few workers is unlikely to produce the level of benefits yielded by a strike involving a very large proportion of the workers of a firm or in an industry.
 3. Step-level functions are, however, not strictly social dilemmas when there is complete information about the exact shape of the function. When individuals perceive themselves as critical to the achievement of a collective good, the game becomes a coordination game rather than a social dilemma.
 4. Step functions characterize facilities such as bridges, tunnels, and roads that have little value if not completed. Some scholars have argued that many public goods are characterized by provision points (Taylor 1987; Hampton 1987; Taylor and Ward 1982).
 5. These experiments were also conducted at Utah State University several years after the first experiments had been conducted at the University of Oregon.

References

Adasiak, A. 1979. Alaska's Experience with Limited Entry. *Journal of the Fisheries Research Board of Canada* 36 (7): 770-82.

Agrawal, A. 1994. Rules, Rule Making, and Rule Breaking: Examining the Fit between Rule Systems and Resource Use. In *Rules, Games, and Common-Pool Resources*, ed. E. Ostrom, R. Gardner, and J. Walker, 267-82. Ann Arbor: University of Michigan Press.

———. 2000. Small Is Beautiful, but Is Larger Better? Forest-Management Institutions in the Kumaon Himalaya, India. In *People and Forests: Communities, Institutions, and Governance*, ed. C. Gibson, M. McKean, and E. Ostrom, 57-85. Cambridge, Mass.: MIT Press.

Allen, P. M., and J. M. McGlade. 1987. Modelling Complex Human Systems: A Fisheries Example. *European Journal of Operational Research* 30: 147-67.

Antilla, S., and A. Torp. 1996. Environmental Adjustment and Private Economic Strategies in Reindeer Pastoralism: Combining Game Theory with Participatory Action Theory. Working paper. Mid-Sweden University.

Benjamin, P., W. F. Lam, E. Ostrom, and G. Shivakoti. 1994. Institutions, Incentives, and Irrigation in Nepal. Decentralization: Finance & Management Project Report. Burlington, Vt.: Associates in Rural Development.

Berkes, F., ed. 1989. *Common Property Resources: Ecology and Community-Based Sustainable Development*. London: Belhaven.

————. 1992. Success and Failure in Marine Coastal Fisheries of Turkey. In *Making the Commons Work: Theory, Practice, and Policy*, ed. D. Feeny, M. McKean, P. Peters, J. Gilles, R. Oakerson, C. Ford Runge, and J. Thomson, 161-82. San Francisco: ICS Press.

Blomquist, W. 1992. *Dividing the Waters: Governing Groundwater in Southern California*. San Francisco: ICS Press.

Blomquist, W., and E. Ostrom. 1985. Institutional Capacity and the Resolution of a Commons Dilemma. *Policy Studies Review* 5 (2): 383-93.

Bromley, D. W., D. Feeny, M. McKean, P. Peters, J. Gilles, R. Oakerson, C. Ford Runge, and J. Thomson, eds. 1992. *Making the Commons Work: Theory, Practice, and Policy*. San Francisco: ICS Press.

Bruce, J. W. 1995. *Legal Bases for the Management of Land-Based Natural Resources as Common Property*. Rome: Forests, Trees and People Programme, Food and Agriculture Organization of the United Nations.

Bruce, J. W., L. Fortmann, and C. Nhira. 1993. Tenures in Transition, Tenures in Conflict: Examples from the Zimbabwe Social Forest. *Rural Sociology* 58 (4): 626-42.

Bruce, J. W., and S. E. Migot-Adholla, eds. 1994. *Searching for Land Tenure Security in Africa*. Dubuque, Iowa: Kendall/Hunt.

Chakravarty-Kaul, M. 1996. *Common Lands and Customary Law: Institutional Change in North India over the Past Two Centuries*. Oxford: Oxford University Press.

Chamberlin, J. 1974. Provision of Collective Goods as a Function of Group Size. *American Political Science Review* 68 (2): 707-16.

Christy, F. T. 1973. *Fisherman Quotas: A Tentative Suggestion for Domestic Management*. Kingston: University of Rhode Island, Law of the Sea Institute.

Clark, C. W. 1980. Restricted Access to Common-Property Fishery Resources: A Game Theoretic Analysis. In *Dynamic Optimization and Mathematical Economics*, ed. P. T. Lin, 117-32. New York: Plenum.

Commons, J. R. 1968. *Legal Foundations of Capitalism*. Madison: University of Wisconsin Press.

Copes, P. 1986. A Critical Review of the Individual Quota as a Device in Fisheries Management. *Land Economics* 62 (3): 278-91.

Cordell, J. C., and M. A. McKean. 1992. Sea Tenure in Bahia, Brazil. In *Making the Commons Work: Theory, Practice, and Policy*, ed. D. W. Bromley, D. Feeny, M. McKean, P. Peters, J. Gilles, R. Oakerson, C. Ford Runge, and J. Thomson, 183-205. San Francisco: ICS Press.

Cornes, R., and T. Sandler. 1994. Are Public Goods Myths? *Journal of Theoretical Politics* 6 (3): 369-85.

Coward, E. W., Jr., ed. 1980. *Irrigation and Agricultural Development in Asia: Perspectives from the Social Sciences*. Ithaca, N.Y.: Cornell University Press.

Dahl, R. A., and C. E. Lindblom. 1963. *Politics, Economics and Welfare: Planning and Politico-Economic Systems Resolved into Basic Social Processes*. New York: Harper.

Demsetz, H. 1967. Toward a Theory of Property Rights. *American Economic Review* 62: 347-59.

Edwards, Steven F. 1994. Ownership of Renewable Ocean Resources. *Land Economics* 9: 253-73.

Ellickson, R. C. 1993. Property in Land. *Yale Law Journal* 102: 1315-44.

Feder, G., and D. Feeny. 1991. Land Tenure and Property Rights: Theory and Implications for Development Policy. *World Bank Economic Review* 5 (1): 135-53.

Feder, G., T. Onchan, Y. Chalamwong, and C. Hangladoran. 1988. *Land Policies and Form Productivity in Thailand.* Baltimore: Johns Hopkins University Press.

Feeny, D. 1993. The Demand for and the Supply of Institutional Arrangements. In *Rethinking Institutional Analysis and Development,* ed. V. Ostrom, D. Feeny, and H. Picht, 159-209. San Francisco: ICS Press.

Feeny, D., F. Berkes, B. J. McCay, and J. M. Acheson. 1990. The Tragedy of the Commons: Twenty-Two Years Later. *Human Ecology* 18 (l): 1-19.

Field, B. C. 1984. The Evolution of Individual Property Rights in Massachusetts Agriculture, Seventeenth-Nineteenth Centuries. *Northeastern Journal of Agricultural and Resource Economics* 14: 97-109.

————. 1985. The Optimal Commons. *American Journal of Agricultural Economics* 67: 364-67.

————. 1989. The Evolution of Property Rights. *Kyklos* 42 (3): 319-45.

Gaffney, M. 1992. The Taxable Surplus in Water Resources. *Contemporary Policy Issues* 10: 74-82.

Ghoshal, S., and P. Moran. 1996. Bad for Practice: A Critique of the Transaction Cost Theory. *Academy of Management Review* 21 (1): 13-47.

Gilles, J. L., and K. Jamtgaard. 1981. Overgrazing in Pastoral Areas: The Commons Reconsidered. *Sociologia Ruralis* 2: 335-58.

Glaser (Picht), C. 1987. Common Property Regimes in Swiss Alpine Meadows. Presented at the Conference on Advances in Comparative Institutional Analysis, Inter-University Center of Postgraduate Studies, Dubrovnik, Yugoslavia, October 19-23.

Gordon, H. S. 1954. The Economic Theory of a Common-Property Resource: The Fishery. *Journal of Political Economy* 62: 124-42.

Grima, A. P. L., and F. Berkes. 1989. Natural Resources: Access, Rights to Use and Management. In *Common Property Resources; Ecology and Community-Based Sustainable Development,* ed. F. Berkes, 33-54. London: Belhaven.

Gupta, A. K. 1986. Socioecology of Stress: Why Do Common Property Resource Management Projects Fail? In *Proceedings of the Conference on Common Property Resource Management, National Research Council,* 305-22. Washington, D.C.: National Academy Press.

Hampton, J. 1987. Free Rider Problems in the Production of Public Goods. *Economics and Philosophy* 3: 245-73.

Hanna, S., and M. Munasinghe. 1995a. An Introduction to Property Rights and the Environment. In *Property Rights and the Environment,* ed. S. Hanna and M. Munasinghe. Stockholm: The Beijer International Institute of Ecological Economics and The World Bank.

————. 1995b. *Property Rights in a Social and Ecological Context; Case Studies and Design Applications.* Stockholm: The Beijer International Institute of Ecological Economics and The World Bank.

Hardin, R. 1976. Group Provision of Goods. *Behavioral Science* 21: 101-6.

————. 1982. *Collective Action.* Baltimore: Johns Hopkins University Press.

Isaac, R. Mark, and James M. Walker. 1988. Group Size Effects in Public Goods Provision: The Voluntary Contributions Mechanism. *Quarterly Journal of Economics* 103: 179-99.

Isaac, R. Mark, James M. Walker, and Arlington W. Williams. 1994. Group Size and the Voluntary Provision of Public Goods: Experimental Evidence Utilizing Large Groups. *Journal of Public Economics* 54 (1): 1-36.

Johnson, O. E. G. 1972. Economic Analysis: The Legal Framework and Land Tenure Systems. *Journal of Law and Economics* 15 (1): 259-76.

Kanbur, R. 1991. Heterogeneity, Distribution and Cooperation in Common Property Resource Management. Background paper. Washington, D.C.: The World Bank.

Lam, W. F. 1998. *Governing Irrigation Systems in Nepal: Institutions, Infrastructure, and Collective Action.* Oakland, Calif.: ICS Press.

Larson, B. A., and D. W. Bromley. 1990. Property Rights, Externalities, and Resource Degradation: Locating the Tragedy. *Journal of Development Economics* 33 (2): 235-62.

Libecap, G. D. 1989a. *Contracting for Property Rights.* New York: Cambridge University Press.

————. 1989b. Distributional Issues in Contracting for Property Rights. *Journal of Institutional and Theoretical Economics* 145: 6-24.

————. 1995. The Conditions for Successful Collective Action. In *Local Commons and Global Interdependence: Heterogeneity and Cooperation in Two Domains*, ed. R. O. Keohane and E. Ostrom, 161-90. London: Sage.

Libecap, G. D., and S. N. Wiggins. 1984. Contractual Responses to the Common Pool: Prorationing of Crude Oil Production. *American Economic Review* 74: 87-98.

Maass, A., and R. L. Anderson. 1986. *. . . and the Desert Shall Rejoice: Conflict, Growth, and Justice in Arid Environments.* Malabar, Fla.: R. E. Krieger.

Martin, E. G. 1986. Resource Mobilization, Water Allocation, and Farmer Organization in Hill Irrigation Systems in Nepal. Ph.D. dissertation. Ithaca, N.Y.: Cornell University.

Martin, E. G., and R. Yoder. 1983a. Review of Farmer-Managed Irrigation in Nepal. In *Water Management in Nepal: Proceedings of the Seminar on Water Management Issues.* July 31-August 2, 82-91. Kathmandu, Nepal: Ministry of Agriculture, Agricultural Projects Services Centre, and the Agricultural Development Council.

————. 1983b. The Chherlung Thulo Kulo: A Case Study of a Farmer-Managed Irrigation System. In *Water Management in Nepal: Proceedings of the Seminar on Water Management Issues*, July 31-August 2, 203-17. Kathmandu, Nepal: Ministry of Agriculture, Agricultural Projects Services Centre, and the Agricultural Development Council.

————. 1983c. Water Allocation and Resource Mobilization for Irrigation: A Comparison of Two Systems in Nepal. Presented at the annual meeting of the Nepal Studies Association, University of Wisconsin, Madison, November 4-6.

Martin, Kent O. 1979. Play by the Rules or Don't Play at All: Space Division and Resource Allocation in a Rural Newfoundland Fishing Community. In *North Atlantic Maritime Cultures: Anthropological Essays on Changing Adaptations.* Raoul Anderson, ed., 276-98. The Hague: Mouton.

Marwell, G., and P. Oliver. 1993. The Critical Mass in Collective Action: A Micro-Social Theory. New York: Cambridge University Press.

McCay, B. J. 1992. Everyone's Concern, Whose Responsibility?: The Problem of the Commons. In *Understanding Economic Process: Monographs in Economic Anthropology*, no. 10, ed. S. Ortiz and S. Lees. Lanham, Md.: University Press of America.

McCay, B. J., and J. M. Acheson, eds. 1987. *The Question of the Commons: The Culture and Ecology of Communal Resources.* Tucson: University of Arizona Press.

McCay, B. J., I. Wright, R. Apostle, and L. Mazany. 1996. Fleet Concentration in an ITQ Fishery: A Case Study of the Southwest Nova Scotia Mobile Gear Fleet. Presented at the sixth annual conference of the International Association for the Study of Common Property, Berkeley, Calif., June 5-8.

McKean, M. A. 1982. The Japanese Experience with Scarcity: Management of Traditional Common Lands. *Environmental Review* 6 (2): 63-88.

————. 1992. Management of Traditional Common Lands (Iriaichi) in Japan. In *Making the Commons Work: Theory, Practice, and Policy*, ed. D. Feeny, M. McKean, P. Peters, J. Gilles, R. Oakerson, C. Ford Runge, and J. Thomson, 63-98. San Francisco: ICS Press.

Merlo, M. 1989. The Experience of the Village Communities in the North-Eastern Italian Alps. In *Collective Forest Land Tenure and Rural Development in Italy*, ed. M. Merlo, R. Morandini, A. Gabbrielli, and I. Novaco, 1-54. Rome: Food and Agriculture Organization of the United Nations.

Migot-Adholla, S. E., P. Hazell, B. Blarel, and F. Place. 1991. Indigenous Land Rights Systems in Sub-Saharan Africa: A Constraint on Productivity? *World Bank Economic Review* 5 (1): 155-75.

Miller, D. 1989. The Evolution of Mexico's Spiny Lobster Fishery. In *Common Property Resources: Ecology and Community-Based Sustainable Development*, ed. F. Berkes, 185-98. London: Belhaven.

Mitchell, R. B. 1995. Heterogeneities at Two Levels: States, Non-state Actors and Intentional Oil Pollution. In *Local Commons and Global Interdependence: Heterogeneity and Cooperation in Two Domains*, ed. R. O. Keohane and E. Ostrom, 223-51. London: Sage.

Montias, J. M. 1976. *The Structure of Economic Systems*. New Haven, Conn.: Yale University Press.

Musgrave, R. A. 1959. *The Theory of Public Finance*. New York: McGraw-Hill.

Netting, R. McC. 1976. What Alpine Peasants Have in Common: Observations on Communal Tenure in a Swiss Village. *Human Ecology* 4: 135-46.

————. 1981. *Balancing on an Alp: Ecological Change and Continuity in a Swiss Mountain Community*. New York: Cambridge University Press.

Nugent, J. B., and N. Sanchez. 1993. Tribes, Chiefs, and Transhumance: A Comparative Institutional Analysis. *Economic Development and Cultural Change* 42: 87-113.

————. 1995. The Local Variability of Rainfall and Tribal Institutions: The Case of Sudan. Presented to the Middle East Economic Association, Washington, D.C., January 7.

Olson, M. 1965. *The Logic of Collective Action: Public Goods and the Theory of Groups*. Cambridge, Mass.: Harvard University Press.

Örebech, P. 1982. *Konsesjoner i fisket*. Oslo, Norway: TANO.

————. 1993. Common and Public Property Rights Regimes to Non-Private Resources. Some Legal Issues on Self-Governing Conservation Systems. In *Common Property Regimes: Law and Management of Non-private Resources; Proceedings of the Conference, Vol. I*, ed. Erling Berge. Ås, Norway: Agricultural University of Norway.

Ostrom, E. 1990. *Governing the Commons: The Evolution of Institutions for Collective Action*. New York: Cambridge University Press.

————. 1992. The Rudiments of a Theory of the Origins, Survival, and Performance of Common-Property Institutions. In *Making the Commons Work: Theory, Practice, and Policy*, ed. D. W. Bromley, D. Feeny, M. McKean, P. Peters, J. Gilles, R. Oakerson, C. Ford Runge, and J. Thomson, 293-318. San Francisco: ICS Press.

————. 1993. The Evolution of Norms, Rules, and Rights. Presented at a Workshop on Social and Ecological System Linkages of the Property Rights and Performance of Natural Resource Systems Group at the Beijer International Institute of Ecological Economics, The Royal Swedish Academy of Sciences, September 2-4.

————. 1996. Incentives, Rules of the Game, and Development. In *Proceedings of the Annual World Bank Conference on Development Economics 1995*, 207-34. Washington, D.C.: The World Bank.

Ostrom, E., R. Gardner, and J. M Walker. 1994. *Rules, Games, and Common-Pool Resources.* Ann Arbor: University of Michigan Press.

Ostrom, E., and E. Schlager. 1996. The Formation of Property Rights. In *Rights to Nature,* ed. S. Hanna, C. Folke, and K.-G. Mäler, 127-56. Washington, D.C.: Island Press.

Ostrom, V., and E. Ostrom. 1977. A Theory for Institutional Analysis of Common Pool Problems. In *Managing the Commons,* ed. G. Hardin and J. Baden, 157-72. San Francisco: W. H. Freeman.

Oye, K. A., and J. H. Maxwell. 1995. Self-Interest and Environmental Management. In *Local Commons and Global Interdependence: Heterogeneity and Cooperation in Two Domains,* ed. R. O. Keohane and E. Ostrom, 191-221. London: Sage.

Pinkerton, E. 1992. Conclusions: Where Do We Go from Here? The Future of Traditional Ecological Knowledge and Resource Management in Canadian Native Communities. In *Traditional Ecological Knowledge and Environmental Assessment,* ed. P. Boothroyd and B. Sadler. Ottawa: Canadian Environmental Assessment Research Council.

———. 1994. Local Fisheries Co-Management: A Review of International Experiences and Their Implications for Salmon Management in British Columbia. *Canadian Journal of Fisheries and Aquatic Sciences* 51 (2): 363-78.

Place, F., and P. Hazell. 1993. Productivity Effects of Indigenous Land Tenure Systems in Sub-Saharan Africa. *American Journal of Agricultural Economics* 75: 10-19.

Putterman, L. 1995. Markets, Hierarchies, and Information: On a Paradox in the Economics of Organization. *Journal of Economic Behavior and Organization* 26 (3): 373-90.

Rapoport, A., and A. M. Chammah. 1965. *Prisoner's Dilemma: A Study in Conflict and Cooperation.* Ann Arbor: University of Michigan Press.

Raychaudhuri, B. 1980. *The Moon and the Net: Study of a Transient Community of Fishermen at Jambudwip.* Calcutta: Government of India Press, Anthropological Survey of India.

Samuelson, P. A. 1954. The Pure Theory of Public Expenditure. *Review of Economics and Statistics* 36: 387-89.

Sandberg, A. 1993. The Analytical Importance of Property Rights to Northern Resources. Colloquium presentation, Indiana University, Bloomington, Workshop in Political Theory and Policy Analysis, September 27.

———. 1996a. A European Debate Revisited. Working paper. Bodö, Norway: Nordland College.

———. 1996b. Against the Wind: On Reintroducing Commons Law in Modern Society. Presented at the sixth annual conference of the International Association for the Study of Common Property, Berkeley, Calif., June 5-8.

Schlager, E. 1990. Model Specification and Policy Analysis: The Governance of Coastal Fisheries. Ph.D. dissertation. Bloomington: Indiana University.

———. 1994. Fishers' Institutional Responses to Common-Pool Resource Dilemmas. In *Rules, Games, and Common-Pool Resources,* ed. E. Ostrom, R. Gardner, and J. M. Walker, 247-65. Ann Arbor: University of Michigan Press.

Schlager, E., W. Blomquist, and S. Y. Tang. 1994. Mobile Flows, Storage, and Self-Organized Institutions for Governing Common-Pool Resources. *Land Economics* 70 (3): 294-317.

Schlager, E., and E. Ostrom. 1992. Property Rights Regimes and Natural Resources: A Conceptual Analysis. *Land Economics* 68 (3): 249-62.

Seabright, P. 1993. Managing Local Commons: Theoretical Issues in Incentive Design. *Journal of Economic Perspectives* 7 (4): 113-34.

Sengupta, N. 1991. *Managing Common Property: Irrigation in India and the Philippines.* New Delhi: Sage.
———. 1993. *User-Friendly Irrigation Designs.* New Delhi: Sage.
Sethi, R., and E. Somanathan. 1996. The Evolution of Social Norms in Common Property Resource Use. *American Economic Review* 86 (4): 766-88.
Singh, K. 1994. *Managing Common Pool Resources: Principles and Case Studies.* New Delhi: Oxford University Press.
Singh, K., and V. Ballabh. 1996. *Cooperative Management of Natural Resources.* New Delhi: Sage.
Siy, R. Y., Jr. 1982. *Community Resource Management: Lessons from the Zanjera.* Quezon City, Philippines: University of the Philippines Press.
Tang, S. Y. 1992. *Institutions and Collective Action: Self-Governance in Irrigation.* San Francisco: ICS Press.
———. 1994. Building Community Organizations: Credible Commitment and the New Institutional Economics. *Human Systems Management* 13: 221-32.
Taylor, M. 1987. *The Possibility of Cooperation.* New York: Cambridge University Press.
Taylor, M., and H. Ward. 1982. Chickens, Whales and Lumpy Goods: Alternative Models of Public Goods Provision. *Policy Studies* 30: 350-70.
van de Kragt, A., J. M. Orbell, and R. M. Dawes. 1983. The Minimal Contributing Set as a Solution to Public Goods Problems. *American Political Science Review* 77: 112-22.
Vincent, L. 1995. *Hill Irrigation: Water and Development in Mountain Agriculture.* London: Overseas Development Institute.
Wade, R. 1992. Common-Property Resource Management in South Indian Villages. In *Making the Commons Work: Theory, Practice, and Policy*, ed. D. Feeny, M. McKean, P. Peters, J. Gilles, R. Oakerson, C. Ford Runge, and J. Thomson, 207-29. San Francisco: ICS Press.
Wilson, J. A. 1995. When Are Common Property Institutions Efficient? Working paper. Orono: University of Maine, Department of Agriculture and Resource Economics.
Wilson, J. A., and L. M. Dickie. 1995. Parametric Management of Fisheries: An Ecosystem-Social Approach. In *Property Rights in a Social and Ecological Context: Case Studies and Design Applications*, ed. S. Hanna and M. Munasinghe. Washington, D.C.: The Beijer International Institute of Ecological Economics and The World Bank.
Wilson, J. A., J. French, P. Kleban, S. R. McKay, and R. Townsend. 1991. Chaotic Dynamics in a Multiple Species Fishery: A Model of Community Predation. *Ecological Modelling* 58: 303-22.

3

Transnational Common Goods: Regulatory Competition for Environmental Standards

Katharina Holzinger

Introduction

As elaborated in the chapter by Elinor Ostrom, two properties are traditionally thought to determine which goods are public ones: the non-rivalry of consumption and the non-excludability from consumption. The necessity for collective provision is based on these two properties. They create an incentive structure for rational individuals that prevents the efficient private provision of such goods. However, a social situation where a common good is to be provided is characterized by many additional properties. The analysis of common goods needs to look very carefully at the properties of the goods and of the social contexts in which they are provided; it also needs to analyze the consequences these properties have on the costs and benefits of the actors. Different cost and benefit structures lead to different strategic constellations, and these, in turn, make different opportunities available for institutional solutions to the problems of common goods provision. Therefore, the provision of common goods does not necessarily imply the incentive structure widely known as the prisoner's dilemma. Because the strategic constellation is determined by many attributes of the social situation, those situations have to be analyzed carefully before predictions are made to determine whether cooperation is possible and which institutions would be appropriate to solve the problem.

A systematic theoretical treatment is thus needed concerning how such attributes influence the strategic constellation. Matrix games are a useful analytical tool for doing this. Basic types of strategic constellations can be captured by two-by-two matrix games, although this a simplification. In an actual common goods problem there are usually more than two actors. There are usually more than two strategies available, too. In general, actors will be confronted with some degree of uncertainty, and measuring costs and benefits will not be easy. Finally, in cases of repeated interaction and ongoing relationships among the actors, the single-shot game does not truly reflect the strategic situation: many equilibria are possible if the game is played repeatedly. However, the two-by-two games have the merit of demonstrating a given strategic structure very clearly; and something can still be learned by the analysis of stage games. It is easy to derive implications for possible institutional solutions to the dilemmas from such clear structures.

This approach will be exemplified by showing how certain properties in the transnational provision of common goods influence the outcomes of regulatory competition in the case of environmental standards. Environmental standards can be viewed as common goods because they are the means for preserving the environmental good concerned. If some states use strict standards and others lax ones, the different states provide a different amount of the good. In case of transboundary or global environmental problems, this poses a second order dilemma because it leads to externalities between the states. It has been claimed that in such a situation regulatory competition between states leads to a *race to the bottom* with regard to environmental standards. Yet there is evidence of a *race to the top* in the environmental domain. As of yet, the analytical conditions under which either one of the two effects arises have not been adequately identified. This chapter analyzes some important factors that influence the outcome. Three properties will be varied in order to show how they determine the result of regulatory competition: the homogeneity or heterogeneity of actors, the type of standards used, and the prevailing trade regime. These variations lead to different strategic constellations, which imply different outcomes for regulatory competition.

Section two starts with an overview of those properties of situations in which common goods are provided that may have an effect on the strategic constellation of actors. In section three the argument for regulatory competition is developed. Section four draws some general conclusions about the requirements for institutional solutions to the different dilemmas.

Characteristics of Common Goods Provision

Public goods are usually defined by two characteristics: there is non-rivalry of consumption and non-excludability from consumption. Both attributes lead to positive or negative externalities, a general characteristic of common goods.[1] As a consequence of the externalities, if the provision of common goods is left to the market, they will not be provided in sufficient quantities. More specifically, non-rivalry is the cause of the undersupply in case of pure public goods, and non-excludability the cause of the overuse in case of common pool resources (Haveman 1973). Provision by the state is traditionally legitimized by this market failure (Samuelson 1954; Musgrave and Musgrave 1976). Game theoretic analysis of common goods leads to a similar result. The provision of common goods is generally thought of as strategic interaction of individuals within a certain strategic constellation, the prisoner's dilemma. Given this incentive structure, rational individuals choose the collectively and individually suboptimal strategy, i.e., they do not contribute to the provision of the common good. In game theoretic terms, this problem can only be solved by an external power, for example, the state.

This view of the problem of common goods must be qualified in three respects. First, it is not always possible for the state to solve common goods problems. When global common goods are at issue, international negotiations are the only way out. Secondly, both economics and game theory diagnose market failure, but it is still not clear whether state intervention leads to better results. The solutions developed by the economic "mechanism design" research (e.g., Blümel, Pethig, von dem Hagen 1986; Holler and Illing 2000) ignore the procedures that the affected groups, states, and multilevel systems actually use in political decision-making on common goods. Thirdly, it has been shown that common goods can be provided and prisoner dilemmas can be solved without the help of the state: in general, experimental research shows that a substantial amount of cooperation takes place (Ledyard 1995); empirical case studies show that commons can be governed without the intervention of an exogenous power (Ostrom 1990).

The empirical studies also show that situations where common goods are to be provided have many different properties. The two basic defining properties are not the only attributes to play a role in the provision of common goods. The need for common goods arises in a given social environment, and those goods have to be provided within a certain social setting. The social situations in which common goods are provided have many properties. In many cases these attributes influence the strategic constellation of actors. This means that these attributes also determine the type of dilemma the actors are exposed to (if there is a dilemma at all) as well as the possibilities for finding an institutional solution to the problem. Some of these attributes—such as group size—have already been theoretically or empirically analyzed, sometimes even extensively. The research question has often concerned how these properties influence the degree of actual cooperation in dilemmas. The strategic constellation will influence the degree of actual cooperation, but it is not equivalent to it. Situations in which common goods are provided vary in many dimensions. The resulting strategic constellations may therefore be very different, and in some cases cooperation may be a part of a rational strategy.

We already know that the strategic constellation associated with the provision of common goods is not necessarily a prisoner's dilemma. For example, Godwin and Shepard (1979) have shown that common property resources (CPR's) have many different characteristics and that the prisoner's dilemma does not properly represent all of them. Also, public goods, CPR's, and other collective-action problems have been analyzed as coordination games (e.g., Ford Runge 1984; Sandler and Sargent 1995), and as volunteer's dilemmas (e.g., Weesie and Franzen 1998; Rapoport 1988; Diekmann 1992). Hirshleifer (1983) has shown how aggregation technology—i.e., the way individual contributions add up to the socially available quantity of the good—affects the structure of the games and thus the equilibrium solutions (cf. Sandler 1997; Holzinger 2001).

However, Aggarwal and Dupont's observation that "the links between the characteristics of goods, the nature of strategic interaction between actors, and the effectiveness or need for international institutions have not been systematically treated" (1999, 393) is still correct, at least in political science research. In economics some work of this kind has been done in recent years, for example, by Sandler (e.g., 1998, 1997), Barrett (e.g., 1998a, 1998b, 1999), or Mäler and De Zeeuw (e.g., 1998). Nevertheless, Aggarwal and Dupont's statement is well-taken, as it implies that much more of this type of work is needed (Sandler 1998, 223).

Before presenting my analysis of regulatory competition, I shall give a short overview of the potential properties exhibited in situations in which common goods are provided (table 3.1). This is neither intended to be a comprehensive list of attributes nor a review of the literature. Only a few examples are mentioned for properties of common good situations and of related research. Broadly, three categories of attributes that influence strategic constellations can be distinguished: properties of the good itself, properties of the actors involved, and properties of the institutional setting.[2]

First, many attributes of the goods themselves have a clear impact on the strategic constellation. First of all, this is true for the "defining properties" of common goods (Samuelson 1954; Musgrave and Musgrave 1976): non-rivalry and non-excludability are the properties which make free riding possible, and which provide the incentive not to contribute. These attributes of goods are the factors which lead to a social dilemma, i.e., a situation where individual rationality does not lead to a collective optimum (cf. Ostrom in this volume). There are other demand-side properties of common goods which may influence the incentive structure; for example, the non-rejectability of a good. The importance of supply-side properties for the incentive structure in the provision of common goods was first shown by Hirshleifer (1983 and 1985); the term *technology of public supply aggregation* was coined by Cornes and Sandler (1996). Whether the contributions of the individual actors to a common good are additive or not, and whether they can be substituted for each another, is of crucial importance for the strategic constellation (cf., for example, Holzinger 2001).

Second, manifold attributes of actors are involved in a common goods problem. For example, many studies are devoted to the question of whether the usual assumption of the individual rationality of actors is empirically valid or not.[3] For the analysis I am proposing, this question is not relevant since the idea of a game theoretic representation of incentive structures presupposes that the assumption of individual rationality be made. Another important strand of research, spawned by Olson (1965), deals with the effects of group size or the anonymity of actors (e.g., Isaac, Walker, and Williams 1993; Güth and Kliemt 1995). The homogeneity or heterogeneity of the actors is a further important aspect. Heterogeneity may stem from the different benefits of the good, the different costs of contributing, the different strategies open to actors, and other things. It has been claimed that it is easier for heterogeneous actors to find a solution to the dilemma (Martin 1995). While this may be valid in certain situations, it is by no means a general truth, as has been shown, for example, by Hausken and Plümper (1999). In the following example heterogeneity seems to change the situation from a dilemma structure to another structure that is problematic from the distributional perspective.

Third, the institutional setting includes rights, rules, and conventions that apply in the respective situation. Property rights provide an important example. So far, not much research has been done on the effects that rules have on the incentive structure for common goods. The work of Ostrom, Gardner, and Walker (1994) is one exception. However, experimental research into public goods has, for example, analyzed the effects of communication (Ledyard 1995) and of sanctions (e.g., Ostrom, Gardner, and Walker 1992). In the remainder of this chapter the effect of trade regimes on regulatory competition shall be analyzed. The common good in question is to be secured through environmental regulations in cases of transboundary pollution.

Table 3.1.   Attributes of Common Goods Provision Situations

_1._	_Attributes of the goods themselves_
	• consumption properties: non-rivalry, non-excludability; non-rejectability • supply or production properties: aggregation function • territorial scope: fixed or adjustable • etc.
_2._	_Attributes of the actors and groups_
	• Small or large groups • Anonymity versus non-anonymity of the involved actors • Single interaction or long-term relationship • Homogeneity or heterogeneity of preferences of the involved actors • Symmetric versus asymmetric strategies • etc.
_3._	_Attributes of the legal, institutional, and social environment_
	• property rights • other legal restrictions • possibility of communication • transparency • possibility of sanctioning • etc.

Regulatory Competition for Environmental Standards

Regulatory Competition as a Common Goods Problem

Here I shall appeal to regulatory competition in the environmental field to show how different attributes of the situation affect the strategic problem and thus the outcome. Three dimensions of the different conditions will be varied. The first dimension is whether the payoffs for the actors are symmetric or asymmetric (homogeneous or heterogeneous preferences), the second is the type of standard used, and the third is the prevailing trade regime. Before I go on to discuss modeling, I shall consider why regulatory competition can be viewed as a common good problem.

The object of regulatory competition is environmental protection standards. It is not necessary to specify the environmental good, because many different goods may be concerned. What they have in common is their transboundary nature. "Purely domestic" regulations, for example, local noise standards, lie outside the scope of the following analysis. They affect several states or several jurisdictions which may regulate the use of the environmental good on their own. However, because of externalities between the jurisdictions that result from the transboundary nature of the goods, in general the individual regulations will not be efficient. Their geographical scope is provided by biological and physical conditions, and it cannot easily be adapted to political borders. Examples of such environmental goods are clean air, transboundary bodies of water, and the climate, to name a few. In many cases they are commons, which means that consumption is rival but not excludable. These goods are increasingly being destroyed as a consequence of productive and consumptive activities, for example, through emissions from products or production processes. The quality of the environmental goods is decreasing, and it may no longer be sufficient for some uses.

The contributions to the preservation or restoration of these goods consist, first of all, in reducing emissions (or, less specifically, in restricting the destructive activities). Since we are talking about common goods, in general the reduction will not be achieved by voluntary or market behavior, but by the regulatory activity of the affected jurisdiction. The regulation—for example, an emission standard—can be viewed as providing the common good within the jurisdiction. At the super-jurisdictional level the regulations of the individual jurisdictions must be viewed as the jurisdictional actors' contributions to the common good. In the following, the analysis will focus on the regulatory level.

In times of a globalized economy not only are environmental goods transboundary, but so are economic processes. Commodities that are subject to environmental regulation are traded internationally. Firms and economies are subject to international competition. In states with stricter environmental regulations, production costs for firms are higher and the firms consequently suffer a competitive disadvantage in comparison to firms in states with laxer standards.

The classical research question about regulatory competition is whether and under which conditions this situation leads to a regulatory *race to the bottom* or to a *race to the top*. In the case of transboundary environmental problems there is evidence of both outcomes (Vogel 1995, 1997; Kern 2000; Zürn 1997; Jänicke 1998). However, a convincing explanation and clarification of the conditions that lead to one or the other result is still missing. Some important factors have been dealt with in the literature, such as the distinction between product and production standards (Scharpf 1996, 1997, 2000), but most factors have not been systematically analyzed. Since this chapter only concentrates on three factors, it will not be able to fill this gap in the research. Its main contribution will consist in systematically analyzing these variables.

Homogeneous and Heterogeneous Actors

The first factor to be varied is the homogeneity and heterogeneity of actors. The problem of regulatory competition will be modeled as a two-by-two matrix game. The players are two states, which regulate the transboundary environmental good by emission standards. They have two strategies: namely, employing high (h) or low (l) standards. This is analogous to making "a large contribution" or "a small contribution" to the common good. Homogeneous states have the same preferences with respect to the two strategies; heterogeneous states have different preferences. The first case represents a symmetric game, as both players not only possess identical strategies, but also identical payoffs. The second case represents an asymmetric game.

I start with the symmetric case. The high standards are assumed to be equivalent to two units of contribution to the environmental good; the low standards are equivalent to one unit. The only further assumptions that must be made concern the relation of the costs and benefits of the standards. Two cases can be distinguished: (1) the benefits (b) per unit of contribution are higher than the costs (c) per unit, and (2) the costs per unit are higher than the benefits. A numerical example will be given along with a general formulation.

Table 3.2. Regulatory Competition in the Symmetric Case

Case 1: b>c   Example: b per unit = 4; c per unit = 3

	strategy combination	benefits	costs	payoff	general payoff
Country A	A: l, B: l	8	3	5	2b − c
	A: l, B: h	12	3	9	3b − c
	A: h, B: l	12	6	6	3b − 2c
	A: h, B: h	16	6	10	4b − 2c

Identical for Country B.   (continued)

Table 3.2.—*Continued*
Game Matrix

Country B

		high standards	low standards
Country A	*high standards*	**10, 10** 4b-2c, 4b-2c	**6, 9** 3b-2c, 3b-c
	low standards	**9, 6** 3b-c, 3b-2c	**5, 5** 2b-c, 2b-c

The game in table 3.2 is usually called a harmony game. There is a unique equilibrium in dominant strategies. At the same time, this equilibrium represents the unique pareto-optimal outcome. From the perspective of both game theory and welfare economics this is an ideal incentive structure. The collectively optimal outcome is achieved, and therefore no exogenous action is necessary. The result is equivalent to the notion of a race to the top: both states apply the high standards.[4] The reason for this is the cost-benefit relation. The cost is less than the benefit of each unit of contribution for each player. Hence, it makes sense to contribute an additional unit. There is no dilemma here. Still, this is a common good, as it is non-rival. Each player also benefits from the others' contributions. Table 3.3 shows what happens if the cost-benefit relation is reversed.

Table 3.3.   Regulatory Competition in the Symmetric Case

Case 2: b<c   Example: b per unit = 2; c per unit = 3

	strategy combination	benefits	costs	payoff	general payoff
Country B	B: l, A: l	4	3	1	2b − c
	B: l, A: h	6	3	3	3b − c
	B: h, A: l	6	6	0	3b − 2c
	B: h, A: h	8	6	2	4b − 2c

Identical for Country A.   (continued)

Table 3.3.—*Continued*
Game Matrix

Country B

	high standards	low standards
high standards	2, 2	0, **3**
	4b-2c, 4b-2c	3b-2c, 3b-c
low standards	**3**, 0	**1, 1**
	3b-c, 3b-2c	2b-c, 2b-c

Country A (high standards, low standards are the row labels for Country A)

The game in table 3.3 is a prisoner's dilemma. There is a unique equilibrium in dominant strategies at the pareto-inferior outcome. This is exactly what is usually expected in the provision of public goods. This is set in conditions of non-rivalry in which the benefit from the individual contribution is lower than its cost. Both states choose the low level regulation; the consequence is a race to the bottom.

More realistic in the context of regulatory competition is an asymmetric situation. The two states have different preferences in respect to the respective environmental good. In practice this will be caused by two factors. First, there are states which place a greater value upon the environmental good. Their benefit from the preservation or restoration of the good is higher than that of other states. Second, there are states which have lower contribution costs than others. It is cheaper for them to achieve a certain environmental standard. For the examples, these two factors need not be distinguished. It is enough to distinguish "rich" and "poor" countries, as has been done the literature (Rehbinder and Stewart 1985; Holzinger 1991; Scharpf 1996). The rich countries have highly developed economies, and their citizens have a preference for a high environmental quality. These countries are able and willing to afford the economic costs of an ambitious environmental policy. The poor countries are economically less developed and the citizens do not consider the clean environment to be a priority. The economic costs of a strict environmental policy are high. These countries will therefore prefer less stringent regulations.

The model is the same as above. The benefit of the environmental good per unit is now higher for the rich country when compared to the poor country. The costs per unit contribution are equal. They imply $c > b$ for the poor country and b>c for the rich one. Thus, the variation in the payoffs is only a result of the different valuation of the environmental good. This way, the asymmetry of payoffs is sufficiently represented. The assumption of different cost structures does not change the incentive structure as long as the poor country values the costs of the contribution more than its benefits and the reverse is true for the rich country.[5]

The result is no surprise. The equilibrium is attained when the poor country chooses low standards and the rich country high standards. It is a pareto-optimal equilibrium in dominant strategies. Since there is a second pareto-optimal outcome (where both states use the high standards), I call this game a weak harmony game. There is no dilemma between individual and collective rationality and there is no problem in selecting the equilibrium. Under the perspectives of welfare and coordination, this game does not pose any problem. There are only reservations from a distributional perspective. While one player is able to push his most preferred outcome through, the other gets only her third preference. This is why this type of incentive structure is sometimes called a Rambo game (Zürn 1992). The poor country gets its first preference, namely, low standards within its own jurisdiction and high standards within the rich country's jurisdiction. As a consequence, different standards apply over the whole area. There are two regulatory areas, and in the case of product standards the market becomes segmented. There is neither a race to the top nor a race to the bottom.

Table 3.4.   Regulatory Competition in the Asymmetric Case

Example: benefits "poor country" $b_P = 2$;
           benefits "rich country" $b_R = 4$;
           costs per unit contribution $c = 3$

	strategy combination	Benefits	costs	payoff	general payoff
Country P	P: l, R: l	4	3	1	$2b_P - c$
	P: l, R: h	6	3	3	$3b_P - c$
	P: h, R: l	6	6	0	$3b_P - 2c$
	P: h, R: h	8	6	2	$4b_P - 2c$
Country R	R: l, P: l	8	3	5	$2b_R - c$
	R: l, P: h	12	3	9	$3b_R - c$
	R: h, P: l	12	6	6	$3b_R - 2c$
	R: h, P: h	16	6	10	$4b_R - 2c$

(continued)

**Table 3.4.—*Continued*
Game Matrix**

	Rich Country R	
	high standards	*low standards*
high standards	2, 10	0, 9
	$4b_P{-}2c$, $4b_R{-}2c$	$3b_P{-}2c$, $3b_R{-}c$
low standards	3, 6	1, 5
	$3b_P{-}c$, $3b_R{-}2c$	$2b_P{-}c$, $2b_R{-}c$

Poor Country P

The Influence of Market Segmentation

So far it has been implicitly assumed that market segmentation or non-segmentation by different standards does not affect the national economies. However, the industries concerned are affected by market segmentation in two respects: the first question is if and in which state differentiated standards lead to competitive advantages or disadvantages for the industries. Different standards, both product or production standards, may cause different costs for the industries concerned. If firms from both states trade their products within the whole market, different standards lead to competitive advantages for the firms in the poor country as well as to competitive disadvantages for the firms in the rich country. The competitive disadvantage regarding product standards vanishes for the rich country if barriers to trade are permitted for environmental reasons. In case of production standards there is no way to escape the disadvantage for the rich state's industry.

The second question is whether a common standard for the whole market implies harmonization advantages (or segmentation costs). Advantages through harmonization can be expected if products are subject to environmental standards which are traded within the whole market, if licensing procedures are different for these products, and if they have to be produced with different variations in each state. This is the case if the prevailing trade regime allows the states to wall off foreign products that do not fulfill the domestic environmental standards. In such a situation the harmonization of standards leads to economic gains for the industries concerned as the average costs decrease. There are no harmonization advantages, but a free trade regime can be pushed through where there is mutual recognition of the products and where the protection from foreign products is not permitted for environmental reasons. Products which are licensed according to different standards can be sold throughout the entire market. However, in such a situation the rich country does not achieve its environmental goal. The regime leads to a positive externality for the poor country and a negative externality for the rich one. However, this is only true with regard to product standards. Production standards do not lead to any harmonization advantages or segmentation costs.

Thus, the incentive structures for the preservation of an international common environmental good vary with two additional properties:

1. Are the instruments used to achieve the common good product standards, or are they production standards?[6]
2. Does the prevailing trade regime permit trade barriers for the sake of the environment, or is it possible to enforce the mutual recognition of products?

Four cases can thus be distinguished (table 3.5). How do the incentive structures in these four cases differ? In case (1) there is a harmonization advantage for both states. However, there are no competitive advantages or disadvantages because the product prices (as far as they are determined by the environmental standard) are the same for both states. In cases (2) and (3) there are no harmonization advantages, as markets are not segmented. The poor country has a competitive advantage, the rich one a disadvantage. It does not make a difference here whether the product or production standards are concerned. In case (4) there are no market segmentation costs, as only production facilities are affected. The poor country has a competitive advantage, as it has lower production costs.

Table 3.5.   Type of Standards and Trade Regime

	product standards	*production standards*
trade barriers	(1) harmonization advantage no competitive dis/advantage	(4) no harmonization advantage small competitive dis/advantage, in/decrease of turnover
free trade	(2) no harmonization advantage competitive dis/advantage	(3) no harmonization advantage competitive dis/advantage

However, the poor country's advantage is restricted to its own territory if the rich country is able to erect trade barriers against products from the poor country where production is subject to low-level regulation. As a consequence, within the rich country's territory there is a loss of turnover for the poor country's industry. The reverse is true for the rich state. Its competitive disadvantage is restricted to the poor country's territory, and its domestic turnover increases.

Case (1): Product standards and trade barriers

The following specific assumptions will be made: the harmonization advantage is the same for both countries. The industries in both states sell their products throughout the entire market and have an equal share of the market. Furthermore, the harmonization advantage is the same for low and high standards.[7] In general, the strategic constellation changes with the presence of a harmonization advantage. It becomes relevant if both states choose the same strategy, i.e., high or low standards, respectively.

Table 3.6. Product Standards and Trade Barriers

Example 1:
bilateral harmonization advantage h = 2

	strategy combination	benefits	costs	harmonization	payoff	general payoff
Country P	P: l, R: l	4	3	2	3	$2b_P - c + h$
	P: l, R: h	6	3	0	3	$3b_P - c$
	P: h, R: l	6	6	0	0	$3b_P - 2c$
	P: h, R: h	8	6	2	4	$4b_P - 2c + h$
Country R	R: l, P: l	8	3	2	7	$2b_R - c + h$
	R: l, P: h	12	3	0	9	$3b_R - c$
	R: h, P: l	12	6	0	6	$3b_R - 2c$
	R: h, P: h	16	6	2	12	$4b_R - 2c + h$

Game Matrix

		Rich Country R	
		high standards	*low standards*
high standards		**4, 12**	0, 9
Poor Country P		$4b_P - 2c + h, 4b_R - 2c + h$	$3b_P - 2c, 3b_R - c$
low standards		3, 6	**3, 7**
		$3b_P - c, 3b_R - 2c$	$2b_P - c + h, 2b_R - c + h$

This game is an assurance game, provided the harmonization advantage is sufficiently large (h > b_i-c). It has two equilibria, one pareto-optimal, the other suboptimal. The optimal equilibrium represents the solution with harmonized high standards, the suboptimal one the outcome with harmonized low standards. Segmentation is no equilibrium. The problem is one of coordination: if the states communicate, they will easily agree to introduce high standards, as both states realize their highest payoff then. This situation leads to a race to the top regarding environmental standards. Without communication, however, there is a certain chance that the states will choose different strategies and "miss each other," although the optimal equilibrium is focal. Only if h is small will the game become a weak harmony game.

The game changes if only one of the countries has a harmonization advantage. If, for example, the poor country's industry does not export its products, it has no harmonization advantage. The poor state has a dominant strategy at low standards. The resulting equilibrium is suboptimal (the upper line in the following example). Both states choose low standards, which means that a race to the bottom will take place. If the rich state has a unilateral harmonization advantage, a unique equilibrium exists where both states choose high standards (lower line in the example).

Table 3.7.   Product Standards and Trade Barriers

Example 2:
unilateral harmonization advantage h = 2
country R (upper line), country P (lower line)

Game Matrix

	Rich Country R high standards	Rich Country R low standards
high standards	2, 12	0, 9
Poor Country P	4, 10	0, 9
low standards	3, 6	1, 7
	3, 6	3, 5

Case (2): Product standards and free trade

In a free trade regime the mutual recognition of products manufactured according to different environmental standards can be pushed through. There are no market segmentation costs for the national industries. However, there is a competitive advantage for the country which applies the low standards if the other country chooses the high ones, and there is a competitive disadvantage for the country applying the high standards if the other country introduces the low ones. This is true as long as different standards lead to different costs and product prices. There is no effect on competition if both states choose high or low standards. For simplicity, a symmetric competition effect (e) is assumed, where the competitive advantage and the disadvantage are the same.

Table 3.8.   Product Standards and Free Trade

Example:
competitive advantage as a result of domestic low standards $e = 2$
competitive disadvantage as a result of foreign low standards $e = -2$

	strategy combination	benefits	costs	competition effect	payoff	general payoff
Country P	P: l, R: l	4	3	0	1	$2b_P - c$
	P: l, R: h	6	3	2	5	$3b_P - c + e$
	P: h, R: l	6	6	-2	-2	$3b_P - 2c - e$
	P: h, R: h	8	6	0	2	$4b_P - 2c$
Country R	R: l, P: l	8	3	0	5	$2b_R - c$
	R: l, P: h	12	3	2	11	$3b_R - c + e$
	R: h, P: l	12	6	-2	4	$3b_R - 2c - e$
	R: h, P: h	16	6	0	10	$4b_R - 2c$

Game Matrix

		Rich Country R	
		high standards	*low standards*
Poor Country P	*high standards*	2, 10 $4b_P - 2c, 4b_R - 2c$	-2, **11** $3b_P - 2c + e, 3b_R - c + e$
	low standards	**5, 4** $3b_P - c + e, 3b_R - 2c + e$	**1, 5** $2b_P - c, 2b_R - c$

In this case the states are in a classical prisoner's dilemma constellation. It has a pareto-inferior equilibrium in dominant strategies, where both countries choose the low standards. If all the above conditions are met, a free trade regime will result in a race to the bottom. If the competition effect is small, the game changes once again to the original weak harmony game.

Case (3): Production standards and free trade

Whenever environmental regulations affect the production processes and not the products themselves, there is no market segmentation, and consequently no harmonization advantage. The production is stationary in each state, but the products are traded throughout the entire territory. The products themselves do not have different properties, but are produced with different manufacturing processes. There is a dilemma for the rich country: on the one hand, in a free trade regime, trade barriers based on environmental considerations are not permitted on product properties themselves. On the other hand, in most cases the production processes cannot be monitored, and even if it is known that the products are produced according to lax production standards, the only possible reaction is to reject the products from this country.[8] In a free trade regime, however, the complete ban on the products is considered discriminatory, thus it is not permitted. As a consequence, the rich country has a competitive disadvantage, while the poor country has a competitive advantage. It is possible that the consumers in the rich country have such a high preference for the environment that they buy the more expensive domestic products because such products are more environmentally friendly. Then the industry in the poor country would experience a decrease in turnover. As it is not very realistic, this possibility will be ignored. The strategic constellation in case (3) is thus the same as in case (2): namely, a prisoners' dilemma. Equilibrium results where both states choose low standards.

Case (4): Production standards and trade barriers for environmental reasons

In general, it is impossible to erect trade barriers against production standards even if they are permitted, because it is difficult to monitor production processes. Nevertheless, there are examples of trade embargoes for environmental reasons (Vogel 1997). If the rich country does not allow the poor country's products to be admitted into its market, the competitive advantage of the poor country is restricted to its own territory. In the same way, the competitive disadvantage of the rich country arises only in the poor country's territory. However, the poor country's industry suffers a loss in turnover, as they cannot sell their product in the rich country. As a consequence, the rich country's industry experiences an increase in domestic turnover.[9] Then, the competition effects are offset by the turnover effects, as long as the symmetry assumptions about market size and market shares are retained. Therefore, the game structure associated with this is once again the weak harmony or Rambo game. There is an equilibrium in dominant strategies, where the rich country chooses the high standards and the poor country the low ones.

Summary of the Results

The analysis has shown that regulatory competition in the environmental field may lead to several different outcomes, depending on the exact conditions. In the symmetric case, the outcome is a result of the relation between costs and benefits of the individual contribution to the common good. If the costs are lower than the benefits, we end up with a harmony game. If the benefits are lower than the costs, the actors are in a prisoner's dilemma, and a race to the bottom of the environmental standards has to be expected. If the actors have heterogeneous preferences, the strategic constellation is a weak harmony game. Each state applies its most preferred standards. This leads to market segmentation.

The analysis becomes more complex if assumptions about the trade regimes and the type of environmental standard are introduced on the basis of heterogeneous preferences. In a free trade regime where mutual recognition of products is the rule, regulatory competition leads to a race to the bottom, as all states choose the low standards, irrespective of the type of standards. The incentive structure is a prisoner's dilemma. In a trade regime where products can be excluded if they are manufactured according to low production standards, the market will become segmented. In the weak harmony game one state will introduce high standards, the other low ones. Finally, if it is also possible to apply domestic product standards to foreign products, it is in the interest of both states to coordinate their action and to apply the high standards. The related game is an assurance game. A race to the top regarding environmental standards will be achieved in this constellation.

These outcomes are a result of varying effects of harmonization and competition. Whenever the harmonization and the competition effects are very small, a weak harmony game results, where each country employs its most preferred standards. In this case neither a race to the bottom nor a race to the top can be expected. This corresponds to empirical observations. In fact, costs of environmental standards are often not high enough to be a relevant competition factor (Vogel 1997).

Table 3.9.   Results

	product standards	*production standards*
trade barriers	(1) assurance	(4) weak harmony
free trade	(2) prisoner's dilemma	(3) prisoner's dilemma

From the perspective of welfare economics, the purely market-based solution is the worst. Free trade leads to inefficiency. With respect to efficiency, the solution which permits protection from negative externalities leads to preferable outcomes. In case of product standards the pareto-optimal solution is one of two possible equilibria; there is a coordination problem. In case of production standards the equilibrium is one of two pareto-optimal solutions. However, this result will be accompanied by distributional consequences which could be considered unfair. The poor state's decision to accept low standards occurs at the cost of the rich state that is forced to bear the negative externalities.

Institutional Response

The variation between the eight conditions discussed in this chapter leads to four different strategic constellations: the prisoner's dilemma, the assurance game, the weak harmony game, and the pure harmony game. The strategic constellations pose different social dilemmas, which require different solutions. The four game structures are of a universal nature. They do not necessarily only arise as a result of the conditions varied here; they may also result from completely different attributes of the contexts in which common goods are provided.

In general, pure harmony games result if the costs of provision are higher than benefits on the aggregate level and if benefits are greater than costs on the individual level. As harmony games pose no dilemma between individual and collective rationality, there is no collective action problem to solve. In the context of regulatory competition the harmony game is associated with a race to the top. There is no need for international collective action.

The prisoner's dilemma is dominated by a problem of defection. Communication between the players is not sufficient to achieve the socially optimal outcome whereby both players contribute to the common good. Even if they negotiate and come to the conclusion that it would be individually and collectively best to contribute, the incentive to free ride remains. In theory a binding contract and an external actor who is capable of securing compliance is required to solve a single shot prisoner's dilemma.[10] In practice this implies a state solution or a self-governance solution "in the shadow of hierarchy," where the state threatens to intervene should the self-governance solution not work. However, experimental and case study evidence has shown that players are able to solve the dilemma without the power of an external actor (Ostrom 1990; Ledyard 1995). In the context of regulatory competition, the prisoner's dilemma structure implies that a common solution for all the countries within the territory affected by the respective environmental problem must be found. The race to the bottom is only able to be stopped by international negotiations and by establishing political institutions in which a common environmental goal can be found—which is easier in the symmetric than in the asymmetric case. The regime that is finally found must include institutions that can secure compliance, as discussed in the chapter by Tanja Börzel in this volume.

What does this imply for regulatory competition in which the prisoner's dilemma structure is a consequence of a particular institution, namely, a free trade regime? In fact, an environmental regime which imposes common standards for the states involved abolishes the free trade regime within the respective environmental domain. Harmonizing standards by a common regime restrains competition.[11] However, this effect has to be weighed against the inefficiency that arises from environmental externalities between the countries. In a normative view the harmonization of standards would be the best solution when there is a transboundary environmental common good. Harmonization is efficient, and it avoids market segmentation.[12]

The assurance game poses a pure problem of coordination. Communication should be sufficient to ensure that both states coordinate at the pareto-optimal equilibrium. As this is not only collectively, but also individually, the best solution, there is no incentive to defect after an arrangement has been made. For the same reason, it should not be difficult to achieve the arrangement. Only consultation is needed. A coordination committee or a similar institution may be sufficient to achieve this. Rating agencies, for example, can be seen as correlating devices in coordination games played by a multitude of anonymous actors (cf. the chapters of Kerwer, Sinclair, and Strulik in this volume). Thus, it is easy to coordinate the standards of several states so that a race to the top is achieved. Coordination is substituted for regulatory competition. From the normative perspective, a regime which allows the erection of trade barriers for environmental reasons would be second best if legal harmonization were not possible—for example, because of a lack of political structures. With respect to product regulation, the result will be harmonization on a voluntary basis.

However, such a regime will lead to market segmentation in case of production standards. The weak harmony constellation does not pose a collective action dilemma. The equilibrium is pareto-optimal and there is no coordination problem, as it is a unique equilibrium. However, the problem with a Rambo game is its distributional consequence. While in our example the poor country gets its first preference, the rich country gets only its third preference. The negative environmental externalities are forced on the rich country. In general, this is a very hard problem to solve, as the poor country has a dominant strategy. In a way, the poor country's payoff can be seen as a result of the "law of the jungle." The rich country might negotiate for the high standards or for a compromise, but if it does not offer compensation, the poor country has no reason to accept these. In our example, the rich country can easily afford compensation payments: for in absolute terms it gains much more from a shift to high standards than the poor country loses. A solution of this type would be a positive sum game, and the contract would be self-enforcing as long as the poor country is better off with this contract than with the weak harmony outcome.[13] However, the compensation payment must be closely coupled with the introduction of the high standards in the poor states, otherwise the poor state still has an incentive to defect. The outcome would then be the harmonized solution with the high standards, in which the payoffs differ from those in the original case (4) game. This solution implies a race to the top and avoids market segmentation.

All in all, for transboundary environmental problems a collective solution which harmonizes the environmental standards for all affected states would be best. It is preferable to individual trade barriers and to a free trade regime. In some cases redistributional measures may be required. The harmonization solution restrains competition. The resulting loss in welfare must be justified by environmental benefits. Whenever the environmental benefits exceed the welfare losses due to restrained competition, regulatory competition is not a desirable option, as it does not enhance efficiency.

Conclusion

The basic idea behind this chapter is that it would be helpful for the analysis of common goods to look much more closely at the properties of the goods and of the social situations in which they are provided and to analyze the consequences of these properties in respect to the costs and benefits for the actors. Different cost and benefit structures lead to different strategic constellations, and these, in turn, lead to different opportunities for institutional solutions to the common goods provision problem. This has been exemplified in the regulatory competition for environmental standards.

It has become clear, however, that the analysis of one specific attribute of a good or one property of the social situation does not capture the strategic constellation in a way that makes it possible to predict empirical behavior. The exact strategic constellation which determines whether regulatory competition leads to a race to the top or a race to the bottom, or to neither one, varies with several factors. It has been shown that the following factors are important: the relation of the costs and benefits caused by environmental regulation, the homogeneity or heterogeneity of the actors' payoffs, the exact object of the regulation—namely, products or production processes—and the prevailing trade regime. Many other factors have been held constant, such as production costs or market shares. All these factors would otherwise also influence the game structure. Additionally there are "hidden" variables. For example, the contributions to the common good were treated as purely additive. Other aggregation technologies might change the game completely. For example, the nature of the common good may be such that it will only be provided if each and every actor contributes. Building a dike is a classic example of this "weakest-link" technology. In such a case the strategic constellation would be an assurance game, given that actors are homogeneous and individual costs exceed benefits.

What we can learn from this analysis is that predicting whether regulatory competition in the environmental field leads to a race to the top or to a race to the bottom is a difficult and tiresome task, which requires that many variables be taken into consideration. Even pure theoretical analysis can only answer this question on a case-by-case basis. Therefore, the main message of this chapter is that predicting behavior in common goods dilemmas is no mean feat, not even at the theoretical level.

Notes

1. The term common goods will be used here as a collective term for goods which are not purely private goods, for example, public goods, common pool resources, or club goods.

2. A similar grouping is made by Ostrom (1999), who goes on to distinguish between "types of actors" and "attributes of the group involved" as well. "Types of actors" refers mostly to their rationality as assumed in Rational choice models, or to their apparent empirical willingness to cooperate, although the theory predicts noncooperation, respectively.

3. An overview of this line of research is given by Ostrom (1998 and 1999).

4. The metaphor of a race to the top (or bottom) implies a dynamic aspect: many states adjust their national standards successively to the level of the highest (or lowest) standards, or they apply ever higher (or lower) standards. There is a move towards an equilibrium. In the logic of two-by-two matrix games there are only two levels of standards and only two countries, which adjust behavior with a single step. The system is in equilibrium after two simultaneous moves. The dynamic aspect of the metaphor is thus lost as a result of analytical reduction.

5. Different costs of implementation of the standards are not very plausible either. The direct costs of applying standards are similar as long as production processes are not too different. If technologies are less developed in poor countries, this probably goes along with lower wages.

6. This aspect has already been analyzed by Scharpf (1996, 1997, 2000).

7. The following models rest on these and further symmetry assumptions, as they assume that all other factors, like market size, production costs, and others, are equal for both states.

8. With product standards the reaction would be to accept only those products which comply with the domestic requirements.

9. Here I shall leave aside the consideration that in political practice the poor country may react to the embargo by erecting a similar barrier.

10. In an infinitely repeated prisoner's dilemma cooperation is at least possible without sanctions or external actors; however, mutual defection also remains possible.

11. If different standards are harmonized although there are no environmental externalities, competition is unnecessarily restrained. Without spillovers there is no justification for harmonization, at least not on environmental grounds. This case is excluded here, since this chapter is about transnational common goods.

12. If harmonization is called efficient here, it is only because the costs of decision-making are neglected. Negotiations over a harmonized standard may take a very long time, or may, for example, impose costs on third parties.

13. For the pros and cons of compensation solutions, see, for example, Raiffa (1985), Frey (1997), and Holzinger (1997).

References

Aggarwal, V. K., and C. Dupont. 1999. Goods, Games, and Institutions. *International Political Science Review* 20: 393-409.

Barrett, S. 1998a. On the Theory and Diplomacy of Environmental Treaty-Making. *Journal of Resource Economics* 11: 317-33.

———. 1998b. Political Economy of the Kyoto Protocol. *Oxford Review of Economic Policy* 14: 20-39.

———. 1999. A Theory of Full International Cooperation. *Journal of Theoretical Politics* 11: 519-41.

Blümel, W., R. Pethig, and O. von dem Hagen. 1986. The Theory of Public Goods: A Survey of Recent Issues. *Journal of Institutional and Theoretical Economics* 142: 241-309.

Cornes, R., and T. Sandler. 1996. *The Theory of Externalities, Public Goods, and Club Goods.* New York: Cambridge University Press.

Diekmann, A. 1992. Soziale Dilemmata. Modelle, Typisierungen und empirische Resultate. In *Theorie, Daten, Methoden: neuere Modelle und Verfahren in den Sozialwissenschaften,* ed. H.-J. Andress, 176-203. Rieden: WB-Druck.

Ford Runge, C. 1984. Institutions and the Free Rider: The Assurance Problem Collective Action. *Journal of Politics* 46: 154-81.

Frey, B. S. 1997. Unerwünschte Projekte, Kompensation und Akzeptanz. *Analyse & Kritik* 19: 3-14.

Godwin, R. K., and W. B. Shepard. 1979. Forcing Squares, Triangles, and Ellipses into a Circular Paradigm: The Use of the Commons Dilemma Examining the Allocation of Common Resources. *Western Political Quarterly* 32: 265-77.

Güth, W., and H. Kliemt. 1995. Competition or Cooperation. On the Evolutionary Economics of Trust, Exploitation, and Moral Attitudes. Working Paper. Berlin: Humboldt University.

Hausken, K., and T. Plümper. 1999. The Impact of Actor Heterogeneity on the Provision of International Public Goods. *International Interactions* 25: 61-94.

Haveman, R. H. 1973. Common Property, Congestion, and Environmental Pollution. *Quarterly Journal of Economics* 87: 278-87.

Hirshleifer, J. 1983. From Weakest-Link to Best-Shot: The Voluntary Provision of Public Goods. *Public Choice* 41: 371-86.

———. 1985. From Weakest-Link to Best Shot: Correction. *Public Choice* 46: 221-23.

Holler, M. J., and G. Illing. 2000. *Einführung in die Spieltheorie.* Berlin: Springer.

Holzinger, K. 1991. Does Legal Harmonization Really "Harmonize" the National Environmental Policies in the European Community? In *The Nation-State versus Continental Integration. Canada North-America—Germany Europe,* ed. L. A. Pal and R.-O. Schultze, 297-313. Bochum: Brockmeyer.

———. 1997. Kompensationen in alternativen Konfliktlösungsverfahren. *Analyse & Kritik* 19: 33-63.

———. 2001. Aggregation Technology of Common Goods and Its Strategic Consequences. Global Warming, Biodiversity, and Siting Conflicts. *European Journal of Political Research* 40: 117-38.

Isaac, R. M., J. Walker, and A. W. Williams. 1993. Group Size and Voluntary Provision of Public Goods: Experimental Evidence Utilizing Large Groups. *Journal of Public Economics* 54: 1-36.

Jänicke, M. 1998. Umweltpolitik—global am Ende oder am Ende global? Thesen zu ökologischen Determinanten des Weltmarktes. In *Perspektiven der Weltgesellschaft*, ed. U. Beck, 332-44. Frankfurt am Main: Suhrkamp.

Kern, K. 2000. *Die Diffusion von Politikinnovationen. Umweltpolitische Innovationen im Mehrebenensystem der USA*. Opladen: Leske + Budrich.

Ledyard, J. 1995. Public Goods: A Survey of Experimental Research. In *The Handbook of Experimental Economics*, ed. J. Kagel and A. E. Roth, 111-94. Princeton, N.J.: Princeton University Press.

Mäler, K.-G., and A. de Zeeuw. 1998. The Acid Rain Differential Game. *Environmental and Resource Economics* 12: 167-84.

Martin, L. 1995. Heterogeneity, Linkage, and Commons Problems. In *Local Commons and Global Interdependence. Heterogeneity and Cooperation Two Domains*, ed. R. O. Keohane and E. Ostrom, 71-91. London: Sage.

Musgrave, R. A., and P. B. Musgrave. 1976. *Public Finance Theory and Practice*. New York: McGraw-Hill.

Olson, M. 1965. *The Logic of Collective Action: Public Goods and the Theory of Groups*. Cambridge, Mass.: Harvard University Press.

Ostrom, E. 1990. *Governing the Commons: The Evolution of Institutions for Collective Action*. New York: Cambridge University Press.

———. 1998. A Behavioral Approach to the Rational Choice Theory of Collective Action. *American Political Science Review* 92: 1-22.

———. 1999. Context and Collective Action: Four Interactive Building Blocks for a Family of Explanatory Theories. Unpublished manuscript.

Ostrom E., R. Gardner, and J. Walker. 1992. Covenants with and without a Sword: Self-Governance Is Possible. *American Political Science Review* 86: 404-17.

———. 1994. *Rules, Games, and Common Pool Resources*. Ann Arbor: University of Michigan Press.

Raiffa, H. 1985. Creative Compensation: Maybe "In My Backyard." *Negotiation Journal* 1: 197-203.

Rapoport, A. 1988. Experiments with N-Person Social Traps: I. Prisoner's Dilemma, Weak Prisoner's Dilemma, Volunteer's Dilemma and Largest Number. *Journal of Conflict Resolution* 32: 457-72.

Rehbinder, E., and R. Stewart. 1985. *Environmental Protection Policy*. Berlin: Walter de Gruyter.

Samuelson, P. A. 1954. The Pure Theory of Public Expenditure. *Review of Economics and Statistics* 36: 387-89.

Sandler, T. 1997. *Global Challenges: An Approach to Environmental, Political, and Economic Problems*. New York: Cambridge University Press.

———. 1998. Global and Regional Public Goods: A Prognosis for Collective Action. *Fiscal Studies* 19: 221-47.

Sandler, T., and K. Sargent. 1995. Management of Transnational Commons: Coordination, Publicness, and Treaty Formation. *Land Economics* 71: 145-62.

Scharpf, F. W. 1996. Politische Optionen im vollendeten Binnenmarkt. In *Europäische Integration*, ed. M. Jachtenfuchs and B. Kohler-Koch, 109-40. Opladen: Leske + Budrich.

———. 1997. Introduction: The Problem-Solving Capacity of Multilevel Governance. *Journal of European Public Policy* 4: 520-38.

———. 2000. *Governing Europe. Effective and Democratic?* Oxford: Oxford University Press.

Vogel, D. 1995. *Trading Up: Consumer and Environmental Regulation in a Global Economy*. Cambridge, Mass.: Harvard University Press.

————. 1997. Trading Up and Governing Across: Transnational Governance and Environmental Protection. *Journal of European Public Policy* 4: 556-71.

Weesie, J., and A. Franzen. 1998. Cost Sharing a Volunteer's Dilemma. *Journal of Conflict Resolution* 2: 600-18.

Zürn, M. 1992. *Interessen und Institutionen der internationalen Politik. Grundlegung und Anwendungen des situationsstrukturellen Ansatzes.* Opladen: Leske + Budrich.

————. 1997. Positives Regieren jenseits des Nationalstaats. Zur Implementation internationaler Umweltregime. *Zeitschrift für Internationale Beziehungen* 4: 41-68.

Part 2

Common Goods and the Role of Private Actors

International Level

4

Governance and Globalization: Conceptualizing the Role of Public and Private Actors

Christoph Knill and Dirk Lehmkuhl

Changing Governance Conditions in the Context of Globalization: The Rise of Private Actors

In recent years a growing number of studies have emphasized the importance of private actors in global governance. In this context a basic observation is that private governance contributions need not be restricted to those types of private actors whose explicit organizational objective lies in the provision of certain public goods, such as humanitarian or environmentalist organizations (see Etkins 1992; Princen and Finger 1994). Rather, private governance contributions or even "private authority" (Cutler, Haufler, and Porter 1999; Higgott, Underhill, and Bieler 2000) might emerge from a more diverse array of private actors, such as business associations (Ronit and Schneider 1999) or multinational companies (Sell 1999; Sinclair 1994; Spar 1999; see also the contributions of Kerwer, Sinclair, and Strulik in this volume).

More specifically, it is argued that private governance contributions might compensate for the decreasing capacities of national governments in defining and providing public goods in light of the internationalization of markets and the emergence of transnational information and communication networks (Cerny 1995; Kobrin 1997).[1] On the one hand, economic and technological interdependencies have created a range of problems that exceed the scope of national sovereignty, and that can therefore no longer be sufficiently resolved by the unilateral action of national governments (examples include the regulation of electronic commerce or the protection of intellectual property rights on digital information). On the other hand, the emergence of globally integrated markets might pose new challenges for the regulation of domestic problems. More specifically, the increasing economic integration is putting pressure on national governments to redesign national regulations in order to avoid regulatory burdens that restrict the competitiveness of domestic industries (regulatory competition).

In this chapter we analyze the impact of these developments—namely, the challenges to the governance capacity of national governments in the context of globalization and the parallel increase in governance contributions of private actors—on the relationship between public and private actors with respect to the definition and provision of public goods. While we do not suppose a hollowing out of the state, we suggest a transformation of patterns of governance—specifically, a decline in hierarchical forms of intervention, and a rise of other forms of governance such as regulated self-regulation, private self-regulation, or interfering regulation. This is not to say that we expect private and public governance capacities to be mutually "driven out." Rather, we observe more synergetic relationships, with private and public activities partially reinforcing each other.

In developing our argument we rely on a broad definition of the term governance, whereby governance includes all modes of co-coordinating individual action, such as hierarchies, networks, associations, or markets. Its meaning is not restricted to specific types of social coordination; namely, attempts at collective problem solving outside of hierarchical frameworks.[2] Governance, as used in this chapter, is not confined to the political guidance and steering actions of governments (*politische Steuerung*); it also covers corresponding activities by societal actors (Mayntz 1998, 7-8). Accordingly, we define governance capacity as the formal and factual capability of public or private actors to define the content of public goods and to shape the social, economic, and political processes by which these goods are provided.[3] This concern with the structural capacities of governance, however, does not imply that we neglect the strategic dimension, i.e., questions of conflict and power in the politics that influence how public goods are defined and provided.

The chapter is structured as follows: in section two our first step will be to identify the basic factors which affect the governance capacity of public and private actors in the context of globalization. Based on these reflections, section three will discuss a combination of different governance capacities which not only make it possible to identify different ideal types of governance patterns, but also to assess the impact of globalization on these distinctive governance patterns. The final section will summarize the results and draw general conclusions.

The Governance Capacity of Public and Private Actors

Generally speaking, we think that a concrete pattern of governance is crucially affected by the distinctive governance capacity of public and private actors. On the one hand, it can be assumed that the general challenge emerging from global markets and transnational networks influences the capacity of national governments to define and provide public goods to a different degree. National governments might still have considerable choice about how to effectively address certain policy problems emerging in the context of internationalization, while for other problems such options are less feasible. In the general debate on global governance, the fact that the state is still a viable actor in the governance of society is generally underestimated. Governments do not only have significant capacities for adjusting governance structures to new requirements; they also dispose of important powers and resources that are not available to other actors: this is particularly evident with respect to their ability to accommodate conflicting interests and define governance priorities (Hirst and Thompson 1996; Peters 1998; Weiss 1998).

On the other hand, the governance capacity of private actors may also vary from case to case. While the classical theory of public goods rests on the assumption that the provision of public goods by private actors is generally characterized by a tension between individual and collective rationality, which can only be overcome by governmental intervention, both empirical and theoretical findings reveal that this classical assumption can hardly be generalized. Rather, the constellation underlying the provision and the production of a certain good is not only affected by the non-rivalry and the non-excludability of consumption, but also by other factors, such as properties of the actors involved (Holzinger forthcoming; Ostrom 1999).

In view of these considerations we suggest that the governance capacity of both public and private actors largely depends on the distinctive *strategic constellation* underlying a certain policy (see also Holzinger in this volume). This constellation is basically affected by three factors: namely, the type of the underlying policy problem; the degree of congruence between the given problem structure and existing regulatory structures; and the institutional context.

The Problem Type

The strategic constellation characterizing the provision of public goods is strongly affected by the attributes of the underlying problem constellation. It has been shown, for instance, that the development of cooperative solutions by the involved actors is more or less likely depending on these attributes. To grasp these different types of public goods problems, we can identify three distinct constellations: coordination, agreement, and defection. For their part, each of these is characterized by a specific problem in resolving conflicts of interests.

Coordination problems arise where there is a relatively strong common interest in the provision of the good and there is agreement on the regulatory solution. In view of this overall compatibility of interests of the involved actors, it is comparatively easy to provide the public good: we assume that both public and private actors have a high governance capacity.

This type of problem constellation can be found in certain areas of technical standardization, namely, in cases where all players benefit from a common standard, but the choice of the solution is not conflictive since no player expects one standard to have a special advantage over another. Here the main problem is to determine a common solution, i.e., to determine the concrete shape of a standard. Thus, standardization requires no more than communication between the involved actors. In addition, once a solution to the coordination problem has been agreed on, it is in everyone's interest to comply, as is the case with driving on the left or the right side of the road (Schmidt and Werle 1997, 100).

However, it becomes more difficult to achieve international agreements between states or collective action by private actors as soon international cooperation involves distributive conflicts. Generally, such *agreement problems* are characterized by a common interest in the provision of a public good and by disagreement about the regulatory solution.

In interaction between states, examples range from the environmental standards in the European Union (EU) and issues such as the data privacy agreement between the United States and the EU to strategic nuclear weapon regimes (Héritier, Knill, and Mingers 1996; Farrell, in this volume; Müller 1993).[4] For private actors, such constellations can often be observed in problems of technical standardization. To ensure the compatibility and interconnectivity of their products, producers are generally interested in common standards. For reasons of economic competitiveness, however, they might prefer different options; i.e., to try to provide their own product as the "solution" to which other companies would have to adjust (Schmidt and Werle 1997). An example often referred to in this context is the "standardization war" in the case of the video recorder technology, where the VHS system developed by Sony and JVC succeeded over the Video 2000 technology developed by Philips and Grundig (see, for instance, Knill and Lehmkuhl 1998).

While, in principle, bargaining between actors can still resolve agreement problems, the requirements for effective governance become even more demanding in the case of *defection problems*. The basic difference between problems of coordination, or agreement, and problems of defection is that, notwithstanding their common interest in the provision of the good and corresponding cooperation agreements, when there are defection problems the involved actors prefer to free ride, taking advantage of the contributions of the others. Among public actors, the risk of defection might either hamper the emergence of an international agreement as such or cause serious compliance problems; consequently, it implies that the public actors have a low governance capacity. Among private actors, this constellation is the underlying problem of most types of negative market externalities, such as environmental pollution or consumer protection. To reduce production costs, industrial actors choose the collectively and individually suboptimal action, namely, not to contribute to the provision of the public good.

Problem Structures and Regulatory Structures

There seems to be a general consensus in the literature that the governance capacity of both public and private actors increases with the degree of congruence between the scope of the underlying problem and the existing regulatory structures; that is, it increases with the congruence between the scope of the problem and the institutional structure established to purposefully influence the behavior of actors in a specific field (see, for instance, Mayntz and Scharpf 1995). On the basis of this argument, it has often been suggested that the internationalization of markets yields a significant reduction of the governance capacity of national governments given that internationalization yields an increasing gap between territorially bound regulatory competencies at the national level and emerging problems of transnational scope (Beck 1998; Zürn 1998). We argue, however, that this statement can hardly be generalized, and in fact it has to be qualified in light of several observations.

With respect to *public* actors, first of all it has to be emphasized that not every problem created by globalization is necessarily of global scope. In other words, not every problem created by globalization exceeds the regulatory scope of national governments. It might well be that a problem created by economic and technological internationalization can still be sufficiently resolved within the territorial boundaries of one nation-state, while such solutions are no longer feasible for other problems.

Moreover, even problems of global scope might be effectively resolved within national boundaries. Such constellations are possible when the extent to which a good is provided is determined by the largest individual contribution: i.e. by the "best shot" (Hirshleifer 1983; Holzinger forthcoming). Despite the fact that the scope of the problem exceeds a single jurisdiction and thus impedes authoritative rule making, other actors might accept the contribution of a single actor. An example of this scenario is the provision of a global system for the administration of Internet addresses and domain names. In this context, one state (the United States) initially resolved the problem for all other states by developing an appropriate system.[5]

However, this is only one of the basic options concerning how individual contributions and the provision of a public good can be linked. In many cases, for instance, the level of provision is based on the sum of the individual contributions. This scenario can be observed, for instance, with respect to the problem of global warming. In this case, the level at which the common good is achieved is determined solely by the total amount of emissions, or by the sum of the contributions of all states in terms of emission reduction, respectively (Holzinger forthcoming). In other words, the problem of global warming cannot be effectively addressed by a single best shot or a "heroic state" which resolves the problem for all other states. In addition, it is conceivable that the provision of the good is determined by the smallest individual contributions (the "weakest link") (Holzinger forthcoming). The problem of controlling illegal and harmful content on the Internet is one good illustration of this scenario. As providers of such material can easily move their services across national borders, the level of protection is factually determined by the country with the lowest regulatory standards. It is obvious that in both examples, i.e., the cases of global warming and Internet content regulation, activities of individual states are no longer sufficient for coping with problems of global scope. In this constellation there is a need for transnational solutions.

The congruence between the structure of global problems and the corresponding regulatory structures is furthermore affected by the degree of development of the international regimes and institutions that address political problems that can no longer be effectively resolved within the territorial boundaries of the nation-state. Thus, national governments frequently try to establish international regimes in order to maintain their capacity to address social and political problems that extend beyond the parameters of national sovereignty. The EU can be viewed as the most developed and institutionally differentiated example of this. Hence the increasing relevance and development of functionally differentiated international regimes over the past few decades indicates that not every problem that demands transnational regulation automatically exceeds the governance capacities of national governments.

Indeed the number, relevance, and regulative activities of international regimes have grown steadily over the past few decades (Zürn 1998). Notwithstanding these developments, there is a strong discrepancy between economic and political integration; i.e., international political coordination and harmonization is able to cope with problems that are emerging from economic and technological challenges. The gap between political and economic internationalization, which, for example, is particularly pronounced in areas characterized by a high demand for international regulation on global ecological problems, or global financial markets, or the Internet, can be traced to the fact that the development, formulation, and implementation of international policies is generally a highly time-consuming and complex process. As a consequence, the project of global "governance without government" (Kohler-Koch 1993; Rosenau and Czempiel 1992; Young 1997) is a reflection of a rather imbalanced development. The successful constitution of transnational markets has coincided with the inability of governments to address social and political problems that are emerging from economic integration, both at the national and the international level.

With respect to the governance capacity of *private* actors, we can principally make the same qualification in terms of the congruence of problem and regulatory structures, as they have been developed for public actors. Not every problem requires the existence of transnational private organizational structures. The private governance capacity might increase in cases in which the distinctive "production function" ("best shot") does not require a congruence between the regulatory structures and the territorial scope of the problem. And, finally, preexisting organizational and regulatory structures might increase the capacity to address global problems. For instance, it is argued that the international orientation of pharmaceutical firms and their experience in associative action increases their capacity to cooperate at the international level (Greenwood 1997).

Institutional Conditions

The governance capacity of both public and private actors is not only affected by the type of the underlying problem and the degree of congruence between problem structure and regulatory structures, but also by the distinctive institutional conditions in which public and private actors operate. In this context several aspects are of analytical relevance.

From the perspective of both national governments and private actors, existing institutional rules, legal rights, and constitutional arrangements define the range of feasible strategies and regulatory options in order to address emerging governance problems. For instance, even when there is congruence between the problem structures and national regulatory structures, economic and technological challenges may imply that public goods can no longer be provided on the basis of existing regulatory arrangements. Rather, fundamental regulatory adjustments at the national level might be necessary. Hence the extent to which such adjustments can be achieved, given the existing institutional opportunities and constraints, has important repercussions on the governance capacity of public and private actors.

The governance constraints that might emerge from existing institutional arrangements can be observed, for instance, in the regulation of Internet content. To cope with this problem, the U.S. government initially confronted Internet providers with similar regulatory restrictions to those applied in the broadcasting sector. This regulatory strategy, however, was rejected by the Supreme Court, which stated that this regulatory option was in conflict with the constitutional guarantee of freedom of information. Similar constitutional constraints to effectively addressing problems of harmful and illegal content on the Internet exist in many other Western democracies.

When focusing on national governments, an additional institutional factor has to be taken into account: it refers to the potential of altering regulatory adjustments even within the existing constitutional constraints. This potential for regulatory adjustment refers to the level of national reform capacity, and it may vary from country to country and from sector to sector.

The level of reform capacity depends on the particular institutional arrangements characterizing a country's legal, administrative, and political system (Knill 1999). It decreases with the number of formal and factual institutional veto points (Immergut 1992) that affect the opportunities for national governments to initiate and push through institutional reforms in the face of political and societal resistance. The number of veto points generally increases the more a political system is characterized by a federalist structure, multiple-party coalition governments, high ministerial autonomy, corporatist decision-making arrangements, and independent institutions such as a constitutional court and a central bank (Scharpf 2000). Although the level of reform capacity does not make it possible to predict the timing or the concrete content and direction of regulatory reforms, it indicates the structural potential of national governments to maintain their governance capacity by adjusting regulatory arrangements in light of the challenges emerging from economic internationalization.

With respect to private actors, the most important institutional factor affecting their governance capacity refers to their organizational structures. In this context we expect the level of private governance capacity to increase with both the strength and the degree of organization of private actors. Organizational strength defines the extent to which organizations are able to influence, monitor, and sanction the behavior of their members; i.e., the extent to which the organizations have sufficient autonomy to make decisions on behalf of their members and are capable of ensuring the members' compliance with these decisions. The level of organizational strength is generally expected to increase with certain organizational properties, such as centralization, and the degree of organization within a specific domain (Schmitter and Streeck 1981).

The degree of organization refers to the extent to which private actors are organized or willing to contribute to the provision of public goods by private organizations. As shown by Olson (1965), for instance, the size of the group and the extent to which organizations might offer "selective incentives" for cooperation can play an important role in this context. The degree of organization may have important repercussions on the resources of the actors involved, including financial, personnel, and technological capacities as well as scientific expertise. Examples of effective private governance reveal that— particularly with respect to complex technological problems—private actors have more appropriate resources for developing corresponding solutions than bureaucracies do. For instance, many stakeholders consider the private sector to be more capable than public authorities at designing the appropriate norms, rules, and standards to govern information and communication networks (Cutler 1999; Knill and Lehmkuhl 1998; Knill 2001).

In summary, our considerations suggest that the extent to which public and private actors will contribute to solving public good problems is crucially affected by the particular context that characterizes the strategic constellation underlying the provision of a certain public good. The question then is what patterns of interaction can be expected given the variations in the governance capacities of private and public actors.

Private Actors and the State: Globalization and Changing Patterns of Governance

Without doubt, the internationalization of economic transactions is inherently a highly dynamic process, characterized by rapid changes in the way in which actors from various regions communicate, exchange resources, and seek to expand their activities. To cope with these dynamics of internationalization analytically requires a model that, on the one hand, is apposite to incorporate this dynamism and, on the other hand, offers a foil against which the impact of internationalization on changes in patterns of governance can be assessed.[6] The Weberian concept of ideal types has the virtue of providing a defined point of reference against which real world observations can be compared and potential differences explained. Relying on them here we distinguish four ideal types of governance constellations, depending on the distinctive level of private and public governance capacities. In so doing, we do not assume that we will find either pure public or pure private forms of governance, but we acknowledge that the concept of policy networks is very useful in describing governance arrangements in complex modern societies (Kenis and Schneider 1991; Mayntz 1993; Rhodes 1997). Rather than challenging this perspective, the following distinction between different ideal types of governance constellations basically seeks to highlight distinctive characteristics and properties of such networks. To label these distinctive characteristics, we refer to a specific mode of regulation in the interaction between public and private actors.

Figure 4.1.   Ideal Type Constellations of Public/Private Interaction

		Governance Capacity of Public Actors	
		Low	High
Governance Capacity of Private Actors	Low	Interfering Regulation	Interventionist Regulation
	High	Private Self-Regulation	Regulated Self-Regulation

Interventionist Regulation

According to traditional theoretical assumptions, public goods are provided by public actors through hierarchical intervention in constellations in which the underlying incentive structure assigns only a limited governance capacity to private actors. Although *interventionist regulation* does not exclude the involvement of private actors, the overall responsibility for the provision of public goods lies with the state, as does the power to decide both the content of public goods and the institutional form for providing them.

From the late 1970s onwards, the dominant concept of an interventionist state came under threat. In accord with that view, the state not only intervened hierarchically to secure the provision of public goods, but it also took the responsibility for producing those goods. This view has now been replaced by concepts of the regulatory state (Majone 1994) or the enabling state (Willke 1995). Along with this shift in the view and function of the state, which has found expression in policies of deregulation, and privatization, and in administrative reforms, there has also been a change in the functional role of interventionist regulation: the government no longer intervenes to provide public goods; instead, it intervenes to enable them to be provided.

This move from an interventionist to an enabling state, however, should neither be equated with a weakening of the hierarchical position of the state (Wright 1994) nor with "withering regulation" as such. Indeed, in many areas that have been subject to policies of deregulation and privatization, in order to protect services of general interest, states have established new institutional capacities both to safeguard market efficiency and to compensate for the negative consequences of market integration (Héritier and Schmidt 2000). Yet, states' efforts to secure both objectives have their costs. With respect to the regulatory reform of the network utilities in many European countries, for instance, there is good reason to claim that the governance costs for states, conceptualized as the administrative efforts of public authorities to change and manage a particular utility regime in terms of "hardware" (personnel, new institutions, subsidies) and "software" (regulations, directives, judicial review), have increased (Bauer 2001).

Regulated Self-Regulation

Our second ideal type refers to a constellation in which both private and public actors have a high level of governance capacity. Given such a constellation, we expect more cooperative patterns of interaction between public and private actors and not simply an interventionist style of regulation. One must, however, be aware of the fact that many of these forms of *regulated self-regulation*, public-private partnerships, or even private-interest governments[7] take place under the "shadow of hierarchy" (Mayntz and Scharpf 1995); that is, the state is still capable of relying on traditional forms of intervention should there be governance failures (Peters 1998; Weiss 1998). What is more, in these more cooperative patterns of interaction between private and public actors, state actors play a central and active role, because they have powers and resources that are not available to societal actors. In particular, governments may provide important incentives (the state may offer financial support, or delegate power, or it may refrain from direct and potentially less effective state intervention) in order to stimulate and increase the integration and organization of societal interests (Streeck 1994, 18; Eichener and Voelzkow 1994; Knill and Lehmkuhl 1998).

The relationship between public and private actors is currently undergoing substantial review at various levels of analysis (in addition to other contributions in this volume, see also Osborne 2000; Powell and Clemens 1998; Reinicke 1998). Most generally, we agree with those studies that assume an enlarged role for regulated self-regulation in the sphere of public policy-making and in the provision of public goods. We consider this increasing importance of regulated self-regulation, that can be described as a transformation from a more hierarchical to a more cooperative relationship between public and private actors, as one of the major ways that globalization has made an impact on patterns of governance. In what follows, we illustrate this transformation in reference to the example of the system for regulating Internet domain names.

The individual name or Internet address has become an important type of property in electronic communication, because it represents position, location, path, and identity. The importance of individual addresses grants great salience to development of a unitary system that administers both the registration and allocation of Internet domain names. As such, this system represents a global public good that can neither be completely left to the market nor exclusively governed by national public authorities (Werle and Leib 2000). Since 1998, a private organization, the Internet Corporation for Assigned Names and Numbers (ICANN), has assumed the responsibility for the provision of this public good. Taking the history of the administration of Internet domain names as an example, we may illustrate the shift from a hierarchical to a cooperative mode of public-private interactions in the provision of a public good that is significant globally.[8]

In a nutshell, the development of the administration of the domain names system has been characterized by a move from private self-organization of Internet freaks to a commercialized national policy objective to a politicized issue of global (transatlantic) public policy-making. In its early days, the development and administration of the Internet domain names system went on largely unobserved as private self-regulation in the U.S. Department of Defense and the National Science Foundation (NSF). Along with the U.S. Congress-driven move towards commercial uses of the Internet and the rapid growth and global expansion of the Internet, however, the domain name system became politicized for two reasons. On the one hand, the U.S. Congress pled for introducing competition and privatization into the management of the infrastructure. On the other hand, European governments no longer accepted a solution under the control of the American government, and they negotiated for greater autonomy in the administration of Internet domain names. Although the U.S. government started to keep a tighter rein on the governance of Internet domain names, it could not prevent this twofold pressure from leading to a re-delegation of the administration of Internet addresses: in 1998 it was delegated to the nonprofit corporation ICANN; subsequently the central role of the U.S. government in governing the Internet was weakened.

The governance arrangement of the Internet domain names system is a good example of regulated self-regulation based on a relative high governance capacity on the part of both public and private actors. Public actors have not only significantly contributed to the emergence of a highly competent private organization; they still have significant influence on ICANN: they provide the framework for the organizational conditions that must be met for ICANN to obtain the authority to control and administer the registration and allocation of Internet domain names (Cuker 1999; Hadfield 2000). At the same time, the strong self-governing capacity of ICANN finds expression in its capacity to govern and implement the substantive and procedural laws within its domain itself. The capacity to authorize new top-level domains is one example; another is the Uniform Domain Name Dispute Policy, a quasi-administrative procedure to authoritatively resolve disputes on the misuse of domain name registrations.[9]

However, two aspects significantly hamper ICANN's position as a free and independent regulatory body. First, its regulatory capacity is based on contracts with the U.S. American Department of Commerce. These contracts have to be renewed annually. Second, the U.S. government has not yet fulfilled its contractual obligation to delegate the final authority over some major root servers to ICANN. This shows that power and conflict among different interests—in the present case between the U.S. government, on the one hand, and European governments and ICANN, on the other—are important dimensions in the analysis of solutions at the international level.

Private Self-Regulation

With the move from the bottom left to the bottom right field of our ideal type constellation, we acknowledge that there can be constellations in which the states' capacity to compensate for regulatory failures by direct intervention is significantly restricted, and in which private self-regulation is clearly dominant. While in reality we expect a more fluid boundary between regulated self-regulation and *private self-regulation*, for analytical reasons it is important to distinguish between the two types.

The specific difference between patterns of regulated self-regulation and private self-regulation refers to the potential of public intervention: in the case of private self-regulation, the state actually has no capacity to directly intervene in private regulation and to provide a specific good itself, whereas in regulated self-regulation it obviously does. The provision of public goods basically depends on the governance capacity of private actors, while governance contributions of public actors are contingent upon the activities of private actors. States might still play a role in providing complementary governance contributions, hence "refining" and guiding societal self-regulation. As examples from various empirical studies have shown, the contributions of public actors range from activities of providing the legitimacy of private self-regulation by officially acknowledging the outcomes of private governance (Ronit and Schneider 1999; Lehmkuhl 2000) to moderating between conflicting interests and stimulating the communication and coordination between different actors (Willke 1995) to midwifery in the process of associational reform, and, finally, to more direct control of cartel-like tendencies that interfere with competition (Knill and Lehmkuhl 1998; Knill 2001). The protection of copyrights on the Internet is one illustration of how globalization might contribute to a simultaneous decrease in the governance capacity of public actors and a relatively high capacity for private self-regulation.

From a historical point of view, the importance of protecting property rights for economic growth has been frequently shown (North and Thomas 1973; Rosenberg and Birdzell 1986). While states have constantly adapted property rights protection to economic and technological changes (North 1981), the specific character of the Internet partly devaluates the set of instruments traditionally applied by states. Texts, ideas, and information in form of software, publishing, and financial services are central areas of Internet activity. What the products of all these branches have in common is that they produce intangible goods that can be easily delivered and cheaply reproduced. While this offers a very interesting commercial perspective, it also entails a number of substantive risks, because it is relatively easy to illegally copy these intangible goods without the risk of detection (Spar 1999, 38). Thus, property-rights protection has become a central issue for information-based economic activities on the Internet.

Although states are quite aware of this problem, they have not yet been able to develop a satisfying solution to the Internet property-rights problem. On the contrary, numerous efforts to reform national or international property-rights regulations have failed. Most prominent was the 1996 effort of the U.S.

government to enhance the protection of digital intellectual property—an effort that failed due to problems at both the international and national level. While the approach toward ensuring property-rights protection within the framework of the World Intellectual Property Organization (WIPO) failed because of resistance, a number of states argued that the approach was too restrictive. The U.S. Congress also rejected the proposals, fearing that the property-rights regulation might have a negative impact on the rights of the individuals for free information.

At the same time, private actors have not waited for public actors to provide a public governance mechanism for solving the problem. Rather, they have developed private initiatives to safeguard property rights on their own. IBM, just to mention one example, has recently launched a project that, by using advanced technologies such as digital watermarks, specific hardware systems, or digital containers, is bound to provide copyright holders with effective control over their property (Spar 1999, 40). In such a constellation, public activities complement private efforts. This complementary role of public actors is finding expression both at the national and the international level in litigation about property rights violations: they are being dealt with before public courts or within the framework of the WIPO and the World Trade Organization (WTO).

Interfering Regulation

Our final ideal type delineates constellations in which public actors are no longer capable of compensating for the low potential of private governance contributions—either by directly providing the public good in question or by effectively altering the opportunity structures for societal actors in order to ensure the private provision of a certain good. Given the limited governance capacity of both public and private actors in this arrangement, it is rather unlikely that political problems can be effectively addressed. Rather than coordinated efforts to ensure the provision of a specific public good, we expect public interference in markets to occur on an ad hoc basis. Thus, we label a constellation in which both public and private governance capacities are lacking as *interfering regulation*.

Interfering regulation neither implies a powerless state nor a retreat of the state. Despite the restrictions on governmental capacities, hierarchical intervention by state authorities still might be able to "disturb" or "obstruct" private activities that create negative externalities. Although a "master plan" is missing in these forms of intervention, and governmental interference will hardly be sufficient to provide effective solutions to problems, the impact of such "policies of pinpricks" should not be underestimated (in terms of educating or persuading private actors).

This said, we are now able to identify the shift from an interventionist to an interfering mode of regulation as the third impact of globalization on patterns of governance. To illustrate this case we refer to the efforts of governments to regulate the content on the Internet. While the hierarchical regulation of broadcasting and television services had traditionally secured the strong regulation of illegal and harmful content, such as violence or pornography, the Internet, with its decentralized and transjurisdictional character, has made it possible to evade territorial regulation. In addition to technical restraints, the attempts to extend the content regulations that were already applied to broadcasting services have been hampered by constitutional provisions in some countries. The U.S. Supreme Court, for example, stated that by extending the existing provisions on broadcasting regulation to the area of the Internet, the Communication Decency Act of 1996 made unconstitutional restrictions on the individual rights to information (Grzeszisk 1998; Schulz 1998).

Given the twofold constraints on traditional hierarchical modes of public regulation, states either try to indirectly regulate extraterritorial activities, or they rely on public/private partnerships. With respect to the first attempt, local damage caused by offshore Internet providers is regulated domestically: in-state end users who obtain and use illegal content are penalized. There are two recent examples of interference by public actors: first, the 1999 verdict of a Bavarian court that made the provider CompuServe responsible for the content offered by its portal; second, the 2000 interim injunction made by a French court according to which the U.S. American provider Yahoo had to block the distribution of Nazi objects on its servers for French users. For some scholars these cases pinpoint that offshore regulation evasion does not prevent a nation from regulating the extraterritorial activity (Goldsmith 1998, 1222). As a second strategy, public actors seek to incorporate private actors in soft regulation or voluntary self-regulation. For instance, Internet service providers may be obliged to install what are known as self-regulatory institutions, i.e., to develop codes of conduct on a voluntary basis (Schulz 1998, 185; CEC 1997), or, for example, providers may only be allowed to transmit content liable to corrupt the young if they have installed filtering protection measures (Grzeszick 1998, 194).

Conclusion: Globalization and Changing Patterns of Governance

The starting point of this chapter was the observation of two major weaknesses of the discourse on globalization and its consequences: on the one hand, there is a lack of systematic empirical research (Elkins 1995, 7) and, on the other hand, the concepts concerning how to analyze and interpret the impact of globalization on the role of states and on the patterns of governance between public and private actors have not been well enough developed. Addressing the latter point, this chapter sets out to reflect theoretically on the impact of globalization on the governance capacity of public and private actors in the provision of public goods. Rather than adopting the view that the demise of the state is near at hand, we have operated with a broad view of the term governance, which includes different types of actor configurations, different combinations of these configurations, and particularly the different interactions between them (Mayntz 1998, 18f). In so doing, we have been able to relate actual patterns of governance to the respective governance capacities of public and private actors, with the latter depending on the strategic constellation underlying the provision of public goods. This specific strategic constellation varies along three dimensions: namely, the type of good problem; the congruence between the scope of the underlying problem and existing regulatory structures of the related actors; and the institutional context.

This procedure has not only allowed us to identify four ideal types of governance, which are distinguished by differing configurations of the governance capacities of public and private actors; what is more, it has made it possible for us to theoretically assess the implications of the economic and political internationalization for the governance capacities of public and private actors. In particular, we suggest that globalization be described as a process in which the patterns of governance are transformed along three paths. According to our model, it is likely that interventionist regulation will increasingly be replaced by regulated self-regulation, by private self-regulation, and by interfering regulation. In all three patterns of transformation, the governance capacity of private actors may vary significantly. In any case, our analytical considerations lead us to expect that private and public governance contributions will generally be mutually reinforcing. In particular, the scenarios of the public-private partnerships and of private self-regulation reveal the mutually reinforcing relationship between public and private governance activities.

This said, it should be clear why we think it is less intriguing to hold on to the idea that the state is weakening or that public and private governance capacities are mutually exclusive. While the relationship between public and private actors is not free of conflict, neither is it paralyzed by conflict. In essence, we are confronted with dynamic, more synergetic relationships, in which public and private contributions might reinforce each other over time. Finally, it is certainly true that we have only addressed one dimension of the problem related to the process of internationalization, i.e., the regulatory dimension. As has been argued by others, however, problems related to accountability and the democratic legitimacy of regulatory structures are at least as important (Scholte 1997; Wolf 2000; Zürn 2000). Thus, a crucial question: how is it possible to ensure that private governance activities will remain responsive to wider societal interests? In principle, as the concern about the legitimacy and the substance of private governance activities increases in importance, the less public actors are able to influence the behavior of private actors.

Notes

Parts of this chapter heavily draw on an earlier article which will be published in *Governance* (Knill and Lehmkuhl 2002). We are particularly grateful to Darrell Arnold, Philip Cerny, Henry Farrell, Adrienne Héritier, Katharina Hölzinger, Andreas Nölke, Volker Schneider, and Klaus-Dieter Wolf for very helpful comments.

1. Despite the broad variety and sometimes confusing conceptions of public goods (Malkin and Wildavsky 1991), in this chapter we stick to the classic economic definition

according to which a public good is defined by the criteria of non-rivalry and the non-excludability of consumption.

2. A more restrictive definition of governance is used, for instance, in the studies of Rosenau and Czempiel 1992; Kooiman 1993; Rhodes 1997.

3. Another conceptual approach to analytically cope with different dimensions describing the context for the provision of public goods distinguishes between the provision, production, and consumption (see McGinnis 1999b, 3f. and other contributions in McGinnis 1999a).

4. Regime analysts with inclinations towards game theory draw a distinction between coordination problems (e.g., battle of the sexes) with stable equilibria and collaboration problems (e.g., prisoner's dilemma, chicken) with equilibria being either suboptimal or absent. In addition, the importance of compliance mechanisms for collaboration problems is emphasized.

5. According to hegemonic stability theory, a hegemonic state might provide a certain good globally when accepting the short-term disadvantage of higher investments for the long-term benefits.

6. The following considerations and examples draw heavily on Knill and Lehmkuhl 2002.

7. Our use of the concept of private-interest government is broader than that of Streeck and Schmitter, who reserve the concept for arrangements in which an attempt is made to make associative, self-interested collective action contribute to the achievement of public policy objectives (Streeck and Schmitter 1985).

8. We thank Marc Hollitscher and Volker Leib for very helpful comments on the ICANN case.

9. In the first six months of its existence (until September 2000), there were 1,573 complaints and 1,012 final decisions (Bettinger 2000, 1110; see also Mueller 2000).

References

Bauer, M. W. 2001. Regulatory Costs of Utility Reforms. Mapping a Framework for Empirical Analysis. Bonn: Max Planck Project Group, unpublished manuscript.

Beck, U. 1998. Wie wird Demokratie im Zeitalter der Globalisierung möglich? Eine Einleitung. In *Politik im Zeitalter der Globalisierung*, ed. U. Beck, 7-68. Frankfurt am Main: Suhrkamp.

Bettinger, T. 2000. Online-Schiedsgerichte für Domainsnamestreitigkeiten. *Wettbewerb in Recht und Wirtschaft* 10: 1109-1116.

Braun, D. 2000. Diskurse zur staatlichen Steuerung. Übersicht und Bilanz. Paper delivered to the Symposium Politische Steuerung, March 1-3, at the Institut für Sozialwissenschaften der Universität Stuttgart.

CEC (Commission of the European Communities). 1997. Towards an Information Society Approach. *Green Paper on the Convergence of the Telecommunications, Media, and Information Technology Sectors*. COM (97) 623 final., Brussels, 3.

Cerny, P. J. 1995. Globalization and the Changing Logic of Collective Action. *International Organisation* 49 (4): 595-625.

Cuker, K. 1999. Global Telecom Rout: As other Nations Struggle for Telecom Dollars, the United States's Superiour Infrastructure is Eating into Their Political Power. www.redherring.com/mag/issue63/news-telecom.html [cited 1999].

Cutler, A.C. 1999. Private Authority in International Trade Relations: The Case of Maritime Transport. In *Private Authority and International Affairs*, ed. A. C. Cutler, V. Haufler, and T. Porter, 283-329. Albany: State University of New York Press.

Eichener, V., and H. Voelzkow. 1994. Ko-evolution politisch administrativer und verbandlicher Strukturen: Am Beispiel der technischen Harmonisierung des europäischen Arbeits-, Verbraucher- und Umweltschutzes. In *Staat und Verbände*, ed. W. Streeck, 256-90. Opladen: Westdeutscher Verlag.

Elkins, D. J. 1995. *Beyond Sovereignty: Territory and Political Economy in the Twenty-First Century*. Toronto: University of Toronto Press.

Etkins, P. 1992. *A New World Order: Grassroots Movements for Global Change*. London: Routledge.

Goldsmith, J. L. 1998. Against Cyberanarchy. *University of Chicago Law Review* 65 (4): 1199-1250.

Greenwood, J. 1997. *Representing Interests in the European Union*. Basingstoke: Macmillian.

Grzeszick, B. 1998. Neue Medienfreiheit zwischen staatlicher und gesellschaftlicher Ordnung. Das Beispiel des Internets. *Archiv des öffentlichen Rechts* 123: 173-200.

Hadfield, G. 2000. Privatizing Commercial Law: Lessons from the Middle and the Digital Ages [SSRN Working Paper Series]. SSRN Electronic Library [cited March 2000].

Héritier, A., and S. Schmidt. 2000. After Liberalization: Public Interest Services and Employment in the Utilities. In *Welfare and Work in the Open Economy, Volume II. Diverse Responses to Common Challenges*, ed. F. W. Scharpf and V. A. Schmidt. Oxford: Oxford University Press.

Héritier, A., C. Knill, and S. Mingers. 1996. *Ringing the Changes in Europe: Regulatory Competition and the Transformation of the State*. Berlin: de Gruyter.

Higgott, R. A., G. R. D. Underhill, and A. Bieler, eds. 2000. *Non-State Actors and Authority in the Global System*. London: Routledge.

Hirshleifer, J. 1983. From Weakest-link to Best-shot : The Voluntary Provision of Public Goods. *Public Choice* 41: 371-86.

Hirst, P., and G. Thompson. 1996. *Globalization in Question: The International Economy and the Possibilities of Governance*. Cambridge: Polity Press.

Holzinger, K. Forthcoming. Aggregation Technology of Common Goods and Its Strategic Consequences. Global Warming, Biodiversity and Siting Conflicts. *European Journal of Political Research* 40.

Immergut, H. 1992. *Health Politics: Interests and Institutions in Western Europe*. Cambridge: Cambridge University Press.

Kenis, P., and V. Schneider. 1991. Policy Networks and Policy Analysis: Scrutinizing a New Analytical Toolbox. In *Policy Networks. Empirical Evidence and Theoretical Considerations*, ed. B. Marin and R. Mayntz, 25-58. Frankfurt am Main: Campus.

Knill, C. 1999. Explaining Cross-National Variance in Administrative Reform: Autonomous versus Instrumental Bureaucracies. *Journal of Public Policy* 19 (2): 113-39.

————. 2001. Private Governance across Multiple Arenas: European Interest Associations as Interface Actors. *Journal of European Public Policy* 8 (2): 227-46.

Knill, C., and D. Lehmkuhl. 1998. Integration by Globalization: The European Interest Representation of the Consumer Electronics Industry. *Current Politics and Economics in Europe* 8 (2): 131-53.

————. 2002. Private Actors and the State: Internationalization and Changing Patterns of Governance. *Governance* 15 (1): 41-63.

Kobrin, S. J. 1997. The Architecture of Globalization: State Sovereignty in a Networked Global Economy. In *Governments, Globalization, and International Business*, ed. J. H. Dunning, 146-71. Oxford: Oxford University Press.

Kohler-Koch, B. 1993. Die Welt regieren ohne Weltregierung. In *Regieren im 21. Jahrhundert. Zwischen Globalisierung und Regionalisierung*, ed. C. Böhret and G. Wewer, 109-41. Opladen: Westdeutscher Verlag.

Kooiman, J., ed. 1993. *Modern Governance: New Government-Society Interactions.* London: Sage.

Lehmkuhl, D. 2000. Commercial Arbitration—A Case of Private Transnational Self-Governance? Bonn: Max Planck Project Group. Common Goods: Law, Politics and Economics. Preprint 2000/1.

Levy, M. A., O. R. Young, and M. Zürn. 1995. The Study of International Regimes. *European Journal of International Relations* 1 (3): 267-330.

Majone, G. 1994. The Rise of the Regulatory State in Europe. *West European Politics* 17: 77-101.

Malkin, J., and A. Wildavsky. 1991. Why the Tradition Distinction between Public and Private Goods Should Be Abandoned. *Journal of Theoretical Politics* 4 (3): 355-78.

Mayntz, R. 1993. Modernization and the Logic of Interorganizational Networks. In *Societal Change between Market and Organisation*, ed. J. Child et al., 3-18. Aldershot: Avebury.

———. 1998. *New Challenges to Governance Theory.* Florence: The Robert Schuman Centre at the European University Institute, Florence.

Mayntz, R., and F. W. Scharpf. 1995. Der Ansatz des akteurzentrierten Institutionalismus. In *Gesellschaftliche Selbstregulierung und politische Steuerung,* ed. R. Mayntz und F. W. Scharpf, 39-72. Frankfurt am Main: Campus.

McGinnis, M. D., ed. 1999a. *Polycentricity and Local Public Economics.* Ann Arbor: University of Michigan Press.

———. 1999b. Introduction. In *Polycentricity and Local Public Economies. Readings from the Workshop in Political Theory and Policy Analysis*, ed. M. D. McGinnis. Ann Arbor: University of Michigan Press.

Mueller, M. 2000. Rough Justice. An Analysis of ICANN's Uniform Dispute Resolution Policy (http://dcc.syr.edu/roughjustice.pdf) www.digital-convergence.org, 2000 [cited 12.12.2000].

Müller, H. 1993. The Internationalisation of Principles, Norms, and Rules by Governments: The Case of Security Regimes. In *Regime Theory and International Relations*, ed. V. Rittberger and P. Mayer, 361-88. Oxford: Clarendon.

North, D. C. 1981. *Structure and Change in Economic History.* New York: Norton.

North, D. C, and R. P. Thomas. 1973. *The Rise of the Western World: A New Economic History.* Cambridge: Cambridge University Press.

Olson, M. 1965. *The Logic of Collective Action: Public Goods and the Theory of Groups.* Cambridge, Mass.: Harvard University Press.

Osborne, S. P., ed. 2000. *Public-Private Partnerships. Theory and Practice in International Perspective.* London: Routledge.

Ostrom, E. 1999. Context and Collective Action: Four Building Blocks for a Family of Explanatory Theories. Unpublished manuscript.

Peters, B. G. 1998. Globalization, Institutions, and Governance. Jean Monnet Chair Papers No. 50. The Robert Schuman Centre at the European University Institute, Florence.

Powell, W. W., and E. S. Clemens, eds. 1998. *Private Action and the Public Good.* New Haven, Conn.: Yale University Press.

Princen, T., and M. Finger. 1994. *Environmental NGOs in World Politics: Linking the Local and the Global.* London: Routledge.

Reinicke, W. R. 1998. *Global Public Policy: Governing without Government?* Washington, D.C.: Brookings Institution Press.

Rhodes, R. W. A. 1997. *Understanding Governance: Policy Networks, Reflexivity, and Accountability.* Buckingham, Pa.: Open University Press.

Ronit, K., and V. Schneider. 1999. Global Governance through Private Organizations. *Governance* 12 (3): 243-66.

———. eds. 2000. *Private Organizations in Global Politics.* London: Routledge.

Rosenau, J. N. and E.-O. Czempiel, eds. 1992. *Governance without Government: Order and Change in World Politics.* Cambridge: Cambridge University Press.

Rosenberg, N., and L. E. Birdzell Jr. 1986. *How the West Grew Rich: The Economic Transformation of the Industrial World.* Boulder, Colo.: Basic Books.

Scharpf, F. W. 2000. Institutions in Comparative Policy Research. Max Planck Institut für Gesellschaftsforschung. Working Paper 00/3.

Schmidt, S. K., and R. Werle. 1997. *Coordinating Technology: Studies in the Standardisation of Telecomunications.* Cambridge, Mass.: MIT Press.

Schmitter, P. C., and W. Streeck. 1981. *The Organisation of Business Interests: A Research Design to Study the Associative Business Action in Advanced Industrial Societies of Western Europe.* Vol. IIMV dp 81-13. Berlin: Wissenschaftszentrum Berlin.

Scholte, J. A. 1997. Global Capitalism and the State. *International Affairs* 73: 427-52.

Schulz, W. 1998. Jugendschutz bei Tele- und Mediendiensten. *Multimedia und Recht* 4: 182-87.

Sell, S. K. 1999. Multinational Corporations as Agents of Change: The Globalization of Intellectual Property Rights. In *Private Authority and International Affairs*, ed. A. C. Cutler, V. Haufler, and T. Porter, 169-98. Albany: State University of New York Press.

Sinclair, T. J. 1994. Passing Judgment: Credit Rating Processes as Regulatory Mechanisms of Governance in the Emerging World Order. *Review of International Political Economy* 1(1): 133-59.

Spar, D. L. 1999. Lost in (Cyber)space: The Private Rules of Online Commerce. In *Private Authority and International Affairs*, ed. A. C. Cutler, V. Haufler, and T. Porter, 313-52. Albany: State University of New York Press.

Streeck, W. 1994. Staat und Verbände: Neue Fragen. Neue Antworten? In *Staat und Verbände*, ed. W. Streeck, 7-34. Opladen: Westdeutscher Verlag.

Streeck, W., and P. C. Schmitter, eds. 1985. *Private Interest Government. Beyond State and Market.* London: Sage.

Weiss, L. 1998. *The Myth of the Powerless State: Governing the Economy in a Global Era.* Cambridge: Polity Press.

Werle, R., and V. Leib. 2000. The Internet Society and Its Struggle for Recognition and Influence. In *Private Organizations in Global Politics*, ed. K. Ronit and V. Schneider, 102-22. London: Routledge.

Willetts, P., ed. 1996. *The Conscience of the World: The Influence of Non-Governmental Organizations in the UN-System.* London: Hurst.

Willke, H. 1995. The Proactive State: The Role of National Enabling Policies in Global Socio-Economic Transformations. In *Benevolent Conspiracies: The Role of Enabling Technologies in the Welfare State. The Cases of SDI, SEMATECH, and EUREKA*, ed. H. Willke, C. P. Krück, and C. Thorn, 325-55. Berlin: de Gruyter.

Wolf, K. D. 2000. *Die neue Staatsraison—Zwischenstaatliche Kooperation als Demokratieproblem in der Weltgesellschaft.* Baden-Baden: Nomos.

Wright, V. 1994. Reshaping the State: Implications for Public Administration. *West European Politics* 17: 102-37.

Young, O. R. 1997. Rights, Rules, and Resources in World Affairs. In *Global Governance: Drawing Insights from the Environmental Experience*, ed. O. R. Young, 1-23. Cambridge, Mass.: MIT Press.

Zürn, M. 1998. *Regieren jenseits des Nationalstaates. Globalisierung und Denationalisierung als Chance.* Frankfurt am Main: Suhrkamp.

―――. 2000. Democratic Governance beyond the Nation-State: The EU and Other International Institutions. *European Journal of International Relations* 6 (2): 183-221.

5

Negotiating Privacy across Arenas: The EU-U.S. "Safe Harbor" Discussions

Henry Farrell

Much recent theoretical attention has been devoted to the provision of common goods across arenas. The normal problems of common good provision (Olson 1968; Hardin 1982) are exacerbated when these problems spill across arenas (there are usually no actors capable of imposing hierarchical solutions), but there are also new difficulties. Solutions in one particular arena of policy-making may be incompatible with the solution or broader regulatory mechanisms in another arena. Furthermore, states, which may solve some common goods problems, seem to be losing some decision-making competencies in the global arena. While non-state actors may provide at least some common goods (Ronit and Schneider 1999), it is unlikely that these forms of provision can be generalized in any meaningful way. Many authors believe that globalization makes it vastly more difficult to solve international common good problems (Cerny 1995).

Yet this pessimism may at least be partly misplaced. The globalization literature argues both that common problems spill over state borders ever more (common good difficulties are internationalized) and that the capacity of states to respond to these problems is ever weaker (there is insufficient capacity to provide common goods internationally). While the first of these claims is true in many areas, the second is at least arguable. States may still try to solve collective action problems through unilateral action, through coordination among themselves, and through new forms of policy which mix public and private action. The second and third of these types of solution typically require negotiations which seek to harmonize forms of common good provision across arenas, or at least to ensure the compatibility of different solutions in different arenas. This layer of international negotiation provides new opportunities for actors in domestic arenas.

The third kind of solution—public actors working together with private actors, or indeed delegating substantial enforcement authority to them—has attracted much recent attention. On the one hand, advocates of this approach (especially in business and government) suggest that it allows a much greater degree of flexibility than "traditional" regulation. On the other hand, critics (who often seek to protect consumer or citizen interests) believe that it is symptomatic of a wider trend towards the abdication of public matters to private self-interested actors, with consequent problems of democratic legitimacy (Cutler, this volume). The differences between these two views of public-private action has given rise to vigorous policy debates and discussions over the introduction of new "hybrid" approaches to common goods problems.

This chapter examines one such set of discussions—the negotiations between the EU and U.S. over the so-called "Safe Harbor" arrangement on data protection and privacy.[1] These negotiations provide a good test case for arguments about common goods provision across national borders (Shaffer 2000). By examining the course of the negotiations, we may come to arrive at a better understanding of the forces dictating both actors' negotiating positions and the bargaining power which they have to realize those positions. The strategic interaction which leads (or does not lead) to a particular form of common good provision involves actors with differing interests and objectives. Insofar as common goods are provided, this will likely emerge from struggles between actors who differ both according to their interests and their conception of how the relevant good is best provided, the latter often being determined by the former. In this particular instance, such an enquiry may help us understand why a hybrid institution involving both public and private actors resulted from negotiations, given the relative goals and bargaining positions.

This chapter adopts an approach which can be characterized as a form of "actor centered institutionalism" (Scharpf 1997). I seek to show that this form of analysis is well suited to the examination of bargaining and negotiation over multi-arena common goods and the agreements reached between actors. I begin by discussing whether privacy can be defined as a common good and the different forms of governance through which it might be provided. I then go on to examine the different approaches to privacy which have arisen in the two arenas under discussion: the European Union and the United States. Next, I describe the different actors involved both indirectly and directly in the negotiations, their preferences, and their power to achieve those preferences given prevailing circumstances. I go on to examine how these positions played out in three interlinked arenas, and conclude by discussing the implications of the Safe Harbor negotiations for common good provision in multi-arena settings.

Privacy as a Common Good

Privacy is an ambiguous concept, with multiple meanings, according both to its context and the philosophical orientations of those discussing it. It is thus difficult precisely to characterize privacy as a common good, given that there is disagreement as to what precisely it involves. One can nonetheless examine how privacy has been discussed and implemented in policy terms and the extent to which this has involved collective action problems. Since the early 1970s, policy-makers have typically conceived of privacy in terms of principles of data protection.[2] Indeed, the 1970s and 1980s saw a substantial degree of policy convergence among industrialized Western democracies as to what such principles should involve (Bennett 1992, 1997). This convergence was marked on the international level by the Organisation for Economic Cooperation and Development's (OECD) nonbinding guidelines on data protection and the Council of Europe's Convention, and on the national level by the adoption of data protection laws in most OECD countries. These principles impose real burdens on the collectors of data: in other words, they are not self-enforcing. Data collectors, if they are guided by rational self-interest, and do not believe they will be punished for failing to abide by these principles, will tend to ignore them.

The observance of fair information principles is a public good problem (Ostrom, this volume). There is non-rivalness of consumption; my observation of privacy principles is unlikely to detract from your observation of privacy principles in most circumstances, but it is difficult to exclude those who seek to free ride on the general perception that fair information principles are observed. Like other public goods, it is likely to be underprovided. Take, for example, privacy on the World Wide Web (WWW).[3] There is substantial opinion poll evidence suggesting that many consumers are unwilling to make purchases or carry out other activities on the WWW because of privacy concerns.[4] The WWW allows new forms of data collection which are often difficult for consumers to detect; furthermore there have been several widely reported cases in which consumers' privacy has indeed been invaded. However, consumers face a serious collective action problem if they wish to mobilize against those firms that do invade their privacy. "Exit" on its own may be insufficient to change firm policy, especially for firms such as profiling firms, which the consumer does not necessarily deal with directly, but which are pervasive on the WWW, and which gather detailed information on consumers' websurfing. But organized collective action may prove difficult given the vast number of consumers involved. The unwillingness of political decision-makers (at least in the United States) to become involved in regulation of e-commerce makes it unlikely that government will serve as a "multiplier" for collective action (Hardin 1982).

Firms, as well as consumers, face a collective action problem. Given the lack of consumer confidence in the WWW, firms may have a common interest in buoying up consumer confidence, and encouraging them to make purchases, through adhering to fair information practices and pressuring other firms to do so too. But this interest is precisely a *collective* one. Insofar as individual firms are unlikely to benefit very much from their own particular contribution to the common good of consumer confidence in the Web, they will have an incentive to free ride on the efforts of others. In the words of Robert Litan,

> In principle, the privacy problem on the Net is a classic "collective action" problem: that is, because all actual and potential Net users would be better off if they were comfortable that the information they provided over the Net was absolutely safe and private, no single firm can capture all of the benefits of guaranteeing that its particular Web site has these characteristics.[5]

This collective action problem might be resolved in various ways. First, reputational incentives alone might encourage firms to adhere to a stringent privacy policy. Insofar as it is the *particular* reputation of a firm which suffers from privacy violations, rather than the *general* reputation of WWW commercial actors as a group, the firm may have an incentive to adhere to privacy practices, even if they are not formally required.[6] Many business representative organizations argue that these reputational effects are sufficient to guarantee consumer privacy: market forces will drive firms with bad reputations out of business or force them to improve their behavior.

A second possible solution is that business self-regulate through its representative organizations, through adherence to uniform privacy standards, through third party bodies, or through some mixture of these three. Knill and Lehmkuhl (this volume) discuss the capacity of private actors to provide common goods, distinguishing between the "strength" of a business organization vis-à-vis its members, and the "degree" to which a particular set of business actors is organized and willing to contribute to the provision of a common good. If self-regulatory schemes are sufficiently "strong," and provide a broad "degree" of coverage, they may be capable of enforcing common good provision.[7]

A third solution is state action—formal regulations which mandate that actors adhere to a certain set of standards. In privacy, one may identify two broad approaches to state regulation. First is the approach of the member states of the European Union and some other OECD states. These states have both omnibus cross-sectoral laws, which lay out privacy practices in detail, and independent, specialized agencies—data protection commissions—which seek to ensure that those laws are enforced. Second is the U.S. approach, with a patchwork of laws and regulations, which differ widely between sectors. In many sectors, there is no legal coverage beyond self-regulation or firms' own commitments. However, there is a mechanism to ensure that firms do at least live up to any promises they may have made to consumers about the privacy of their information. The Federal Trade Commission (FTC), under Section 5 of the FTC Act, can issue "cease and desist" orders to firms who are violating their stated commitments and impose substantial fines. It has taken action against firms such as Geocities, which has violated its privacy statements. One should note that the FTC cannot either force firms to issue a privacy policy or dictate what the terms of any privacy policy should involve; it can merely police those commitments that firms have voluntarily made.

I do not wish to discuss the respective strengths and weaknesses of these approaches in this chapter; instead, I wish to repeat the suggestion that the mode (or mix of modes) which prevails in a particular policy setting is likely to be the end result of struggles between different actors with competing end goals. Most firms would ideally prefer a situation in which privacy protection is left to them, either through pure market mechanisms or through some form of self-regulation in which they set the rules. Equally, other actors such as consumer organizations or data protection authorities may prefer an end result in which privacy is protected through legally binding rules mandating fair information practices. State actors will have their own interests and objectives, which may vary between different policy areas within the state apparatus. The question of which set of preferences prevails is an empirical one, which will depend in part on the prevailing institutional setting and its effect on the relative bargaining positions of the relevant actors.[8]

Thus, in summary, it is clear that privacy (or, more precisely, data protection) may give rise to collective action issues. Adherence to data protection principles is a public good. Consumers face a linked collective action problem if they wish to ensure that these principles are lived up to. There exist different mechanisms through which these common good problems might be resolved—reputation and market forces, self-regulation by firms, and government regulation. Each of these different modes has different implications and possibility conditions. These different mechanisms reflect the interests and objectives of different actors within those governance systems. As discussed in the next section, globalization and the advent of e-commerce are resulting in problems of governance, as common good problems become internationalized. But insofar as these problems must be resolved in a multi-arena setting, there are new opportunities for actors strategically to act across arenas in order to attain their goals.

Privacy and Data Protection in Europe and the United States: The Background

Europe and the United States have very different approaches to data protection and privacy. The United States, as discussed above, has eschewed an omnibus approach to privacy protection, and in many areas, most notably e-commerce, there is little substantial legal protection.[9] Furthermore, legislation in the area of e-commerce is a highly sensitive topic. The United States administration has concluded that regulation is inappropriate, given how swiftly e-commerce is evolving and has instead sought to encourage self-regulation in areas such as privacy in the belief that self-regulation would be more flexible and responsive. In Europe, in contrast, data protection legislation has been enacted in a number of waves (Mayer-Schönberger (1997), culminating in the European Union's *Directive on the Protection of Individuals with Regard to the Processing of Personal Data and on the Free Movement of Such Data*, the so-called "Data Protection Directive," which came into effect in October 1998. This Directive was intended to prevent differences in how member states protected data from impeding the integration of the single market. The Directive thus provided a framework for omnibus protection for privacy across different sectors, the specifics of which were to be implemented in national law.

The United States and EU approaches came into conflict because of overspill between the two arenas; modern communications technology made it relatively easy to transfer information from the EU to third party states such as the United States. This could potentially have undermined the EU's attempts to provide data protection for its citizens, if it were possible to transfer personal data outside the jurisdiction of the EU, and then to process it without fulfilling the requirements of the Directive. Accordingly, the Directive only allowed the export of data (with some tightly worded exceptions) under two circumstances: where the data was contractually protected or the jurisdiction to which it was being exported had "adequate" protection.[10] Contractual protection was more suited for some forms of data transfer (such as personnel records) than for others, and there was furthermore some doubt as to what contractual forms were necessary: the EU has only very recently finalized a set of model contractual clauses.[11]

The Data Protection Directive describes in some detail the process by which adequacy or non-adequacy is to be determined. The Commission, under Article 25 [6] of the Directive, may find that a third country gives an adequate level of protection "by reason of its domestic law or of the international commitments it has entered into." Where the Commission finds that a third country provides an inadequate level of protection, member states are enjoined to prevent data transfers to that third country (Article 25 [4]). At the same time, the Commission is instructed to enter into negotiations as appropriate with the third country (Article 25 [5]). The "international commitments" provided by a third country may result directly from these negotiations; indeed the language of the relevant clause seems to suggest that this is the primary sense of the term as employed in the Directive.

In its negotiations with a third country, the Commission must also consult with the Article 31 Committee, which is composed of representatives of the member states and chaired by the Commission.[12] This Committee is a comitology procedure which votes by qualified majority on measures to be taken with regard to adequacy. If the Committee votes against the proposed measure, the Commission must defer application of the measure for three months and communicate this to the Council forthwith. The Council may act under qualified majority to take a different decision during that three-month period. The European Parliament has procedural oversight, in order to ensure that neither Commission nor Council has overstepped its competences.

It was clear from an early stage that the United States was unlikely to be considered an "adequate" jurisdiction as matters stood. However, U.S. experts hoped that some sectors, with specific legal protections, could be considered "adequate," and that the EU might consider certain self-regulatory codes of conduct sufficient for an adequacy finding. The importance of EU-U.S. trade in services meant that the Commission had to seek some mutually tolerable modus vivendi. Structured EU-U.S. discussions over adequacy started in early 1998, some six months before the Directive was due to come into effect. Initially, these discussions were not especially fruitful. Prominent U.S. decision-makers viewed the Directive as a fundamental threat to U.S. commercial interests, and to the expansion of e-commerce, and they sought to force the European Union to back down. Other figures in the Department of Commerce were aware of how unlikely an EU climb down was, and engaged in serious discussions with the European Union as to how adequacy might be reached. Ambassador David Aaron, the undersecretary for international trade in the Department of Commerce, had been briefed by U.S. businesses about the possible consequences of the Directive, and began discussions with John Mogg, the director general for the Internal Market. The EU-U.S. discussions were initially frustrating. The European Union maintained that it was interested only in legislation drafted to provide adequate protection to the data of European citizens which had been exported, while the United States sought to postpone the implementation of the Directive, and to gain a recognition of adequacy for the U.S. system as it then stood. In this early stage of discussions, negotiators were pessimistic: the best likely outcome was some form of damage limitation. However, a suggestion by Aaron that the adequacy judgment need not extend to the entire U.S. system, but rather to a set of firms which had voluntarily agreed to embrace a set of privacy principles, proved to be the basis for a potential compromise. EU negotiators found the approach interesting enough to merit further negotiations, and the EU undertook to be as flexible as possible in its interpretation of the Directive (i.e., to avoid data blockages unless absolutely necessary) while discussions were still under way. On November 4, 1998, Aaron wrote a public letter to U.S. businesses, setting out draft principles for a so-called "Safe Harbor" for U.S. firms: the intention was that firms would not be subject to EU action as long as they adhered to these principles. In summarized form, the principles were

Notice – Organizations must inform individuals about what type of personal information is collected, how it was collected, whom it was disclosed to, and the choices individuals have for limiting this disclosure.

Choice – Organizations must give individuals the opportunity to opt out when information is used for purposes unrelated to the use for which they originally disclosed it. Individuals must be given opt in choice with regard to certain sorts of sensitive information.

Onward transfer – Individuals must be able to choose whether and how a third party uses the information they provide. When information is transferred to third parties, these parties must provide at least the same level of privacy protection originally chosen.

Security – Organizations must take reasonable measures to assure the reliability of information and prevent loss or misuse.

Data integrity – Personal data must be kept accurate, complete, current, and used only for the purposes for which it is gathered.

Access – Individuals must have reasonable access to data about them, and be able to correct it when it is inaccurate, subject to the sensitivity of the information and its dependent uses.

Enforcement – There must be mechanisms for assuring compliance with the principles, recourse for individuals, and consequences for the organization when the principles are not followed. Enforcement could take place through compliance with private sector privacy programs, through compliance with legal or regulatory authorities, or by committing to cooperate with the data protection authorities in Europe.

The United States hoped that the EU would accept these principles relatively swiftly; instead, negotiations were to last over eighteen months. When the Commission presented the U.S. proposal, certain member states expressed their difficulties with the package, in particular on the questions of access and enforcement. Lengthy negotiations followed, which only reached a final resolution in June 2000. The Safe Harbor principles themselves saw very significant amendment, mostly in response to European demands that they be tightened and made more workable. In addition to the principles themselves, a series of Frequently Asked Questions (FAQs) was negotiated, which provided authoritative interpretation of the principles in specific instances.

The final agreement reached on Safe Harbor involves both the principles themselves and enforcement mechanisms designed to back them up. Enforcement is provided on three levels. The first line of enforcement is intended to handle complaints about possible breaches of their privacy. Organizations may sign up to third party dispute resolution bodies, which should fulfill certain stated criteria, or commit to cooperate with data protection authorities within the European Union member states; in the future they may also be able to commit to work together with appropriate U.S. regulatory authorities.

The second line of enforcement is intended to ensure both that organizations do not fail to fulfill their Safe Harbor commitments and that third party dispute resolution mechanisms work as they are supposed to. The FTC has oversight powers under the FTC Act: signing up to Safe Harbor is a public commitment, and firms which fail to abide by such commitments can be penalized.[13] The same is true of third party dispute resolution bodies, insofar as they act on behalf of for-profit bodies. The FTC has undertaken to deal with complaints from third party dispute resolution bodies and from European data protection authorities on an accelerated basis.

The third line of enforcement is provided by the European Union itself. Under certain restricted circumstances, European data protection authorities can still block the flow of data. Further, the Safe Harbor arrangement itself is a unilateral determination of adequacy on the part of the European Union rather than an international agreement, which means that it can be suspended or abrogated unilaterally if it is clear that it is not working.

At the time of writing (June 2001), the Safe Harbor has come into effect, so far has attracted some sixty firms. Interviews suggest that firms are behaving cautiously: Safe Harbor involves serious obligations, which many firms are reluctant to take on without fully considering alternatives. While involved actors suggest that Safe Harbor will play a substantial role for U.S. firms, this is still uncertain.[14]

Privacy and Data Protection: Arenas and Actors

The process leading up to Safe Harbor can be characterized in terms of three interlinked arenas, or in Tsebelis's term, "nested games" (Tsebelis 1990). The first of these arenas is the obvious one: the EU-U.S. negotiations. But the second of these arenas was more important for many of the U.S. actors involved: domestic politics within the United States itself. Privacy had suddenly become an important policy issue, in part because of the publicity surrounding the EU's Data Protection Directive and its external effect, but mostly because of consumer concern both about privacy on the WWW and new technologies allowing the offline gathering and use of personal information. Further, these two arenas potentially intersected: many actors who sought to influence developments in the first arena (EU-U.S. negotiations) were motivated by goals that they were pursuing in the second (the domestic U.S. debate). In particular, actors who were less powerful in the second sought to use their influence in the first to increase their bargaining strength. Finally, there was a third arena, that within the European Union itself, where any adequacy arrangement would have to receive approval in terms of its substance (Article 31 Committee/Council) and process (European Parliament).

To develop this argument, it is first necessary to describe actors involved in the negotiation process in greater detail. The remainder of this section describes these actors and their goals. The subsequent three sections will look in closer detail at each of the three games—first, the EU-U.S. negotiations, next the domestic policy debate within the United States, and finally the debate within the EU institutions.

On the European side, four main actors (or sets of actors) can be identified— the Commission, the member states, the European Parliament, and the data protection commissioners of the individual member states.[15]

The *Commission* did not have unified preferences on Safe Harbor, but internal critics of its negotiating stance did not play a major role in determining its policy. The Commission negotiators' primary concern was to resolve what they saw as a potentially dangerous situation for the implementation of the Directive. Officials believed that many firms were ignoring the Directive, and transmitting personal information to the United States, because it was necessary to their business, and because the benefits outweighed the risks of being caught. The Commission effectively had three alternatives. First was to ignore what was happening, which would have undercut the intent and credibility of the Directive. Second was to encourage a harsher attitude to enforcement, which might have prompted more compliance on the part of firms, but which also might have led to U.S. retaliation, as well as domestic difficulties. Third was to negotiate with the United States in order to try to reach an adequacy finding which would allow firms to comply with the Directive. The third of these was the most attractive to the Commission, which retained the option of more stringent enforcement as a bargaining tool.

The *member states* differed in their attitudes to data protection and to the kinds of compromise that would be necessary to reach an agreed solution with the United States. Some member states, most prominently the U.K. and Ireland, had no difficulties in principle with a self-regulated, nonlegislative compromise of the sort that finally emerged. Germany and France, in contrast, were more skeptical about self-regulation and more difficult to persuade. In the absence of formal legal protections, they preferred not to grant adequacy to the United States, and instead to oblige firms to provide contractual protections to information transfers outside the United States. Member states were represented in the process through the Article 31 Committee.

The *European Parliament* did not become formally involved until after the Commission and the Article 31 Committee had decided to grant adequacy. The Parliament was politically split on the merits and drawbacks of a compromise solution with the United States. This split cut across party lines. On the one hand, many Parliament members were distrustful of self-regulation and were influenced by the jaundiced view of data protection commissioners. Furthermore, because the process of determining adequacy did not involve an international agreement as such, the Parliament's role was limited to procedural oversight, which rankled some Members of European Parliament (MEPs), who felt that they should have a more direct say. On the other hand, other Parliament members viewed the process as a political opportunity to demonstrate that a more flexible approach to consumer protection issues could work, and thus to influence ongoing policy debates within Europe. Throughout the negotiations, Commission officials sought to keep MEPs on both sides of the debate informed of developments.

The *data protection commissioners* were formally represented in the policy discussions surrounding the negotiations through the so-called Article 29 Working Party. This body was constituted of representatives of the data protection commissions, one from each member state. Votes took place on the basis of a simple majority procedure. The Working Party's role, however, was purely advisory; while the Commission was obliged to inform the Working Party about how it had responded to the Party's proposals and suggestions, it was under no obligation to implement them. The Working Party was deeply skeptical of the proposition that the "patchwork of narrowly-focused sectoral laws and voluntary self-regulation" (Data Protection 1998) that characterized the United States could provide comprehensive protection to the data of European citizens.

On the U.S. side, the main actors were those within the administration (I include independent agencies in this category), concerned businesses and business organizations, and consumer groups. While some figures in Congress maintained a strong interest in privacy, and a watching brief, they did not play a direct role.

The *administration* was relatively slow to react to the Data Protection Directive and initially was internally divided about how best to respond. Many figures in the administration saw the Directive in terms of the ongoing policy debate about the regulation of privacy on the WWW, and the regulation of e-commerce more generally. The White House had sought to forestall government regulation of the Internet, and saw the Data Protection Directive as an antithetical approach, which involved an extensive role for government in e-commerce and a heavy regulatory burden for firms. Thus, it advocated a hard-line position which would seek to force the EU to back down. Another body of opinion shared the basic presumption that self-regulation was the best way to regulate e-commerce, but did not believe that the EU or its member states could be pressured to put the Directive into abeyance. Negotiations would be necessary to find some mutually acceptable modus vivendi. This perspective was most clearly articulated by the Department of Commerce where the National Telecommunications and Information Administration had already sought to carve out a leadership role in the debate on self-regulation and e-commerce. [16] A third approach was embodied in the FTC, an independent agency. The FTC too had sought to shape the debate on privacy through a series of reports, and had strongly hinted that it wished to expand its ambit to include privacy issues. While the FTC moved back and forth on the issue of whether self-regulation was sufficient to protect privacy, tacking to the prevailing political winds, it saw privacy on the WWW as a consumer protection issue, which might eventually be handled best through formal legislation and an enforcement role for the FTC itself.

Business, like the administration, was divided, but initially hostile to the Directive. U.S. firms had lobbied heavily while the Directive was working its way through the EU decision-making process, and had been successful in persuading lawmakers to water down some of its requirements (Regan 1999). However, it still remained threatening to U.S. business, especially in its extraterritorial aspects. Business had strong relationships with the U.S. administration, and a direct voice in the EU-U.S. relationship, through the TransAtlantic Business Dialogue (TABD), a process through which EU and U.S. businesses could reach common positions on outstanding issues in the transatlantic relationship and voice them to policy-makers (Peterson and Green Cowles 1998). U.S. firms had two, partially conflicting aims. On the one hand, they wished to see a regime which would allow stability in data transfers. On the other hand, they wished to firewall EU-U.S. discussions from the nascent domestic debate about whether formal privacy standards should be implemented on the WWW. At the same time that the Directive's extraterritorial impact was becoming a political issue, businesses were having mixed success in creating credible self-regulatory schemes to forestall domestic privacy legislation. Firms feared that the two debates might become enmeshed, and that EU pressure might increase the leverage of groups lobbying for legislation on online privacy.

Finally, U.S. *consumer organizations* favored strong legislation to protect individual privacy, both in the online and offline worlds. A small group of privacy advocacy groups, most prominently the Electronic Privacy Information Center (EPIC), had successfully highlighted privacy problems within the United States, and sought to persuade policy-makers to take a more proactive approach to privacy protection. More broadly focused consumer groups, including the Public Interest Research Group (PIRG) and the Consumer Project on Technology (CPTech), had also become involved in the issue. While these groups had succeeded in placing privacy on the policy agenda, consumer groups had relatively limited access to policy-makers within the administration, who typically saw privacy as an issue of e-commerce confidence, and took their lead from business. Like business, consumer groups had an official voice in the transatlantic relationship through the TransAtlantic Consumer Dialogue (TACD), initiated in 1998.

Arena I: The EU-U.S. Negotiations

The EU-U.S. negotiations had its start in a kind of confrontation that is analytically tractable: its structure resembled the "Chicken" game form. Important figures within the United States wanted the European Union to back down and suspend application of the extraterritorial aspects of the Directive. Ira Magaziner, the White House information technology "czar," embarked on a series of speeches and briefings where he threatened WTO action should the EU stop data flows. He also suggested that the Directive was unpopular among member states, many of which had no previous data law of their own, and were relatively slow to adopt required legislation. The implication was that the Europeans should recognize the U.S. system as adequate under the Directive, if they did not indeed themselves embrace a self-regulatory approach. For their part, the Europeans wanted the United States to back down and create a formal system of domestic data protection which would provide adequacy under the Directive. In the Chicken game, each player wants the other player to play Cooperate (to back down), while she plays Defect. The danger is that if both players play Defect, the result is mutually disastrous. And this seemed to be the most likely scenario[17]—the EU refusing to back down, but the U.S. refusing to introduce formal legislative changes which would have provided adequacy.

Of course, neither side prevailed as such. There is some reason to believe that the U.S. threat of WTO action was not a credible one. Legal scholarship[18] suggests that the European Union, provided it did not act in a discriminatory fashion in blocking data, would have had a good chance of prevailing in any WTO case. The relevant treaty, the General Agreement on Trade in Services (GATS), provides a specific exemption for the protection of personal information.[19] EU officials were confident that they would prevail in any action, and on the U.S. side, the United States Trade Representative (USTR) appeared reluctant to become involved. Thus, the international institutional environment did not provide the United States with sufficient leverage to force the EU to climb down. Further, the EU could credibly claim that its hands were tied by the Directive; the Commission was legally bound to make adequacy judgments on the basis of a more or less objective set of criteria.

Similarly, however, the United States could credibly refuse to introduce formal federal legislation. The multitude of veto points in the U.S. political system would have made it difficult for the United States to introduce extensive omnibus legislation, even had it wanted to (Scharpf 2000). And it was clear that there was no political consensus within the administration to legislate on privacy, let alone at the behest of a foreign supranational entity.

The squaring of the circle came about through an imaginative U.S. proposal to provide the kinds of adequacy that the EU was looking for, but through means that both (1) were closer to the current U.S. approach of self-regulation, and (2) did not require formal legislation, and thus did not have to be shepherded through the numerous veto points. As described by a senior U.S. negotiator, "the basic deal was we will accept your high standards, if you will accept our self-regulation."[20] But the package, as European negotiators stressed, was not standard self-regulation—it involved governmental officials negotiating the content of rules, and regulatory authorities ensuring that they were enforced. Rather than seeking to harmonize two radically different approaches to privacy regulation, Safe Harbor seeks to provide an interface between them.

To say that the solution is an interface between the two systems is not to imply that there was not vigorous bargaining between the EU and the United States as to the form that this interface should take. The Safe Harbor Principles and accompanying FAQs were submitted to detailed parsing and negotiation. Furthermore, the particular institutional arrangements of the adequacy procedure had implications for the respective bargaining strength of the EU and the United States. A recent body of literature in international relations has examined the effect of institutional arrangements on both the EU's bargaining strength and the likelihood of agreement in international negotiations where the EU is involved (Jupille 1999; Meunier 2000). However, this literature focuses on trade negotiations, where the issues are more readily captured using simple spatial models; one of the key difficulties of the Safe Harbor negotiations was precisely that negotiators' bargaining positions could not be mapped onto a simple continuous issue space. In the words of an EU negotiator:

> you can't negotiate very easily on these issues. First of all, because they are fundamental rights, that you can't just negotiate away . . . you've got access or you've got no access, you can't have half access. You really have to define very specifically when access has to be given, when access can be denied.[21]

Or as David Aaron described it, "the solution we're seeking is not a balance or a tradeoff. It's more like resolving simultaneous equations" (Aaron 1999). This said, as Meunier and Jupille have suggested, the institutional structures governing Safe Harbor did have an important effect on the bargaining power of the parties. In particular, the EU was able to use the complications of the adequacy procedure to wring concessions from their U.S. counterparts. The European Union both had ultimate veto power, and some (more limited) power in agenda setting, through the Commission's role in the negotiations.

More specifically, if adequacy was to be granted, the Commission had to have the approval of the Article 31 Committee, or at the very least, the benign neglect of the Council. But key member states such as Germany and France had signaled their skepticism about the principles and enforcement aspects of Safe Harbor. These countries, together with other doubters, were capable of blocking approval of adequacy under the qualified majority procedure: thus, they held an implicit veto over the adequacy decision. And Commission negotiators used these states' reluctance on certain issues as bargaining ammunition in their discussions with their U.S. counterparts. By keeping the member states informed, and by reporting their doubts back to the Americans, Commission negotiators were able to secure important concessions. This continued until the Article 31 Committee finally issued a unanimous decision in favor of the Safe Harbor in June 2000: the EU was successful in demanding some concessions even after an outline deal had been agreed upon in March of the same year. The skepticism of data protection commissioners also proved useful at times: the perception that U.S. firms might face the unconstrained zeal of independent-minded data protection commissions in the absence of an agreement helped concentrate the minds of U.S. negotiators. Finally, the European Parliament's doubts about the Safe Harbor had less influence in the negotiations because their formal role was less important: their oversight of the adequacy finding was supposed to be limited to its procedural aspects (although see below). But the approval of Parliament is important for the long-run political legitimacy of the arrangement, which may have important consequences for the continuation of Safe Harbor, especially if any scandals erupt about the misuse of EU citizens' data by U.S. firms.

Thus, in summation, the possibility of EU-U.S. confrontation over privacy was averted by an "interface" solution. In bargaining over the particular form of this solution, the European Union enjoyed a position of structural advantage. The adequacy procedure allowed it to accept or reject any U.S. proposal. Furthermore, the European Commission was able to shuttle back and forth between the negotiations (Arena I) and the other actors within the European Union (Arena III). The obduracy of actors with veto power within the European Union strengthened its bargaining hand in negotiations with the Americans. If most of the changes made in subsequent drafts of Safe Harbor went the way of the EU rather than the United States, this reflects the structural advantage which EU negotiators enjoyed given the institutional framework governing the adequacy finding, rather than any lack of skill on the part of the U.S. negotiating team.[22]

Arena II: The Domestic Debate on Privacy within the United States

Even before the Directive came into effect, it had already begun to have reverberations in the U.S. debate over online and offline privacy. The game between the EU and the United States began at an early stage to intersect in complicated ways with the wider political battles within the United States about how privacy should be protected in the information age. By mid-1998, when the Directive began to loom large, privacy had already become a charged issue in the United States. Both those who argued in favor of formal legislation to protect privacy (privacy advocates), and those who argued for self-regulation (firms and the administration) had already taken cognizance of the EU adequacy ruling and its possible consequences. Marc Rotenberg, the director of EPIC, perhaps the most important privacy advocacy group in the debate, spoke of the EU Directive in broadly positive terms in congressional testimony, arguing that the EU's Directive should alert the United States to how far it lagged behind in privacy protection.[23] Business, unsurprisingly, had a different analysis of the Directive. The TABD initially criticized the Directive, warning that "Data protection standards should not be used to establish new trade barriers which could hinder the development of electronic commerce between the EU and the U.S." (Trans Atlantic Business Dialogue 1997). Within the United States, industry groups had already mobilized both to lobby against possible legislation and to argue that the adequacy requirements of the European Union would be perfectly well met by existing self-regulatory initiatives. The Online Privacy Alliance (OPA) was founded by a group of major firms following a meeting in April 1998, with the aim both of convincing EU and U.S. regulators that self-regulation was providing adequate protection to individual privacy on the WWW, and of persuading other firms to sign up to self-regulatory schemes while there was still a chance of influencing the policy agenda. The administration too was eager to persuade businesses to sign up to self-regulation, in part because of long-standing policy, but also in part to strengthen its hand in negotiations with Brussels. If the United States was successfully to persuade the EU that self-regulation could protect privacy, it had to be able to point to existing and relatively widespread mechanisms of self-regulation (Magaziner 1998). In mid-1998, the U.S. administration was clearly disappointed at how slow businesses had been to respond to this challenge. One so-called "privacy seal organization," TrustE, had commenced operation, but still had relatively few members. Administration pressure led a number of large firms to approach the Better Business Bureau (BBB) to set up a privacy seal program, but this took time to launch; the BBB had ample experience in dispute resolution, but little to none in privacy related issues.

The Safe Harbor Principles drew vigorous public and private comment. Aaron's covering letter for the draft principles had stressed that they were "not intended to govern or affect U.S. privacy regimes, which are being addressed by other government and private sector efforts," seeking to draw a line between the EU-U.S. negotiations and the ongoing domestic privacy debate. It was clear, however, from the comments of firms and business organizations that many of them disagreed. Most explicitly, TrustE and the Information Technology Association of America (ITAA) stressed in public comments that the Safe Harbor principles were likely to set the floor for domestic privacy practice, regardless of the intent of their negotiators, a fact which the ITAA urged Commerce to bear in mind during negotiations. The OPA vehemently opposed the Safe Harbor principles, implying that the Department of Commerce had almost entirely capitulated to their European counterparts in drafting the principles, and forcefully suggesting that Commerce rethink its whole approach and adopt the OPA's own (rather less demanding) privacy guidelines as a baseline for negotiation. Finally, American negotiators in practice were forced to recognize the intersection of the international and national debates. At one point in the negotiations, the U.S. team had to deliberately slow pedal discussions with the Europeans on the principle of onward transfer, for fear that any agreement would be seen as setting a precedent for debate over financial services reform in Congress.

U.S. consumer advocates also objected strongly to the draft Safe Harbor standards, but from the opposite standpoint; they felt that the standards were too weak in many important aspects, and were in any event highly suspicious of the suggestion that privacy protection could be achieved through self-regulation. Privacy advocates had hoped that the external pressure of the Directive could increase pressure towards a more stringent legal approach to privacy protection in the United States. In pressing their objections, the existence of TransAtlantic Consumer Dialogue (TACD) proved invaluable. Business interests remained more influential than consumer groups and were better able to make themselves heard to policy-makers. But by the same token, TACD was more important to consumer groups than TABD was to firms, who usually had individual channels to important decision-makers. Many consumer advocates had difficulty in gaining access to a policy-making process that was almost entirely dominated by commercial interests.[24] Consumer associations were also highly fragmented, making it more difficult for them to present a unified front to government; deep divisions had developed between consumer groups over the NAFTA agreement. TACD allowed these groups to overcome both hurdles in the Safe Harbor debate. First, these groups now had an official voice in the process and opportunities to press their concerns in person on decision-makers in the administration. Second, they could reach common positions on issues such as the Safe Harbor, presenting a unified perspective. Finally, the TACD process allowed U.S. consumer groups to exploit new channels to European officials and Members of the European Parliament (MEPs) as well as American ones. EU consumer groups, unlike their U.S. counterparts, frequently had strong relationships with officials at the European level, thanks to the Commission's creation of policy networks on various consumer issues. U.S. consumer and privacy groups could now use these relationships to press their concerns on EU officials involved in the Safe Harbor process, and thus seek indirectly to influence outcomes in Arena II (the U.S. domestic debate) through acquiring leverage in Arena III (the internal EU debate) and consequently Arena I (the EU-U.S. negotiations).

Thus, in short, the EU-U.S. negotiations (Arena I) had an important impact on domestic U.S. discussions on privacy (Arena II), despite the efforts of the Department of Commerce to firewall them from each other. Even before the Safe Harbor approach was articulated, privacy advocates sought to use the Directive's likely extraterritorial effects to push for formal legislation, while businesses were hostile to the Directive, in part just because they feared it would strengthen the argument for such legislation. Furthermore, actors in Arena II sought to influence negotiations in Arena I because these might in turn have knock-on effects in Arena II. Thus, businesses sought to persuade Commerce negotiators to maintain a tough line, while privacy advocates used the official channels of TACD and the unofficial channels between European consumer groups and European officials to press their case. More generally, the institutional framework of the transatlantic relationship clearly had a substantial impact on the capacity of consumer interests to make their case on privacy issues, even within the American context.

Arena III: The EU Approval Process

The granting of adequacy, as has been observed, involves a long and complicated procedure. The veto points in this procedure strengthened the Commission in its negotiations in Game I; the unwillingness of the member states and the suspicions of the Parliament and data protection commissioners were useful ammunition in its discussions with the Americans. But they were sometimes problematic for the Commission, forcing it to engage in a multisided set of discussions, representing the U.S. position to European decision-makers, and vice versa, in a process which consumed valuable time and resources. Indeed, when the Commission had finally reached an agreement with the U.S. side that it thought was workable, the strengths turned into weaknesses. After having sold a deal to the Americans on the basis that this was the best available, given the intransigence of member states and other actors, it now had to turn around and sell the deal to those self-same intransigent actors. The Commission's adequacy decision had to meet the approval of the member states and the procedural approval of the Parliament if it was to hold.

The Commission, anticipating this, had been careful to prepare its ground. It had kept key figures in the Parliament briefed as to the state of negotiations. Even more importantly, it had sought to educate members of the Article 31 Committee as to the benefits of a deal. One key turning point in this process was a meeting in January 2000, where selected members of the Committee were invited to Washington, D.C. for three days of consultations with U.S. officials and representatives of self-regulatory organizations, most importantly TrustE and BBBOnline.

However, the Parliament proved rather more difficult to persuade, even though Parliament's role was supposed to be limited to procedural oversight. The initial response to the adequacy finding came from the Parliament's Committee on Citizens' Freedoms and Rights, Justice and Home Affairs, where the rapporteur was an Italian MEP, Elena Paciotti. Paciotti was influenced in her report by the Article 29 Working Party's largely negative appraisal of the arrangement, as well as by the critical comments of the FTC, which had recently issued a harsh assessment of the effectiveness of self-regulation in providing online privacy. Further, the efforts of American privacy and consumer groups to argue against Safe Harbor in Brussels had borne fruit; the Committee "took on board the concerns of the representatives of American consumers regarding the inadequacy of the American protection system" in its discussions.[25] In referring to these, and to other principled objections, the report went considerably beyond procedural oversight, demanding that the Commission renegotiate the substance of the Safe Harbor, which it saw as insufficient in several important aspects.

The plenary debate in Parliament on the adequacy finding, which followed the rapporteur's report and its adoption in committee, showed that many parliamentarians held the hope that the Safe Harbor could be renegotiated, and that withholding an adequacy judgment would encourage the United States to adopt formal legislation. Commissioner Fritz Bolkestein, seeking to undermine this analysis, argued that

> To make approval of the determination of adequacy conditional on
> these changes is more likely to end up sinking the safe harbor than
> achieving hoped-for improvements. I would like to leave you in ab-
> solutely no doubt about this. The United States has no desire to re-
> visit the discussions again and the Commission also takes the view
> that the talks are over.[26]

The Commission adopted precisely the opposite tactic to that which it had
adopted in the negotiations. Now, rather than using inflexibilities in Arena III
(the EU approval process) in order to improve its bargaining position in Arena I
(the EU-U.S. negotiations), the Commission sought to use inflexibilities in
Arena I to improve its bargaining position in Arena III. The Commission sought
to represent reality as it saw it: it was convinced that it had exhausted the concessions that the U.S. side might have to offer, and believed that the EU could
essentially take or leave the deal.[27] In the event, it was successful, but only just.
Parliament passed the report by an extremely narrow majority, but without an
amendment that would have made it clear that the Commission had overstepped
its authority in making the adequacy decision. This could have caused a major
institutional crisis between the Commission and Parliament: as MEP Palacio
Vallelersundi noted in plenary, the Parliament was substantially overstepping its
legal powers in seeking to require the Commission to renegotiate the substance
of the arrangement.[28] Bolkestein, who was well aware that Parliament was split
over the Safe Harbor, took the position that since the Parliament had not explicitly stated that the Commission had overstepped its powers, it had exercised its
powers of oversight and not judged against the adequacy decision, which therefore stood. Parliament, not willing to start institutional warfare, tacitly acqui-
esced.

Thus, the approval process within the European Union was deeply intercon-
nected with the other two arenas of decision-making. Not only did institutional
inflexibilities in the process of determining adequacy (Arena III) strengthen the
Commission's hand in its negotiations with the United States (Arena I), but the
opposite also was true; inflexibilities in the deal reached with the United States
(Arena I) helped the Commission to make its case in Parliament that the arrangement could not be renegotiated (Arena III). Furthermore, U.S. privacy advocates, in their efforts to win formal privacy legislation in the United States
(Arena II) had sought to make their objections to the Safe Harbor deal heard in
Brussels (Arena III) in order to keep the U.S. administration under pressure.
They were successful in that they influenced parliamentary debate against Safe
Harbor and helped ensure that Parliament remains vigilant for cracks and flaws
that might appear in the Safe Harbor process over time.

Conclusion

In this chapter, I have sought to examine the processes leading up to the provision of one common good—privacy—across multiple arenas. I have suggested

that these processes are inherently *political*; that is, that they involve conflict between actors with different perceptions of how the good in question is best provided, and even of whether the good should be provided at all.

This suggests a mode of analysis that does not examine common good provision in functionalist terms; rather, it sees common good provision as the possible result of political conflict. This clearly implies that common good provision in multiple arenas involves at least two different sorts of interrelationships. The first is that which is most frequently discussed in the literature; that is, the extent to which multiple arenas make it more or less possible for certain kinds of common goods to be provided (Cerny 1995). Thus, in the case at hand, the ease of data exchange between the EU and the United States meant that it was impossible for the EU to enforce a Directive with strong legislative protections for personal data without somehow preventing the external misuse of that data.

Yet there is a second kind of interrelationship too, which is the one that I have emphasized in this chapter. Not only does the increasing importance of multi-arena governance pose policy *problems*, but it also provides political *opportunities* for various actors. To the extent that one arena of decision-making intersects with another, it may allow actors to find new ways of achieving goals that might otherwise have been impossible. More generally, through its effects on the relative bargaining power of actors, it has substantial (and differential) effects on the political constellations of the various arenas that have become related to each other. This is clearly demonstrated in the case studied in this chapter. Actors in one game may seek to use leverage in another in order to pursue their goals. Safe Harbor is a continuing process; at this point it is difficult to predict its final outcome. Debate continues over the efficacy (or lack of same) of hybrid institutions, which rely in part on private actors for enforcement. What is clear from the history of Safe Harbor is that the intersections between policy arenas have had an important influence on the relative power of actors on both sides of that debate to make their voices heard and to strive for policy results close to their preferred outcome.

Notes

1. This chapter is one of three linked papers discussing Safe Harbor. The second links the negotiations into broader discussions of change in the EU-U.S. relationship. The third will examine the solution reached in terms of broader arguments in international relations theory about regime formation.

2. Many privacy advocates believe that such data protection principles do not either capture the concept of privacy or protect it in practical terms. See Davies (1997). In my argument, I bracket this debate, as I seek to examine the policy implications of privacy rather than its normative dimensions.

3. I use the example of firms on the WWW, both because it highlights many of these issues, and because it is highly relevant both to the main topic of this chapter and to policy discussions on privacy more generally. Many, and perhaps most, of the arguments that I make can be extended to non-WWW firms.

4. See, for example, a poll carried out by Odyssey, cited in the *New York Times*,

which finds that a massive 92 percent of respondents agreed, or agreed strongly, with the statement, "I don't trust companies to keep personal information about me confidential, no matter what they promise." Cited in "Survey Shows Few Trust Promises on Online Privacy," *New York Times*, April 17, 2000. There have been a number of widely publicized privacy breaches or potential privacy breaches by major e-commerce firms and technology firms, including Geocities, Real Networks, Doubleclick, Intel, and Microsoft.

5. Robert E. Litan, Testimony: The European Union Privacy Directive, given before the House Committee on International Affairs, May 7, 1998.

6. For a reputation-based account of the persistence of firms, see Kreps (1990).

7. On compliance, see Tanja Börzel, this volume.

8. I note that ideational factors also play an extremely important role, so that "simple" institutional arguments have only limited explanatory power. I explore ideational factors in greater detail in forthcoming work.

9. There are however safeguards for the online privacy of children in the Children's Online Privacy Protection Act (1999).

10. The term "adequate" had been substituted after heavy lobbying from business interests for the term "equivalent," which was used in the original draft of the directive. See Regan (1999). Adequacy clearly presupposed a lower standard than equivalency, and a wider variety in the approaches that could be considered to meet the requirements of the directive.

11. Discussions have been ongoing between the European Union and the International Chamber of Commerce on the subject of model contracts. At the time of writing, a draft set of clauses has been issued for public discussion; business has indicated its dissatisfaction with them.

12. The Article 31 Committee should not be confused with the Article 29 Working Party, which I describe below.

13. The FTC act does not cover firms in certain sectors (although in air transport, for example, there is an equivalent set of obligations and enforcement mechanisms), leading to serious worries among privacy advocates.

14. I limit my remarks here to Safe Harbor's *direct* effects, as measured in terms of the number of firms adhering to it. As I hope to elaborate in later work, Safe Harbor's *indirect* effects appear to be substantial, and may in the long run be more important.

15. Consumer groups were not directly involved to the same extent as their U.S. counterparts.

16. See Department of Commerce (1997). Reidenberg (1999) has a useful short discussion of policy debates on privacy within the U.S. administration during this period.

17. More accurately I should say "disastrous for some." A standoff between the EU and the United States would have had substantial negative implications for commercial exchange, and consequently for state actors responsive to the needs of commerce. But it may well have had advantages for players in other games. Some U.S. privacy advocates, for example, might well have preferred a continuing and volatile stalemate on the international level: this would have helped increase the pressures on domestic legislators to introduce formal privacy protection.

18. Shaffer (2000). For a somewhat different emphasis, see Reidenberg (1999) and Swire and Litan (1998).

19. Magaziner's threat of WTO action may, interpreted in another way though, as a signaling device to show that the United States viewed this issue seriously, and was prepared to make life highly uncomfortable for the EU if it actually blocked data flows. Interview with Ira Magaziner, conducted September 21, 2000. Certainly, EU negotiators were highly worried about how the administration would respond to substantial blockages in data flow between U.S. companies and their European subsidiaries.

20. Interview with U.S. negotiator.

21. Interview with Commission negotiator.

22. Of course, the Europeans could not persuade the United States to move further than its minimum acceptable position. Further, the U.S. side did have substantial agenda-setting power, which it used—the fact that it persuaded the EU side finally to accept a solution with substantial self-regulatory elements is evidence of this.

23. Marc Rotenberg, testimony given before the House Committee on International Relations, May 7, 1998.

24. See, for example, the complaints in the "Letter Regarding a Proposed White House Conference on Privacy" sent to the secretary for commerce by various advocates, scholars, and experts in the field of privacy on February 26, 1998. <http://www. epic.org/privacy/internet/daley_ltr_2_26_98.html> (checked January 14, 2001).

25. Available at http://www3.europarl.eu.int/omk/omnsapir.so/debats?FILE=00-07-03&LANGUE=EN&LEVEL=DOC&GCSELECTCHAP=8&GCSELECTPERS=92 (checked January 14, 2001).

26. See the discussions in the Parliament's Plenary debate, July 3, 2000, available at http://www3.europarl.eu.int/omk/omnsapir.so/debats?FILE=00-07-03&LANGUE=EN& LEVEL=DOC&GCSELECTCHAP=8&GCSELECTPERS=94 (January 14, 2000).

27. Interviews with Commission negotiators.

28. Available at http://www3.europarl.eu.int/omk/omnsapir.so/debats?FILE=00-07-03&LANGUE=EN&LEVEL=DOC&GCSELECTCHAP=8&GCSELECTPERS=89 (January 14, 2000).

References

Aaron, D. 1999. Remarks of David L. Aaron. Under Secretary of Commerce for International Trade before the Information Technology Association of America Fourth Annual IT Policy Summit, March 15.

Bennett, C. 1992. *Regulating Privacy: Data Protection and Public Policy in Europe and the United States.* Ithaca, N.Y.: Cornell University Press.

———. 1997. Convergence Revisited: Toward a Global Public Policy for the Protection of Personal Data? In *Technology and Privacy: The New Landscape,* ed. M. Rotenberg and P. Agre. Cambridge, Mass.: MIT Press.

Cerny, P. 1995. Globalization and the Changing Logic of Collective Action. *International Organization* 49: 595-625.

Data Protection Working Party. 1998. Working Document: Transfers of Personal Data to Third Countries: Applying Articles 25 and 26 of the EU Data Protection Directive. Brussels. European Commission, Directorate General XV, D/5025/98.

Davies, S. 1997. Reengineering the Right to Privacy: How Privacy Has Been Transformed from a Right to a Commodity. In *Technology and Privacy: The New Landscape,* ed. M. Rotenberg and P. Agre. Cambridge, Mass.: MIT Press.

Department of Commerce. 1997. Privacy and Self Regulation in the Information Age. Washington, D.C. Department of Commerce NTIA.

Hardin, R. 1982. *Collective Action.* Baltimore, Md.: Johns Hopkins University Press.

Jupille, J. 1999. The European Union and International Outcomes. *International Organization* 53: 403-25.

Kreps, D. 1990. Corporate Culture and Economic Theory. In *Perspectives on Positive Political Economy,* ed. J. Alt and K. Shepsle. Cambridge: Cambridge University Press.

Magaziner, I. 1998. Speech Given in Context of IBM Privacy Symposium <http://www.ibm.com/iac/transcripts/internet_privacy_symp/iramagaziner.html> (checked October 10, 2000).

Mayer-Schönberger, V. 1997. Generational Development of Data Protection in Europe. In *Technology and Privacy: The New Landscape*, ed. M. Rotenberg and P. Agre. Cambridge, Mass.: MIT Press.

Meunier, S. 2000. What Single Voice? European Institutions and EU-U.S. Trade Negotiations. *International Organization* 54: 103-35.

Olson, M. 1968. *The Logic of Collective Action.* New York: Schocken.

Peterson, J., and M. Green Cowles. 1998. Clinton, Europe, and Economic Diplomacy: What Makes the EU Different? *Governance* 11: 251-71.

Regan, P. 1999. American Business and the European Data Protection Directive: Lobbying Strategies and Tactics. In *Visions of Privacy*, ed. C. Bennett and R. Grant. Toronto: University of Toronto Press.

Reidenberg, J. 1999. The Globalization of Privacy Solutions: The Movement towards Obligatory Standards for Fair Information Practice. In *Visions of Privacy*, ed. C. Bennett and R. Grant. Toronto: University of Toronto Press.

Ronit, K. and V. Schneider. 1999. Global Governance through International Organizations. *Governance* 12: 243-66.

Scharpf, F. 1997. *Games Real Actors Play: Actor-Centered Institutionalism in Policy Research.* Boulder, Colo.: Westview Press.

————. 2000. Institutions in Comparative Policy Research. *Comparative Political Studies* 33(6/7): 762-90.

Shaffer, G. 2000. Globalization and Social Protection: The Impact of EU and International Rules in the Ratcheting Up of U.S. Privacy Standards. *Yale Journal of International Law* 25: 1-88.

Swire, P., and R. Litan. 1998. None of Your Business: World Data Flows, Electronic Commerce, and the European Privacy Directive. Washington, D.C.: Brookings.

Trans Atlantic Business Dialogue. 1997. TABD Priorities for the Mid-Year U.S.-EU Summit, 13 May. < http://www.tabd.org/recom/97priority.html> (checked January 13, 2001).

Tsebelis, G. 1990. *Nested Games.* Berkeley: University of California Press.

6

The Privatization of Global Governance and the Modern Law Merchant

A. Claire Cutler

Introduction

Notions of governance and authority are usually associated with the activities of governments and public officials in the pursuit of public purposes and the provision of "public goods." "Public goods" are generally defined by their indivisibility and non-exclusivity, which basically mean that they are open to enjoyment by all.[1] In contrast, the economic and market activities of individuals and corporations are associated with private and non-governmental interests, purposes, and goals. Indeed, the separation of the public and private domains constitutes a fundamental postulate of liberalism, which is the dominant approach to international law and international relations.[2] In both disciplines, liberalism links political authority with democratically accountable public offices and eschews notions of private interest governance. Liberal political and legal theories associate legitimate authority with the operation of democratically representative institutions of government. Only public officials are competent to function authoritatively through representative democratic institutions that ensure their accountability, at least in theory.[3] Liberal political economy complements this analysis by problematizing the provision of public goods by private mechanisms and institutions.[4] Neoliberal economic theory suggests that public goods tend to be underproduced by private actors who, by virtue of the above-described character of public goods, are able to free ride and enjoy them without contributing to their provision. Consequently, the intervention of governments is theorized to be necessary in order to provide public goods.

However, significant transformations in governance arrangements in both local and global political economies suggest that the distinction between public and private realms is becoming increasingly difficult to sustain. Three significant trends that are linked to deeper transformations in local and global political economies are challenging conventional, liberal notions of political authority and governance. The first is the increasing *juridification* of political, social, and economic life as law is utilized to legitimate increasingly more varied claims to authority.[5] The second is the increasing heterogeneity of and *pluralism* in forms of regulation and governance, while the third is the enhanced significance of *privatized* governance arrangements. These trends in governance are evident in the findings of a proliferating number of studies focusing on the governance of local and global political, economic, social, and legal relations.[6] The increasing salience of law and the heterogeneity of and pluralism in regulatory arrangements in some cases defy easy classification as public or private. Indeed, the foundational distinction between public and private international law threatens to dissolve as private corporations develop public international law in the form of binding legal codes and as governments increasingly enter the market place.[7] My contribution analyzes an important example of these trends in the legal regime governing transnational economic relations. This regime is known variously as the modern law merchant, transnational commercial law, or the law of private international trade. It comprises the corpus of law and practice that regulate international commercial relations of a private nature. This regime is undergoing increasing juridification, pluralization, and privatization in response to deeper transformations in the global political economy. However, before addressing the nature and operation of this regime, the discussion will briefly review these three trends in governance.

Juridification, Pluralization, and Privatization

Both governmental and non-governmental authorities are participating locally and globally in the development of governance and regulatory frameworks and institutions. This is resulting in the increasing juridification of economic, social, and political life,[8] a development that some refer to as the "legalization of world politics."[9] Indeed, the unprecedented expansion of efforts to regulate the increasing complexity of both domestic and international relations through law has generated considerable interest in the notion of "global governance." "Global governance" may well be the catchphrase for the turn of the century. The idea of multiple sources of global governance is analytically attractive as a means of capturing the broad range of public and private actors and institutions creating regulatory and governance arrangements. In some instances, these arrangements intersect with more general processes of globalization, privatization, and deregulation, contributing to the expansion of *privatized* regulatory authority in global political, economic, social, and legal relations.[10]

The increasing multiplicity of public and private governance arrangements wrought by forces of globalization and the privatization and deregulation of industries, sectors, commodities, and services is creating a plurality of authority relations. For some, this is reminiscent of the medieval political economy and the heterogeneity and pluralism of medieval authority structures.[11] The analogy is based on the increasing diversity in, and multiplicity of, authority structures that are suggestive of the diffuse and heterogeneous nature of authority relations in the medieval age.[12] In some cases the diffusion of authority is said to attenuate authority relations between governments and their societies and to strengthen other non-governmental, but authoritative relations.[13] These non-governmental or private regulatory arrangements may range from highly informal industry norms and practices, coordination service firms,[14] production and strategic alliances, joint ventures, networks, and business associations, to highly institutionalized private international regimes.[15] Such authority structures might include transnationally organized private business associations, like the International Chamber of Commerce; transnationally organized crime and crime enforcement through transnationally organized private means; subnational groups that operate across national boundaries, like labor unions and industries, and non-state actors who are organized and operate globally, like global social human rights and environmental movements.[16]

The notion that private entities may claim legitimacy as political authorities is inconsistent with liberal democratic political and economic theory and yet it appears to be an increasingly common trend. The privatization of governance, when embodied in juridical forms as legal regimes, whether they be trade, investment, environmental, or human rights regimes, must have serious implications for political accountability and the future of democratic institutions. Even more profound are the implications of privatized lawmaking and enforcement for the rule of law, both locally and globally. In its classic conception, the rule of law is associated with the equal application of law to all subjects.[17] The law is required to be general in character, clear, stable, prospective, and, importantly, public.[18] This conception is inconsistent with discretionary, arbitrary, secretive, or private lawmaking. It is precisely the orderly, predictable, and public promulgation of law that gives law legitimacy and authority in democratic societies.

This chapter focuses on an important although undertheorized body of *private* law that is of growing concern in the regulation of local and global political economies. The law governing private international trade, or the new law merchant, evokes images of the medieval *lex mercatoria*, or law merchant, which operated as a universalized private system of law amongst the European trading world.[19] This chapter argues that the globalization of the rules of private international law is an important element in the juridification and legalization of world politics. Increasingly, privatized legal disciplines are finding their way into both international and national commercial legal orders, structuring domestic and foreign economic relations in ways that have an impact on state-society relations within states and relations between and among states.[20] The globalized law merchant provides a good illustration of the trends toward juridified, pluralized, and privatized social relations. Moreover, it raises significant problems for the future of democratically accountable institutions and the rule of law in both domestic and international relations.

The first part of the chapter addresses the modern *lex mercatoria* and considers its nature as the juridical link mediating local and global political economies. This section compares medieval and modern forms of the law merchant, illustrating the historical specificity of each form in terms of the analytical processes of law-creation and dispute resolution. The modern law merchant is argued to constitute a unique and essential element embedded within the emerging global political economy. The second part focuses on developments in the modern law merchant that are associated with key transformations in the global political economy, the juridification of international commercial relations, and the expansion of privatized governance. It will address some of the distributional consequences and normative issues raised by the privatization of governance in terms of the future of democratically accountable processes of lawmaking and dispute resolution and the implications for the rule of law.

The Medieval and Modern Law Merchant

This section first describes the nature and operation of the modern law merchant in general terms and then proceeds to analyze the modern and medieval regimes in terms of the analytical processes of law-creation and dispute resolution. The analysis seeks to establish the historical specificity and unique character of the modern law merchant as a regime of private governance.

Nature and Operation

The modern law merchant mediates local and global political/legal orders by providing juridical links that are essential to the regulation of the global political economy.[21] It provides the constitutional foundations of the global political economy through rules governing the protection and enforcement of private property and contractual rights and obligations across a range of international commercial activities, including international trade, investment, and finance, transportation, insurance, and dispute resolution.[22] These rules articulate the principles and procedures that structure international commercial relations. Although they are termed rules of private international *trade* law, they extend far beyond the governance of exchange relations to include the full range of productive relations. They include, for example, the governance of international licensing, joint ventures, partnerships, distributorship and construction contracts, and the extraterritorial application of antitrust, tax, securities, and intellectual property laws. While the operation of private international trade law is a complex matter, it may be usefully regarded as functioning in at least two ways.[23] In one way, the rules of private international law operate as a conflict of laws system, providing rules that determine what national law applies to transactions involving persons or corporations from different states when there is uncertainty as to the law that should govern.[24] In this sense, private international law operates as a domestic conflict of laws system and derives its authority from, and is an extension of, the domestic political/legal order. As a conflict of laws system, the rules of private international law serve to localize international transactions in one national system of law, thus linking international and national political/legal arenas. These links derive from the domestic application of foreign law under the rules of private international law and the extraterritorial application of domestic law under the rules of comity. However, private international trade law also operates in another way as a more or less independent source of governance through the application of international law generally by domestic and/or international tribunals. In this application, private international trade law operates neither as a conflict of laws system nor as an extension of domestic law, but as a source of governance that is formulated internationally and transnationally and is accepted voluntarily by commercial participants. In this regard, it exhibits similarities to public international law. In some cases the legal rules are adopted by states into their national legal systems, becoming embedded in national political/legal orders. The laws of private international trade, or the law merchant, thus link local and global political/legal orders, providing merchants from diverse political/legal systems with a uniform business language and culture.

Beyond the above description, there is very little analytical or theoretical clarity on the nature and function of the law merchant regime. As Patterson notes, trade lawyers and negotiators rarely stop to examine the assumption that the rules governing international commerce contribute to increased prosperity in the world.[25] It is simply assumed that uniform commercial law facilitates commerce by reducing the costs and uncertainties of transacting.[26] As William Scheuerman suggests, it is generally assumed that there is a natural affinity between capitalism and the rule of law.[27] Indeed, the development of legally uniform laws regulating international commerce is for many, at least in the developed world, regarded as a welcome and positive development. The globalization of legal relations is generally considered to provide societies throughout the world with the much needed public goods of stability, predictability, and security in production and exchange.

A few economic historians have analyzed the medieval law merchant institutions through public goods theory and provide much theoretical insight into the reasons why law merchant institutions developed as they did. For example, Douglass North and others have examined the emergence of the law merchant norms and institutions as a response to the transaction and information costs and insecurity experienced by traders engaging in trade over wide geographical regions.[28] Students of international relations have examined the theoretical and analytical relevance of public goods theory for global governance.[29] However, there has been scant attention to the relevance of this theory for the modern law merchant. Nor has there been significant analysis of the political and distributional dimensions of the law merchant. In fact, leading scholars attribute the success of the law merchant in ordering international commerce by unifying the world through a global common law and a universal commercial code to its essentially private, apolitical, and neutral character.[30] As we turn to consider the processes of law-creation and dispute resolution, it becomes evident that private institutions and actors have figured prominently in creating and enforcing both the medieval and modern law merchant regimes.

Law-Creation and Dispute Resolution

The law merchant is conventionally regarded as having passed through three phases in its historical development. The first phase, lasting from the eleventh to sixteenth centuries, is characterized as one of medieval internationalism and the universality of merchant laws and mechanisms for dispute resolution. A second phase, lasting from the seventeenth to nineteenth centuries, is marked by the localization and nationalization of the merchant law and institutions as modern territorial states developed and assumed greater control over international commercial activities. The third phase, from the nineteenth century to the present, is regarded as one of modern internationalism as states move to adopt uniform commercial laws and uniform institutions for dispute resolution. Our main concern will be with the first and third phases in the development of merchant laws and institutions for dispute resolution.

During the medieval phase merchants exhibited almost complete autonomy in both the creation of merchant laws and in settling disputes amongst themselves.[31] Merchants created laws governing the sale of goods, transportation, finance, and insurance, some of which drew on ancient and Roman customs and sources. There was considerable normative and institutional pluralism, in that medieval merchants could pursue commercial claims in the royal courts, ecclesiastical courts, common law courts, or law merchant courts.[32] However, the law merchant courts provided the most utilized institutional framework for settling commercial disputes in the medieval period and operated privately more like contemporary arbitration tribunals than like courts of law. According to the folklore of the law merchant, the courts were known for their speed, informality, efficiency, and justice.[33] The merchant courts sat in fairs, market, and seaport towns and enforced unique commercial transactions, like bare promises, bills of lading, charter parties, partnership agreements, insurance principles, and financial transactions that were not enforceable in other local courts. Juries comprised of merchants sat and arbitrated disputes, applying principles from the law merchant, which was predominantly customary in origin.[34] Some of theses customs were recorded in codes and compilations that came to provide the foundation for later codifications, like the Laws of Oléron that formed the basis for the Sea Laws of Wisby.[35] These codes were associated with key commercial centers in the Mediterranean, like Venice, Amalfi, and Genoa, Barcelona, and the North Sea and Baltic port towns and the fair and market towns of Champagne and Lyons.[36] In the late medieval period, private merchant associations, like the merchant guilds, developed to assist in the regulation of international commerce. They disciplined their members and imposed trade embargos against political authorities who did not respect the property rights of guild members.[37] The medieval law merchant regime thus formed a private system of law and institutions. Local authorities were generally incapable of enforcing merchant law and deferred to the merchant courts. The former did not participate in the regulation of international trade, beyond the granting of charters to hold fairs and markets, the general provision of safe conduct for merchants in their transit to the fairs and markets, and awarding exemptions from local laws in return for the payment of customs and duties.[38]

Today, there is considerable pluralism and a complex mix of both public and private authority in the creation of merchant law and in the resolution of commercial disputes. Institutionally, the movement for the unification and harmonization of international commercial law is at the center of norm-creation and dispute settlement.[39] The unification movement forms part of broader moves to "unify the world as a whole"[40] and is an integral aspect of what David Kennedy refers to as the general "move to institutions" born with the efforts to create global governance arrangements in the League of Nations after the First World War.[41] The unification movement was initiated to re-create the unity and coherence lost during processes of state-building during the second phase in the development of the law merchant regime. With the emergence of the state system and the incorporation of the medieval law merchant and court system into domestic legal systems, significant differences in commercial law developed. European in origin, the unification movement has expanded to include most regions of the world and most legal systems. The movement involves both private and public authorities and engages in the harmonization and unification of increasingly more areas of private international trade law.[42] Although both public and private participants are involved in the unification movement, the emphasis is on preserving a broad scope for merchant autonomy and private ordering in law-creation and dispute settlement.[43] The movement is driven by the *mercatocracy*, which is an elite association of transnational merchants, private lawyers, insurers, financiers, business associations, government officials, and representatives of governmental and non-governmental international organizations.[44] The *mercatocracy* operates through private business associations, law, accounting, financial, and insurance firms and a host of other private and public organizations engaged in the development of a common commercial law and culture and a unifying commercial ideology.

The United Nations Commission for International Trade Law (UNCITRAL) and the International Institute for the Unification of Private Law (UNIDROIT) are the two most significant intergovernmental bodies engaged in the unification and harmonization of international commercial law, while the International Chamber of Commerce is the most significant private association involved.[45]

UNCITRAL has created uniform law governing a number of commercial matters, the most significant being the unification of international sales law (*Vienna Sales Convention*).[46] Unification efforts in this area had proceeded unsuccessfully prior to the creation of UNCITRAL in 1968 and the assumption of a leadership role in UNCITRAL by the United States.[47] The primarily European and civil law character of earlier unification efforts had failed to generate interest in common law countries. However, under the leadership of the United States other common law states followed suit and the unification effort produced what is regarded by many as the most "successful" unification initiative ever undertaken.[48] Today the *Vienna Sales Convention*, which trade experts say "resembles" American commercial law "more than the law of any other country," has substantially worldwide acceptance.[49]

UNIDROIT, the other most important intergovernmental institution involved in formulating uniform law, has also engaged in considerable unification efforts in a number of areas, including contracts for the international sale of goods, agency in the international sale of goods, international leasing and factoring, franchising, and security interests in mobile equipment.[50] UNIDROIT produced a very successful set of uniform principles for contracting, the *Principles of International Commercial Contracting*.[51] Although the *Principles* are not *hard law*, in the form of binding international agreements, like the *Vienna Sales Convention*, they have been adopted by many countries and operate as *soft law* or as a nonbinding statement of principles.[52]

The ICC is a private body comprised of representatives from national Chambers of Commerce. It has produced uniform laws governing documentary credits, contract guarantees, arbitration, and conciliation. As a non-governmental body, the ICC lacks the international legal personality required to create international law. Only states or their representatives may enter into treaties and create customary rules of international law, the two main sources of law.[53] However, as *soft* law the ICC's unification efforts have been extremely successful. In some cases, as in the law governing the terms of trade (*Incoterms 1980*) and the law governing documentary credits and collections (*Uniform Customs and Practices for Documentary Credits and Credits*), the voluntary adoption by commercial participants is so great that they have over time acquired the status of customary international law.[54]

Dispute resolution is also characterized by significant institutional pluralism. The variety of legal options available to commercial participants for settling their disputes today is proliferating with the creation of regional, global, and national trade arrangements. Merchants may settle their disputes publicly by litigating in national courts of law, or they may choose to deal with their differences privately, through international commercial arbitration. They may choose to settle their disputes under national law, international law, laws created through multilateral or regional negotiations, or negotiated privately amongst themselves. In fact, there are many dispute settlement institutions and rules available for resolving international commercial disputes, including those operating under the North American Free Trade Agreement (NAFTA), the Canada-U.S. Free Trade Agreement (FTA) and the European Union (EU), global rules governing trade and investment and intellectual property under the General Agreement on Tariffs and Trade (GATT) and World Trade Organization (WTO), and national rules adopting UNCITRAL Model Arbitration Law and Rules or those of the increasingly numerous arbitration institutions in the world.[55] However, the majority of international commercial disputes are settled by private international commercial arbitration tribunals and not by adjudication in domestic courts of law.[56] Moreover, governments, at least in the developed world, are participating enthusiastically in limiting their powers of review by providing a hospitable legal and regulatory framework for private and closed arbitration proceedings. States are limiting the powers of their national courts to review the decisions of private international commercial arbitrations, while simultaneously committing public offices to the enforcement and execution of foreign and domestic arbitration awards. States are adopting uniform and mandatory legislation that provides for the national recognition and enforcement of foreign arbitral awards. This legislation curtails the authority of national courts to intervene in private arbitration proceedings and limits judicial authority to set aside awards.[57] Today, private actors arbitrate the disputes and produce awards that are then enforced through the offices of public authorities under domestic laws and procedures governing the execution of judgments. The world of international commercial arbitration, which is increasingly transnational in its operation, institutional structures, and culture, is thus comprised by an interesting mixture of private and public authority.[58]

The significant role that private authority has played in the creation and enforcement of merchant law in the medieval and modern phases of the law merchant suggests considerable symmetry and unity between the periods. It is thus not difficult to see how the predominantly *private* nature of the medieval law merchant system is suggestive of the contemporary expansion of private authority in the governance of the global political economy. However, there are significant differences in the political economies of the medieval and contemporary worlds that limit the analytical utility of this analogy. Private merchant authority operated in the medieval period largely because of the general inability or unwillingness of local political authorities to regulate international commerce in any comprehensive manner. What is striking about the medieval period is the contrast between the very limited authority that political leaders exercised over the foreign commercial activities of merchants and the intensity with which they regulated local markets and domestic commercial relations.[59] The bifurcation of authority over local and long-distance commerce is consistent with the diffuse, multiple, overlapping, and parcelized nature of medieval authority relations, more generally, and with the limited jurisdictional reach of local political authorities. Local political authorities shared authority with other political and religious authorities in a system mediated by customary laws and historic entitlements. This reflected the conditions of the feudal political economy wherein ownership of property was subject to multiple claims through the institutions of subinfeudation.[60] The reach of rulers, both temporal and ecclesiastical, was predominantly limited to local commercial centers engaged in retail exchanges and did not extend to overseas long-distance or wholesale trade. In fact, foreign merchants and merchant guilds were most often exempted from local laws in exchange for the payment of customs or other dues and taxes.[61] Thus, medieval merchants, their law, and institutions operated *outside* the political economy of the time.

While medieval merchants operated autonomously and privately by virtue of the general incapacity of local rulers to regulate their activities, today merchants operate autonomously and privately with the full sanction and support of political authorities. Moreover, the *mercatocracy* does not operate outside the contemporary political economy, but in a space that is *insulated within* the global political economy. The shift in the locus of merchant authority is part of a much broader development in the movement from feudal to capitalist political economies and the emergence of distinctions between the public and private realms, or politics and economics, respectively.[62] In the feudal political economy, merchant authority was not part of an integrated system wherein "all production is subordinated to the self-expansion of capital, to the imperatives of accumulation, competition, and profit maximization," which it was to become under capitalism.[63] The feudal system, as Ellen Wood argues, was characterized by a fusion of political and economic authority in the feudal lords and depended upon the private appropriation of value.[64] Indeed, Wood characterizes feudalism as an early but significant step in the "privatization of political power," because it legitimized private property as the legitimate political foundation for the distribution of economic and social goods.[65] Under feudalism, merchant autonomy was neither constitutive of, nor subordinate to, feudal economic and political relations, but operated outside of the feudal political economy. Wood argues that merchants depended upon the private appropriation of value from the sale of luxury goods to the rulers and upon the fragmentation of markets and political authority, which enabled them to operate autonomously, buying cheap in one locale and selling dear in another.[66] Even more important, however, was the constitution of the merchant class as a social order that functioned *outside* the ambit of the political economy of the day. As we have noted, merchant laws and transactions were not enforceable in the local courts and merchant activities were exempted from the application of the laws governing the local political economies. International merchants thus stood outside the political economy as a separately constituted and autonomous class. So significant was *merchant autonomy* that authorities on the law merchant identify this as a foundational attribute of the law merchant order.[67]

As Karl Polanyi notes in his classic analysis of the emergence of the private sphere, it was to take the emergence of market society, subordinating land, labor, and money to the discipline of the free market to complete the transition from feudalism to capitalism.[68] During this process, the law merchant and its institutions were reconstituted as an integral part of the political economy in the private sphere of civil society. There merchant laws were neutralized of political or distributional function, and privatized, as integral and natural elements of the economy and the private sphere of market exchange. The law merchant courts were absorbed into national legal systems, while merchant laws were integrated into the national laws governing property and contract.[69] These laws in turn provide the foundation for productive and exchange relations under capitalism. In the words of E. P. Thompson, these laws were "deeply imbricated within the very basis of productive relations."[70] Simultaneously, the merchant class was reconstituted through " a long process in which certain *political* powers were gradually transformed into *economic* powers and transferred to a separate sphere."[71] This was the sphere of the economy and civil society, as differentiated from the sphere of politics and the state.

Jürgen Habermas also analyzes the emergence of the distinction between the public and private spheres and their associations with politics and economics, respectively. He shows how the process of differentiating between the private and public domains was inextricably bound up with the emergence of capitalism and the creation of a private sphere insulated from political control. In law, the transition from feudalism to capitalism marked a transition from economic exchange relationships based on estate and birth to relations based upon "fundamental parity among owners of commodities in the market."[72] Private law "secured the private sphere in the strict sense, a sense in which private people pursued their affairs with one another free from impositions by estate and state, at least in tendency."[73] There, in the sphere of private exchange, they pursued their economic activity insulated from political interference or control. This transition from feudal to capitalist legal regulation is also captured nicely by the juristic adage "from status to contract," which depicts the movement of legal relations emanating from social and political controls to those emanating from free exchange in economic markets.[74]

With the emergence of centralized and territorially localized political authority in states and the association of state authority with the public sphere, merchant law was incorporated into domestic legal systems where it was privatized and neutralized of political content as part of the private domain of economic activity. Private international trade law developed as an autonomous and politically "neutral" legal order as part of the economic realm, "purified of public, social function,"[75] but one embedded deeply within capitalism and the global political economy.

These developments are central to understanding analytical differences between the medieval and modern law merchant. Moreover, they also provide insight into the significance of contemporary transformations in the global political economy that are giving rise to the expansion of privatized governance in both law-creation and dispute resolution, to which attention will now turn.

The Privatization of Governance

Thus far we have argued that the new law merchant system constitutes an important source of privatized governance, but it is to be distinguished from its medieval ancestor. This emphasis on private regulation is associated by many with the creation of a new "global business civilization."[76] This civilization is globalizing neoliberal legal norms that constitutionalize the privatization and deregulation of key industries, sectors, and commercial practices and that impose market discipline on domestic societies.[77] The discipline resulting from the operation of trade, investment, financial, intellectual property, securities, competition, consumer and environmental protection laws is being shaped under private regimes quite removed from public review. Stephen Gill refers to this as a "new constitutionalism" that is restructuring the global political economy along neo-liberal lines.[78] "The aim of the new constitutionalism is to allow dominant economic forces to be increasingly insulated from democratic rule and popular accountability."[79] It operates through processes that "reconfigure state apparatuses," making governments "facilitators" of market values and market regulations, and that discipline societies into accepting the legitimacy of these processes.[80] The expansion of legal regimes that institutionalize private processes of law-creation and enforcement, like the GATT, NAFTA, the FTA, the ICC, and UNCITRAL, are an integral element of this new constitution and the increasing juridification of international commerce. Their success in promoting market values and in providing rules believed to be necessary for the expansion of trade and investment is generally attributed to their character as private and, hence, neutral and apolitical regimes in which technical expertise rather than political acumen determine outcomes.[81] The modern law merchant is heralded as a great success, and most trade experts believe that it successfully unifies diverse legal, political, economic, and cultural systems because of its nature as *private* and essentially *apolitical* regime.[82] As a system of private law it is said to operate neutrally amongst commercial actors, constituting a powerful mechanism of global governance. Indeed, the *mercatocracy* is committed in principle to the privatization of processes of norm-creation and dispute settlement, for private ordering is regarded as the most natural, consensual, efficient, and just means for regulating international commerce.[83] This view, however, suffers from the misconception that private, economic matters are inherently *apolitical*. It overlooks the important insight provided by significant scholars of political theory that politics is about "who gets what, when, where, and how" and that all activity that has distributional consequences is inherently *political*.[84] The law merchant rules have significant distributional consequences which we are only beginning to understand.[85] Indeed, important developments in law-creation and dispute settlement under the modern law merchant illustrate that it is a significant element in the politics of the new constitutionalism. The neoliberal order is redistributing economic and political authority by restructuring and attenuating state-society relations through processes that involve the law merchant. These processes, in turn, are linked to deeper transformations in the global political economy.

Developments in Law-Creation and Dispute Resolution

The regulation of international economic relations has been challenged, more generally, by those who regard international economic law as a mechanism for the domination and control of weaker commercial participants.[86] William Scheuerman argues that the transnational economic regulation of international trade, finance, banking, taxation, and commercial arbitration is "not only weak on the traditional liberal virtues of generality, clarity, prospectiveness, and stability, but its democratic credentials are unimpressive as well. Too often transnational economic law primarily serves the interests of the most privileged sectors of the global economy."[87] Such criticism suggests that the unification of commercial law, while no doubt providing security, stability, and predictability for some parties involved in commercial transactions, does not necessarily equalize the playing field or guarantee equal interest representation. The law merchant may, indeed, reduce information costs, negotiating costs, and enforcement costs, as suggested in the literature,[88] but these public goods may be distributed quite inequitably amongst commercial participants. The criticisms also suggest that there might not be a natural affinity between unified law and the rule of law.

These criticisms gain greater specificity and force when one considers two developments in lawmaking and dispute resolution that are integral elements of the new constitutionalism and neoliberal discipline. In the area of law-creation, there is a marked trend toward soft, informal, nonbinding, and discretionary regulation, while in the area of dispute resolution, the private arbitration of commercial disputes has eclipsed their adjudication in national courts of law and is expanding in scope. Each development will be addressed in turn.

Trade specialists note a trend toward the increasing reliance on soft over hard law and the application of discretionary, flexible, and ad hoc standards in the unification and regulation of international commercial law and practice.[89] Some explain or justify this development in terms of the need to remain adaptable in a turbulent economic climate and to be able to rely on the technical expertise of private lawyers, accountants, insurers, bankers, and the like.[90] In contrast, others from predominantly developing states argue that flexible, soft, and discretionary standards work against their interests. The latter believe that hard law, while more difficult to achieve agreement over, tends to level the playing field for participants by conducting the lawmaking process in multilateral forums with rules governing participation and voting. Samson Sempasa notes that African countries would have preferred that arbitration laws be unified through hard law rather than soft law because this would have ensured "widespread discussion and more intense scrutiny and debate on a broader multilateral basis."[91] He also contrasts the limited participation of African countries with the overwhelming influence of multinational corporations in the creation of international commercial arbitration law and institutions.[92] According to another trade specialist, "[e]ssentially, the Western industrialized world's view of the arbitral process is embodied in the rules of practice of arbitral institutions, non-governmental organizations such as the ICC, national non-governmental arbitral agencies like the AAA [American Arbitration Association] and the various national and transnational trade systems."[93]

This trend toward increasingly flexible and soft legal standards in lawmaking is thus regarded by some as strengthening the already dominant commercial actors at the expense of the weaker. It should be noted, however, that the hardness of the unification effort is no necessary guarantee of equal representation. Hard laws, too, have been subject to criticism for representing the interests of powerful at the expense of weaker commercial participants. For example, the *Vienna Sales Convention* is faulted for representing the interests of commercial participants from developed countries, at the expense of those in the developing world.[94] It is said to work to the advantage of exporters of heavy equipment and those who possess technical expertise. This is a problem that has also been associated with historical efforts to unify sales law and with the unification of maritime transport laws, which are said to favor the interests of large shipping, insurance, and financial companies.[95] The ICC *Incoterms*, which are curiously soft in origin but have acquired durability as hard standards through their evolution into customary law, are regarded as benefiting trading partners asymmetrically. The *Incoterms* are said to block the entry of new transport carriers into the maritime transport market by strengthening the position of existing multi- and transnational carriers.

Concerns over the limited representation of weaker trading partners in the creation of international commercial law also extend into the institutional practices of international commercial arbitration. Commercial participants from developing states characterize international commercial arbitration as a private club that limits entry to commercial participants from the developed world.[96] Studies of the institutional foundation of international commercial arbitration support that it constitutes a very exclusive, private, and elite club dominated by corporate lawyers, bankers, and accountants who represent powerful corporate interests.[97] The privacy in which arbitration proceedings are conducted compounds the problem of limited entry for others who are not privy to private proceedings, like public interest groups representing consumers or environmentalists. Unlike in judicial proceedings where judges are bound to produce judgments and reasons and have a duty to admit interested parties as interveners, private arbitrations are conducted in secret with no publication requirement or rights of public access. Such privacy, it is argued, is fundamentally antithetical to the rule of law.[98] Moreover, when coupled with the expansion of arbitral subject matter, arbitral secrecy forms a powerful challenge to democratically accountable institutions. The scope of arbitration has expanded to govern mandatory legislation which was previously regulated judicially. Increasingly, matters addressed by mandatory domestic laws, like disputes over antitrust and competition laws and policies, consumer and environmental protection laws, intellectual property and securities laws and regulations are being held to be arbitrable subject matter.[99] The arbitration of such disputes in closed, secret, and private proceedings subject to no publication requirement is a significant departure from the past where they would be resolved in public, judicial forums. This marks a significant transformation in dispute resolution from a predominantly judicial and public activity in the second phase in the development of the law merchant to a predominantly private activity in the contemporary phase. Furthermore, there are significant political implications of the private arbitration of mandatory legislation. The ability of parties to sidestep the application of mandatory national antitrust, taxation, securities, consumer protection, and intellectual property regulations or to have their rights and responsibilities under such laws determined privately, in secret, and the general difficulty of holding transnational corporations accountable under international law reflect a significant accretion in private power and authority.[100] As one legal scholar notes, "the very purpose of most mandatory economic regulation legislation is to constrain private commercial activity in ways believed to be essential to the greater public good."[101] The private arbitration of such mandatory regulations infuses the private sphere with public functions, raising crucial problems of the distinction between judicial and arbitral functions and important concerns about political accountability. While judges operate as part of the public sphere and are duty bound to protect the unrepresented public interest, private arbitrators are not: their duties go to resolving the differences of the parties before them.

The increasing reliance on soft discretionary standards and private international commercial arbitration are thus strengthening private institutions and processes, while weakening mechanisms that work toward public participation and democratic accountability. These developments in law-creation and dispute resolution are in turn linked to transformations the global political economy associated with the advent of the "competition state," the transnationalization of capital, and processes of "flexible accumulation." These transformations are of crucial significance to the juridification of commerce and the expansion of privatized commercial law for they provide the ideological and material foundations for the unification movement. One transformation involves the replacement of the "welfare state" by the "competition state" in response to enhanced international commercial competition and the imposition of the new constitutionalism of disciplinary neoliberalism.[102] The new constitutionalism constitutes a new ideological context for the unification movement for it provides the theoretical rationale for privileging the expansion of private legal regulation and the subordination of domestic policy concerns to neoliberal market discipline. We noted earlier that Gill associates the new constitutionalism with the insulation of dominant economic forces from democratic rule and popular accountability. Neoliberal discipline "operates in practice to confer privileged rights of citizenship and representation to corporate capital and large investors" subordinating the interests of society and public policy more generally to the needs of capital.[103] The goal is to produce internationally competitive industries and services as distributional concerns of equity or justice in commercial transactions are subordinated to concerns of efficiency and enhanced competitiveness. Competition states have in turn shifted their public policy focus from the provision of social welfare to "the promotion of enterprise, innovation and profitability in both private and public sectors."[104]

A related transformation involves the transition from an international political economy based on national patterns of capital accumulation to a global political economy based upon the transnationalization of capital.[105] Competition states facilitate transnational patterns of capital accumulation by undertaking to minimize barriers to the mobility of goods, services, and capital through entry into binding legal arrangements like the WTO and the GATT, NAFTA, the FTA, the Maastricht Treaty and European Monetary Union (EMU), and bilateral investment treaties under the auspices of the International Center for the Settlement of Investment Disputes (ICSID). These legal agreements create hard obligations that cut deeply into the autonomy of public policy and national legislative processes.[106] Contemporaneously, disputes over mandatory national legislation that might impede the mobility of goods, services, and capital through the imposition of environmental or consumer protection laws or legislation governing taxation, securities, and intellectual property rights are increasingly being determined in private by corporate lawyers and accountants, beyond the scrutiny of governments and public policy processes.

Significantly, the unification and harmonization of private international trade law plays a major role in ensuring that national differences in legal rules and legal culture do not create additional barriers to the free flow of goods, services, and capital. The adoption by states of binding commitments to enforce the awards of foreign arbitration tribunals under the *New York Convention on the Enforcement of Foreign Arbitral Awards (New York Convention)* and the adoption of rules harmonizing investment, financial, banking, insurance, and transport practices through UNCITRAL, UNIDROIT, and ICC and other formulating agencies go a long way in facilitating the transnational activities of corporate actors.

A third and related development concerns the advent of patterns of "flexible accumulation" associated with post-Fordist production and efforts to improve productivity and competitiveness.[107] Post-Fordism involves enhanced capital mobility and flexibility or "flexible accumulation" and "flexibility with respect to labour processes, labour markets, products, and patterns of consumption"; the emergence of new sectors of production, new financial services and markets; intensified rates of technological, commercial, and organizational innovation; and the resulting time-space compression as the time horizon for decision-makers shrinks.[108] Soft, flexible, discretionary, and ad hoc rules that are able to accommodate instantaneous transacting and are responsive to fast changing economic conditions are mechanisms of flexible accumulation. In some cases the compression of time and distance render commercial transactions instantaneous and simultaneous, creating a dynamism that renders traditional forms of unified law quite irrelevant and dated.[109] This is evident in the growing commercial preference for nonbinding soft law in the form of voluntary statements of principle, model laws, and optional codes that provide a certain degree of unification without binding parties whose competitive interests and goals might shift over the course of a transaction. Soft law agreements are easier to negotiate, require less compromise, are less restrictive of domestic autonomy, and are easier to breach.[110]

The trend toward soft lawmaking appears to contrast sharply with the deepening of hard law under regimes like the WTO and NAFTA, suggesting that the juridification and privatization of governance involves complex and even contradictory trends. However, a closer inspection of the GATT, for example, illustrates that it is substantively highly ambiguous, indeterminate and riddled with exceptions, which belie its characterization as *hard law*.[111] Importantly, what *is* hard about such agreements is their enforcement. The private and secretive nature of dispute resolution through arbitration under these and other agreements guarantees that the deals struck remain private, beyond intervention and scrutiny by the public, consumers, environmentalists, governments, and public policy officials, and others not party to the proceedings. Moreover, governments and public officials are committed to avoid intervening into the arbitral process and are duty bound by *hard* obligations to enforce the final arbitration award through domestic enforcement procedures. Governments are thus utilizing public offices to enforce awards over which they have little or no substantive control.

The unification movement and the expansion of privatized governance function as integral elements of the corporate strategy used by the *mercatocracy* to adapt to patterns of flexible accumulation, intensified international competition, and the movement from national to transnational patterns of capital accumulation. This strategy involves the dissemination of neoliberal discipline through merchant laws and institutions that promote "the restructuring of state and capital on a world stage towards a more globally integrated and competitive market-driven system," which transforms the state "so as to give greater freedom to the private aspects of capital accumulation in the extended state at the local, national and transnational levels."[112] Preferences for unification through soft law rather than hard law and permissive rather than mandatory legal standards,[113] discretionary and ad hoc legal regulation,[114] declining corporate-control *functions* of states through privatization and deregulation,[115] and arbitral privacy and secrecy[116] are key attributes of these corporate strategy mechanisms of flexible accumulation.

The law merchant thus operates as a system of private governance, promoting corporate interests and creating a permissive, facultative, and flexible regulatory framework for the expansion of transnational capital. It provides the normative infrastructure for the movement from a world economy, based upon linked national economies, to an "emergent transnational or global society predicated on a *global economy*."[117] As a system of private governance, it displaces legislative and judicial checks on authority with a private arbitral regime that leads some to characterize international arbitration as "virtually lawless" and driven by "market forces."[118] When considered in the context of the expansion of corporate authority to challenge national policies under legal regimes like the FTA, NAFTA, and the failed Multilateral Agreement on Investment (MAI), this suggests a formidable expansion of corporate power. Under these agreements, disputes are settled through mechanisms that operate very much like private arbitrations, independent of national courts of law and national public policy processes.[119] As one analyst predicted, "arbitration is power" in the service of private interests.[120]

Together these transformations encourage the development of legal rules and processes that assist commercial actors in operating more competitively. Enhanced efficiency and competitiveness are thus added to the unification goals of greater certainty, predictability, and security providing an obvious distributional dimension to rule-making and enforcement, infusing the supposedly neutral, private sphere with overtly public functions. Simultaneously, the expansion of porous, discretionary, malleable, and private rule-making and enforcement threatens to undermine democratic notions of the rule of law. As Scheuerman observes, the global political economy relies "overwhelmingly on *ad hoc*, discretionary, closed, and non-transparent legal forms, fundamentally inconsistent with a minimally defensible conception of the rule of law."[121] Moreover, he concludes after a review of the legal regulation of international commercial arbitration, international business taxation, international finance and banking, and international trade that there is little evidence that the legal substructure of global capitalism is "strengthening classical rule of law virtues."[122]

The suggestion that the law merchant constitutes a source of *global* governance providing public goods must thus be tempered by recognizing tendencies toward

A. Claire Cutler

biased distributional consequences. In addition, while the reach of the regime may be global, its interest representation is not: "international arbitration is a Western institution intended to serve exclusively Western interests,"[123] while porous and discretionary standards serve the interests of capital.[124] Moreover, the law merchant is a product of Western, Anglo-American, and European law, and its globalization raises important questions about global legal hegemony and imperialism.[125] The ability of this essentially private global regime to represent the interests of non-Western commercial participants is highly questionable, particularly in commercial transactions involving standard form contracts where the terms of the agreement are already determined.[126] The *mercatocracy* and the law merchant are central institutions for the dissemination of neoliberal discipline throughout the world. However, this role is obscured by notions of multiple sources of global governance and the re-medievalization of the world. These notions tend toward the assumption that a plurality of interests are represented and that no one interest dominates. This is quite simply not an accurate representation of the centrality of the merchant elite and its law in the expansion of capital into new forms and into new transnational or non-national spaces. The expansion is not reflective of a reversion to an earlier, feudal political economy, but is constitutive of a new political economy that is the handiwork of a systematic and global unification movement organized by a transnational merchant class. Moreover, this new political economy involves the infusion of the private sphere with public purposes through processes of juridification and privatization that are reordering state-society relations in complex ways. Notions of multiple and plural sources of governance thus obscure the unity and coherence of contemporary global capitalism and threaten to dissolve "capitalism into an unstructured and undifferentiated plurality of social institutions and relations."[127] They also obscure the extent to which state-society relations are being reconfigured by a "privatization of public power" and the creation of an entirely new "'private' realm, with a distinctive 'public' presence and oppression of its own, a unique structure of power and domination, and a ruthless systemic logic."[128] The normative implications of this development are profound in terms of the role that the juridification and privatization of governance play in producing or deepening global inequalities, constraining governments public policy autonomy, and undermining the rule of law in international relations. At the very least what is required is a critical reappraisal of privatized governance as a source of global governance.

Notes

1. Mancur Olson, *The Logic of Collective Action: Public Goods and the Theory of Groups* (Cambridge, Mass.: Harvard University Press, 1965).
2. Liberalism constitutes the most significant and enduring approach in both disciplines. For the classic statement of the public/private distinction in liberal political theory, see Michael Walzer, "Liberalism and the Art of Separation," *Political Theory* 12, no.

3 (1984): 315-30. For the liberal foundations of the distinction between public and private international law, see Mark Janis, "Jeremy Bentham and the Fashioning of International Law," *American Journal of International Law* 78 (1984): 405-18, and A. Claire Cutler, "Artifice, Ideology, and Paradox: The Public/Private Distinction in International Law," *Review of International Political Economy* 4, no. 2 (Summer 1997): 261-85.

3. For further discussion of liberal theory, see A. Claire Cutler, "Locating 'Authority' in the Global Political Economy," *International Studies Quarterly* 43 (1999): 59-81, and Cutler, "Private Authority in International Trade Relations: The Case of Maritime Transport," in *Private Authority and International Affairs,* ed. A. Claire Cutler, Virginia Haufler, and Tony Porter (Albany: State University of New York Press, 1999), 283-329.

4. Olson, *The Logic of Collective Action,* and J. S. Coleman, *Foundations of Social Theory* (Cambridge, Mass.: Harvard University Press, 1990).

5. The term *juridification* is used to denote the use of legal and juridical concepts, institutions, and ideologies to create and substantiate claims to legitimate political authority. In part, this usage incorporates the meaning ascribed to juridification in the early work of Jürgen Habermas as the use of law to expand the scope of administrative power, but it goes beyond to include a much broader set of claims to legitimate authority coming from private corporations or business associations and other non-state entities. See Jürgen Habermas, *The Theory of Communicative Action, Vol. II, Lifeworld and System: A Critique of Functionalist Reason,* trans. Thomas McCarthy (Boston: Beacon Press, 1987), 375ff, and Stephen R. White, "Reason, Modernity, and Democracy," in *The Cambridge Companion to Habermas,* ed. Stephen R. White (Cambridge: Cambridge University Press, 1995), 11.

6. Analysts are studying the globalization of a broad range of economic and social matters. See, for example, Philip Cerny, "Embedding Global Financial Markets: Securitization and the Emerging Web of Governance," in *Private Organizations, Governance, and Global Politics,* ed. Karsten Ronit and Volker Schneider (London: Routledge, 2000); Robert Cox, *Production, Power, and World Order: Social Forces in the Making of History* (New York: Columbia University Press, 1987); Stephen Gill and David Law, "Global Hegemony and the Structural Power of Capital," in *Gramsci, Historical Materialism and International Relations,* ed. Stephen Gill (Cambridge: Cambridge University Press, 1993), 93-124; A. Claire Cutler, "Historical Materialism, Globalization, and Law: Competing Conceptions of Property," in *The Point Is to Change the World: Socialism through Globalization?* ed. Mark Rupert and Hazel Smith (London: Routledge, forthcoming); Phil Williams, "Transnational Organized Crime, the State, and International Society," in *Private Authority and Global Governance,* ed. Thomas Bierksteker and Rodney Hall (Cambridge: Cambridge University Press, forthcoming); Mark W. Zacher, with Brent Sutton, *Governing Global Networks: International Regimes for Transportation and Communications* (Cambridge: Cambridge University Press, 1996).

7. See Cutler, "Artifice, Ideology, and Paradox;" J. Fried, "Globalization and International Law—Some Thoughts for States and Citizens," *Queen's Law Journal* 23, no. 1 (1997): 259-76; and William Twining, "Globalization and Legal Theory: Some Local Implications," *Current Legal Problems* 49 (1996): 1-42.

8. See Alan Hunt, *Explorations in Law and Society: Toward a Constitutive Theory of Law* (New York: Routledge, 1993), ch. 12 for a compelling analysis of the increasing centrality of law in modern society in the context of trends identified in contemporary social theory.

9. See the special issue on legalization and world politics of *International Organization* 54 no. 3 (Summer 2000).

10. See Cutler, Haufler, and Porter, eds., *Private Authority and International Affairs;*

Richard Higgott, Geoffrey Underhill, and Andreas Bieler, eds., *Non-State Actors and Authority in the Global System* (London: Routledge, 1999); Bierksteker and Hall, eds., *Private Authority and Global Governance*; Karsten Ronit and Volker Schneider, "Global Governance through Private Organizations," *Governance: An International Journal of Policy and Administration* 12, no. 3 (July 1999): 243-66, and Ronit and Schneider, eds., *Private Organizations, Governance, and Global Politics.*

11. Hedley Bull, *The Anarchical Society: A Study of Order in World Politics* (London: Macmillan, 1977): 254-55 and 264-76; Susan Strange, *The Retreat of the State: The Diffusion of Power in the World Economy* (Cambridge: Cambridge University Press, 1996); and Philip Cerny, "Neomedievalism, Civil Wars, and the New Security Dilemma: Globalization and Durable Disorder," *Civil Wars* 1, no. 1 (Spring 1998): 36-64.

12. See John G. Ruggie, "Territoriality and Beyond: Problematizing Modernity in International Relations," *International Organization* 47, no. 1 (Winter 1993): 139-74 for a description of the medieval power structure.

13. Strange, in *The Retreat of the State*, probably makes the strongest case for the diffusion of power and authority in the world and the consequent loss of governmental control over society.

14. These include multinational law, insurance, management, consultancy firms, debt-rating agencies, stock exchanges, and financial clearing houses. See Cutler, Haufler, and Porter, *Private Authority and International Affairs*, 10.

15. See Cutler, Haufler, and Porter, *Private Authority and International Affairs*, ch. 1; A. Claire Cutler, "Interfirm Cooperation and Private International Regimes," in *Private Authority and Global Governance,* ed. Bierksteker and Hall; and Strange, *The Retreat of the State.*

16. See Cutler, "Private Authority in International Trade Relations"; Volker Schneider, "Global Economic Governance by Private Actors: The International Chamber of Commerce," in *Organized Business and the New Global Order,* ed. J. Geenwood and H. Jacek (London: Macmillan, 1998); Ann Marie Clarke, Elisabeth Friedman, and Kathryn Hochstetler, "The Sovereign Limits of Global Civil Society: A Comparison of NGO Participation in UN Conferences on the Environment, Human Rights, and Women," *World Politics* 51(October 1998): 1-35.

17. A. V. Dicey, *Introduction to the Study of the Constitution [1885]* (London: Macmillan, 1967).

18. William Scheuerman, "Economic Globalization and the Rule of Law," *Constellations: An International Journal of Critical and Democratic Theory* 6, no. 1 (March 1999): 3-25.

19. Analysts use a variety of terms to describe and define the law merchant, including "a set of general principles and customary rules," B. Goldman, "The Applicable Law: General Principles of the Law—the *lex mercatoria*," in Julian Lew, ed., *Contemporary Problems in International Commercial Arbitration* (London: School of International Arbitration, Center for Commercial Studies, 1986): 116; "the rules of the game of international trade," Eugen Langen, *Transnational Commercial Law* (Leiden: A. W. Sijthoff, 1973), 21; "common principles in the law relating to international commercial transactions," Clive Schmitthoff, "Nature and Evolution of the Transnational Law of Commercial Transactions," in *The Transnational Law of International Commercial Transactions,* ed. Clive Schmitthoff and Norbert Horn (Deventer: Kluwer, 1982), 19; "uniform rules accepted in all countries," Schmitthoff, "International Business Law: A New Law Merchant," *Current Law and Social Problems* 2 (1961), 139; "an international body of law, founded on the commercial understandings and contract practices of an international community composed

principally of mercantile, shipping, insurance, and banking enterprises of all countries," Harold Berman and Colin Kaufman, "The Law of International Commercial Transactions *(Lex Mercatoria),*" *Harvard International Law Journal* 19, no. 1 (Winter 1978), 272-73. These definitions do not disclose the extent to which the existence of the law merchant as an autonomous legal order is debated by legal scholars. In general, European scholars tend to accept the existence of the law merchant as an autonomous legal order much more readily than do Anglo-American scholars. The latter tend to see it as an extension of domestic legal systems; see Cutler, "Artifice, Ideology and Paradox"; Christoph Stoecker, "The *Lex Mercatoria:* To What Extent Does It Exist?" *Journal of International Arbitration* (1990): 101-25; Keith Highet, "The Enigma of the *lex mercatoria,*" *Tulane Law Review* 63 (1989): 613-28. Additionally, some scholars tend to define the law merchant very narrowly, limiting it to harmonized or universalized customs and practices accepted by the merchant community. This chapter adopts the more expansive approach common in Anglo-American commercial law, regarding the law merchant as coterminous with the law of private international trade. See Schmitthoff, "Nature and Evolution of the Transnational Law of Commercial Transactions" and "International Business Law."

20. See A. Claire Cutler,"Globalization, Law, and Transnational Corporations: The Deepening of Market Discipline," in *Power in the Global Era: Grounding Globalization,* ed. Theodore Cohn, Stephen McBride, and David Wiseman (Houndmills, Basingstoke, U.K.: Macmillan, and New York: St. Martin's, 2000), 53-66 for an analysis of the embedding of regional and international trade law regimes in domestic legal orders.

21. For fuller analysis of the nature and operation of the law merchant regime, see A. Claire Cutler, "Global Capitalism and Liberal Myths: Dispute Settlement in Private International Trade Relations," *Millennium: Journal of International Studies* 24, no. 3 (Winter 1995): 377-97. And Cutler, "Locating 'Authority' in the Global Political Economy." This section follows closely on the analysis in A. Claire Cutler, "Global Governance and the Modern *Lex Mercatoria,*" *Of Global Governance: Culture, Economics and Politics,* ed. Claire Turenne Sjolander and Jean François Thibault (University of Ottawa Press, forthcoming).

22. Cutler, "Locating 'Authority,'" 48.

23. See generally, Cutler, "Artifice, Ideology, and Paradox."

24. See generally, Marvin Baer, Joost Blom, Elizabeth Edinger, Nicholas Rafferty, Geneviève Saumier, and Catherine Walsh, *Private International Law in Common Law Canada: Cases, Texts, and Materials* (Toronto: Emond Montgomery, 1997), and Horn and Schmitthoff, eds., *The Transnational Law of International Commercial Transactions.*

25. Elizabeth Patterson, "United Nations Convention for Contracts for the International Sale of Goods: Unification and the Tension between Compromise and Domination," *Stanford Journal of International Law* 23, no.1 (1986): 263-303.

26. See Cutler, "Global Capitalism and Liberal Myths."

27. Scheuerman, "Global Law in Our High Speed Economy."

28. Paul Milgrom, Douglass North, and Barry Weingast, "The Role of Institutions in the Revival of Trade: The Law Merchant, Private Judges, and the Champagne Fairs," *Economics and Politics* 2, no. 1 (1990): 1-23.

29. A pioneering effort in this regard is Robert Keohane, *After Hegemony: Cooperation and Discord in the World Political Economy* (Princeton, N. J.: Princeton University Press, 1984). And see Zacher with Sutton, *Governing Global Networks.*

30. Schmitthoff, "International Business Law."

31. For good accounts of medieval merchant law and institutions, see William Mitchell, *An Essay on the Early History of the Law Merchant* (Cambridge: Cambridge University

Press, 1904); Wyndham Bewes, *The Romance of the Law Merchant* (London: Sweet and Maxwell, 1923); and René David, "The International Unification of Private Law," *International Encyclopaedia of Comparative Law: Legal Systems of the World, Their Comparison and Unification*, Vol. II, (The Hague: Mohr, Tubingen Martinus Nijhoff, 1972).

32. Bruce Benson,"To Arbitrate or to Litigate: That Is the Question," *European Journal of Law and Economics* 8, no. 2 (September 1999): 114 and 120-27; Schmitthoff, "International Business Law."

33. Leon Trakman, *The Law Merchant: The Evolution of Commercial Law* (Littleton, Col.: Fred B. Rothman, 1983).

34. See generally, Berman and Kaufman, "The Law of International Commercial Transactions."

35. Cutler, "Private Authority in International Trade Relations," 304.

36. Milgrom, North, and Weingast,"The Role of Institutions."

37. Avner Greif, Paul Milgrom, and Barry Weingast, "Coordination, Commitment, and Enforcement: The Case of the Merchant Guild," *Journal of Political Economy* 102, no. 4 (1994): 745-76. See also Avner Greif, "Contract Enforceability and Economic Institutions in Early Trade: The Maghribi Traders' Coalition," *American Economic Review* 83, no. 3 (1993): 525-48 for even earlier regulatory associations developed by merchants.

38. See generally, Shepard Clough and Charles Cole, *Economic History of Europe*, revised ed. (Boston: D. C. Heath, 1946), and Henri Pirenne, *Economic and Social History of Medieval Europe* (London: Kegan Paul, 1937).

39. The most authoritative review of the history of the unification movement is still that provided by David, "The International Unification of Private Law." See also A. Claire Cutler, "Public Meets Private: The International Unification and Harmonization of Private International Trade Law," *Global Society* 13, no. 1 (1999): 25-48.

40. Roland Robertson, *Globalization: Social Theory and Global Culture* (London: Sage, 1992), 4.

41. David Kennedy, "The Move to Institutions," *Cardozo Law Review* 8 (1987): 841-988. See generally, Cutler, "Public Meets Private."

42. See generally, David, "The International Unification of Private Law," and John Honnold, "International Unification of Private Law," in *United Nations Legal Order*, Vol. 2, ed. Oscar Schachter and Christopher Joyner (Cambridge: Grotius Publications, 1995): 1025-56.

43. For a classic statement of the need to preserve merchant autonomy, see Trakman, *The Law Merchant*, 97, and Kazuaki Sono, "Restoration of the Rule of Reason in Contract Formation: Has There Been a Civil and Common Law Disparity?" *Cornell International Law Journal* 21, no. 3 (1988), 485.

44. I derive the term *mercatocracy* from the Latin term, *lex mercatoria*, or law merchant. See Cutler, "Public Meets Private" for analysis of the *mercatocracy* as a transnational merchant class and for elaboration of its institutional foundations. And see Yves Dezalay and Bryant Garth, *Dealing in Virtue: International Commercial Arbitration and the Construction of a Transnational Legal Order* (Chicago: University of Chicago Press, 1996) for the elite nature of the international commercial arbitration world. See William Robinson and Jerry Harris, "Towards a Global Ruling Class? Globalization and the Transnational Capitalist Class," *Science and Society* 64, no. 1 (Spring 2000): 11-54; Kees van der Pijl, *Transnational Classes and International Relations* (London: Routledge, 1998); and Stephen Gill, ed., *Gramsci, Historical Materialism, and International Relations* (Cambridge: Cambridge University Press, 1993) for discussion of the formation of a transnational capitalist class.

45. See Rudolf Dolzer, "International Agencies for the Formulation of Transnational Economic Law," in *The Transnational Law of International Economic Transactions*, 61-80.

46. *United Nations Convention on Contracts for the International Sale of Goods*, UN Doc. A/Conf.97/18. Annex 1, reprinted in *International Legal Materials* 19 (1980): 668- 95.

47. Paul Lansing, "The Change in American Attitude to the International Unification of Sales Law Movement and UNCITRAL," *American Business Law Journal* 18, no. 4 (1980): 270-71.

48. Cutler, "Public Meets Private," cf. 73.

49. Peter Pfund, Assistant Legal Advisor for Private International Law, U. S. Department of State, cited in Patterson, "United Nations Convention for Contracts," cf. 55, and Honnold, "International Unification of Private Law," 1038.

50. See M. J. Bonell, "The UNIDROIT Initiative for the Progressive Codification of International Trade Law," *International and Comparative Law Quarterly* 27 (1987): 423-41.

51. *Principles of International Commercial Contracts* (Paris: UNIDROIT, 1994). See M. J. Bonell, "The Unidroit Principles of International Commercial Contracts and CISG-Alternatives or Complementary Instruments?" in *Harmonization and Change: Workshop Papers from the Twenty-Fifth Annual Workshop on Commercial and Consumer Law* (Faculty of Law, University of Toronto, 1995), 327-41.

52. Hard law comprises international treaties, conventions, and agreements that are formally binding, while soft law comprises nonbinding model laws, codes, and statements of principles that are voluntarily adopted by commercial actors. See Peter Malanczuk, ed., *Akehurst's Modern Introduction to International Law*, 7th revised ed. (London: Routledge, 1997), 54.

53. See generally, Malanczuk, *Akehurst's Modern Introduction to International Law*, ch. 3.

54. See Michael Rowe, "The Contribution of the ICC to the Development of International Trade Law," in *The Transnational Law of International Commercial Transactions*, 51-60.

55. Dezalay and Garth, *Dealing in Virtue*, 6.

56. Cutler, "Global Capitalism and Liberal Myths."

57. The *United Nations Convention on the Recognition and Enforcement of Foreign Arbitral Awards* (*New York Convention*), 10 June 1958, UN Doc. A/Conf.9/22 is in force in some 123 states (as of 4 October 2000) and curtails the power of national courts to intervene in private arbitration proceedings. In addition, states are voluntarily adopting the UNCITRAL *Model Law on International Commercial Arbitration* (adopted by some 32 states as of 4 October 2000) which together with the *New York Convention* provides a comprehensive body of international commercial arbitration law. (See UNCITRAL Homepage<http://www.UNCITRAL.org/en-index.html> 4 October 2000.)

58. See Dezalay and Garth, *Dealing in Virtue*, and Cutler, "Public Meets Private."

59. See Cutler, "Global Capitalism and Liberal Myths," 388-89 for a review of the various market offenses.

60. See Cutler, "Historical Materialism, Globalization, and Law."

61. Greif, Milgrom, and Weingast, "Coordination, Commitment, and Enforcement."

62. See Jürgen Habermas, *The Structural Transformation of the Public Sphere: An Inquiry into a Category of Bourgeois Society*, trans. T. Burger (Cambridge, Mass.: MIT Press, 1994), and Ellen Meiksins Wood, *Democracy against Capitalism: Renewing Historical Materialism* (Cambridge: Cambridge University Press, 1995).

63. Wood, *Democracy against Capitalism*, 156.

64. Wood, *Democracy against Capitalism*, 37-39.

65. Wood, *Democracy against Capitalism*, 37, defines the "privatization of political power" as "the process by which this authority of private property asserted itself, uniting the power of appropriation with the authority to organize production in the hands of a private proprietor for his own benefit."

66. Wood, *Democracy against Capitalism*, 165.

67. See Trakman, *The Law Merchant*, and Schmitthoff, "International Business Law."

68. *The Great Transformation: The Political and Economic Origins of Our Time* (Boston: Beacon, 1944).

69. See generally, Berman and Kaufman, "The Law of International Commercial Transactions."

70. E. P. Thompson, *Whigs and Hunters: The Origin of the Black Act* (New York: Pantheon Books, 1975), 359. And see Cutler, "Historical Materialism, Globalization, and Law," and A. Claire Cutler, "Critical Historical Sociology and International Law," in *Bringing Historical Sociology Back into International Relations*, ed. John Hobsen and Stephen Hobden (Cambridge: Cambridge University Press, forthcoming) for discussion of the law merchant as part of the base and not the superstructure of capitalism.

71. Wood, *Democracy against Capitalism*, 36.

72. Habermas, *The Structural Transformation of the Public Sphere*, 75.

73. Habermas, *The Structural Transformation of the Public Sphere*, 75.

74. Habermas, *The Structural Transformation of the Public Sphere*, 77.

75. Wood, *Democracy against Capitalism*, 39.

76. Robert Cox, "Civilizations in World Politics," *New Political Economy* 1, no. 2 (1996): 141-56; Susan Strange, "The Name of the Game," in *Sea Changes: American Foreign Policy in a World Transformed*, ed. N. X. Rizopoulos (New York: Council on Foreign Relations, 1990), 238-73, and Schmitthoff, "International Business Law."

77. See Stephen Gill, "Globalization, Market Civilization, and Disciplinary Neoliberalism," *Millennium: Journal of International Studies* 24, no. 1 (Winter 1995): 399-423, and Gill, "New Constitutionalism, Democratization and Global Political Economy," *Pacifica Review* 10, no.1 (February 1998): 23-38.

78. Gill, "New Constitutionalism."

79. Gill, "New Constitutionalism," 23.

80. Gill, "New Constitutionalism," 25-26.

81. See Schmitthoff, "Nature and Evolution of the Transnational Law of Commercial Transactions."

82. Schmitthoff, "International Business Law," and "Nature and Evolution of the Transnational Law of Commercial Transactions," and see Cutler, "Artifice, Ideology, and Paradox," and "Locating 'Authority.'"

83. For the ideological foundations of the *mercatocracy* see Cutler, "Global Capitalism and Liberal Myths," and "Public Meets Private."

84. This is Harold Lasswell's famous definition of politics, which is cited by Susan Strange, *The Retreat of the State*, 45, in making her case for the "political" nature of corporate and market activities. See my discussion of the analytical and normative problems associated with drawing a rigid separation between economics and politics in "Theorizing the 'No-Man's-Land' between Politics and Economics," *Strange Power: Shaping the Parameters of International Relations and International Political Economy*, ed. Thomas Lawton, James Rosenau, and Amy Verdun (Aldershot, U.K.: Ashgate, 2000), 159-74.

85. See Cutler, "Private Authority in International Trade Relations," 309-10.

86. Patterson, "United Nations Convention for Contracts," Arthur Rosett, "Critical

Reflections on the United Nations Convention on Contracts for the International Sale of Goods," *Ohio State Law Journal* 15, no. 2 (1984): 265-305.

87. Scheuerman, "Global Law in Our High Speed Economy," in *The Legal Culture of Global Business Transactions*, ed. Volkmar Gessner (Oxford: Hart, 2000).

88. See Cutler, Haufler, and Porter, "The Contours and Significance of Private Authority," and Milgrom, North, and Weingast, "The Role of Institutions."

89. See Malanczuk, *Akehurst's Modern Introduction to International Law*, ch. 3, and P. T. Muchlinski, *Multinational Enterprises and the Law* (Oxford: Blackwell, 1995).

90. John Kline, "Advantages of International Regulation: The Case for a Flexible, Pluralistic Framework," in *International Regulation: New Rules in a Changing World Order*, ed. Carol Adelman (San Francisco: Institute for Contemporary Studies, 1988).

91. Samson Sempasa, "Obstacles to International Commercial Arbitration in African Countries," *International and Comparative Law Quarterly* 41 (1992): 399.

92. "Obstacles to International Commercial Arbitration," 393.

93. Quoted in Sempasa, "Obstacles to International Commercial Arbitration," 392, note 17.

94. See Patterson, "United Nations Convention on Contracts," and Alejandro Garro, "Reconciliation of Legal Traditions in the UN Convention on Contracts for the International Sale of Goods," *International Lawyer* 23, no. 2 (1989): 443-83.

95. See Horacio Grigera Naon, "The UN Convention on Contracts for the International Sale of Goods," in *The Transnational Law of International Commercial Transactions*; Gyula Eörsi, "Contracts of Adhesion and the Protection of the Weaker Party in International Trade Relations," in UNIDROIT, *New Directions in International Trade Law*, Vol. I (New York: Oceana Publications, 1977), 155-76.

96. See Sempasa, "Obstacles to International Commercial Arbitration," and see Dezalay and Garth, *Dealing in Virtue*.

97. See Dezalay and Garth, *Dealing in Virtue* and *Professional Competition and Professional Power: Lawyers, Accountants, and the Social Construction of Markets*, ed. Yves Dezalay and David Sugarman (London: Routledge 1995).

98. Scheuerman, "Economic Globalization," and Scheuerman, "Global Law in Our High Speed Economy."

99. Philip McConnaughay, "The Risks of Lawlessness: A 'Second Look' at International Commercial Arbitration," *Northwestern University Law Review* 93, no. 2 (1999): 403-23.

100. See A. Claire Cutler, "Critical Reflections on Westphalian Assumptions of International Law and Organization: A Crisis of Legitimacy," *Review of International Studies* 27, no. 2 (2001): 133-50.

101. McConnaughay, "The Risks of Lawlessness," 495.

102. See Gill, "New Constitutionalism," and Gill, "Globalization, Market Civilization, and Disciplinary Neoliberalism," and Philip Cerny, *The Changing Architecture of Politics: Structure, Agency, and the Future of the State* (London: Sage, 1990), and Cerny, "Paradoxes of the Competition State: The Dynamics of Political Globalization," *Government and Opposition* 32, no. 2 (1997): 251-74.

103. Gill,"New Constitutionalism," 23.

104. Cerny, *The Changing Architecture of Politics*, 205.

105. For the transnationalization of capital, see Stephen Gill and David Law, "Global Hegemony and the Structural Power of Capital," and William Robinson, "Globalization: Nine Theses on Our Epoch," *Race and Class* 38, no. 2 (1996): 13-31, and Robinson, "Beyond the Nation-State Paradigms: Globalization, Sociology, and the Challenge of

Transnational Studies," *Sociological Forum* 13, no. 4 (1998): 561-94.

106. For discussion of the impact of these legal agreements on the autonomy of domestic public policy processes and legislative authority, see Twining, "Globalization and Legal Theory"; Fried, "Globalization and International Law'; Gill, "New Constitutionalism"; and Cutler, "Globalization, Law, and Transnational Corporations."

107. David Harvey, *The Condition of Postmodernity: An Enquiry into the Origins of Cultural Change* (Cambridge, Mass.: Blackwell, 1990).

108. Harvey, *The Condition of Postmodernity,* 147.

109. See Scheuerman, "Global Law in Our High Speed Economy," and for a discussion of time-space compression, see Harvey, *The Condition of Postmodernity.*

110. Kenneth Abbott and Duncan Snidal, "Hard and Soft Law in International Governance," *International Organization* 54, no. 3 (2000): 421-56, and Cutler, "Public Meets Private."

111. Scheuerman, "Economic Globalization and the Rule of Law," 13.

112. Stephen Gill, "Theorizing the Interregnum: The Double Movement and Global Politics in the 1990s," in *International Political Economy: Understanding Global Disorder,* ed. Björn Hettne (Halifax, Nova Scotia: Fernwood and London: Zed Books, 1995), 85, and see Cerny, "Paradoxes of the Competition State."

113. Cutler, "Public Meets Private."

114. Scheuerman, "Economic Globalization and the Rule of Law."

115. Muchlinski, *Multinational Enterprises and the Law.*

116. Dezalay and Garth, *Dealing in Virtue.*

117. Robinson,"Beyond the Nation-State Paradigms," 563.

118. McConnaughay, "The Risks of Lawlessness: A 'Second Look' at International Commercial Arbitration," 453 and 462; Benson, "To Arbitrate or to Litigate," 93.

119. Case law is only beginning to come out under Chapter 11 of NAFTA, which provides investor corporations the right to seek compensation directly from a host state if the state is found to have adversely affected the investors interests. Canadians became acutely aware of the ability of foreign corporations to undermine national legislative and policy measures designed to protect the environment when the Canadian government paid $19.5 million to settle a Chapter 11 claim brought by Ethyl Corp., in 1998.

120. Heinrich Kronstein, "Arbitration Is Power," *New York University Law Review* 38 (June 1963): 699.

121. Scheuerman, "Economic Globalization and the Rule of Law," 3.

122. Scheuerman, "Economic Globalization and the Rule of Law,"15.

123. McConnaughay, "The Risks of Lawlessness," 523.

124. Scheuerman, "Economic Globalization and the Rule of Law," and Scheuerman, "Global Law in Our High Speed Economy."

125. Patterson, "United Nations Convention for Contracts"; Susan Silbey,"Let Them Eat Cake: Globalization, Postmodern Colonialism, and the Possibilities of Justice," *Law and Society Review* 31, no. 2 (1997): 207-35; and Sempasa, "Obstacles to International Commercial Arbitration."

126. See Eörsi,"Contracts of Adhesion," 155-76, and Cutler, "Interfirm Cooperation and Private International Regimes."

127. Wood, *Democracy against Capitalism,* 247.

128. Wood, *Democracy against Capitalism,* 254.

References

Abbott, K., and D. Snidal. 2000. Hard and Soft Law in International Governance. *International Organization* 54 (3): 421-56.

Baer, M., J. Blom, E. Edinger, N. Rafferty, G. Saumier, and C. Walsh. 1997. *Private International Law in Common Law Canada: Cases, Texts, and Materials*. Toronto: Emond Montgomery.

Benson, B. 1999. To Arbitrate or to Litigate: That Is the Question. *European Journal of Law and Economics* 8 (2): 91-151.

Berman, H., and C. Kaufman. 1978. The Law of International Commercial Transactions (Lex Mercatoria). *Harvard International Law Journal* 19 (1): 221-77.

Bewes, W. 1923. *The Romance of the Law Merchant*. London: Sweet and Maxwell.

Biersteker, T., and R. Hall, eds. Forthcoming. *Private Authority and Global Governance*.

Bonell, M. J. 1987. The UNIDROIT Initiative for the Progressive Codification of International Trade Law. *International and Comparative Law Quarterly* 27: 423-41.

———. 1995. The Unidroit Principles of International Commercial Contracts and CISG-Alternatives or Complementary Instruments? Workshop Papers from the Twenty-Fifth Annual Workshop on Commercial and Consumer Law. Faculty of Law, University of Toronto.

Bull, H. 1977. *The Anarchical Society: A Study of Order in World Politics*. London: Macmillan.

Cerny, P. G. 1990. *The Changing Architecture of Politics: Structure, Agency, and the Future of the State*. London: Sage.

———. 1997. Paradoxes of the Competition State: The Dynamics of Political Globalization. *Government and Opposition* 32 (2): 251-74.

———. 1998. Neomedievalism, Civil Wars, and the New Security Dilemma: Globalization and Durable Disorder. *Civil Wars* 1 (1): 36-64.

———. 2000. Embedding Global Financial Markets: Securitization and the Emerging Web of Governance. In *Private Organizations, Governance, and Global Politics*, ed. K. Ronit and V. Schneider. London: Routledge.

Clarke, A. M., E. Friedman, and K. Hochstetler. 1998. The Sovereign Limits of Global Civil Society: A Comparison of NGO Participation in UN Conferences on the Environment, Human Rights, and Women. *World Politics* 51: 1-35.

Clough, S., and C. Cole. 1946. *Economic History of Europe*. Revised edition. Boston: D. C. Heath.

Coleman, J. S. 1990. *Foundations of Social Theory*. Cambridge, Mass.: Harvard University Press.

Cox, R. 1987. *Production, Power, and World Order: Social Forces in the Making of History*. New York: Columbia University Press.

———. 1996. Civilizations in World Politics. *New Political Economy* 1 (2): 141-56.

Cutler, A. C. 1995. Global Capitalism and Liberal Myths: Dispute Settlement in Private International Trade Relations. *Millennium: Journal of International Studies* 24 (3): 377-97.

———. 1997. Artifice, Ideology, and Paradox: the Public/Private Distinction in International Law. *Review of International Political Economy* 4 (2): 261-85.

———. 1999. Locating 'Authority' in the Global Political Economy. *International Studies Quarterly* 43: 59-81.

———. 1999. Private Authority in International Trade Relations: The Case of Maritime Transport. In *Private Authority and International Affairs*, ed. A. C. Cutler, V. Haufler, and T. Porter, 283-329. Albany: State University of New York Press.

———. 1999. Public Meets Private: The International Unification and Harmonization of Private International Trade Law. *Global Society* 13 (1): 25-48.

———. 2000. Theorizing the 'No-Man's-Land' between Politics and Economics. In *Strange Power: Shaping the Parameters of International Relations and International Political Economy*, ed. T. Lawton, J. Rosenau, and A. Verdun, 159-74. Aldershot, U.K.: Ashgate.

———. 2000. Globalization, Law, and Transnational Corporations: The Deepening of Market Discipline. In *Power in the Global Era: Grounding Globalization*, ed. T. Cohn, S. McBride, and D. Wiseman, 53-66. Houndmills, Basingstoke, U.K.: Macmillan.

———. 2001. Critical Reflections on Westphalian Assumptions of International Law and Organization: A Crisis of Legitimacy. *Review of International Studies* 27 (2): 133-50.

———. Forthcoming. Global Governance and the Modern Lex Mercatoria. In *Of Global Governance: Culture, Economics, and Politics*, ed. C. T. Sjolander and J.-F. Thibault. Ottawa: University of Ottawa Press.

———. Forthcoming. Interfirm Cooperation and Private International Regimes. In *Private Authority and Global Governance*, ed. T. Bierksteker and R. Hall. Cambridge: Cambridge University Press.

———. Forthcoming. Historical Materialism, Globalization, and Law: Competing Conceptions of Property. In *The Point Is to Change the World: Socialism through Globalization?* ed. M. Rupert and H. Smith. London: Routledge.

———. Forthcoming. Critical Historical Sociology and International Law. In *Bringing Historical Sociology Back into International Relations*, ed. J. Hobsen and S. Hobden. Cambridge: Cambridge University Press.

Cutler, A. C., V. Haufler, and T. Porter, eds. 1999. *Private Authority and International Affairs*. Albany: State University of New York Press.

David, R. 1972. *The International Unification of Private Law. International Encyclopaedia of Comparative Law: Legal Systems of the World, Their Comparison and Unification, Vol. II.* The Hague: Martinus Nijhoff.

Dezalay, Y., and B. Garth. 1996. *Dealing in Virtue: International Commercial Arbitration and the Construction of a Transnational Legal Order*. Chicago: University of Chicago Press.

Dezalay, Y., and D. Sugarman, eds. 1995. *Professional Competition and Professional Power: Lawyers, Accountants, and the Social Construction of Markets*. London: Routledge.

Dicey, A. V. 1967. *Introduction to the Study of the Constitution* [1885]. London: Macmillan.

Dolzer, R. 1982. International Agencies for the Formulation of Transnational Economic Law. In *The Transnational Law of International Economic Transactions*, ed. N. Horn and C. Schmitthoff, 61-80. Deventer: Kluwer.

Eörsi, G. 1977. Contracts of Adhesion and the Protection of the Weaker Party in International Trade Relations. In *UNIDROIT, New Directions in International Trade Law. Vol. I*, 155-76. New York: Oceana.

Fried, J. 1997. Globalization and International Law—Some Thoughts for States and Citizens. *Queen's Law Journal* 23 (1): 259-76.

Garro, A. 1989. Reconciliation of Legal Traditions in the UN Convention on Contracts for the International Sale of Goods. *International Lawyer* 23 (2): 443-83.

Gill, S., ed. 1993. *Gramsci, Historical Materialism, and International Relations*. Cambridge: Cambridge University Press.

———. 1995. Globalization, Market Civilization, and Disciplinary Neoliberalism. *Millennium: Journal of International Studies* 24 (1): 399-423.

————. 1995. Theorizing the Interregnum: The Double Movement and Global Politics in the 1990s. In *International Political Economy: Understanding Global Disorder*, ed. B. Hettne, 65-99. Halifax, Nova Scotia: Fernwood.

————. 1998. New Constitutionalism, Democratization, and Global Political Economy. *Pacifica Review* 10 (1): 23-38.

Gill, S., and D. Law. 1993. Global Hegemony and the Structural Power of Capital. In *Gramsci, Historical Materialism, and International Relations*, ed. S. Gill. Cambridge: Cambridge University Press.

Goldman, B. 1986. The Applicable Law: General Principles of the Law—The *lex mercatoria*. In *Contemporary Problems in International Commercial Arbitration*, ed. J. Lew. London: School of International Arbitration, Center for Commercial Studies.

Greif, A. 1993. Contract Enforceability and Economic Institutions in Early Trade: The Maghribi Traders' Coalition. *American Economic Review* 83 (3): 525-48.

Greif, A., P. Milgrom, and B. Weingast. 1994. Coordination, Commitment, and Enforcement: The Case of the Merchant Guild. *Journal of Political Economy* 102 (4): 745-76.

Habermas, J. 1987. *The Theory of Communicative Action, Vol. II, Lifeworld and System: A Critique of Functionalist Reason*. Trans. T. McCarthy. Boston: Beacon Press.

————. 1994. *The Structural Transformation of the Public Sphere: An Inquiry into a Category of Bourgeois Society*. Trans. T. Burger. Cambridge, Mass.: MIT Press.

Harvey, D. 1990. *The Condition of Postmodernity: An Enquiry into the Origins of Cultural Change*. Cambridge, Mass.: Blackwell.

Higgott, R., G. Underhill, and A. Bieler, eds. 1999. *Non-State Actors and Authority in the Global System*. London: Routledge.

Highet, K. 1989. The Enigma of the *lex mercatoria*. *Tulane Law Review* 63: 613-28.

Honnold, J. 1995. International Unification of Private Law. In *United Nations Legal Order, Vol. 2*, ed. O. Schachter and C. Joyner, 1025-56. Cambridge: Grotius.

Horn, N., and C. Schmitthoff, eds. 1982. *The Transnational Law of International Commercial Transactions*. Deventer: Kluwer.

Hunt, A. 1993. *Explorations in Law and Society: Toward a Constitutive Theory of Law*. New York: Routledge.

Janis, M. 1984. Jeremy Bentham and the Fashioning of International Law. *American Journal of International Law* 78: 405-18.

Kennedy, D. 1987. The Move to Institutions. *Cardozo Law Review* 8: 841-988.

Keohane, R. 1984. *After Hegemony: Cooperation and Discord in the World Political Economy*. Princeton, N.J.: Princeton University Press.

Kline, J. 1988. Advantages of International Regulation: The Case for a Flexible, Pluralistic Framework. In *International Regulation: New Rules in a Changing World Order*, ed. C. Adelman. San Francisco: Institute for Contemporary Studies.

Kronstein, H. 1963. Arbitration Is Power. *New York University Law Review* 38: 661-700.

Langen, E. 1973. *Transnational Commercial Law*. Leiden: A. W. Sijthoff.

Lansing, P. 1980. The Change in American Attitude to the International Unification of Sales Law Movement and UNCITRAL. *American Business Law Journal* 18 (4): 270-71.

Malanczuk, P., ed. 1997. *Akehurst's Modern Introduction to International Law*, 7th rev. edition. London: Routledge.

McConnaughay, P. 1999. The Risks of Lawlessness: A 'Second Look' at International Commercial Arbitration. *Northwestern University Law Review* 93 (2): 403-23.

156 A. Claire Cutler

Milgrom, P., D. North, and B. Weingast. 1990. The Role of Institutions in the Revival of
Trade: The Law Merchant, Private Judges, and the Champagne Fairs. *Economics and
Politics* 2 (1): 1-23.
Mitchell, W. 1904. *An Essay on the Early History of the Law Merchant.* Cambridge:
Cambridge University Press.
Muchlinski, P. T. 1995. *Multinational Enterprises and the Law.* Oxford: Blackwell.
Olson, M. 1965. *The Logic of Collective Action: Public Goods and the Theory of Groups.*
Cambridge, Mass.: Harvard University Press.
Naon, H. G. 1982. The UN Convention on Contracts for the International Sale of Goods. In
The Transnational Law of International Commercial Transaction, ed. N. Horn and
C. Schmitthoff, 89-124. Deventer: Kluwer.
Patterson, E. 1986. United Nations Convention for Contracts for the International Sale of
Goods: Unification and the Tension between Compromise and Domination. *Stanford
Journal of International Law* 23 (1): 263-303.
Pirenne, H. 1937. *Economic and Social History of Medieval Europe.* London: Kegan Paul.
Polanyi, Karl. 1944. *The Great Transformation: The Political and Economic Origins of Our
Time.* Boston: Beacon Press.
Principles of International Commercial Contracts. 1994. Paris: UNIDROIT.
Robertson, R. 1992. *Globalization: Social Theory and Global Culture.* London: Sage.
Robinson, W. 1996. Globalization: Nine Theses on Our Epoch. *Race and Class* 38 (2): 13-
31.
———. 1998. Beyond the Nation-State Paradigms: Globalization, Sociology, and the
Challenge of Transnational Studies. *Sociological Forum* 13 (4): 561-94.
Robinson, W., and J. Harris. 2000. Towards a Global Ruling Class? Globalization and the
Transnational Capitalist Class. *Science and Society* 64 (1): 11-54.
Ronit, K., and V. Schneider. 1999. Global Governance through Private Organizations.
Governance: An International Journal of Policy and Administration 12 (3): 243-66.
Rosett, A. 1984. Critical Reflections on the United Nations Convention on Contracts for the
International Sale of Goods. *Ohio State Law Journal* 15 (2): 265-305.
Rowe, M. 1982. The Contribution of the ICC to the Development of International Trade
Law. In *The Transnational Law of International Commercial Transactions*, ed.
N. Horn and C. Schmitthoff, 51-60. Deventer: Kluwer.
Ruggie, J. G. 1993. Territoriality and Beyond: Problematizing Modernity in International
Relations. *International Organization* 47 (1): 139-74.
Scheuerman, W. 1999. Economic Globalization and the Rule of Law. *Constellations: An
International Journal of Critical and Democratic Theory* 6 (1): 3-25.
———. 2000. Global Law in Our High Speed Economy. In *The Legal Culture of Global
Business Transactions*, ed. V. Gessner. Oxford: Hart.
Schmitthoff, C. 1961. International Business Law: A New Law Merchant. *Current Law and
Social Problems* 2: 129-53.
———. 1982. Nature and Evolution of the Transnational Law of Commercial Transactions.
In *The Transnational Law of International Commercial Transactions*, ed. N. Horn and
C. Schmitthoff, 19-31. Deventer: Kluwer.
Schneider, V. 1998. Global Economic Governance by Private Actors: The International
Chamber of Commerce. In *Organized Business and the New Global Order*, ed.
J. Geenwood and H. Jacek. London: Macmillan.
Sempasa, S. 1992. Obstacles to International Commercial Arbitration in African Countries.
International and Comparative Law Quarterly 41: 387-413.
Silbey, S. 1997. Let Them Eat Cake: Globalization, Postmodern Colonialism, and the

Possiblities of Justice. *Law and Society Review* 31 (2): 207-35.

Stoecker, C. 1990. The Lex Mercatoria: To What Extent Does It Exist? *Journal of International Arbitration*: 101-25.

Strange, S. 1996. *The Retreat of the State: The Diffusion of Power in the World Economy.* Cambridge: Cambridge University Press.

———. 1990. The Name of the Game. In *Sea Changes: American Foreign Policy in a World Transformed*, ed. N. X. Rizopoulos, 238-73. New York: Council on Foreign Relations.

Thompson, E. P. 1975. Whigs and Hunters: The Origin of the Black Act. New York: Pantheon.

Trakman, L. 1983. *The Law Merchant: The Evolution of Commercial Law.* Littleton, Colo.: Fred B. Rothman.

Twining, W. 1996. Globalization and Legal Theory: Some Local Implications. *Current Legal Problems* 49: 1-42.

United Nations Convention on Contracts for the International Sale of Goods (Vienna Sales Convention). 1980. UN Doc. A/Conf.97/18, Annex 1, reprinted in *International Legal Materials* 19: 668-95.

United Nations Convention on the Recognition and Enforcement of Foreign Arbitral Awards (New York Convention). 10 June 1958, UN Doc. A/Conf.9/22.

UNCITRAL Homepage. October 4, 2000. <http://www.UNCITRAL.org/en-index.html>.

Van der Pijl, K. 1998. *Transnational Classes and International Relations.* London: Routledge.

Walzer, M. 1984. Liberalism and the Art of Separation. *Political Theory* 12 (3): 315-30.

Williams, P. Forthcoming. Transnational Organized Crime, the State, and International Society. In *Private Authority and Global Governance*, ed. T. Bierksteker and R. Hall.

Wood, E. 1995. *Democracy against Capitalism: Renewing Historical Materialism.* Cambridge: Cambridge University Press.

Zacher, M. W., and B. Sutton. 1996. *Governing Global Networks: International Regimes for Transportation and Communications.* Cambridge: Cambridge University Press.

7

Non-State Actors and the Provision of Common Goods: Compliance with International Institutions

Tanja A. Börzel

Introduction

Are private actors on the rise, crowding out the states as the traditional stakeholders in world politics? There is a growing body of literature observing an increasing presence of multinational corporations, International Non-Governmental Organizations, epistemic communities, transnational advocacy coalitions, terrorist groups and other criminal organizations, transnational social movements, and corporate private regimes (Cutler in this volume). Some go as far as to argue that we are witnessing the emergence of a global (capitalist) civil society, which is overtaking the state-world as we have known it (Omahe 1990; Strange 1996; Amin 1997; Boli and Thomas 1999).

Yet, there is little evidence for the claim that nation-states are doomed to become, at best, side players in world politics. Transnational private actors have a role in global politics. But their influence varies significantly, both across time and issues. Moreover, the relationship between state and non-state actors is not necessarily zero-sum. The major challenge for theorizing about non-state actors in world politics, therefore, is not only to demonstrate that they matter, but to explain where, when, and how they matter. This chapter takes issue with these challenges by looking at the role of private actors in compliance with international institutions for the provision of common goods.

Compliance is crucial for the provision of common goods, as many collective action problems are in fact compliance problems. The prisoner's dilemma prohibits cooperation because actors are uncertain about whether others will not defect. For a rational actor, defection (noncompliance) becomes more rewarding than cooperation as the costs of being cheated are higher than the benefits obtained from cooperation (Ostrom and Holzinger in this volume). Many empirical studies point to the importance of non-state actors in bringing about compliance (Cook 1996; Korey 1998; Wapner 2000). But these explanations have rarely been turned into generalizable propositions. Nor have they been tested systematically against more state-centered explanations of compliance.

The first part of the chapter clarifies the concept of compliance applied in this study and the distinction made between public and private actors. The second part reviews prominent theories of compliance in the International Relations literature. I contrast systemic, state-centered theories with subsystemic, society-based approaches. The different approaches allow me to derive a series of hypotheses about the role of private actors in compliance with international institutions. The chapter concludes with some reflections on how the different hypotheses may relate to and interact with each other.

Compliance and the Distinction between Public and Private Actors

What Is Compliance?

The literature on compliance presents a wide variety of understandings and definitions of the concept. Moreover, the distinction between compliance and related concepts, such as implementation and effectiveness, is often not clear. For the sake of this study, compliance is defined as *rule-consistent behavior of those actors to whom a rule is formally addressed and whose behavior is targeted by the rule*.[1] While states are the addressees of most international norms and rules, and, hence, are formally responsible for compliance, they are not necessarily the main or exclusive targets. Many rules target the behavior of non-state actors, too.

The distinction between addressees and targets of a rule is important for defining the relative role of public and private actors in compliance. If states are only the addressees of a rule but not the main targets, the ultimate responsibility for compliance lies with private actors. Beyond formal incorporation into national law, the role of public actors is confined to effectively monitoring and enforcing international rule in order to ensure compliance. Unlike in cases where states are both addressees and targets of a rule, problems of "involuntary non-compliance" are more likely to arise.

Many studies explore the extent to which international norms and rules are complied with by their addressees, i.e., they focus on states only (Jacobsen and Brown Weiss 1995; Weiler 1988; Krislov, Ehlermann, and Weiler 1986). The distinction between addressees and targets of a rule helps to clarify the relationship between *compliance*, on one hand, and *implementation* with its three major elements, *output*, *outcome*, and *impact/effectiveness*, on the other hand. *Implementation* refers to putting policies or rules into practice.

Table 7.1. Public and Private Actors as Addressees and Targets of International Rules

Rule addressee Rule target	*Public Actors*	*Private Actors*
Public Actors	human rights security free trade	international criminal law
Private Actors	environment health and safety	political risk insurance commercial arbitration

Drawing on Easton's system theory approach, implementation studies often distinguish between three different stages of the implementation process:

- *output*: the legal and administrative measures required to achieve the policy goal (formal and practical implementation);
- *outcome*: the effect of the policy measures on the behavior of the target actors;
- *impact*: the effect of the policy on the socioeconomic environment (*effectiveness*).

This typology, however, is far from being consensual. Parts of the international regimes literature refer to *outcome* as *regime effectiveness*, although the equation is not complete because regime effectiveness is defined as rule-consistent behavior of states only, neglecting the behavior of private actors as potential targets of a regime (Rittberger 1995; Zürn 1997). Others, by contrast, measure *effectiveness* in terms of the *impact* of a regime or policy defined as the extent to which it makes a difference to its environment as compared to what would have occurred in the absence of the regime or policy (Levy, Young, and Zürn 1995; Nollkämper 1992). The distinction between *outcome* and *impact/effectiveness* seems justified if a change in the behavior of target actors is not assumed to necessarily solve the problem to which the regime or policy is addressed. *Effectiveness*, thereby, becomes an important measure for the *problem-solving capacity* of a regime or policy, which some scholars, however, refer to as *regime impact* (Rittberger 1995; Müller 1993).

Given the definition of compliance as rule-consistent behavior of both the addressees and the targets of a rule, this study focuses on *output* and *outcome*, while impact, effectiveness, and problem-solving capacity are excluded. With respect to *output*, compliance with a rule requires that:

- the rule is completely and correctly incorporated into national legislation and/or conflicting national rules are amended or repealed (formal compliance);
- the administrative infrastructure and resources are provided to put the objectives of the rule into practice and to monitor the rule-consistent behavior of the target actors of the rule (practical compliance);
- the competent authorities encourage or compel rule-consistent behavior of the target actors by effective monitoring, positive and negative sanctions, and compulsory corrective measures (practical compliance, monitoring and enforcement).

Concerning *outcome*, compliance with a rule presupposes that:

- the target actors take the necessary action to make their behavior consistent with the requirements of the rule;
- the target actors refrain from action violating the rule.[2]

The definition of compliance as "output + outcome" entails a procedural understanding, which contrasts with a conceptualization of compliance as a binary category. The simple dichotomy of compliance versus noncompliance is usually too static to measure a dependent variable, which consists of multiple dimensions. Rule-consistent behavior is the ultimate measure for compliance. But it is often the result of a process of interpretation, contestation, and negotiation, of cooperation and conflict, whose main purpose is to reconcile divergent interests, interpretations, and problem perceptions (Chayes and Chayes Handler 1995; Snyder 1993; Mayntz 1983). On one hand, states often seek more time for implementation because of strong domestic opposition or the lack of necessary resources, or both. Noncompliance may be also justified by "recalcitrant" subnational authorities if they bear the main responsibility for implementation or by political changes, such as a change in government. In such cases of "involuntary noncompliance," where states are willing to comply but lack the necessary economic, administrative, or political capacity, the issue of noncompliance as such is not contested. On the other hand, member states often object that their (refraining from) action constitutes an issue of noncompliance. They argue, for instance, that the rule is not applicable to the issue under consideration or they claim that the issue qualifies as one of the exceptions permitted by the rule. In order to understand and explain the mechanisms through which compliance evolves, one has to study the whole process rather than merely focusing on the outcome of it. Ambiguous and imprecise rules are particularly prone to become subject of contesting interpretations.

Public and Private Actors

The distinction between public and private actors departs from state-centric approaches to compliance, which have been dominant in the field of International Relations (see below). In order to explore the role of private actors in compliance with international rule, the state cannot be treated as a unitary actor but has to be unpacked. Public (state) actors (policy-makers, bureaucracies) are distinguished from private (non-state) actors, who do not operate on behalf of a state or an international organization. Within private actors, we can differentiate between *for-profit, economic actors* (e.g., corporations, interest groups) and *non-profit, societal actors* (e.g., voluntary organizations, social movements, advocacy coalitions). Economic actors aim foremost to produce financial wealth and are driven by the goal of maximizing profit. They are less concerned with solving common problems or advancing a particular political agenda. Societal actors, by contrast, are usually devoted to addressing public issues. Needless to say, these public issues are not necessarily "progressive" or in the general interest of the public good. The organization of Aryan Nations, which strives to generate solidarity across borders among white people of European descent, is only one example of an International Non-Governmental Organizations (INGO) pursuing a "public bad" (racism) rather than a "public good" (Ridgeway 1995).

Explaining Compliance with International Institutions

Organizing the Field

Admittedly, traditional International Relations (IR) theories are a poor basis for exploring the role of private actors in compliance because of their state-centric perspective. But they serve as the null hypotheses against which more complex, society-centered approaches shall be examined. Moreover, liberalism as one of the major IR paradigms as well as constructivist approaches, which, by now, have firmly established themselves in the field, provide ample room for developing private-actor based explanations of compliance. There is a comprehensive body of implementation research from the 1970s and 1980s, whose findings are broadly reflected in the IR literature (Pressman and Wildavsky 1984; Ingram and Schneider 1990; Sabatier 1986). But unlike those carrying out implementation studies in the field of public policy, IR scholars have not given up on developing generalizable claims about compliance, in spite, or maybe because of, the complexity of the issue.

For the research on compliance, it is useful to distinguish IR theories according to their level of analysis and the logic of action to which they subscribe: level of analysis—*systemic* versus *subsystemic* versus *integrative* theories; logic of action—*rationalist* versus *constructivist* versus *integrative* theories.

Figure 7.1. **International Relations Theories and the Role of Private Actors**

Systemic State-centered	Neorealism		
	Neoliberal Institutionalism	Statist Constructivism English School of Realism	
Do private actors matter? *Privileged actors*	Two-level games	Transnational Relations	Sociological Institutionalism
Subsystemic Society-centered	Liberalism	Domestic Structures	Society-centered Constructivism

rationalist	constructivist
logic of consequentialism	logic of appropriateness

How do private actors matter?
Dominant compliance mechanism

The level of analysis makes it possible to differentiate between theories according to the relative role that they attribute to public and private actors in compliance (do private actors matter). The logic of action that actors follow refers to differences between theories with respect to the way in which they see private actors influence compliance (how do private actors matter). The relationship between the two dimensions is orthogonal. Rationalist and constructivist approaches can be either systemic or subsystemic. The various combinations of the two dimensions generate different compliance mechanisms privileging different types of actors.

Systemic versus Subsystemic Approaches

The level of analysis refers to the location of the causes of state behavior by classifying competing explanations according to the units in which they are conceptualized (Singer 1960; 1961).

Systemic theories focus on the international level for explaining state behavior. The structure of the international system—the distribution of power, economic dependencies, international institutions—define both the interests of states and their capacity to pursue these interests. Neorealist theories emphasize the distribution of material capabilities in the international system as well as its anarchic nature. In the absence of a central power able to enforce state commitments, states face the constant threat of being conquered, occupied, or made subservient. As a result, states are most concerned about maximizing the chances of their survival by increasing their political and economic power vis-à-vis their rivals (Waltz 1979; Grieco 1988). Neoliberal Institutionalist approaches share the neorealist assumption about the anarchic structure of the international system and the emphasis on the distribution of material capabilities among states. Yet, they stress that the structure of the international system does not merely give rise to competing interests among states. Due to relations of interdependence, states develop mutual interests, e.g., in liberalizing trade or protecting the environment (Keohane 1984; Oye 1986). Statist constructivists, like Alex Wendt (Wendt 1992; 1999), as well as the English School of Realism (Wight 1966; Bull 1977), finally, do not limit international structures to material and economic features but stress that socially constructed norms and rules, and shared beliefs, also shape and motivate states.

Despite considerable differences, systemic approaches share some basic assumptions. The causes of state behavior are external, that is, located in the international system. States are treated as if there were unitary actors. For their predominantly state-centric perspective,[3] systemic approaches do not attribute any significant role to (trans)national private actors in international politics, either in the formulation or the implementation of international rules. Therefore, they will provide the null-hypotheses for this study.

Subsystemic theories open the black box of the state. They focus on the political institutions, the society, and the culture of individual states to explain state behavior in world politics. Andy Moravcsik aptly summarized the major difference between systemic and subsystemic approaches: "State behavior does not respond to the international system—it constitutes it" (Moravcsik 1993, 5). There are two major strands of subsystemic theories.

First, actor-centered approaches focus on the pressure from domestic social groups through legislatures, interest groups, elections, and public opinions in explaining state behavior. Liberal pluralist theories conceive of states as political systems for the authoritative allocation of values in a given society (Easton 1965). Public actors are constrained by societal pressures which evolve from the political process in which societal interests compete. Political decisions are analyzed predominantly in terms of the preferences and strength of private actors (Dahl 1961). Rationalist liberal theories in International Relations derive state preferences from demands by domestic actors, who strive to maximize their material and immaterial welfare (Moravcsik 1997; Milner 1988). Constructivist liberal approaches, by contrast, point to the importance of collectively shared values, beliefs, and identities of societal actors which shape state interests and identities (Risse-Kappen 1995b; Katzenstein 1996).

Second, more institution-centered subsystemic theories concentrate on the institutions of representation, education, and administration that link state and society. They emphasize the different degrees of state strength and autonomy vis-à-vis society. Such domestic structure approaches mainly developed in the field of comparative foreign economic policy in order to explain variations in state responses to similar challenges in the international system (Katzenstein 1976; 1985; Gourevitch 1986). The notion of domestic structures refers to "the political institutions of the state, to societal structures, and to the policy networks linking the two" (Risse-Kappen 1995a, 20). The central argument is that the political influence of private and public actors depends on the domestic structures of a particular state that mediate, filter, and refract their interests.

Subsystemic approaches privilege private actors in explaining state behavior. State preferences are ultimately derived from domestic interests, even if they may be mediated by domestic structures. Therefore, they provide the starting point for private-actor based explanations of compliance.

There has been a lively debate in the field of IR about which theories, systemic or subsystemic, are superior in analyzing state behavior in international politics (Keohane 1990, 192; Waltz 1979; 1986; Moravcsik 1993, 14-15). Out of this debate, a third perspective emerged that maintains that the growing presence of non-state actors in world politics increasingly blurs the distinction between the international and the domestic sphere and, therefore, requires an integrative approach, which systematically combines system-level and subsystem level explanations of state behavior (Moravcsik 1993; Risse-Kappen 1995a; but see already Deutsch et al. 1957).

Integrative theories can be divided into two major "camps." International bargaining theories conceptualize international negotiations as a two-level game (Putnam 1988; Evans, Jacobson, and Putnam 1993; Moravcsik 1993). Two-level game approaches explain state behavior as the interplay of powerful socioeconomic interests at the domestic level and the bargaining constraints at the international level. The chiefs of government form the crucial link between the two levels. Transnational relations criticize two-level game approaches for ignoring transnational, transgovernmental, and cross-level activities which undercut the gatekeeping position of governments between the domestic and international level. Transnational and transgovernmental alliances are said to limit both the autonomy and the strategy options of state actors in international negotiations (Knopf 1993; Risse-Kappen 1995a; Keck and Sikkink 1998; Risse, Ropp, and Sikkink 1999).

While private actors still feature prominently, integrative theories put private and public actors on a more equal footing. Two-level game approaches assume that state interests cannot be entirely reduced to societal demands. The balancing of international and domestic concerns in a process of "double-edged diplomacy" (Evans, Jacobson, and Putnam 1993) allows state executives to increase their autonomy vis-à-vis their domestic constituencies in pursuing their own interests. Transnational actors undermine the autonomy of national governments in international politics by forming coalitions across national boundaries. But state actors remain one of the major targets of transnational activities.

Table 7.2. Level of Analysis and Privileged Actors

Level of Analysis	*Privileged Actors*
Systemic Theories	State actors
Subsystemic Theories	National private actors
Integrative Theories	(Trans)national private actors and state actors

Rationalist versus Constructivist Approaches

International Relations Theories are embedded in different meta-theories of social action, which lead to different, and sometimes competing, assumptions about (state) behavior, particularly with respect to the role of institutions. James March and Johan Olsen introduced the distinction between two fundamental modes of social action, the logic of consequentialism and the logic of appropriateness (March and Olsen 1989; 1998). The former is the realm of *rational choice approaches* that treat the interests and preferences of actors as mostly fixed during the process of interaction. Rational choice focuses on strategic interaction, in which actors engage to maximize their utilities on the basis of given and fixed preferences. They follow a logic of instrumental rationality by weighing the costs and benefits of different strategy options, taking into account the (anticipated) behavior of other actors.

Constructivist or social structure approaches in IR emphasize the logic of appropriateness as the mode of social action. "Human actors are imagined to follow rules that associate particular identities to particular situations, approaching individual opportunities for action by assessing similarities between current identities and choice dilemmas and more general concepts of self and situations" (March and Olsen 1998, 951). Rule-guided behavior differs from instrumentally rational behavior in that actors try "to do the right thing." Rather than maximizing their given interests, actors strive to figure out what would be the appropriate behavior in a given situation. Stressing the constitutive effect of social norms and institutions, constructivist approaches distance themselves from rationalist approaches by rejecting methodological individualism, which treats actors, their capabilities and preferences as given and derives the social structure from their interaction. The ontological priority of agent over structure is replaced by the assumption that agency and structure are mutually constitutive. Social structures do not only regulate behavior, but they also define the social identities and interests of actors. While individuals do not exist outside social structures, they constantly create, reproduce, and change them.

These rather abstract assumptions about human behavior and the effect of norms and institutions have significant repercussions for the dominant mechanisms through which compliance with international rules is brought about as well as the ways in which private actors can effect compliance with international rules.

The rationalist logic of consequentialism points to the *redistribution of resources* as the dominant compliance mechanism. International institutions empower actors who favor compliance vis-à-vis those who oppose it. States, international organizations, or (trans)national actors obtain resources (e.g., sanctioning power, expertise, money, allies) through which they can constrain the strategy choices of other actors by rendering noncompliance more costly. Consequently, *social mobilization and pressure* are the major ways by which non-state actors influence compliance. Domestic actors, often in transnational alliances with international non-governmental organizations, exploit international norms and organizations to generate pressure for compliance on public actors. International institutions offer an authoritative venue for private actors to challenge state behavior. They provide new political opportunities to private actors, "encouraging their connections with others like themselves and offering resources that can be used in intra-national and transnational conflict" (Tarrow forthcoming; cf. Haas 1989; Klotz 1995b; Keck and Sikkink 1998). By exploiting these political opportunities, private actors mobilizing for compliance become empowered vis-à-vis public actors (and private actors opposing compliance). Through pressure "from below and from above" (Brysk 1993), private actors change the cost-benefit calculations of public actors in favor of compliance, essentially by increasing the costs of noncompliance (cf. Börzel 2000).

The constructivist logic of appropriateness specifies an alternative compliance mechanism, which relies on *socialization* and *habitualization* (Mayntz in this volume). Through processes of social learning and persuasion, actors internalize new norms and rules of appropriate behavior and redefine their interests and identities accordingly. *Social learning* and *persuasion* are the major ways by which private actors influence compliance. Private actors do not so much constrain public actors' choices by making noncompliance more costly. Rather than merely pressuring actors into compliance, private actors strive to persuade public and private actors, who oppose compliance, to change their interests (Finnemore 1996; Risse, Ropp, and Sikkink 1999). They attempt to engage opponents of compliance in a (public) discourse on why compliance with a particular norm constitutes appropriate behavior. The appeal to collectively shared norms and identities plays a crucial role in such processes of persuasion. For states, for instance, which perceive themselves as modern and liberal, violations of human rights can be framed as seriously contradicting their identity. The same is true for noncompliance with environmental regimes by states that pride themselves as progressive environmental leaders. Reputational mechanisms ("naming and shaming") may play a crucial role in inducing the behavioral changes necessary for compliance (Héritier in this volume). By engaging addressees and targets in processes of social learning and persuasion, private actors aim at the internalization of an international rule so that it is eventually "taken for granted" (Risse and Sikkink 1999, 5-6).

Integrative approaches do not privilege one compliance mechanism with its respective way of private actors' influence over the other. Differential empowerment and socialization capture and explain different, yet equally important elements of the compliance process (Checkel 1999; Finnemore and Sikkink 1998). Not only can differential empowerment be as effective as socialization in bringing about compliance with international rules. Social mobilization plays a crucial role in promoting socialization processes. Yet, there is still little research that systematically explores the relationship between the two logics of social action.

Table 7.3.   Logic of Actions, Private Actor Influence, and Dominant Compliance Mechanisms

Logic of Action	Dominant Compliance Mechanisms	Source of Private Actor Influence
Rationalist (consequentialism)	Redistribution of resources; Differential empowerment	Pressure, social mobilization
Constructivist (appropriateness)	Socialization and habitualization	Persuasion, social learning
Integrative (consequentialism/appropriate-ness)	Redistribution of resources and socialization	Pressure and persuasion

Formulating Hypotheses

The previous section distinguished major theories in International Relations in accord with the actors they privilege (level of analysis), on one hand, and the dominant compliance mechanism they identify, on the other hand (logic of action). The role of private actors in compliance with international rules varies along these two dimensions. The different combinations of the two dimensions make it possible to formulate a series of hypotheses about whether and how private actors matter in the compliance with international rules.

Table 7.4. Dominant Compliance Mechanisms and Privileged Actors

Dominant Compliance Mechanism Privileged Actors	Redistribution of Resources	Socialization
State actors	Neorealism Neoliberal Institutionalism Managed Compliance ⟹	 Statist Constructivism
Domestic private actors	Liberalism Domestic Structures ⟹ ⇩	Society-centered Constructivism Sociological
State actors and domestic private actors	Two-Level Games	Institutionalism
Transnational actors	Transnational Liberalism	Transnational ⟸ Constructivism

Misfit as the Precondition for Noncompliance

While IR approaches differ in regard to the compliance mechanism and the actors they privilege, they share one major assumption, which provides the starting point for this study: only "inconvenient" rules, that is, rules which impose significant compliance costs (material and immaterial), give rise to compliance problems. Irrespective of the theoretical approach they adhere to, most scholars agree that international norms and rules are most likely to be implemented and observed if they fit, i.e., if they are compatible with the domestic context, such as regulatory standards, political and administrative institutions, problem-solving approaches, and collectively shared identities (Börzel 2000; Duina 1999; Risse and Ropp 1999, 271; Keck and Sikkink 1998).

Hypothesis 1:
State compliance with international rules is less likely, the less the international rules fit corresponding domestic rules.

Compliance through State Power and Coercion

Power-based approaches, such as Neorealism, assume that states do not comply with international rules if high costs of compliance are involved. In the absence of a central enforcement power, retaliation and rewards by a hegemon are the sole means to deter noncompliance with "inconvenient" rules (Downs, Rocke, and Barsoom, 1996; Fearon 1998; O'Connell 1992). Hegemonic states change the cost-benefit calculations of less powerful states by increasing the costs of noncompliance (stick) and lowering the costs of compliance (carrot), respectively.

Hypothesis 2:
State compliance with inconvenient international rules is more likely, the more a hegemonic state provides positive and negative incentives for compliance.

Compliance through International Institutions

Neoliberal institutionalism and functionalist regime theory argue that institutions can prevent noncompliance. Free riding, i.e., reaping the benefits of an international agreement without complying, only pays as long as (most of the) other states do comply. Otherwise, the agreement breaks down, which is to the detriment of all participants. International institutions provide a solution to this social dilemma. Effective monitoring and sanctioning mechanisms can deter free riding by increasing the likelihood of getting caught and being punished (Stein 1983; Snidal 1985; Keohane 1984; Ostrom 1990; Abbott et al. 2001).

Hypothesis 3:
State compliance with inconvenient international rules is more likely, the more elaborated the monitoring mechanisms and the more autonomous the international institutions are in settling disputes and imposing sanctions.

Compliance through a Low Number of Veto Players

As Liberalism derives state preferences from domestic interests, pressure from domestic actors with intense distributional concerns explains whether states are likely to comply with international rules. Inconvenient international rules conflict with state interests because they impose significant compliance costs on powerful domestic actors. Those actors are likely to mobilize and pressure state actors to refrain from initiating the institutional and policy changes necessary for compliance. The number of domestic veto players (regions, parties, interest groups, courts) is, hence, crucial for the capacity of states to change the status quo in order to achieve compliance with misfitting international rules (Tsebelis 1995; cf. Alesina and Rosenthal 1995; and Knill and Lehmkuhl in this volume).

Hypothesis 4:
State compliance with inconvenient international rules is more likely, the lower the number of veto players at the domestic level.

Compliance through Double-Edged Diplomacy

The ratification of international agreements theoretically links the international and the domestic level in two-level games. The domestic constituents decide whether to ratify and implement the tentative international agreement bargained by their governments in the first stage of the negotiation process. Problems of involuntary defection may arise when domestic actors override or subvert an international agreement against the opposition of their government. Thus, the size of the win-set, defined by the number of agreements that are likely to be ratified at the domestic level, is crucial for compliance. The size of the win-set depends on three factors: (1) the domestic interests (heterogeneous vs. homogeneous; (2) the political institutions (veto points, autonomy of government); and (3) the strategies of the chief of government (Putnam 1988; cf. Moravcsik 1993; Evans 1993).

Hypothesis 5:
State compliance with inconvenient international rules is more likely, the larger the domestic win-set (the more homogeneous domestic interests, the fewer veto points, the more autonomous the chief of government, and the less the chief of government manipulates the domestic win-set).

Compliance through Pressure from Above and Below

Transnational actors (TNAs) influence state compliance with international rules by mobilizing pressure on states from "above," through coalitions with international organizations (monitoring, verification), and from "below," through coalitions with domestic actors. Domestic private actors are not only empowered through information, expertise, moral support, and financial assistance provided by TNAs. TNAs offer them a possibility to circumvent their governments and mobilize support at the international level (Keck and Sikkink 1998; Risse, Ropp, and Sikkink 1999; Brysk 1993; Klotz 1995a).

Hypothesis 6:
State compliance with inconvenient international rules is more likely, the more pressure through mobilization is exerted by pro-compliance transnational networks from "above" and from "below."

Compliance through State Socialization

Statist constructivism focuses on collectively shared norms, values, and beliefs, which shape state interests and identities. Compliance, then, depends on the successful internalization of international norms and rules up to the point that states take them for granted. Some authors argue that state compliance with international norms becomes "contagious" after a critical mass of states (norm leaders) adopt the norms. A "norm cascade" sets in, driven by a process of socialization, through which norm leaders persuade other states to adhere. Giving in to peer pressure, other states comply to demonstrate that they conform with the group of states to which they want to belong and whose esteem they care about. The "compliance pull" (Franck 1990) or norm cascade is reinforced if the international institution promoting the norm or rule enjoys high legitimacy (Finnemore and Sikkink 1998, 901-905).

Hypothesis 7:
State compliance with inconvenient international rules is more likely, the more states adhere to them and the higher the legitimacy of the international institutions supporting the rules is, and the more the rules are considered part of a general legal system.

Compliance through Social Learning and Legitimacy

For society-centered constructivism, domestic rather than state actors have to internalize international norms and rules to achieve compliance. Through processes of social learning and persuasion, domestic actors internalize new norms and change their beliefs, interests, and behavior accordingly. To foster learning and persuasion, many authors emphasize the importance of dense interaction facilitated by nonhierarchical (informal) relations (Risse 2000, 19; Börzel 1998, 264). At the same time, legal scholars and political scientists argue that *deliberative* processes that involve all relevant interests, i.e., the rule addressees and rule targets in rule-making and rule implementation, significantly increase the legitimacy of the rule-motivating, voluntary compliance (Franck 1990; 1995; Joerges and Neyer 1997; Héritier in this volume). Actors do not comply because of fear or self-interest but because they accept a rule on the grounds of its normative rightfulness. Next to procedural fairness and justice (Tyler 1997), legitimacy can also result from a process of deliberation, rational discourse, or arguing, in which actors justify their claims and challenge those of other actors by appealing to collectively shared norms and values rather than their power or economic interests (bargaining, cf. Risse 2000).

Hypothesis 8:
State compliance with inconvenient international rules is more likely, the more the addressees and the target actors of the rules participate in their formulation, adoption, and implementation, the more rule-making is based on arguing and deliberation (legitimacy), and the denser the interaction between the actors involved (learning).

Compliance through Institutional Isomorphism

Sociological Institutionalism treats the global social structure formed by coherent and all-encompassing norms and values (world culture) as the major determinant of state interests and state identities. Like the norm cascade in state constructivism, cultural isomorphism predicts a compliance pull of international norms and values, where it becomes increasingly inappropriate for states and their societies not to adhere. Yet, norm internalization by national societies is not automatic. The institutionalization of international norms is not equated with rule-consistent behavior in terms of a habitualization and taken-for-grantedness by domestic actors. Institutional decoupling, where individual behavior does not conform to institutional norms and rules in which actors are embedded, can deflect the logics of cultural isomorphism (Meyer and Rowan 1991). Institutional decoupling, thereby, points to a major problem in ensuring compliance with international rules. Output (formal and practical implementation) does not automatically lead to the desired outcome (change in behavior of target actors). Unfortunately, sociological institutionalism does not specify conditions under which institutional decoupling is likely to occur nor when and how it is overcome. Beside the important insight about the problem of institutional decoupling, sociological institutionalism gives rise to a hypothesis similar to that of statist constructivism:

Hypothesis 9:
State compliance with inconvenient international rules is more likely, the higher their degree of international institutionalization (giving rise to institutional isomorphism).

Compliance through Transnational Mobilization and Persuasion

Transnational constructivism combines the constructivist compliance mechanism of socialization with the rationalist mechanism of differential empowerment. Transnational pressure can be instrumental in ensuring the adoption and institutionalization of international rules (output). Sustainable behavioral changes (outcome), however, require the full internalization of an international rule with actors redefining their interests rather than their strategies only. Transnational norm entrepreneurs do not exclusively rely on pressure; they also use socialization mechanisms to achieve their goals. They engage norm violators and opponents of compliance in a (public) discourse, challenging the appropriateness of their norm-violating behavior by appealing to collectively shared norms and identities.

Hypothesis 10:
State compliance with inconvenient international rules is more likely, the more transnational networks manage to engage norm violators in a reasoned discourse about the (in)appropriateness of their behavior.

Domestic Structures: Compliance through Domestic Mobilization

Domestic Structure approaches emphasize that the political influence of private actors depends on the domestic structures of a state. The less access private actors have to the political system, the higher the autonomy of the state vis-à-vis its society (Katzenstein 1978; Kitschelt 1986). But easier access for private actors does not necessarily mean more influence, because the coalition-building requirements for reaching a certain policy outcome increase. The easier the political access, the higher the requirements for winning coalitions, and vice versa (Risse-Kappen 1995a). Moreover, the political culture of a state significantly influences the requirements for coalition building. In a strongly decentralized political system, the formation of a winning coalition may be facilitated by a cooperative political culture, which favors consensus over majority decisions (Katzenstein 1984).

Hypothesis 11:
State compliance with inconvenient international rules is more likely, the more domestic actors favoring compliance have access to the implementation process and are able to form winning coalitions to change

the status quo. This will be the likely, the more open the political system is and the more cooperative its political culture.

Compliance through Capacity Building

Management approaches conceive of noncompliance mostly as a problem of "involuntary defection." States do not so much lack the willingness as the capacity, i.e., the necessary resources to comply (technology, expertise, administrative manpower, financial means, etc.). Capacity building (financial and technical assistance), rather than sanctioning, becomes the primary means to ensure compliance with international rules (Keohane, Haas, and Levy 1993; Mitchell 1996; Underdal 1998; Jänicke 1990).

Hypothesis 12:
State compliance with inconvenient international rules is more likely, the more resources a state has, and the more resources it receives from the outside to ensure compliance, respectively.

The twelve hypotheses about state compliance do not claim to be encompassing. Nor do they always provide competing explanations. Some of the hypotheses complement rather than supplement each other, as they share core assumptions. The concluding section will reflect on how the various hypotheses may relate to each other.

Conclusion

This chapter has theoretically explored the role of private actors in compliance with international rules. Taking "misfit" as a precondition of noncompliance, it derived eleven hypotheses about state compliance with inconvenient international rules, which specify different causal mechanisms through which state actors, international institutions, and private actors make an impact on compliance. These causal mechanisms are neither complete, nor are they necessarily mutually exclusive. Rather, they make it possible to identify and analytically separate causal factors that may be relevant to explaining state compliance and the respective role of private actors.

How the various explanations may interact with and relate to each other is ultimately an empirical rather than theoretical question. Yet, we can deductively derive some preliminary propositions. Causal explanations are either competing or complementary. Competing hypotheses draw on the same explanatory factors, but predict opposing outcomes because their underlying theories emphasize different causal processes. The state power hypothesis, for instance, assumes that the less power resources a state has, the more compliant it will be. A powerful state, like the United States of America, can hardly be forced to comply with international rules. Small states, by contrast, are much more vulnerable to sanctions by the international community or a hegemon. Drawing on the same explanatory factors (capabilities), the capacity hypothesis comes to a diametrically opposed conclusion from that reached by the power hypothesis—here, a sufficient number of resources is the precondition for compliance. Poor countries often simply lack the financial, administrative, and technological capacity to comply with international rules. Both the state power and the capacity hypotheses grant private actors no influence on promoting or impairing compliance. Another set of hypotheses are more sensitive to the role of private actors, but they disagree on the direction of their impact. The veto player hypothesis predicts that the likelihood of compliance decreases if there are a high number of domestic actors, public and private, involved in the implementation process. Ratification of international agreements is less difficult in a parliamentary system, like Great Britain, where the government enjoys a majority in Parliament, than in a presidential system, like the United States, where the president cannot automatically count on the support of Congress. The double-edged diplomacy hypothesis, on the contrary, contends that a high number of veto players may be conducive to compliance because it helps to prevent misfit, the major cause of noncompliance. The mobilization of private actors reduces a government's scope of negotiation and thus increases its bargaining power needed to reach a favorable agreement. The United States will hardly be expected to sign an international agreement whose ratification is likely to fail in the U.S. Senate and/or to face serious opposition from powerful interest groups. The legitimacy hypothesis, finally, suggests that the inclusion of potential veto players increases the chance of compliance, not because it reduces the size of the win-set, but because it increases the acceptance of international rules by those involved in their implementation. This is particularly true for the rule targets, which are in most cases private actors.

Hypotheses are also competing, if their causal explanations mutually exclude each other. If the coercive power of a hegemonic state is the only way to ensure compliance, international institutions, transnational actors, or domestic interests have no role to play. While liberal approaches would argue that the Serbian ex-president Milosevic was finally ousted by domestic protest movements, power-based theories would always claim that the influence of societal mobilization was epiphenomenal and that it was NATO, under the leadership of the United States, which bombed Milosevic out of power. Likewise, if the internalization of international norms and rules is the prerequisite for sustained compliance, it was the work of transnational advocacy coalitions acting as norm entrepreneurs that brought down the apartheid regime of South Africa rather than international sanctions.

Most hypotheses, however, appear to complement rather than exclude each other. Their explanatory factors point towards the same outcome but emphasize different processes. Transnational approaches agree that private actors are crucial for achieving compliance with inconvenient international norms and rules. Often they induce rule-consistent behavior by mobilizing domestic interests and international pressure *and* by inducing learning and socialization processes. Human rights networks do not merely mobilize national and international protest against oppressive regimes. Often, they strive to engage representatives of the regime in a public discourse on the appropriateness of human rights violations. Transnational constructivism explicitly combines the different causal processes specified by the transnational mobilization, socialization, learning, and persuasion hypotheses. The interaction of different causal factors is another form of complementarity. Causal factors frequently reinforce each other. Thus, capacity building through the transfer of resources can increase the legitimacy of international institutions. EU financial assistance has fostered the willingness of lowly regulated member states, such as Greece, Portugal, or Spain, to comply with rather demanding EU environmental standards, which impose significant compliance costs and do not always address the most pressing environmental problems in these countries. Likewise, international sanctions are most effective if complemented by domestic pressure "from below." Human rights networks have effectively used international sanctions to shame their oppressive governments and challenge their legitimacy. At the same time, domestic actors and transnational coalitions serve as "watchdogs" of compliance with international norms. More than half of the European infringement proceedings against member states are initiated by complaints of citizens, companies, and public interest groups. Finally, causal factors can undermine each other's effects. If states are willing to comply but lack the necessary capacities, sanctions, such as financial penalties, may reinforce rather than alleviate the problem. Rewarding voluntary defection by providing financial assistance, by contrast, could create further incentives for noncompliance. Severe sanctions can also undermine the legitimacy of international norms and hamper the capacity of private actors to invoke the normative power of international institutions to persuade other actors into compliance.

In sum, private actors may have a crucial impact on compliance with international institutions for the provision of common goods. But their influence is often reinforced or deflected by other causal factors. Consequently, it may be more fruitful to explore the mutual relationship between the various hypotheses than to pitch them against each other. The question is not so much whether private actors matter for compliance, but when and how they matter. What is needed, therefore, is empirical research that systematically tests the explanatory powers of the various hypotheses and finds out to what extent they compete with or complement each other.

Notes

For comments on earlier versions of this chapter I am thankful to Christoph Engel, Adrienne Héritier, Katharina Holzinger, Christian Joerges, Markus Lehmann, Dirk Lehmkuhl, Leonor Moral, Stefan Oeter, Thomas Risse, Anne-Marie Slaughter, Jens Steffek, Cornelia Ulbert, Jacques Ziller, Michael Zürn, and the anonymous reviewers.

1. Actors targeted by a rule are not identical with actors affected by a rule. Unlike affected actors, a rule directly requires targeted actors to change their behavior.

178 Tanja A. Börzel

Consumers are affected by foodstuff regulations, but it is the food industry which has to change its production behavior.

2. Note that outcome is not measured in terms of effectiveness. The extent to which, for instance, industry complies with air pollution regulations is not measured by an improvement of the air quality in a given region (which could also be caused by external factors) but by whether the polluters have implemented measures to reduce air pollution as required by the regulation. Whether these measures actually help fight air pollution is an altogether different matter, which relates to questions of effectiveness rather than compliance.

3. This is not to argue that all systemic approaches are necessarily state-centered while all subsystemic approaches are society-centered. Strictly speaking, the two distinctions are orthogonal. Yet, with the exception of world systems theories and interdependence theories, systemic approaches are predominantly state-centered, particularly when it comes to explaining compliance. The same holds true for the society-centered focus of most subsystemic approaches, perhaps with the exception of bureaucratic politics (see below).

References

Abbott, K. W., R. O. Keohane, A. Moravcsik, A.-M. Slaughter, and D. Snidal. 2001. The Concept of Legalization. *International Organization* 55 (1): 121-47.

Alesina, A., and H. Rosenthal. 1995. *Partisan Politics: Divided Government, and the Economy.* Cambridge: Cambridge University Press.

Amin, S. 1997. *Capitalism in the Age of Globalization.* London: Zed Press.

Boli, J., and G. M. Thomas. 1999. *Constructing World Culture: International Nongovernmental Organizations since 1875.* Stanford, Calif.: Stanford University Press.

Börzel, T. A. 1998. Organizing Babylon: On the Different Conceptions of Policy Networks. *Public Administration* 76 (2): 253-73.

———. 2000. Why There Is No Southern Problem: On Environmental Leaders and Laggards in the European Union. *Journal of European Public Policy* 7 (1): 141-62.

Brysk, A. 1993. From Above and from Below: Social Movements, the International System, and Human Rights in Argentina. *Comparative Political Studies* 26 (3): 259-85.

Bull, H. 1977. *The Anarchical Society: A Study of Order in World Politics.* London: Macmillan.

Chayes, A., and A. C. Handler. 1995. *The New Sovereignty: Compliance with International Regulatory Agreements.* Cambridge, Mass.: Harvard University Press.

Checkel, J. T. 1999. Why Comply? Constructivism, Social Norms, and the Study of International Institutions. Working Paper. Oslo: Arena.

Cook, H. 1996. Amnesty International at the United Nations. In *The Conscience of the World: The Influence of Non-Governmental Organizations in the UN System,* ed. P. Willets, 181-213. London: Hurst & Company.

Dahl, R. 1961. *Who Governs: Democracy and Power in an American City.* New Haven, Conn.: Yale University Press.

Deutsch, K. W. et al. 1957. *Political Community and the North Atlantic Area: International Organization in the Light of Historical Experience.* Princeton, N.J.: Princeton University Press.

Downs, G. W., D. M. Rocke, and P. N. Barsoom. 1996. Is the Good News about Compliance Good News about Cooperation? *International Organization* 50 (3): 379-406.

Duina, F. G. 1999. *Harmonizing Europe: Nation-States within the Common Market.* New York: State University of New York Press.

Easton, D. 1965. *A Systems Analysis of Political Life.* New York: Wiley & Sons.

Evans, P. B. 1993. Building an Integrative Approach to International and Domestic Politics. In *Double-Edged Diplomacy: International Bargaining and Domestic Politics,* ed. P. B. Evans, H. K. Jacobsen, and R. D. Putnam, 397-430. Berkeley: University of California Press.

Evans, P. B., H. K. Jacobson, and R. D. Putnam, eds. 1993. *Double-Edged Diplomacy: International Bargaining and Domestic Politics.* Berkeley: University of California Press.

Fearon, J. 1998. Bargaining, Enforcement, and International Cooperation. *International Organization* 52 (2): 269-305.

Finnemore, M. 1996. *National Interests in International Society.* Ithaca, N.Y.: Cornell University Press.

Finnemore, M., and K. Sikkink. 1998. International Norm Dynamics and Political Change. *International Organization* 52 (4): 887-917.

Franck, T. M. 1990. *The Power of Legitimacy among Nations.* Oxford: Oxford University Press.

———. 1995. *Fairness in International Law and Institutions.* Oxford: Clarendon Press.

Gourevitch, P. A. 1986. *Politics in Hard Times: Comparative Responses to International Economic Crisis.* Ithaca, N.Y.: Cornell University Press.

Grieco, J. M. 1988. Anarchy and the Limits of Cooperation: A Realist Critique of the Newest Liberal Institutionalism. *International Organization* 42 (3): 485-507.

Haas, P. M. 1989. Do Regimes Matter? Epistemic Communities and Mediterranean Pollution Control. *International Organization* 43: 377-403.

Ingram, H., and A. Schneider. 1990. Improving Implementation through Framing Smarter Statutes. *Journal of Public Policy* 10 (1): 67-88.

Jacobsen, H. K., and E. Brown Weiss. 1995. Strengthening Compliance with International Environmental Accords: Preliminary Observations from a Collaborative Project. *Global Governance* 1 (2): 119-48.

Jänicke, M. 1990. Erfolgsbedingungen von Umweltpolitik im international Vergleich. *Zeitschrift für Umweltpolitik* 3: 213-32.

Joerges, C., and J. Neyer. 1997. From Intergovernmental Bargaining to Deliberative Political Processes: The Constitutionalization of Comitology. *European Law Journal* 3 (3): 273-99.

Katzenstein, P. J. 1976. International Relations and Domestic Structures: Foreign Economic Policies of Advanced Industrial States. *International Organization* 30 (1): 1-45.

———.ed. 1978. *Between Power and Plenty: Foreign Economic Policies of Advanced Industrial States.* Madison: Wisconsin University Press.

———. 1984. *Corporatism and Change: Austria, Switzerland, and the Politics of Industry.* Ithaca, N.Y.: Cornell University Press.

———. 1985 *Small States in World Markets: Industrial Policy in Europe.* Ithaca, N.Y.: Cornell University Press.

———. 1996. *Cultural Norms and National Security: Police and Military in Postwar Japan.* Ithaca, N.Y.: Cornell University Press.

Keck, M., and K. Sikkink. 1998. *Activists beyond Borders: Advocacy Networks in International Politics.* Ithaca, N.Y.: Cornell University Press.

Keohane, R. O. 1984. *After Hegemony: Cooperation and Discord in the World Political Economy.* Princeton, N.J.: Princeton University Press.

———. 1990. International Liberalism Reconsidered. In *The Economic Limits to Modern Politics,* ed. J. Dunn, 165-94. Cambridge: Cambridge University Press.

Keohane, R. O., P. M. Haas, and M. A. Levy. 1993. The Effectiveness of International Environmental Institutions. In *Institutions for the Earth: Sources of Effective International Environmental Protection,* ed. P. M. Haas, R. O. Keohane, and M. A. Levy, 3-26. Cambridge, Mass.: MIT Press.

Kitschelt, H. P. 1986. Political Opportunity Structures and Political Protest: Antinuclear Movements in Four Democracies. *British Journal of Political Science* 16: 57-85.

Klotz, A. 1995a. Norms Reconstituting Interests: Global Racial Equity and U.S. Sanctions against South Africa. *International Organization* 49: 451-78.

———. 1995b. *Norms in International Relations: The Struggle against Apartheid.* Ithaca, N.Y.: Cornell University Press.

Knopf, J. W. 1993. Beyond Two-Level Games: Domestic-International Interaction in the Intermediate-Range Nuclear Forces Negotiations. *International Organization* 47 (4): 599-628.

Korey, W. 1998. *NGOs and the Universal Declaration of Human Rights: "A Curious Grapevine."* New York: St. Martin's Press.

Krislov, S., C.-D. Ehlermann, and J. Weiler. 1986. The Political Organs and the Decision-Making Process in the United States and the European Community. In *Integration through Law, Methods, Tools, and Institutions: Political Organs, Integration Techniques, and Judicial Process,* ed. M. Cappelletti, M. Seccombe, and J. Weiler, 3-112. Berlin: de Gruyter.

Levy, M. A., O. R. Young, and M. Zürn. 1995. The Study of International Regimes. *European Journal of International Relations* 1 (3): 267-330.

March, J. G., and J. P. Olsen. 1989. *Rediscovering Institutions.* New York: Free Press.

———. 1998. The Institutional Dynamics of International Political Orders. *International Organization* 52 (4): 943-69.

Mayntz, R., ed. 1983. *Implementation politischer Programme II. Ansätze zur Theoriebildung.* Opladen: Westdeutscher Verlag.

Meyer, J. W., and B. Rowan. 1991. Institutional Organizations: Formal Structure as Myth and Ceremony. In *The New Institutionalism in Organizational Analysis,* ed. W. W. Powell and P. J. DiMaggio, 41-62. Chicago: University of Chicago Press.

Milner, H. V. 1988. *Resisting Protectionism: Global Industries and the Politics of International Trade.* Princeton, N.J.: Princeton University Press.

Mitchell, R. B. 1996. Compliance Theory: An Overview. In *Improving Compliance with International Environmental Law,* ed. J. Cameron, J. Werksman, and P. Roderick, 3-28. London: Earthscan.

Moravcsik, A. 1993. Introduction: Integrating International and Domestic Theories of International Bargaining. In *Double-Edged Diplomacy: International Bargaining and Domestic Politics,* ed. P. Evans et al., 3-42. Berkeley: University of California Press.

———. 1997. Taking Preferences Seriously: A Liberal Theory of International Politics. *International Organization* 51 (4): 513-53.

Müller, H. 1993. *Die Chance der Kooperation.* Darmstadt: Wissenschaftliche Buchgesellschaft.

Nollkämper, A. 1992. On the Effectiveness of International Rules. *Acta Politica* 27 (1): 49-70.

O'Connell, M. E. 1992. Enforcing the New International Law of the Environment. *German Yearbook of International Law* 35: 293-332.

Omahe, K. 1990. *The Borderless World: Power and Strategy in an Interlinked Economy.* New York: Harper.

Ostrom, E. 1990. *Governing the Commons: The Evolution of Institutions for Collective Action.* Cambridge: Cambridge University Press.

Oye, K., ed. 1986. *Cooperation under Anarchy.* Princeton, N.J.: Princeton University Press.

Pressman, J., and A. Wildavsky. 1984. *Implementation.* Berkeley: University of California Press.

Putnam, R. 1988. Diplomacy and Domestic Politics. The Logic of Two-Level Games. *International Organization* 42 (2): 427-60.

Ridgeway, J. 1995. *Blood in the Face: The Ku Klux Klan, Aryan Nations, Nazi Skinheads, and the Rise of a New White Culture.* New York: Thunder's Mouth Press.

Risse, T. 2000. Let's Argue: Communicative Action in International Relations. *International Organization* 54 (1): 1-39.

Risse, T., and S. C. Ropp. 1999. Conclusions. In *The Power of Human Rights: International Norms and Domestic Change,* ed. T. Risse, S. C. Ropp, and K. Sikkink, 234-78. Cambridge: Cambridge University Press.

Risse, T., S. C. Ropp, and K. Sikkink, eds. 1999. *The Power of Human Rights: International Norms and Domestic Change.* Cambridge: Cambridge University Press.

Risse, T., and K. Sikkink. 1999. The Socialization of International Human Rights Norms into Domestic Practices: Introduction. In *The Power of Human Rights: International Norms and Domestic Change,* ed. T. Risse, S. C. Ropp, and K. Sikkink, 1-38. Cambridge: Cambridge University Press.

Risse-Kappen, T. 1995a. Bringing Transnational Relations Back In: Introduction. In *Bringing Transnational Relations Back In: Non-State Actors, Domestic Structures, and International Institutions,* ed. T. Risse-Kappen, 3-33. Cambridge: Cambridge University Press.

———. 1995b. Democratic Peace—Warlike Democracies? A Social Constructivist Interpretation of the Liberal Argument. In special issue of *European Journal of International Relations,* ed. N. P. Gleditsch, and T. Risse-Kappen, 489-515.

Rittberger, V., ed. 1995. *Regime Theory and International Relations.* Oxford: Clarendon Press.

Sabatier, P. A. 1986. Top-down and Bottom-up Approaches to Implementation Research. *Journal of Public Policy* 6: 21-48.

Singer, D. J. 1960. International Conflict: Three Levels of Analysis. *World Politics* 12: 453-61.

———. 1961. The Level-of-Analysis Problem in International Relations. *World Politics* 14: 77-92.

Snidal, D. 1985. Coordination versus Prisoners' Dilemma: Implications for International Cooperation and Regimes. *American Political Science Review* 79 (4): 205-39.

Snyder, F. 1993. The Effectiveness of European Community Law: Institutions, Processes, Tools, and Techniques. *Modern Law Review* 56: 19-54.

Stein, A. A. 1983. Coordination and Collaboration: Regimes in an Anarchic World. In *International Regimes,* ed. S. D. Krasner, 115-40. Ithaca, N.Y.: Cornell University Press.

Strange, S. 1996. *The Retreat of the State: The Diffusion of Power in the World Economy.* Cambridge: Cambridge University Press.

Tarrow, S. Forthcoming. Beyond Globalization: Why Creating Transnational Social Movements Is So Hard and When Is It Most Likely to Happen? *Annual Review of Political Science.*

Tsebelis, G. 1995. Decision Making in Political Systems: Veto Players in Presidentialism, Parliamentarism, Multicameralism, and Multipartism. *British Journal of Political Science* 25 (3): 289-325.

Tyler, T. R. 1997. Procedural Fairness and Compliance with the Law. *Schweizerische Zeitschrift für Volkswirtschaft und Statistik* 133 (2/2): 219-40.

Underdal, A. 1998. Explaining Compliance and Defection: Three Models. *European Journal of International Relations* 4 (1): 5-30.

Waltz, K. 1979. *Theory of International Politics.* Reading, Mass.: Addison-Wesley.

————. 1986. Reflections on Theory of International Politics: A Response to My Critics. In *Neorealism and Its Critics,* ed. R. Keohane, 322-45. New York: Columbia University Press.

Wapner, P. 2000. The Transnational Politics of Environmental NGOs: Governmental, Economic, and Social Activism. In *The Global Environment in the Twenty-First Century: Prospects for International Cooperation,* ed. P. S. Chasek, 87-108. Tokyo: United Nations University.

Weiler, J. 1988. The White Paper and the Application of Community Law. In *1992: One European Market?* ed. R. Bieber, R. Dehousse, J. Pinder, and J. H. H. Weiler, 337-58. Baden-Baden: Nomos.

Wendt, A. 1992. Anarchy Is What States Make of It: The Social Construction of Power Politics. *International Organization* 88 (2): 384-96.

————. 1999. *Social Theory of International Politics.* Cambridge: Cambridge University Press.

Wight, M. 1966. Western Values in International Relations. In *Diplomatic Investigations,* ed. H. Butterfield and M. Wight, 89-131. London: Allen & Unwin.

Zürn, M. 1997. Positives Regieren "jenseits des Nationalstaates." *Zeitschrift für Internationale Beziehungen* 4 (1): 41-68.

Part 2

Common Goods and the Role of Private Actors

European Level

8

New Modes of Governance in Europe: Policy-Making without Legislating?

Adrienne Héritier

Introduction

Under conditions of problem interdependence across boundaries, collective action to provide common goods[1] has to take place vertically across multiple levels of government and horizontally across multiple arenas[2] involving public and private corporate actors. No single actor, public or private, has sufficient potential for action and/or sufficient power to solve problems of interdependence on her own, nor has she all the knowledge and information required to solve complex, dynamic, and diversified problems. Hence actors have to rely on each other (Kooiman 1993, 4). Problem interdependencies create incentives to cooperate: the very potential to mutually obstruct solutions promotes the willingness to come to agreements (van Vliet 1993, 110). Europe is such a multilevel and multi-arena polity, faced with complex problems of interdependence against a background of diverse social and economic conditions in which public and private actors with very diverse interests depend on each other to provide common goods. In short, it is faced with a need for governance across multiple arenas.

In the literature the concept of governance is used in two different ways: one broad, the other more restricted. In the encompassing sense it implies every mode of political steering involving public and private actors, including the traditional modes of government and different types of steering from hierarchical imposition to sheer information measures. In the restricted sense it only comprises types of political steering in which nonhierarchical modes of guidance, such as persuasion and negotiation, are employed, and/or public and private actors are engaged in policy formulation.

Private actors may be engaged in a variety of forms of policy formulation:[3] they may "regulate" themselves on a voluntary basis; a regulatory task may have been delegated to them by a public actor; or they may be engaged in "co-regulation," regulating jointly with public actors (see also Knill and Lehmkuhl in this volume). The focus of this analysis is on new modes of governance and government in the European Union that (1) include private actors in policy formulation, and/or (2) while being based on public actors, (3) are only marginally based on legislation (these are hierarchical insofar as they are subject to a majority decision) or that are not based on legislation at all. In recent years non-legislative modes of policy-making and modes of governance including private actors in policy formulation have gained in salience in European policy-making, and they have been advocated as a panacea for speeding up European decision-making, which has so often ended up in a gridlock (Héritier 1999). The European integration project has reached a stage where core areas of the welfare state such as employment policy, social policy, and education are directly affected. These are areas where member state political support is very difficult to gain (Jacobsson 2001). Hence a method of cooperation has been developed to avoid the classical form of legislation through directives and regulations; instead, it relies on the open method of coordination, that is, target development and published scoreboards of national performance, as measured by the policy objectives that have been agreed upon, as well as voluntary accords, that is, the self-regulation of private actors. Many statements praising the new modes of governance have come out of the Commission. To quote just two examples here: the sixth Environmental Action Program promises that "voluntary initiatives will certainly have a key role to play" in European environmental policy in the coming years (DG XI official, *European Voice*, 11-17 January 2001). Additionally, employment and social policy Commissioner Diamantopoulos now calls legislation an "outdated" form of policy-making and points to the need for voluntary agreements among social partners (*European Voice*, March 2001).

While the Commission sees the new modes of governance as offering a possibility to expand European policies in the face of national governments' resistance, member-state governments prefer them to legislation because they allow member states more autonomy in shaping policy. Trade associations support the new modes of policy-making because they have an important role in it. The European Parliament is more skeptical because they circumvent the Parliament's rights of co-decision.

The aim of this chapter is to raise the following issues regarding the "new" modes of multilevel/multi-arena governance: first, different types of new governance and their individual elements are identified. The theoretical discussion about them points out the reasons for their emergence, their mode of operation, and the links to the "classical" hierarchical forms of decision-making. Second, the new modes of governance that provide common goods—in European policy measures—are empirically examined for a certain period of time; they are also gauged, both according to their political-institutional and their instrumental capacity. And finally, another issue is raised: namely, how do these new modes of governance fit into the overall context of European government and governance across multiple arenas, and what are their implications for the European polity as such.

New Modes of Governance

There has been an increase in the political salience of the new modes of governance (CEC White Paper), in particular, of target definitions and the publications of performance, on the one hand, and of voluntary accords with and by private actors, on the other. These new modes of governance are guided by the principles of voluntarism (nonbinding targets and the use of soft law), subsidiarity (measures are decided by member states), and inclusion (the actors concerned participate in governance). The mechanisms of governance are diffusion and learning, persuasion, standardization of knowledge about policies, repetition (iterative processes of monitoring and target readjustment are employed), and time management (setting of time tables) (Jacobsson 2001, 11ff.).

These modes are thought to have specific advantages: they evade the lengthy, unwieldy, and cumbersome process of legislative decision-making. At the same time, the threat of legislation is used to increase the willingness of actors to act voluntarily. Since these new forms of governance avoid regulatory requirements, it is expected that they will meet with less political resistance from the decision-makers and the implementing actors alike. After all, the latter would have to carry the costs of regulation. At the substantive level the advantages are seen in the greater flexibility of the policy measures and the greater adaptability of those measures to a rapidly changing social, economic, and technological environment.

Two basic new modes of governance are distinguished here: the first type—including two subtypes—develops substantive targets. The first subtype seeks to reach these targets exclusively by using reputation mechanisms and mutual learning (the open method of coordination). The second subtype seeks to reach the targets by using voluntary accords. The second type only defines procedural norms. It does not specify substantive policy targets. Each type/subtype is itself composed of several elements. It seems analytically useful to distinguish between the instruments employed—that is, the mechanism used in order to reach a particular policy goal—and the decision-making/participatory structure in which these instruments are defined and then applied.

The individual types are discussed against the background of all the empirical instances of the new modes of governance—as defined above—that were initiated, developed, and decided upon from January 2000 to July 2001. First, the number of new governance measures of this type are set in relation to measures in all policy areas,[4] that is, Commission regulations, decisions, directives, and recommendations, Council conclusions, resolutions, regulations, decisions, common positions, and recommendations, European Parliament and Council directives and decisions. Of course, these individual decisions are of very different scope and importance, something not grasped by a sheer quantitative comparison. A total of 926 measures have been counted on the basis of the monthly *Official Journal* summary in *Agence Europe* (January 2000 until July 2001); 99 of these measures can be strictly considered "new modes of governance" as defined above: community action programs comprising a few but not all the elements of the Open Method of Coordination (OMC) and voluntary accords.[5] Most of the new measures are to be found in the areas of social policy and environmental policy.

Target Development: Implementation by Publication, Reputation Mechanisms, and Learning (Open Method of Coordination)

The theoretical background for target development as a novel method of policy-making has been formulated in the literature on the exchange of information, monitoring, and learning and deliberation as well as the theory of policy diffusion and transfer (Radaelli 2000). The linking of target development with these mechanisms and processes is thought to be well adapted to collective problem solving under conditions of local and regional diversity and under conditions in which problems are volatile (Dorf and Sabel 1998, 314). Under the notion of a "deliberative polyarchy," problem-solving experience is pooled, and the diverse pragmatic solutions practiced by various political actors and their respective performances are compared; this may trigger a learning process that benefits all the participants, informing separate, independent decisions (Dorf and Sabel 1998, 321). Under a somewhat stricter view, a reputation mechanism (naming and shaming) may induce a behavioral change accommodating the desired policy goals. The tool of benchmarking, applied in assessing organizations, has played an important role in the development of this instrument. Benchmarking implies comparing how an organization performs relative to other organizations in view of a defined target. The targets can be defined and benchmarking can be initiated by an organization itself (bottom-up), or this can be imposed (top-down) (de la Porte et al. 2001). "It involves searching for best practices, organizational learning and continuous improvement in order to eliminate performance gaps" (de la Porte et al. 2001, 2). In terms of different forms of control (hierarchy: command and control, competition/rivalry; design: contrived randomness and architecture), and community: (social control) (Baldwin, Scott, and Hood 1998; Scott 2001), benchmarking is based on a loose form of community-based control (Scott 2001, 16).

With respect to decision-making costs, target setting and publicizing performance have the advantage of not requiring a lengthy formal decision-making process before a consensus can be reached in the first place; instead, information pooling may begin informally and spread step by step. However, if performance is to be seriously monitored and evaluated, targets have to be defined and measured clearly, and third-party administrative support is required. A further condition for effective functioning is that the individual participants be willing to provide the necessary information (Dorf and Sabel 1998, 338).

In a more encompassing and long-term view, a successful ongoing exchange of information on practices may lead to transnational decentralized learning networks (de la Porte et al. 2001, 11). In Europe these possibilities have raised the expectation that the European polity, as such, might eventually turn into a "confederation of (learning) policy-networks" (Beresford Taylor 2000), or epistemic communities (Haas 1992) promoting "communicative rationality in practice" (Dryzek 1987, 437). Policy standards have been developed through consultation with member-state representatives. Such standards can be adapted to different institutional environments, and legal and national contexts (Mosher 2000).

From these general considerations it may be expected that little political opposition will arise from actors who bear the implementation costs, if they are involved in target-definition, if they are free to choose the instruments to reach these targets, and if supranational implementation limits itself to publishing and comparing performance. The actors involved are quite willing to participate in the decision-making processes that shape the governmental instruments, as they are willing to politically support the introduction of the instruments. In other words, this mode of governance has a high political-institutional capacity: it is able to generate both participation and political support.

Similarly, the instrumental capacity is expected to be high, i.e., the involved actors have strong incentives to apply the proposed instruments, and the instruments are likely to contribute to solving the problem at hand; for watching the performance of others will induce member states to step up their endeavors to reach the set targets, using reputational mechanisms and/or integrating similar successful practices.

In the European context, benchmarking—that is, target development, mutual information, and learning—has been introduced as an "open method of coordination" aimed at orienting member-state activities towards a specific policy target within set timetables. It started with the Monetary Union, Best Economic Policy Guidelines, and, more recently, Social Europe—that is, employment policy, income distribution, working time, social protection, education and lifelong learning, social infrastructure, regional cohesion, poverty and social inclusion. Instruments applied to reach the policy targets are chosen by member-state governments. Indicators of achievement (benchmarking) and guidelines for action are formulated and defined by the responsible actors—i.e., member-state governments—on the basis of a Commission proposal. They are then evaluated by a permanent high-level committee of national civil servants and the Commission (Scharpf 2000, 25). The performance is measured by the specified indicators. Member states have to report annually on the actions taken to implement these guidelines. The reports are subsequently monitored by peer review, officials of member-state governments, and the Commission. The outcomes are published and ranked (scoreboards; hit lists). The monitoring committee and the Commission may then propose specific recommendations to the Council. By publicizing and exchanging information about different practices, it is hoped that processes of mutual learning among member states will be set in motion. A reputation mechanism is at work: and it is expected that those showing a poor performance will be shamed into performing better. To facilitate reaching the defined targets, in some instances European funds are offered to finance special measures. By providing information on and comparing the policy performances of individual member states, the Commission takes on the role as the adjudicator and assessor of member-state achievements (de la Porte et al. 2001, 11). This mode of governance in itself is not novel, but has been employed at the national level. However, its use in the European context, with its highly diverse national policy practices, does constitute a novelty.

Looking more specifically at the individual components of target development and benchmarking, the following elements emerge.

Table 8.1.   Target Development and Benchmarking: Implementation by Publication/Monitoring/Learning

Instruments:
developing substantive targets; plus timetables; instruments to reach targets chosen by member states; monitoring and publicizing performance; exchanging information on policy measures; loss of reputation as a sanctioning instrument.
Actor involvement and participatory structure:
targets defined by private actors (self-regulation; peer review); targets defined by public actors; targets jointly defined by public and private actors (co-regulation).

Target Development and Implementation by Reputation Mechanisms and Learning: Empirical Examples

From January 2000 until July 2001 target setting and monitoring as forms of open method of coordination linked with national action plans are to be found in the following measures:

In social policy:
The "gender equality" program (2001-2005) provides for targets to be formulated to achieve gender equality in all community policies. Benchmarks will be used with clear criteria for assessing behavior; in addition, practices will be monitored, and all the programs will be evaluated (*Agence Europe*, December 2000, 58).
The "social services programme" has formulated indicators to measure social exclusion. More specifically, in health policy, targets have been defined by member states to reduce the waiting lists for the provision of health services. Transparency is to be established regarding the waiting times in the different national health systems.
Under the "employment guidelines," labor market policies are to be evaluated according to quantitative and qualitative indicators. They are then to be subject to peer review. An exchange of information on good

practices ought to initiate mutual learning (*Agence Europe*, June 2000, 13).

An EP recommendation established a program for a quality evaluation of school education (*Official Journal*, 1 March 2000).

Educational benchmarks have been established, in particular for electronic learning (*Agence Europe*, May 2000). Member states' school systems will be measured in reference to these (*Agence Europe*, December 2000, 55-56).

The draft regulation on "public interest services" provides a monitoring mechanism for public service performance. It is proposed that member-state governments report to the Commission every six months.

A Youth Community Action Program has been established by the EP and the Council (*Official Journal*, 20 May 2000).

A Community Action Program has been introduced to combat discrimination based on religion, sexual orientation, and age (*Official Journal*, 2 December 2000).

A Decision of the EP and the Council introduced a training program for professionals in the European audiovisual program industry (*Official Journal*, 27 January 2001).

The Commission decided to monitor job satisfaction and stress levels as part of its annual evaluation of the Union's labor market (*European Voice*, 14-20 June 2001).

These measures are all examples of pure target development/benchmarking. Substantive targets are formulated by member states, the Commission taking part in the process. No particular instruments are recommended. Information is just exchanged on the performance and practices employed in member states.

Environmental policy is the second area in which examples of target setting and monitoring are found:

Under the "safety at sea/maritime pollution" measure the Commission proposes banning all ships from EU ports that have been held in an EU port for safety checks twice in the last two years. A blacklist, which will be updated every six months, is to be set up to facilitate this (*Agence Europe*, March 2000, III, 54).

In the "noise assessment" measure, noise indicators are to be developed which will make it possible for the member states to create noise cards and corresponding action plans to limit noise (*Agence Europe*, August/September 2000, III, 57).

A pollutant emission register has been established under the Integrated Pollution Prevention and Control Directive.

A Commission recommendation introduced monitoring levels of radioactivity to assess the exposure of the population (*Official Journal*, June 2000).

In contrast to the pure measures in social policy mentioned above, the environmental policy measures are mostly hybrids. They are closely linked to "hierarchy": in the case of the safety at sea measure, the scoreboard approach constitutes only one element in an otherwise straightforward regulatory command-and-control measure. The blacklist is to speed up safety checks; at the same time, it is a necessary precondition for banning ships. In the case of "noise assessment," the gathering and comparing of information is to be linked with action plans, which may subsequently lead to variable legislative measures, devised by member states.

Other measures:

Ireland "was shamed" under the broad economic policy guidelines: the Council in February 2001 adopted a recommendation according to which Ireland "should end the inconsistency with the Broad Economic Policy Guidelines, engendered by the Budget Plans for 2001 to prevent a further boost to demand in Ireland aggravating overheating and inflationary pressure." The Commission will be mandated to monitor Ireland's economy on a monthly basis and report back to the Council during the course of 2000. Responding to the Recommendation, the Irish finance minister said that he had no intention of changing his economic policy and that Ireland's budget aimed to achieve economic stability with measures to curb wage increases, among others. The economic and monetary affairs commissioner was confident that Ireland would bow to pressure. However, there are no sanctions (*Agence Europe*, III, February 2001, 14-15).

The Commission recommendation of June 2000 was issued concerning the disclosure of information on financial instruments (*Official Journal*, 27 June 2000).

The Commission initiated an Action Plan "Europe," supported by member states at the dotcom summit in Lisbon, to accelerate the Internet penetration of schools (*European Voice*, 3 May–6 June 2001).

Discussion of Political-Institutional and Instrumental Capacity

On the basis of the general discussion, I concluded that the political-institutional capacity is expected to be high, that is, the involved actors are quite willing to participate in a decision-making process that shapes the instrument and to politically support the introduction of the instrument. In the context of target development/monitoring, publication, scoreboards, and learning, member states are free to define and adopt their own measures for reaching the set target. The defined goals are not mandatory in the strict sense, and nonperformance does not lead to formal sanctions. Hence low costs are expected for political decision-making; that is, it is expected that political support can be easily mustered up. There is a great willingness to take part in target definition, and the process is not long and drawn out. Because of the voluntary commitment, the instrumental institutional capacity is also expected to be high. While this may hold in general, a closer look at the political background of the development of some of the individual empirical cases reveals that this is not true under all circumstances. Rather, in social policy-making, target formulations have been very contested when attempts have been made to precisely define goals (de la Porte et al. 2001, 9). For instance, while the Commission is only too happy to start up a scoreboard with well-defined and measurable objectives, which will allow it to regularly monitor how much progress has been made in implementing the social agenda, member-state governments do not want clear targets to be set, which will make it possible to measure progress (*European Voice*, 31 May–7 June 2000, 7). Instead, they prefer for target formulation to remain rather vague, in particular when the member states are pursuing conflicting goals and individual participants are tempted to free ride and not to contribute to the provision of common goods. Thus the employment goals decided upon at the Lisbon summit in 2000—that is, "lifelong learning," "increasing employment in services," "modernizing social protection," and "promoting social inclusion" (Scharpf 2000, 25, n. 20)—are rather fuzzy. Yet, there is also some indication that the pressure resulting from European measures—as soft as these may be— may help overcome domestic resistance to starting the reform of some institutionally deeply entrenched policies. Thus, in view of stalled domestic decision-making processes, some countries welcome the Commission initiative on the exchange of information about the functioning of old-age pension systems (von Maydell 2001, personal communication).

Of course, the mode of target formulation relates directly to the instrumental capacity, the extent to which incentives for implementation can be set, and the instrument's likely contribution to solving the problem at hand. Vague targets make monitoring, combined with voluntariness and the choice of instruments, a duller weapon than was originally planned (Beresford Taylor 2000, 21). National action plans may merely report on the ongoing activities, without moving in new directions. In particular, when policy traditions are deeply embedded in institutions, such as those typically found in the national welfare-state practices, or when redistributive issues are at stake in dealing with the question of who contributes how much to the provision of a common good, there is a rather limited willingness to learn from member states with other practices. Learning seems to be restricted to minor points among countries with basically similar systems (Scharpf 2000) and/or to problems of a coordinative nature where all stand to win from providing the common good.

Viewing, in general, the development of European policy-making, social policy has been notoriously resistant to the influence of Europeanization. Against this background, the significance of target setting and publication is presently difficult to gauge. Only over a longer time period will it be possible to say whether it is only a first step, meant to prepare the ground for European legislative policy-making—the Commission's "foot in the door," as it were—in an area of policy-making which has thus far been jealously guarded by member states, or whether it is a new policy mode in its own right that will remain in place. The particular character of the link to "hierarchy" in the individual policy measures may throw some light on this question: where a measure is explicitly under the proviso that a legislative proposal will follow should the measure fail, it is likely that the measure is a first step towards legislation.

Target Development and Implementation by Voluntary Accords

Instead of just publishing performance data and exchanging information on policy practices, voluntary accords may be set up by the involved public and private actors to reach the specified targets. Co-regulation and self-regulation may have different origins and take on different forms: when private organizations establish and manage their own rules without outside interference, voluntary self-regulation (unilateral and negotiated agreements—Lévêque 1998) has emerged. Delegated self-regulation, by contrast, is an arrangement imposed on private organizations, and the rules under which it functions are defined by a public authority (public voluntary agreements—Lévêque 1998; Ronit and Schneider 2000, 23). Some voluntary accords function entirely independently; typically, targets are set in a collective decision process, and the industry is held collectively liable for implementation. In case of policy failure, the industry is collectively sanctioned, independently from individual firms' efforts (DeClercq et al. 2001, 19). Others function in the shadow of hierarchy and fulfill a "support function" (DeClercq et al. 2001, 19); that is, should there be mismanagement or policy failure, public authorities may take on the regulatory functions. They are instituted on a parallel private and public basis.

The theoretical discussion of voluntary accords points to various advantages that they have as steering instruments: for one, from the vantage point of political-institutional capacity, a voluntary commitment to an accord by a private actor implies lower political decision-making costs because the affected private actors and their associations will mobilize less political resistance than they would in a legislative procedure. Another important advantage is that private accords may be reached more quickly, particularly if—given problem interdependence—there is a need to act across national boundaries and across governmental levels, where public decision-making is notoriously slow. Additionally, in terms of instrumental capacity, once commitment is secured, compliance is more likely both because private actors have participated in putting up the accord in the first place and may have developed an intrinsic motivation to carry it out (DeClercq et al. 2001, 16) and because they are better at mobilizing the necessary resources for implementation (Streeck and Schmitter 1985; Streeck 1995; Mayntz and Scharpf 1995). The private actors' resources cover a vast spectrum, ranging from the possibility of obliging members to comply with an accord ("Verpflichungsfähigkeit" or "governability" in the case of business associations) to financial resources, to technical expertise.

Additionally, the interdependence between firms provides them both with extensive information about other market actors and with leverage to sanction noncompliance. All these elements help overcome the informational asymmetry between regulators and regulatees and prevent industry from information closure (DeClercq et al. 2001, 16).

Why would private actors, for their part, be interested in committing themselves to such voluntary accords? At the political level, firms generally prefer voluntary agreements to legislation because such measures offer them more possibilities to shape the instruments used (Umweltgutachten 1998); indeed, by forming an institution under private authority, firms can influence public policies to their own advantage, more adjusted to the specific sectoral needs. They may also avoid some requirements associated with public authorities: for instance, the demands for accountability and the need to interact with other stakeholders (Cutler, Haufler, and Porter 1999, 353; Kerwer in this volume). Such cooperative agreements also entail some advantages over strategies of noncooperation with other private actors: by creating a commitment to joint activities, they reduce transaction costs by providing information about other firms; they make it possible to more effectively cope with the problem of strategic interdependence; furthermore, such accords enhance the confidence of the industry's customers (Cutler, Haufler, and Porter 1999, 352), environmental NGOs, and insurance companies (DeClercq et al. 2001, 16).

Voluntary accords to achieve specific policy targets may also be the first attempts to initiate European policy-making in an area previously entirely reserved to member states. They have a "bridging or transition function" (DeClercq et al. 2001, 18) and constitute a stage preliminary to legislation (Sairinen and Teittinen 1999, 5; cited in DeClercq et al. 2001, 18).

The individual instrumental and decision-making components of this mode of governance are the following:

Table 8.2. Target Development and Implementation by Voluntary Accords

Instruments:

  target development plus timetables;
  definition of contributions to reaching the target;
  monitoring mechanisms;
  sanctions in case of noncompliance.

Actor involvement and participatory structure:

  targets and contributions set solely by private actors (self-regulation);
  targets and contributions set jointly by private and public actors (co-regulation).

Empirical Examples

In environmental policy about twenty such accords are already in place
(OECD 1999, 61). In the period under investigation, the following examples
were found:

The new "Sixth Environmental Action Programme," which the Commission
agreed to at the end of January 2001, emphasizes the need for
cooperation between industry, green groups, and national authorities
when tackling major environmental problems. Wherever possible,
voluntary agreements among various stakeholders are to be used rather
than binding rules (*European Voice*, 11–17 January 2001, 6).

Under the "energy efficiency programme," new voluntary agreements
between the Commission and a number of industries are prepared to
boost the energy efficiency and to support the European Union climate-
change strategy. Voluntary agreements with big industrial consumers,
such as the chemical, steel, pulp and paper, and cement and textile
industries, are seen as making it possible to tailor mandatory energy
efficiency objectives to the need(s) of the specific industry (*Agence
Europe*, May 2000, III, 58).

Minimum energy efficiency standards are also to be used more effectively
by linking them with labeling schemes for certain products (household
appliances, commercial and other end-use equipment).

Another new voluntary accord is being prepared between the "automobile
and oil industries" to reduce vehicle emissions. The first automobile oil
initiative was negotiated and set up in the beginning of the 1990s.

Under the "road safety programme," the Commission announced measures
to make cars safer for pedestrians; the automobile industry announced
that it is beginning work on a voluntary agreement. Here a deal is being
negotiated with the Commission to ensure the manufacture of safer
vehicles with softer bumpers and low-impact metals. If this attempt at
co-regulation fails, in which policy-makers set informal targets and
leave it to industry to meet them, industry may be threatened with
binding rules (*European Voice*, 14–20 June 2001). The Belgian
presidency is very critical of the voluntary code (a system testing the
impact of a car in a collision with a pedestrian) and calls for binding
rules in the form of a directive (*European Voice*, 28 June–4 July 2001).

The "End-of-life Vehicles Directive" of 1999 proposes using voluntary
agreements as an instrument to implement this in member states.

The other policy area in which both target setting and implementation by
private accords are frequent is social policy. In the period under investigation the
particular instances of new modes of governance are the following:

Under "social dialogue," negotiations went on between social partners for
nine months to hammer out a deal on the "working conditions for
temporary staff" ("temps"). However, the negotiations quickly reached
an impasse, and the deadline expired without a compromise being

struck. Under Union rules it is expected that legislative steps will now be initiated by the Commission (*European Voice*, 8–14 March 2001, 8). While the European Trade Union Confederation, ETUC, demands that agency workers be treated the same way as their full-time counterparts, the European employers' association, UNICE, wants agencies to grant only minimum employment standards. UNICE also questions the EU's role in decision-making on this issue in the first place; it argues that this matter should not be decided by the Union's social partners, but by member states individually (*European Voice*, 4–10 January 2001, 6). However, Social Commissioner Diamantopoulos promised members of the European Parliament "firm action"—that is, legislation—should the negotiations stall (*European Voice*, 31 May–6 June 2001).

European airlines are presently negotiating an agreement to limit the flight time of pilots and crew. The EP has demanded that the agreement be integrated into a harmonized civil-aviation standard that incorporates technical requirements agreed upon by the aviation authorities. This standard is to be transposed into European Union law. However, for over a decade industry has failed to agree to modernized standards. If industry does not reach a deal, the EP will try to impose an agreement after the May deadline (*European Voice*, 11–17 January 2001, 3).

In February 2001 the European social partners agreed to guidelines to grant teleworkers equal rights with other employees (*Agence Europe*, February 2001, III, 61; *European Voice*, 26 April–2 May 2001).

In both cases there is a clear link to hierarchy: that is, the Community is used to link control and hierarchy (Scott 2001, 11). In the case of "temps," legislation is planned should the social dialogue agreement fail. In the case of airline flight time regulation, a model of "encapsulated legislation" is provided for: the agreement reached is to be incorporated into a standard that regulates the industry. Then, by reference to the European legislation, it will be given a legal character. In some instances, from the very beginning, accords are meant to be incorporated into legislation after they are concluded (see also Falkner 2000; 1998).

Other measures:

An antifraud program for noncash payments has established a partnership between the payment-systems industry, retailers, infrastructure network providers, and national and international authorities. The Commission plans to organize a forum on technical security and will launch a fraud prevention webpage to encourage exchange of information between the payment industry and retailers (*Agence Europe*, February 2001, III, 23-24).

A program to fight cyber crime has been introduced. An EU Forum with the participation of service providers, networks operators, consumer groups, data protection authorities, and representatives from law enforcement agencies are to enhance cooperation and raise public awareness of risks (*Agence Europe*, February 2001, III, 70).

Discussion

While the popularity of these measures generally speaks for their political-institutional capacity—at least in comparison to the alternative of classical legislation—the de facto political, institutional capacity is lower than has been claimed; that is, the costs for political decision-making are higher than theoretically anticipated. Several elements point to their possible costliness: for one thing, voluntary accords frequently have to be initiated by the Commission; that is, they would not emerge spontaneously. Further, industry, for its part, considers the Commission to have too much influence in shaping the guidelines and views the Commission as foisting requirements upon them, without allowing them a say (Chapman 2000, 2). Additionally, if negotiations among private actors drag on and are long-winded, the accords are frequently linked to hierarchical decision-making. The participatory structure of the negotiations has given rise to criticism as well. Industry points to a bias in the participatory structure in the development of the regulatory arrangements. In its view, that structure is selective and nonrepresentative. For these reasons a formal review process at the EU level has been called for in which all sides—from industry, public interest groups, and government—are to have a voice (Chapman 2000, 2).

With respect to instrumental capacity, voluntary accords have met with criticism because legal certainty is considered to be unsatisfactory. Industry is split in its view: Some have leveled criticism because of the lack of legal certainty offered to those who are involved and the lack of accountability for the decisions made. In response to that, the Commission's environmental and legal-service officers have proposed drawing up a Union-wide regulatory framework before any new accords are struck. Such a framework, they argue, would give legal certainty to those involved; at the same time it would not detract from the flexibility or voluntary nature of such accords. This judicial framework for voluntary accords is supported by members of Parliament, who point to the lack of accountability under private accords. Other representatives of industry argue, by contrast, that a legal framework would make it more difficult for them to join in such agreements (Cordes 2000, 2).

Seen in the overall context of European policy development, in using these new modes of governance, environmental policy and social policy come from different directions. In the past—that is in the 1980s and part of the 1990s—environmental policy was an area of direct European intervention, of command-and-control legislation. Since the mid-1990s, however, voluntary modes have increasingly been used. It was particularly under the pressure of Great Britain and the Netherlands that soft modes of environmental policy-making with legally nonbinding targets were introduced (Héritier, Knill, and Mingers 1996). The general direction of policy development, therefore, has shifted from hierarchy to self-regulation,[6] with a "second generation" of European policy instruments. However, the shadow of hierarchy still looms large when there is regulatory failure and when voluntary accords and public intervention mutually support one another. In social policy, by contrast, policy development shows a different pattern. Social policy has long been, and in principle still is, the exclusive territory of member states. Here, voluntary agreements constitute one of the first steps in European policy-making.

Procedural Norms/Codes of Best Practice

As opposed to target setting and implementation by monitoring and private accords, the new modes of governance that issue procedural norms or codes of best practice focus on *how* to properly deal with a problem or how to solve conflicts between participants, but they do not focus on specific substantive outcomes. Such codes might only be recommended; or they can be obligatory. Procedural norms may be backed up by a third party's authority (e.g., by the Commission or experts). In case of failure in the negotiation process or implementation failure, they may be followed by a legislative solution. Some procedural norms are formulated solely by industry.

In terms of political-institutional capacity, private actors have the same incentives to participate as they do in target setting linked with voluntary accords. Additionally, they should be motivated by the fact that no policy targets are imposed upon them. Moreover, in technologically complex areas, such activity also presents an opportunity to gain access to the expertise of competitors, that is, to gain knowledge about what those competitors are doing (Haufler 1999, 202). In terms of instrumental capacity, there are the same advantages as in the case of target setting and voluntary accords: commitment to such codes makes compliance more likely. They are considered to be more flexible and therefore adjustable to rapid technological and economic changes, and they are thus thought to fit better to the exigencies of a particular industry.

Procedural norms contain the following elements:

Table 8.3.   Procedural Norms/Codes of Best Practice

Instruments:
the instrumental element is identical with the procedure recommended.
Actor involvement and participatory structure:
private actors only (self-regulation); private and public actors (co-regulation).

Empirical Examples

In the period under scrutiny, only four new procedural norms or codes of practice are found in the fields of social policy, environmental policy, and consumer policy.

In social policy:
As a part of the social agenda, a high-level group of public actors has drawn up "best practice guidelines" for dealing with the problems of pensions. They have sought to encourage an exchange of ideas between countries on how to deal with the problem of the "social time bomb," and by doing so they monitor the success of individual governments' schemes.
By urging companies to take on similar responsibilities for working conditions throughout Europe (in particular regarding the use of child labor), the Commission invites companies to formulate a code of conduct related to those issues for themselves. Should firms fail to do so, legislative steps will be taken (*European Voice*, 11-17 January 2001, 6).

Norms of organizational procedure are quite frequently to be found in environmental policy—such as in the Eco-Audit and Management Regulation (EMAS) and the Seveso Directive—and in product safety, where quality management systems are used (Spindler 2000; Engel 1998).

The EMAS scheme is presently being revised. In 1993 it was originally set up with the aim of establishing common standards for auditing the environmental aspects of the activities of industrial companies. The aim of the revision is to broaden the involvement in the scheme, particularly to include small and medium-sized industrial firms as well as nonindustrial companies. Approved companies may use the EMAS logo. The EP now urges taking the informational needs of all stakeholders into account. It recalled an agreement with the Council stipulating that the environmental statements under EMAS were to consider the particular interests of all the relevant parties and that the information was to be presented in a clear and coherent manner in printed form. At least every three years the Commission is to report to the Parliament EP and the Council on the functioning of EMAS (*Agence Europe*, December 2000, III, 76).

Consumer policy applies voluntary codes of conduct, too:
Under the guidelines of the Commission and member states, voluntary codes of conduct are to be established by Internet-based firms to boost consumer confidence. A core group of specially invited firms and consumers have been selected to discuss the details of the proposal. While consumer organizations have welcomed the step, larger industry

groups have been critical of this "separate co-regulation scenario," developed by the commissioner for consumer affairs.

Discussion

In terms of political-institutional capacity, the political decision-making costs necessary to bring a code about—for the above stated reasons—are expected to be lower. In the empirical cases under scrutiny here, however, costs have often been higher than expected. In particular in the case of EMAS there was a long drawn out negotiation process between private and public actors in some countries, such as Germany, when the specific aspects of implementation were hammered out. This makes it clear that, even when no costs are involved with agreeing on a substantive policy target, there may be substantial costs connected with introducing and operating new institutions in order to apply the procedure (see the administrative resistance in the case of access to information in environmental policy—Bugdahn 2001).

The participatory structure under which such procedural codes are developed has also been heavily criticized by stakeholders for the imbalanced involvement of affected interests in the development of the instrument. In one instance (EMAS) industry is seen to be favored to the detriment of environmental associations. In consumer policy, too, the interest groups involved are considered to be selective and non representative. To prevent this and to allow for the balanced involvement of the actors concerned, industrial associations call for formalizing the participation of the stakeholders, specifically by formulating the guidelines to be followed.

To increase the instrumental capacity, there is usually a link to hierarchy: specifically, there is parallel supervision by public authorities, among other things, to increase transparency in utilizing the instrument in case the privately established code should fail to function as expected. The shadow of hierarchy is criticized by industry as a Commission attempt to force guidelines upon it.

Conclusion

In this contribution four questions have been addressed regarding the new modes of governance in Europe that aim at providing common goods. The first question raised the simple issue of the relative importance of new modes of governance in European policy-making in view of the fundamental shift in the mode of policy-making. Looking at the policy measures from the beginning of 2000 until July 2001, the analysis found that only a minority of measures can be considered new modes of governance, defined in terms of target development, benchmarking, monitoring, voluntary accords, and codes of practices. Hence, the new modes are by no means on their way to becoming the predominant forms of European policy-making. Further, the large majority of these measures are to be found in the areas of social and environmental policy. The new modes are of especially great importance in the area of employment and social policy.

After estimating the relative quantitative importance of the new types of governing and governance, the second question was raised: it concerned political institutional capacity. It is generally argued that target development linked with publicizing the participation of those bearing the costs of implementation increases their willingness to take part in shaping these instruments and reduces political opposition. Some evidence to that effect is provided: industries' quick acceptance of the open method of coordination, voluntary accords for environmental matters, and the greater frequency of such measures in social policy. The information gathered on the decision-making process involved in shaping new instruments shows that it is not as insignificant as expected. Three aspects of the decision-making process point to this: first, member states involved in target development and private actors involved in setting up voluntary accords are frequently engaged in lengthy negotiations over the contents of these targets, preferring soft targets, while the Commission pushes for specific ones. Second, these "new" modes often need an element of "hierarchy" in order to be brought about in the first place; that is, they are either initiated and guided by the Commission, or when private actors lag behind in decision-making, the Commission, the Council, and the EP step in and proceed to legislation. Hence, in setting the right incentives for actors to sway them to participate in policy formulation, their political-institutional capacity is strongly linked with legislative policy-making. Thus, although the new modes of governance extensively rely on voluntariness and private actors, as is evident in the voluntary accords and codes of practices, these actors are moving around "on a leash," so to say. Third, another type of "political cost" emerges, which has not remained unchallenged, namely, a certain selectiveness in the institutional context of policy formulation in voluntary accords. Private actors have been voicing criticism of this because of the selective involvement of private actors in policy formulation. They advocate a regulatory framework to balance participation.

Effectiveness was the third issue raised, specifically the instrumental capacity of new modes of governance, defined as a congruence of the incentive structure of the instrument and the central implementing actors, on the one hand, and the capacity to reach the defined policy target, on the other. On theoretical grounds, an enhanced instrumental capacity is expected because the actors bearing the costs of implementation have a say in shaping the policy instrument and are therefore willing to provide their expertise in that area and to commit the members of their organizations to implementation. The sources of information looked at here do not allow us to come to a systematic assessment of the quality of implementation and the effectiveness of the new modes. What has emerged about the particular structure of the new modes, however, is that they are frequently hybrids: the instrumental capacity of new modes is often backed up by "hierarchy," that is, the threat is voiced that traditional legislation will ensue if implementation should be unsatisfactory.

Also, there is an inherent conflict between targets that can easily be agreed upon, and carry few decision-making costs, on the one hand, and the effectiveness of those targets, on the other. If targets are formulated in a general way, which may make them politically easy to achieve, then they often have "no bite" when implemented, and they remain without much effect. Against this background it has also been pointed out that these soft instruments do not purvey legal certainty and that frequently there is a lack of accountability for the impact of applying these instruments.

In brief, viewing institutional and instrumental capacity on the basis of the empirical cases under scrutiny here indicates that, in order to fully deploy both capacities, the new modes of governance would have to rely on an entire "infrastructure" aimed at establishing the following conditions: the right incentives for those bearing the costs of regulation; the right participatory structure for shaping the instruments so that all those affected have a voice in shaping them; the guarantee of legal certainty; and the possibility to hold actors accountable for the consequences of particular actions. Hence, as easy as the new modes of governance may seem at first glance, when they are analyzed in detail it becomes clear that they are more demanding than expected.

In view of the above, the question of the significance of the new modes in the overall context of the European polity has to be discussed. Two aspects help to put them into perspective: on a time scale, the role of target development, benchmarking, and monitoring has yet to be properly assessed. It may turn out not to be a new type of policy-making at all and that such mechanisms have long been employed when the Commission has sought to move into a new national policy area that has long proven to be particularly resistant to Europeanization. Hence we might also find it to be a first step on the way to European legislation.

At an overall political decision-making level, the attempt to push European policy-making forward by the open method of coordination and voluntary accords may be seen as a "third way" between supranationalism and intergovernmentalism, which is needed when moving into core areas of member states' policy-making (Jacobsson 2001, 2). It offers a possibility to overcome the "joint decision trap" (Scharpf 1999), i.e., that trap encountered by member states which desire a closer cooperation in social issues, but are not willing to embark upon supranational decision-making (Jacobsson 2001, 5; Streeck 1995).

From the viewpoint of democratic legitimation, advantages and disadvantages of the open method of coordination exist, too:[7] members of the European Parliament view the process with some skepticism since they are not involved in this soft mode of policy-making, and they opt for legislation instead. Yet, at the same time, if the public is strongly involved in debating cross-national performance in the areas chosen for benchmarking and best practices, this could create a European policy space. It could also add political credibility and legitimacy to national policy-makers, since open coordination would lend itself to avenues that press for accountability from below and help improve "good governance" in Europe (de la Porte et al. 2001, 14-15). However, it may still be premature to advocate that the future of the European policy-making system ought to become "a confederation of learning networks" (Beresford

Taylor 2000, 21), centered on sharing knowledge and experience, and characterized by benchmarking, peer review, and public pressure.

Notes

1. Common goods include: public goods, characterized by accessibility and non-rival consumption; common pool resources, characterized by accessibility and rival consumption; and club goods, characterized by limited access and rival consumption.
2. Since the term "arena," in contrast to the term "level," encompasses both the vertical and horizontal dimension, it is used as the more general term.
3. In policy implementation, private actors are regularly involved in the realization of policy measures, since they frequently are important addressees of these measures, as ultimate target groups or as instrumental organizations needed to realize the targets (Windhoff-Héritier).
4. Exceptions are security and defense policy, enlargement policy, and trade policy with respect to third countries, as well as decisions related to European bodies and decision-making rules in European bodies.
5. About half of the 99 new modes measures are not fully developed, open methods of coordination or voluntary accords; in these cases, a target is formulated by a European body, and then applications for projects funds are solicited in order to realize these targets, or mere recommendations are formulated.
6. However, in some member states, such as Spain, where environmental policies did not play an important role before influence was wielded by the European Union, the direction of development is reversed. Here voluntary accord plays a role in familiarizing industry with environmental measures and enhancing compliance with national and European legislation (DeClercq et al. 2001, 19).
7. However, it is also contested: the Commission's employment General Directorate advocates these tools rather than legislation, considering the latter to be outdated and too slow in a fast-moving economy. Yet, there is resistance from some member states, and in the specific case, from France. Its labor minister, for example, argues for more legislation in social policy. This position is supported by heads of governments at the subnational level in Germany (e.g., Wolfgang Clement) who are afraid that the new modes of governance will undermine their legal competences in shaping European policy-making.

References

Baldwin, R., C. Scott, and C. Hood. 1998. *A Reader on Regulation*. Oxford: Oxford University Press.
Beresford Taylor, A. 2000. EU Moves towards the Creation of a Network Europe. *European Voice*. 15-21 June: 21.
Bugdahn, S. 2001. *Freedom of Access to Information on the Environment: The EU Directive and its Implementation*. Thesis manuscript, European University Institute, Florence.
CEC European Governance: A White Paper, Brussels, July 2001.
Chapman, P. 2000. Industry Voices Concerns over Co-Regulation. *European Voice*. 26 October–1 November: 2.
Cordes, R. 2000. Argument Rages over Voluntary Energy-Saving Industry Accords. *European Voice*. 4-10 May: 2.

Cutler, C., V. Haufler, and T. Porter, eds. 1999. *Private Authority and International Affairs.* New York: SUNY Press.

DeClercq, M. et al. 2001. *National Patterns in the Use of Voluntary Approaches in Environmental Policy.* International Policy Workshop on the Use of Voluntary Approaches.

De la Porte, C., P. Pochet, and G. Room. 2001. Social Benchmarking, Policy-making, and the Instruments of New Governance in the EU. Paper presented at European Community Studies Association Conference, Madison, Wisconsin, May 31-June 2.

Dorf, M., and C. Sabel. 1998. A Constitution of Democratic Experimentalism. *Columbia Law Review* 2: 267-473.

Dryzek, J. 1987. Complexity and Rationality in Public Life. *Political Studies* 35: 424-42.

Engel, C. 1998. Selbstregulierung im Bereich der Produktverantwortung. Instrumente und deren Ausgestaltung. Preprint of the Max Planck Project Group. Common Goods: Law, Politics and Economics 1998/7.

Falkner, G. 1998. *EU Social Policy in the 1990s: Towards a Corporatist Policy Community.* European Public Policy Series. London: Routledge.

————. 2000. The Council or the Social Partners? EC Social Policy between Diplomacy and Collective Bargaining. *Journal of European Public Policy* 7 (5): 705-24.

Haas, P. 1992. Epistemic Communities and International Policy Co-ordination. *International Organization* 46: 1-35.

Haufler, V. 1999. Self-Regulation and Business Norms: Political Risk, Political Action. In *Private Authority and International Affairs,* ed. C. Culter, V. Haufler, and T. Porter. New York: SUNY Press.

Héritier, A. 1999. Elements of Democratic Legitimation in Europe: An Alternative Perspective. *Journal of European Public Policy* 6 (2): 269-82.

Héritier, A., C. Knill, and S. Mingers. 1996. *Ringing the Changes in Europe: Regulatory Competition and the Transformation of the State: Britain, France, Germany.* Berlin: de Gruyter.

Jacobsson, K. 2001. Employment and Social Policy Coordination: A New System of EU Governance. Paper for the Scancor workshop on "Transnational Regulation and the Transformation of the States." Stanford, 22-23 June.

Kooiman, J. 1993. Social-Political Governance. In *Modern Governance: New Government-Society Interactions,* ed. J. Kooiman. London: Sage.

Lévêque, F. 1998. Voluntary Approaches. Environmental Policy Research Briefs, No. 1.

Mayntz, R., and F. W. Scharpf. 1995. Steuerung und Selbstorganisation in Staatsnahen Sektoren. In *Gesellschaftliche Selbstregelung und politische Steuerung,* ed. R. Mayntz and F. W. Scharpf. Frankfurt am Main: Campus.

Mosher, J. 2000. Open Method of Coordination: Functional and Political Origins. *ECSA Review* 13: 3.

OECD. 1999. Voluntary Approaches for Environmental Policy. An Assessment. Policy Paper.

Radaelli, C. 2000. Policy Transfer in the European Union; Institutional Isomorphism as a Source of Legitimacy. *Governance* 13 (1): 25-43.

Ronit, K., and V. Schneider, eds. 2000. *Private Organizations, Governance, and Global Politics.* London: Routledge.

Sairinen, R., and O. Teittinen. 1999. *The Voluntary Agreements as an Environmental Policy Instrument in Finland.* Paper for the CAVA Workshop in Ghent, November 26-27.

Scharpf, F. W. 1999. *Governing in Europe: Effective and Democratic?* Oxford: Oxford University Press.

———. 2000. *Notes toward a Theory of Multilevel Governing in Europe*, MPIfG Discussion Paper 2000/5.

Scott, C. 2001. EU Governance as Control: Promoting Effectiveness and Legitimacy? Paper presented at European Community Studies Association Conference. Madison, Wisconsin, May 31-June 2.

Spindler, G. 2000. Recht und Organisationsnormung. Presentation at the Max Planck Project Group. Common Goods: Law, Politics and Economics, November 20.

Streeck, W. 1995. From Market Making to State Building? Reflections on the Political Economy of European Social Policy. In *European Social Policy: Between Fragmentation and Integration*, ed. S. Leibfried and P. Pierson, 389-431. Washington, D.C.: Brookings.

Streeck, W., and P. Schmitter. 1985. Gemeinschaft, Markt und Staat—und die Verbände? *Journal für Sozialforschung* 25 (2): 133-57.

Umweltgutachten. 1998. Umweltschutz: Erreichtes Sichern—Neue Wege gehen. Der Rat von Sachverständigen für Umweltfragen. Stuttgart: Metzler-Poeschel.

Van Vliet, M. 1993. Environmental Regulation of Business: Options and Constraints for Communicative Governance. In *Modern Governance: New Government-Society Interactions*, ed. J. Kooiman, 106-18. London: Sage.

Windhoff-Héritier, A. 1980. *Politikimplementation—Ziel und Wirklichkeit politischer Entscheidungen*. Königstein: Hain Verlag.

9

The Case of Public Mission versus Competition Rules and Trade Rules

Leonor Moral Soriano

Introduction

Network industries provide a particular common good, namely, accessibility to services such as rail transport, energy supply, or telecommunications. Network industries provide access to universal services: they benefit all users throughout the territory at uniform tariffs and with similar quality conditions. The liberalization of network industries poses a conflict between unrestricted free trade and undistorted competition, on the one hand, and universal services, on the other, for providing such services may justify restrictions to free trade and distortions of competition. This contribution analyzes the role of one major player in European politics, namely, the European Court of Justice (hereafter referred to as the Court). Here I shall specifically examine its role in solving the conflict posed between market values (free trade and competition) and non-market values (universal services).

Rules for free movement and competition set the limits of states' discretionary powers, since both types of rules are intended to safeguard the European market from member states' intervention.[1] These rules provide thresholds according to which the Court controls the legality of national measures—i.e., they establish the compliance of these measures with European law. By so doing, they establish the level of discretion of member states that is compatible with European law. The effects upon competence issues make free movement and competition rules the keystones of the European Constitution; the case law of the Court concerning the interpretation and application of these rules is the axis of the institutional design of Europe.

Regulated sectors and, in particular, public utilities sectors (telecommunications, rail transport, and energy) are most appropriate for analyzing some constitutional and institutional aspects of European law. First of all, both free movement rules and competition rules apply to public utilities sectors. This means that attention has to be paid to whether these two bodies of rules compete with each other, complement each other, or are hierarchically organized.

Second, the privatization of traditionally public monopolies for the provision of public services (telecommunication, transport, energy, post, etc.) generates a clear conflict between institutions: namely, between the Commission, which aims at adapting public monopolies to European free movement and competition rules, and the member states, which aim at maintaining their discretionary powers to intervene in national economies. In this sense, attention should be paid to the way in which the Court of Justice deals with the conflict between free competition and the free movement of goods and services, on the one hand, and the public mission assigned to public monopolies and privileged undertakings, on the other hand. This issue is directly related to the setting of limits on the state's intervention.

Third, the liberalization process of public utilities sectors has generated re-regulation and new regulatory structures which involve member states, European institutions, independent regulatory bodies (national, supranational and European), private undertakings, and (since the White Paper of the Commission on competition policy) consumers associations. Attention should be paid to the way in which the Court of Justice shapes new regulatory structures in the public utilities sectors. This question is deeply related with Böllhoff's contribution in this volume on the developments of new regulatory regimes in the utilities. How far does the Court challenge and change the macro- and micro-organizatorial design that member states have developed across sectors?

Competition between rules, and competition between jurisdictions and new regulatory structures in the area of public utilities, are some of the constitutional and institutional issues this chapter deals with. To deal with them, the contribution focuses on the case law of the European Court of Justice concerning a particular type of competition law case: namely, it focuses on those cases challenging the member states' conferrals of exclusive or special rights to undertakings which are entrusted with the performance of a task of general economic interest. Since exclusive and special rights are known to distort competition and affect trade between member states, the Court is called to assess both anticompetitive and intra-Community trade effects. However, do free trade rules and competition rules establish different thresholds according to which the states' intervention is controlled? What derogation clause does the Court apply to justify state intervention? Does the derogation clause on competition rules, known as the public mission exception, also suspend the application of free trade rules, or is the opposite rather the case? Does the application of the public mission derogation clause reveal a negative integration bias on the part of the Court? To what extent does the case law of the Court on the application of the public mission exception determine a particular regulatory structure?

The Tension Enshrined in Article 86

At the Intergovernmental Conference for the Amsterdam Treaty, Article 16 was introduced. It declares that *services of general economic interest* occupy a place in the shared values of the Union, and it stresses their role in promoting social and territorial cohesion. This proviso also declares that the Community and the member states shall take care of such services, *each within the scope of their respective powers* and within the scope of the application of the Treaty. Article 16 does not aim at designating Community and member states' competences in the provision of services of general economic interest; it rather proclaims that services of general economic interest are a value of the Union, which has to be weighed by both the Community and the member states against other (colliding) values of the Union. This means that the Commission, for example, should not only promote competition, but also services of general economic interest, even though providing them may distort competition; still, member states should take account of free market and nondistorted competition principles when issuing measures for the provision of public services.

Article 16 could be seen as a sign of new airs blowing in Europe, since it recognizes that state intervention does promote Community values. However, this deferential attitude towards member states' discretionary powers contrasts with the original provisos of the Treaty, and in particular with Article 31(1). This provision is addressed to the star of state intervention measures, namely, public monopolies.

> Member States shall adjust any state monopolies of a commercial character so as to ensure that no discrimination regarding the conditions under which goods are procured and marketed exists between nationals of Member States.
> The provisions of this Article shall apply to any body through which a Member State, in law or in fact, either directly or indirectly supervises, determines or appreciably influences imports or exports between Member States. These provisions shall likewise apply to monopolies delegated by the State to others.

This proviso presupposes, on the one hand, that public monopolies are legal under Community law and, on the other hand, that they do not quite comply with Community law, because they cause discriminatory market restrictions. This schizophrenic character of Article 31(1) and the deliberate ambiguity of the text are the result of the thorny political problem this proviso tries to solve: the limits of national economic policy in the context of a common market (Buendía Sierra 1999, 77). Indeed, whereas national monopolies were a policy instrument widely used by the founding member states, this was incompatible with the idea of creating a single market, free from restrictions and barriers, imposed by member states. As Böllhoff explains in his contribution, the liberalization of the utilities led to a competition-based provision of universal services. This model causes administrative reforms affecting the monopoly-based model of the provision of universal services. Indeed, the compromise between member states' interests, on the one hand (i.e., protecting their discretionary powers), and Community's interests, on the other hand (i.e., unrestricted intra-Community trade), consists in the obligation to adjust state monopolies of a commercial character[2] to the principle of nondiscrimination in intra-Community trade.

Whereas Article 31(1) expresses the compromise between the State's monopolies and free trade rules, Article 86 points towards the compromise found between public and privileged undertakings and competition rules. This proviso establishes that in the case of public undertakings and privileged undertakings member states shall neither enact nor maintain in force any measure contrary to the rules contained in the Treaty, and in particular those concerning competition. Article 86(2) provides the derogation clause: limits on competition are justifiable in the provision of services of general economic interest. Finally, Article 86(3) privileges the Commission, for it attributes to this European institution the power to address directives or decisions to member states in order to ensure the application of Articles 86(1) and 86(2).

Article 86 has been defined as "a delicate balance" between the presumption that public monopolies and privileged undertakings are legal, and the recognition that they may be illegal if they fall foul of the EC competition rules (Gardner 1995). However, Article 86 does not mirror a "delicate balance," for unlike Article 16, it does not contain a command to balance conflicting interests, nor does it provide criteria according to which a balance can be found. Rather than a balance, Article 86 mirrors the tension between (1) the presumption that member states are free to create public monopolies and privilege undertakings (the sovereign approach), (2) the presumption that monopolies are illegal because they restrict competition (the competition approach)[3] and, since the *Manghera* case,[4] (3) the presumption that monopolies are illegal because they restrict free trade (the trade approach).

The tension between the power of member states which hold public monopolies and can grant exclusive or special rights to undertakings in order to guarantee the provision of services of general economic interest and the power of the Commission, which aims at eliminating all barriers to the free market and undistorted competition, is to be solved by the Court. To this aim, the derogation clause enshrined in Article 86(2), known as the *public mission exception*, has been referred to as the legal framework in which a balance between public monopolies and competition rules, and between public monopolies and trade rules, ought to be struck. The outcome of this balance, and the criteria to strike it, seems to benefit member states and the Commission equally: the Court backs the discretionary powers of member states to grant special or exclusive rights; it also backs the quasi-legislative powers of the Commission under Article 86(3), and in this sense it backs the enhancing competence of the Commission in competition policy.[5]

Special or Exclusive Rights: Compatibility with EC Law

The Court has consistently held that, in principle, the Treaty does not prohibit public monopolies and privileged undertakings. In the *France v Commission* case,[6] the Court established that member states can use certain undertakings, in particular in the public sector, as an instrument for economic or fiscal policy. However, the conferral of special or exclusive rights has to be compatible with competition rules and the preservation of the unity of the Common Market (§ 12). Rather than solving the problem, this statement of the Court points to the core of the problem: when are special and privileged undertakings compatible with the Treaty? There are a number of clashes between the Treaty provisions and the concession of special or exclusive rights to undertakings which are entrusted with the provision of services of general public interest such as water or electricity supply, telecommunications, post, rail transport, and others. These clashes raise several questions concerning the compatibility of special and exclusive rights with the prohibitions on the prevention, restriction, or distortion of competition (Article 81[1] EC Treaty), with the prohibition of the abuse of dominant position (Article 82 EC Treaty), and with the principle of free trade between member states.

Clashes between the conferral of special and exclusive rights, and free trade rules are straightforward, since the prohibition restricting competition according to Article 86(1) and the prohibition restricting free trade according to Articles 28 and 29 are addressed to member states. However, the prohibitions of Article 81(1) and 82 are addressed to private undertakings, rather than to member states. This means that, in principle, member states cannot be accused of distorting competition or abusing their dominant position.[7] However, the Court linked Articles 81 and 82 together with Article 86, and by so doing, linked the prohibitions on preventing, restricting, or distorting competition, and the prohibition on abusing dominant position to state intervention. The Court referred to the doctrine of the effectiveness of Community law and the doctrine of direct effect and concluded that member states infringe on Articles 81 and 82 either by issuing anticompetition measures, or when privileged undertakings had an anticompetitive behavior.

The doctrine of the *effet utile* was applied in the *GB-INNO v ATAB*[8] case, where the Court asserted that "the Treaty imposes a duty on Member States not to adopt or maintain in force any measure which could deprive that provision [prohibition of abuse of dominant position] of its effectiveness (§ 31)."

So far, Article 86(1) has imposed a prohibition on member states: they are not to enact or maintain measures contrary to competition rules as far as *public undertakings and privileged undertakings* are concerned. The prohibition is expanded to include any sort of state intervention by the application of the *effet utile* doctrine.

Further, the Court has attributed direct effects to the prohibition enshrined in Articles 81 and 82 of the Treaty. In the *Sacchi* case[9] concerning exclusive rights to broadcasting, granted by Italy to a single undertaking, the Court stated that:

> The national court has in each case to ascertain the existence of such abuse and the Commission has to remedy it within the limits of its powers.
>
> Even within the framework of Article 90 {new Article 86}, therefore, the prohibitions of Article 86 {new Article 82} have a direct effect and confer on interested parties rights which the national courts must safeguard. (§ 18)

Hence, even though Articles 81 and 82 are addressed to undertakings, and therefore cannot derive direct effects, when they are read along with the obligations that the Treaty imposes on member states, they do confer rights which can be vindicated before the national courts.[10]

Since both the effectiveness and direct effect of competition rules are recognized, member states have to comply with the obligations imposed by them in the same way as they have to comply with the obligations imposed by free trade rules.

Compatibility Special or Exclusive Rights/Prohibition on the Prevention, Restriction, or Distortion of Competition

Companies entrusted with the provision of services of general interest use most profitable activities (provision of electricity in big cities) to subsidize loss-making activities (provision of electricity in rural areas). By using this cross-subsidizing technique, entrusted undertakings are able to provide services which benefit all users throughout the territory of the member state at uniform tariffs and with similar quality conditions; that is, cross-subsidies are required to provide services of general economic interest. Cross-subsidizes, however, are possible only if member states grant special or exclusive rights, so that the most profitable sectors are closed to competition (e.g., the exclusive right to supply electricity in city areas).

In the *Corbeau* case,[11] the Court dealt with the compatibility of cross-subsidizing in relation to European competition law. The case arose when Mr. Corbeau established a courier business consisting of the collection and distribution of mail at home before noon the next day in or around Liège. The courier business competed with *Régie de Postes*, a public monopoly which, according to the Law on Postal Service of 1956, was granted exclusive rights over mailing activities in Belgium. The exclusive rights granted to *Régie de Postes* aimed at guaranteeing that the most profitable sectors of the postal service were not creamed off by competing undertakings. The national court dealing with the judicial action brought by Mr. Corbeau addressed a preliminary question to the Court concerning the compatibility of unrestricted competition (Article 81) and the conferral of special or exclusive rights to undertakings (Article 86[1]).

The Court solved the former conflict between free competition (Article 81) and the power of member states to grant special or exclusive rights by referring to the public mission exemption contained in Article 86(2): conferring special or exclusive rights has to be justified by the provision of services of general economic interest.

In particular the Court held that "the questions which falls to be considered is therefore the extent to which a restriction on competition or even the exclusion of all competition from other economic operators is *necessary* in order to allow the holder of the exclusive right to perform its task of general interest and in particular to have the *benefit of economically acceptable conditions* (§ 16)."

The Court has consistently held that the answer to the former question is up to national courts. To assist them and to guarantee that European law is applied homogeneously across Europe, the Court provided some criteria to assess the necessity of anticompetition measures. It held that the starting point of such examinations is the *economic equilibrium* of the undertaking, that is, the equilibrium which should exist between less profitable sectors and the profitable sectors (§ 17).[12] Such equilibrium justifies restrictions on competition by granting exclusive and special rights. The great novelty of this judgment is the deferential attitude of the Court towards privileged undertakings. This operates first by the chosen criterion of necessity: unlike in the field of free movement of goods, the Court did not consider that the necessary measure was the least restrictive one. Rather, the Court upheld that in order to guarantee the economic stability of a firm entrusted with the provision of a public service, restrictions on competition are justified.

To Gardner, the focus on the economic equilibrium of the privileged undertaking would encourage a more restrictive interpretation of when restrictions on competition are compatible with EC competition rules, and therefore, it would also encourage a more restrictive policy toward public monopolies and privileged undertakings (Gardner 1995, 78). So far, however, this has not been the case. In the *Gas and Electricity Monopolies* cases, for example, the Court has rejected this approach, which was held by the Commission, and most of the attention was directed to the task of providing a service of general economic interest entrusted to the privileged undertaking. In the *Albany* case,[13] the Court paid no attention to the economic equilibrium of the firm and focused on the economically acceptable conditions under which the privileged company ought to perform the social task entrusted to it.

The evaluation of the economically acceptable conditions under which a privileged undertaking has to perform a social task requires the analysis of highly complex issues: what constitutes a cross-subsidy? Is a cross-subsidy taking place? What are the combined effects of all competing undertakings upon the privileged one?[14] By leaving the evaluation of these complex economic questions to the national courts, Gardner says, the Court may have opened a Pandora's box, given the differing familiarity of national judges with economic issues and with European competition rules (Gardner 1995, 82).

Despite these criticisms, the contribution of the *Corbeau* judgment is of great importance. Before the *Corbeau* judgment, the conflict between competition policy and public services was considered a conflict between opposed aims, that is, it was conceived as a sort of either/or conflict. However, the innovation in *Corbeau* was that, instead of focusing on the conflict, the Court focused on the aims/end relationship existing between competition policy and the provision of public services. Indeed, restrictions on competition are thought of as a necessary means for providing services of general economic interest. The proportionality test is the tool for applying the derogation clause of Article 86(2).

Compatibility of Exclusive Rights/Prohibition on Abusing Dominant Position

Special or exclusive rights may clash with a different prohibition established by the EC Treaty: namely, the abuse of the dominant position (Article 82). Although it is placed under the title of "Rules on Competition," the prohibition on abusing dominant position is connected to both the common market and the principle of free trade. This is clear from the wording of Article 82: "Any abuse by one or more undertakings of a dominant position . . . shall be prohibited as incompatible with the *common market* insofar as it may *affect trade* between Member States." The main question is whether these effects can be justified by the provision of services of general economic interest—that is, by applying the derogation clause of Article 86(2).

Although it is not in the field of public utilities, the *Höfner* case[15] casts light on the direction that the Court has taken when scrutinizing state intervention. This case is concerned with the legality of public monopolies under European law, and in particular, the interpretation of the prohibition to abuse the dominant position (Article 82) in relation to the power of member states to grant special or exclusive rights (Article 86[1]). The case arose when a German private recruitment agency brought forth a judicial action questioning the validity of the German Law on the Promotion of Employment, which grants the exclusive right to offer job placement services to the German Federal Employment Office.

The Court starts reasoning by declaring that: "[t]he simple fact of creating a dominant position by granting an exclusive right within the meaning of Article 90(1) {new Article 86(1)} of the Treaty is not as such incompatible with Article 86 {new Article 82} (§ 29)."

According to the Court, the simple fact that special or exclusive rights are granted creates a dominant position.[16] Despite this causal relationship (between conferring special or exclusive rights and the creation of a dominant position), member states are not in breach of EC law, for only the *abuse* of dominant position by the privileged undertaking is prohibited by the Treaty. This implies that the focus of the Court's judicial control should be on the attitude of the privileged undertaking, rather than simply on the fact that exclusive and special rights are granted by the member states.[17] Therefore, the fact that a privileged undertaking abuses its dominant position means that this undertaking is in breach of EC law, whereas the member state is not, because conceding special or exclusive rights is compatible with the EC Treaty.

The Court, however, has stretched the boundaries of the traditional interpretation of Article 82 (Gardner 1995, 83) farthest by adopting a peculiar understanding of when a dominant position is abused. The Court declared that: "[a] Member State is in breach of the prohibitions contained in those two provisions [Articles 82 and 86(1)] if the undertaking in question, *merely by exercising* the exclusive rights granted to it, cannot avoid abusing its dominant position (§ 29)."[18]

Rather than describing the *active* abuse of dominant position, the Court described the *passive* abuse of dominant position,[19] according to which the mere existence of special or exclusive rights induces the privileged undertaking to abuse its dominant position: "[s]uch an abuse may in particular consist in limiting the provision of a service to the prejudice of those seeking to avail themselves of it (§ 30)."

The already tight judicial control upon member states granting special or exclusive rights is tightened even further by the end of the *Höfner* judgment. According to the Treaty, the member states are only held responsible if the abusive conduct of the privileged undertaking affects the trade between member states; in this sense, the Court further argued that: "[I]t is sufficient to establish that that *conduct is capable* of having such an effect (§ 32)."[20]

There are a number of presumptions which the Court has adopted when interpreting Articles 82 and 86(1) together, and which work against the discretionary powers of member states: the Court presumes that the conferral of special or exclusive rights generates a dominant position; it also presumes that the mere existence of a dominant position induces the privileged undertaking to abuse it; and finally, for the Court, it is enough when the abuse of a dominant position is capable of affecting trade between member states—there is no need to prove that this has occurred.

The *Höfner* case has resulted in the erosion of the state monopolies (Reich 1992, 887), which also leads to the erosion of the notion of public service. This explains that the public mission exceptions contained in Article 86(2) have hardly been applied in cases where public monopolies are accused of abusing their dominant position. Such a derogation clause would lead to a balanceable solution of the conflict between public service monopolies, on the one hand, and European competition rules, on the other. However, if rather than a balance, the Court focuses on the compatibility of State's intervention with Community rules, a higher threshold of legality is being established.

Compatibility Exclusive Rights/Free Trade

The European competition law model differs from other legal models (the American one, for example) since it mainly looks at market integration. In the XXIXth Report on competition policy,[21] the Commission declares that the primary objective of competition policy is the maintenance of competitive markets. The second objective is the single market: having an internal market is an essential condition for the development of an efficient and competitive industry.[22]

However, this does not mean that competition among jurisdictions (namely, conflicts between competition rules and free trade rules) may not occur. The question of the compatibility of competition rules and free trade rules rose in the *Gas and Electricity Monopolies* cases, three judgments concerning the compatibility under European law of exclusive import rights granted by member states (Netherlands, Italy, and France) to electricity and gas companies. These judgments deal with competition between European rules, and in particular between the free movement of goods (Article 28), the restriction on the free movement of goods justified by mandatory requirements (Article 30), and nondiscrimination regarding State monopolies (Article 31); they also deal with the exclusive rights to provide services of general economic interest: Article 86(1) and restriction to competition rules justified by the performance of a task in the public interest Article 86(2).[23]

This chapter focuses on the Court's reasoning in the case against the Netherlands, since the Court repeated its reasons in the other two *Gas and Electricity Monopolies* cases. In this case, the Commission held that by granting exclusive import rights for electricity to the Dutch firm SEP, the Netherlands had failed to fulfill obligations under Articles 28 and 31(1). By contrast, the Dutch Government argued that exclusive import rights were justified according to Articles 30 and 86(2). The question was whether restrictions on trade caused by exclusive rights granted for the provision of services of general economic interest (electricity supply) should be evaluated either under the rule of reason of Article 30 or under the derogation clause of Article 86(2).

The first issue the Court dealt with concerned the compatibility between exclusive import rights and Article 31(1). To evaluate such compatibility, two questions have to be answered: (1) has the member state granted an exclusive import right (§ 17)? And (2) does the right affect import, keeping in mind that it is not necessary to affect all imports, but rather, it is sufficient if those rights have an appreciable influence on imports (§ 18)? If the answer to both questions is affirmative, then the ruling of the *Manghera* case[24] applies: exclusive import rights give rise to discrimination prohibited by Article 31(1) against exporters in other member states because economic operators or sellers in other member states are thereby deprived of the possibility of offering their products to customers of their choice in the member state where the exclusive import right has been granted (§ 15 and § 23).[25]

Despite the fact that exclusive import rights are contrary to the prohibition against discrimination regarding the conditions of the procurement and marketing of goods, the Court thought that it was not necessary to evaluate whether such restrictions were also incompatible with Article 28 (free movement of goods), or whether the restriction on trade between member states could be justified under the rule of reason contained in Article 30.[26] That is, under European law, discriminatory restrictions on trade caused by public monopolies and privileged undertakings cannot be justified under the rules for the free movement of goods; *however*, the conferral of special and exclusive rights can be justified under European competition rules. By deciding in this way, the Court rescues national regulatory powers—in particular, those related to services of general economic interest—from the stricter control of Article 30, and places the judicial scrutiny under competition law, and in particular, under the derogation clause of Article 86(2) of the EC Treaty. Moreover, the Court establishes that the correct framework within which the legality of public monopolies and privileged undertakings is to be evaluated is Article 86(2). Emphasis is given to the cause of the restrictive effects, rather than to the nature of the restriction (either on intra-Community trade or on competition).

The Public Mission Exception 86(2)

Article 86(2) contained a derogation clause on the competition rules of the Treaty. According to it, restrictions on competition are justified by the provision of services of general economic interest. This is known as the *public mission exception*. In the *Gas and Electricity Monopolies* cases the Court has enhanced the importance of Article 86(2), for it not only applies when special and exclusive rights are incompatible with competition rules (in particular Articles 81 and 82); it also applies when these rights are incompatible with free trade rules (in particular Articles 28 and 31).

The Court has consistently held that it is up to the national courts to assess whether or not the exception of Article 86(2) applies; that is, national courts have to assess whether the violation of competition rules and trade rules may be justified because a service of general economic interest is provided by a privileged undertaking. The Court, however, has provided some criteria which may guide the Commission when it brings judicial actions against member states, and the national judges when they have to deal with judicial actions brought by particular individuals against privileged undertakings.

To apply the derogation clause of Article 86(2), three requirements have to be met: the firm has to be entrusted with the operation of services of general economic interest; competition laws should be incompatible with the performance of a public mission task; trade should not be affected to an extent which is contrary to the interests of the Community.

Services of General Economic Interest

Article 86(2) refers to two types of enterprises: those entrusted with the operation of *services of a general economic interest*, and those having the character of a *revenue-producing monopoly*. As to the first group, it is not relevant whether the company is private or public, but rather whether the public authority has *entrusted* the operation of services of general economic interest. "Services" is interpreted in a broad sense, for even the provision of certain goods, such as gas and electricity, would enter into this category (Buendía Sierra 1999, 227). The service has to have an "economic" nature, which also has been interpreted in a broad sense to include, for example, cultural activities (Buendía Sierra 1999, 278). The service must also be of interest for the general economic activity. For example, a service related to the regional development of a particular area is a general service in nature, even though its application is addressed to a certain region or a certain group.

The former criteria do not specify which particular services are of general economic interest. It is up to the Court to decide, on a case-by-case basis, which services can benefit from the derogation clause of Article 86(2). This has been very much the case since the Court attributed direct effect to Articles 81(1) and 82 in 1974 (in the *Sacchi* judgment), and an increasing number of preliminary questions have been addressed to the Court concerning the application of the public mission exception. What counts as a service of general economic interest was not decided upon in comprehensive terms, but rather for the particular case. The following activities have been accepted as being of general economic interest in character: the operation of a river port which handles the majority of the river traffic of goods in a member state; the establishment and operation of a public telecommunication network; water distribution; the operation of television services; electricity distribution; the operation of certain transport lines; employment recruitment; basic postal services; the maintenance of a postal service network in rural communities; regional development within a member state; processing building waste. The list is by no means exhaustive.

In the *Corbeau* judgment the Court provided a definition more suitable for universal services than for services of general economic interest. It established that services (such as the collection, carrying, and distribution of mail) are of general economic interest if (1) they benefit all users (2) throughout the territory of the member state (3) at uniform tariffs and (4) in similar quality conditions, irrespective of the specific situations or the degree of economic profitability of each individual operation (§ 15).[27]

Much is to be done by the Court to explore the implications of the former definition, and in particular of the requirement that universal services benefit all users at uniform tariffs. Universality has a geographic dimension which is very well encapsulated in the definition of the Court: electricity should be supplied to users in remote areas. However, universality of the service also has a social dimension, for electricity should be supplied to all groups of society, regardless of financial and physical disadvantages (Sauter 1998, 121); it should also be supplied to other groups such as immigrants, political refugees seeking asylum, homeless people, and others. Universal services will penetrate a society if such services can be realized, if these services are offered at affordable prices (rather than at uniform tariffs), and if non-profitable investments are made to adapt the service to the less favored groups of society.

No doubt, the social penetration of universal services is going to be elaborated in the future by the Court, since one of the aims attached to the provision of services of general economic interest is social and territorial cohesion (Article 16 EC). No doubt, reading Articles 16 and 86(2) together will generate a horizontal regulatory space which the Commission and the member states should share to grant access to services which (1) benefit all social groups (2) throughout the territory of the member state (3) at uniform and affordable tariffs, and (4) in similar quality conditions, irrespective of the specific situations or the degree of economic profitability of each individual operation.

The second type of undertaking to which Article 86(2) applies is that of a revenue-producing monopoly. It is an enterprise that aims at producing revenue for the State, rather than offering a service of general economic interest. For example, an enterprise to which the State has granted an exclusive right in order to obtain revenue. These undertakings can be either public or private. Little attention has been paid to this type of undertaking, since member states justify privileged undertakings by the performance of a service of general economic interest, rather than in reference to their revenue-producing character.[28]

Incompatibility with the Performance of a Public Mission Task

The derogation clause of Article 86(2) applies if the application of competition rules is *incompatible* with the provision of a service of general economic interest.

In the landmark cases *Höfner*, *ERT*,[29] and *Merci*, the Court offered its interpretation of when a member state is in breach of the rules prohibiting the abuse of dominant position: namely, when the privileged undertaking, *merely by exercising the exclusive right, cannot avoid* abusing its dominant position (*Höfner*, at § 29). In the *ERT* case the Court referred to the fact that exclusive rights create a situation in which the company *is led* to abuse its dominant position (*ERT*, at § 37) or even *induced* to do so (*Merci*, at § 19). According to this strict interpretation, it is very likely that the activities of privileged undertakings could be declared illegal, and member states be found to be in breach of Community law.

Neither was the Court less stringent when interpreting the application of the public mission derogation clause. In all three cases, the Court repeated that privileged undertakings entrusted with the provision of public services are exempted from the obligations imposed by competition rules if the application of these rules is *incompatible* with the provision of the public service (*Höfner*, at § 24) or it *obstructs* its provision (*ERT*, at § 38; and *Merci*, at § 26). The Court did not elaborate these terms, probably because more attention was paid to *how to bring anticompetition state intervention under judicial scrutiny* than *how to evaluate anticompetition state measures.*

The *Corbeau* and *Almelo*[30] cases are meant to serve as the turning point in the application of the public-mission exception. The major innovation was the way in which the Court constructed and interpreted the derogation clause: namely, as a balancing exercise. The Court adopted a sort of "rule of reason": the focus is not on whether the application of competition rules is incompatible or obstructs the task entrusted to the privileged undertaking; instead, what is going to be assessed is whether restrictions on competition are *necessary* in order to realize the requirements of public interest. Member states can confer exclusive rights which may hinder the application of European competition rules, "in so far as restrictions on competition, or even the exclusion of all competition by other economic operators are necessary to ensure the performance of the particular task assigned to the undertakings possessed of the exclusive rights (§ 14)."

The change is very subtle, but powerful. Before the *Corbeau* judgment, the conflict between competition policy and public services was considered a conflict between opposed aims, that is, it was conceived of as a sort of either/or conflict. However, after *Corbeau* the focus was on the aims/end relationship existing between competition policy and the provision of public services. Indeed, restrictions on competition are thought of as a necessary means to provide services of general economic interest.

Then, the question turns out to be whether restrictions are necessary to provide such services. Although it is up to the national courts to decide this—the *Corbeau* case arrived at the Court via the preliminary question procedure—the Court provided some criteria; and in particular it referred to the *conditions of economic equilibrium* (§ 17) or the *economically acceptable conditions* (§ 16) under which the entrusted undertaking should perform its public mission task.

Despite the economic expertise which the mentioned criteria may require, the Court had in mind a lay notion of what amounts to "conditions of economic equilibrium": the undertaking entrusted with the provision of a public service should be able to compensate for less profitable sectors, delivering post to remote areas, against the profitable sectors, delivering post in urban areas. That is, exclusive rights in profitable areas are conferred in order to finance loss-making activities required under universal service obligations.

Although some authors have viewed the *Corbeau* case as implying a choice for applying an economic test which focuses on the economic viability of the privileged undertaking (Gardner 1995, 81), the intention of the Court was not to substitute the strict test of "obstructing the performance" or "making impossible the performance" (*Höfner, ERT,* and *Merci*) with the strict (and far too complex) economic test of the "economic viability" of the undertaking. Indeed, the Court did not hold that competition rules apply as long as the economic stability of the undertaking is assured; it upheld that in order to guarantee the economic stability of a firm entrusted with the operation of a public service, restrictions on competition are justified. Advocate General Darmon interprets the ruling of the *Corbeau* case in this sense: "The competition rules may be disapplied not only where they make it impossible for the undertaking in question to perform its public service task but also where they jeopardize its financial stability (Advocate General Darmon's Opinion in *Almelo,* § 146)."

The outcome is looser judicial control on State intervention. This is further confirmed by the *Almelo* case, where the application of the public mission exception was at stake in the field of electricity supply. The Court repeated the doctrine of *Corbeau*: restrictions on competition are allowed if they are necessary in order to make possible the performance of a task of general interest. It argued that: "In that regard, it is necessary to take into consideration the economic conditions in which the undertaking operates, in particular the costs which it has to bear and the *legislation*, particularly concerning the environment, to which it is subject (§ 49)."[31]

If in the *Corbeau* case the Court showed a deferential attitude towards member states' discretionary powers, this attitude is definitively strengthened in *Almelo,* for the Court explicitly referred to the national regulation of the discussed public service. This means that the economic, social, and policy choices that member states made when regulating services of general economic interest ought to be taken into account to decide whether or not competition rules apply. It also means that national regulatory space is left unchallenged by European law, and in particular by competition rules.

Apart from the looser control on member states' regulatory powers, the *Corbeau* and *Almelo* cases confirm that when applying the public-mission exception (Article 86[2]), the proportionality test provides the framework within which conflicts between incommensurable goods—namely, competition and the performance of tasks of public interest—ought to be solved. Proportionality, being the chosen model of reasoning, leaves the door open to nonmarket values, and in particular to the value intrinsically bound to the provision of universal services, independent of their economic viability (Ross 2000, 25) or their anti-competition effects.

Another victory for member states' discretionary powers is clear in the definition of the burden of proof as established in the *Gas and Electricity Monopolies* cases. First of all, those who invoke the public mission exemption should demonstrate that all conditions are met. Member states have to prove that by eliminating the restrictive measures (exclusive import rights) the performance of the public task under economically acceptable conditions is going to be jeopardized. This burden, the Court added, cannot be extended to further ask that member states be forced to prove that no other conceivable measure could enable the public mission task to be performed under the same conditions (§ 58). As such, the former definition of the burden of proof leaves a wide margin of discretion for the member states (Slot 1998, 1200). They can concentrate on the justification of the restrictive measure rather than on evaluating other (possibly more efficient) alternatives.

The large leeway attributed to member states contrasts with the tougher attitude of the Court towards the Commission. The Court ruled that the Commission failed to fulfill its obligation as a judicial applicant, namely, that Treaty obligations have not been fulfilled by the Netherlands, France, and Italy.

The Court blamed the Commission for concentrating too much on the legal reasons which backed its claim, and too little on the facts.[32] The Court devoted many words (§§ 59-63 and § 71) to the lack of a reasonable and coherent statement from the Commission, to its failure to provide evidence, and finally, to the failure to offer clearer initiatives. This tough attitude on behalf of the Court may be explained by the fact that the Commission's action was indeed very poorly justified, which raised suspicions as to its aim. Indeed, the Commission was growing impatient with the slow-moving deliberation concerning the liberalization of the electricity and gas sectors. Instead of using the legislative powers conferred by Article 86(3) of the EC Treaty, the Commission brought about judicial action which aimed at boosting the deliberation process, not at prosecuting these member states for failure to fulfill their Treaty obligations. The Court clearly aborted the Commission's strategy and reminded the parties that in the absence of a common policy for liberalizing the electricity sector, the Court was not the arena for overcoming this deficiency:

> It is certainly not for the Court, on the basis of observations of a general nature made in the reply, to undertake an assessment, necessarily extending to economic, financial and social matters, of the means which a Member State might adopt in order to ensure the supply of electricity on the basis of costs that are as low as possible and in a socially responsible manner. (§ 63)

Interests of the Community

The final requirement which Article 86(2) establishes is that the development of trade must not be affected to such an extent that it is *contrary to the interests of the Community*. This requirement imposes a limit to a national public sectors' operations in the European market (Ehrike 1998, 746), and by so doing it prevents the derogation clause contained in Article 86(2) from being (ab)used by member states to avoid compliance with the Treaty's obligations.

The Court is very keen on leaving open a definition of "Community interests." For example, in the *Ufex* case,[33] the Court was confronted with this issue. The appellants of the case (three private undertakings of the courier sector) brought an appeal against a previous decision of the CFI. Among the pleas submitted by the appellants, it was argued that the CFI legally erred in assessing the Community interest. The appellants expected the CFI to spell out the necessary criteria to be used in assessing the Community interest. Otherwise, this concept would become vague, and defined on a case-by-case basis by the Commission rather than by the European courts. The Court answered the plea by establishing that: "In a field such as competition law, the factual and legal circumstances may differ considerably from case to case, so that it is permissible for the Court of First Instance to apply criteria which have not hitherto been considered" (§ 80).

This refusal to spell out what is considered a Community interest was also shown in the *Gas and Electricity Monopolies* cases. Moreover, in these cases the

Court indicated that it was up to the Commission to prove that the national measures (e.g., exclusive rights granted to electricity undertakings) were contrary to the interest of the Community. As the Commission failed to do so, an opportunity was missed to elaborate a qualitative or quantitative threshold which gives content to the Community-interest notion. However, in general terms the aims of the European Community (Articles 2 and 3) and the principles of the Treaty (nondiscrimination and proportionality among others) provide useful clues as to what is to be considered a Community interest.

Sending "Messages"

The case law concerning the application of Article 86(2) deals with a particular conflict of interests, namely, that existing between free competition and free trade, on the one hand, and state intervention justified by the provision of a service of general economic interest, on the other hand. This tension has been sorted out by adopting a rule of reason similar to that adopted in the *Cassis de Dijon* case: public monopolies and privileged undertakings are prima facie contrary to the European competition rules, unless it can be shown both that their existence is justified because they provide a service of general economic interest, and that the consequent restrictive effects on competition and trade are limited to what is necessary to achieve this service (Edward and Hoskins 1995, 168).

Attention has to be paid to the messages that the Court seems to be sending to the Commission, the Council, the member states, and the national courts in applying the public mission exception. These messages can be read as indicating the "passive activism" of the Court (Flynn 1995, 228): their main interest seems to be to indicate the scope of the competence of the Commission, the Council, and member states. The Court acts like a referee who has to remind the players of the rules of a (political) game which has been played somewhere else, but not yet in the new field of regulated utilities services.

Message to the Commission

The *electricity* cases can be read as the Court's warning to the Commission that it should take clearer initiatives and provide more evidence, for in a number of pleas, the Court pointed out the lack of reasoning or the lack of proofs provided by the Commission to support its actions. Moreover, the Court was sending a clear message to the Commission: not to use proceeding actions as an instrument to put pressure on the (slow) negotiations concerning the common rules for the internal market in electricity and natural gas. Indeed, the Commission wanted the Court to take the lead in the regulation of the electricity and gas market; however, the Commission got a quite different answer from the Court, for it focused on the (political) role of the institutions and on their performance.

By imposing heavy burdens of proof on the Commission, in Article 226 the Court made the monitoring of State intervention more onerous for the Commission. By so doing, another message was sent to the Commission: namely, to use Article 86(3), rather than Article 226, to give impetus to the legislation on the regulation of public monopolies and privileged undertakings. The Commission employed this legislative path in the telecommunication sector. This was totally backed by the Court (e.g., case *France v Commission*).

Message to Member States

The Court seems to have sent an optimistic message to the member states: public monopolies and privileged undertakings are neither threatened by the application of rules for the free movement of goods, nor by the application of the strict interpretation of the mandatory requirements derogation clause (Articles 28 and 30 respectively). Why? Because the compatibility of special and exclusive rights with the rules of the Treaty is to be evaluated under Article 86(2). The way the Court interpreted the requirements for applying this derogation clause clearly benefits the discretion of member states under Community rules.

The fact that the Court's interpretation or Article 86(2) points to the protection of member states' discretionary powers, whereas the interpretation of Article 86(3) points to the protection of the Commission's legislative powers are not contradictory outcomes of case law. Rather they are two sides of the same coin: the emphasis on the institutional and political (rather than juridical) arena. The liberalization of utilities sectors should take place in these arenas. Indeed, the Court reminded the Commission that it ought to use its quasi-legislative powers in a clear and well-reasoned way. This legislation cannot successfully be implemented unless the Commission allows member states to become involved in the earlier consultation stages. Although the Commission seeks the participation of member states, the states may feel that their discretionary powers are being threatened by Commission's quasi-legislative competence in regard to competition issues. To counterbalance this autonomous legislative power, member states may become more active within the Council of Ministries in order to boost European legislation. Thus, the Council becomes a player taking part in two different games: that between member states and the Community, and that between the Community's institutions.

Message to National Courts

The Court of Justice consistently holds that under European competition rules it is up to the national courts to evaluate the compatibility of public monopolies and privileged undertakings. The decentralized application of Article 86(2), supported by the Court, coheres with the decentralized application of European competition rules, promoted by the Commission. Indeed, in its

White Paper on Competition policy, the Commission proposed a reform according to which the current system of notification and exemption, which implements Articles 81(2) and (3), should be replaced by a decentralized ex post control system.[34] This reform, proposed by the Commission, will boost the decentralized application of European competition rules[35] because national authorities and national courts will apply Article 81 in full.[36]

The decentralized application of European competition, which the Court (and the Commission) supports, leads to a number of consequences. First, due to the national courts' sympathetic attitude towards the parties[37] and the varying familiarity with European competition law, one could fear an uneven application of the public service exception. In this sense, the Court and the Commission hold that it will be necessary to establish measures that aim at training national judges in competition law.

Second, due to the complexity of competition cases, national courts may address the Commission as an expert in competition law. The Court has indicated this possibility,[38] and the Commission has elaborated the notice concerning cooperation with national courts.[39] Moreover, in the Commission's White Paper on Competition law, it has declared the need to reform the existing procedure for cooperation in order to adapt it to the decentralized application of European competition rules. Consequently, the Commission will be at the center of a network made up by itself, national authorities, and national courts; once again, this network will enhance the Commission's powers.

Third, the decentralized application of Article 86(2) imprints the Community character on national courts. To explain this consequence, it is necessary to remember the requirements established by Article 86(2). This derogation clause applies (1) to undertakings providing services of general economic interest; (2) if the application of competition rules obstructs the performance of their task, in law or in fact; and (3) if trade is not affected in a manner contrary to the interest of the Community. The later requirement means that the Community interest threshold does not delimit the jurisdiction of national courts; it rather stamps them with a further community role: national courts not only apply Community law—supremacy, direct effect, and the effective implementation of Community rights being the main tools that the Court elaborates for this purpose.[40] They also have to take into account and to evaluate the Community interest; by so doing, national courts come close to assuming the role of a Community institution.

More than Setting the Stage and Stepping Out?

Flynn holds that the Court has not only declared which regulatory competence member states and European institutions have; it has gone beyond this and constructed regulatory structures (Flynn 1995, 228). He refers to the Court-established separation between operational and regulatory activities in the utility sectors. Although this differentiation was strongly defended in the *GB-INNO v ATAB* case, further Court judgments undermine this statement. In the

Almelo case, the Court held that: "In that regard, it is necessary to take into consideration the economic conditions in which the undertaking operates, in particular the costs which it has to bear and the *legislation*, particularly concerning the environment, to which it is subject" (§ 49).[41]

The Court explicitly referred to the national regulation of the discussed public service. This means that the economic, social, and policy choices that member states made when regulating services of general economic interest ought to be taken into account to decide whether or not competition rules apply. It also means that national regulatory space is left unchallenged by European law, and in particular by competition rules.

In the *Albany* case the Court ruled that it is compatible with European law that a privileged undertaking that has been entrusted with performing a social task—namely, the management of supplementary compulsory pension funds—can fulfill a dual role: it can manage the pension scheme; and as an authority, it can grant exemptions. The Court distinguished its previous ruling in the *GB-INNO v ATAB* case, and held that: "[t]he exercise of exemption involves an evaluation of complex data relating to the pension schemes involved and the financial equilibrium of the fund, which necessarily implies a wide margin of appreciation" (§ 120).

Given the complexity of the evaluation and the risks that the exemptions presuppose for the financial equilibrium of the privileged undertaking, the Court held that member states should consider that the power of exemption should not be attributed to a different entity. The Court has not only backed member states' regulatory powers in the field of public services, but it also has backed the regulatory structure established by member states.

Conclusion

This chapter has argued that whenever the Court is called to assess the legality of member states' measures under European law, it decides upon the degree of intrusion into the economic, financial, and social choices that can be made by member states. In a particular economic field—namely, market integration—the Court has consistently adopted a quite strict degree of judicial scrutiny. The Court's nondeferential attitude towards national measures that affect fundamental freedoms, and in particular the free movement of goods, has promoted market integration, for obstacles to trade imposed by member states are eliminated. Is the Court's negative integration bias maintained in other economic fields? If competition law cases are analyzed, it is clear that there is no negative integration bias. One could argue that, indeed, it should not exist since competition law may be thought of as a policy which is independent from the already concluded internal market project. This is not the case. As free trade rules, competition rules concern access to the market. If a member state grants exclusive rights to distribute electricity to a privileged undertaking, it restricts access to the market. As in free trade law, the question is whether such a restriction is lawful, that is, whether it is nondiscriminatory and necessary in order to pursue certain values (e.g., the universality of certain services of general economic interest). In answering these questions a bias towards negative integration cannot be perceived, but a quite different one can be.

The *Gas and Electricity Monopolies cases* provide a clear signal that when the Court seeks to assess State intervention regarding public interest it applies a lower threshold than that used in the case law regarding the free movement of goods. Why? Because the legality of those national measures that have both discriminatory effects on intra-Community trade and restrictive effects on competition are going to be evaluated according to competition rules. Indeed, in the mentioned cases, the Court held that the discriminatory effects on intra-Community trade that arise from granting exclusive import rights could not be justified under free trade rules. The fact that granting an exclusive import right cannot be justified under free trade rules does not imply that the state measure is illegal. To fully assess the legality of the measure it is necessary to determine whether granting exclusive rights can be justified in light of competition rules, and in particular in light of the public mission derogation clause of Article 86(2).

Article 86(2) establishes that restrictions on competition can be justified if a service of general economic interest is provided. However, to what extent does the performance of a public task justify restrictions on competition? The Court has answered this question by adopting a sort of rule of reason: restrictions on competition are accepted if they are necessary to guarantee the performance of a task of public interest under economically acceptable conditions. The way the Court has applied the threshold of necessity and the criterion of "economically acceptable conditions" indicates that the Court has a deferential attitude towards member states' discretionary powers.

The way the burden of proof is defined in the *Gas and Electricity Monopolies* cases is a final sign that there is no negative integration bias. This benefits member states, which are not bound to demonstrate that granting exclusive rights is the least restrictive measure. Indeed, the stringent "least restrictive measure" threshold largely applied in the area of free trade does not have such relevance in competition cases concerning public services.

The deferential attitude towards member states' discretionary powers in the public service sectors does not simultaneously imply that the Commission's powers have been reduced in competition matters. Attention is paid to the way the Commission carries out its competence: it is necessary to elaborate better reasoning and to provide more evidence if this institution is to function properly.

Notes

1. This opening statement obviously holds in the case of rules for free movement of goods and services, which aims at eliminating obstacles to free trade that the member states might create. It also holds in the case of competition rules addressed to member states, because, rather than a general rule on the elimination of distortions to competition, the Treaty focuses on the elimination of those anticompetitive practices—originated by member states—which represent an obstacle to free trade. Not only the Treaty, but also the Court of Justice is willing to combine the free movement rules with competition rules.

This combination can be summarized by the principle of free trade under conditions of fair competition established by the Court in the *Consten and Grundig* case (joined cases 56 & 58/64 *Consten SARL & Grundig v Commission* [1966] ECR 299). See P. Pescatore 1987, 383.

2. The "commercial nature" of monopolies means that such bodies are undertakings; that is, they carry out economic activities. If a body carries out economic activities and at the same time has regulatory functions, it is a state monopoly of commercial character (Buendía Sierra 1999, 81).

3. Edward and Hoskins differentiate four different models of judicial control over public monopolies: the Absolute Sovereignty approach—member states have exclusive competence in granting legal monopolies; the Limited Sovereignty approach—member states can grant legal monopolies if they do necessarily contravene the rules of the Union; the Absolute Competition approach—legal monopolies are per se a violation of competition rules; and the Limited Competition approach—member states may create legal monopolies and distort competition as long as this distortion is necessary to achieve the public mission objective (Edward and Hoskins 1995, 159).

4. Case 59/75 *Pubblico Ministero v Flavia Manghera and others* [1976] ECR 91.

5. The Commission has two alternative law-making paths to implement its liberalization policy in the utilities sectors: namely, internal market legislation and competition legislation. If the Commission follows the first option, legislation implementing the liberalization of the utilities sectors will be issued by majority voting at the Council (Article 95) and in accord with the co-decision procedure of Article 251, which involves both the Council and the Parliament. This is the path chosen to liberalize the energy sector (electricity and gas). A more successful path, at least for the interests of the Commission, is the competition legislation established in Article 86(3). This path has been chosen to liberalize the telecommunication sector, and it has received the support of the Court.

6. Case C-202/88 *France v Commission* [1991] ECR I-1223.

7. Undertakings, and in particular public and privileged undertakings, have to comply with the prohibitions against distorting competition and abusing dominant position; the responsibility for the bad-doing lies with the company and not with the state that granted the special and exclusive rights that led to a distortion of competition or an abuse of the dominant position.

8. Case 13/77 *GB-INNO v ATAB* [1977] ECR 2115.

9. Case 155/73 *Giuseppe Sacchi* [1974] ECR 409.

10. The major consequence of allowing national courts to be involved in the application of Community competition law is the decentralization of adjudicative powers that reinforce the constitutional role of the Court in relation to national courts.

11. Case C-320/91 *Criminal proceedings against Paul Corbeau* [1993] ECR I-2533.

12. This position is also held in further cases such as the *Almelo* case and the *Gas and Electricity Monopolies* cases (Case C-157/94 *Commission v Kingdom of the Netherlands* [1997] ECR I-5699; Case C-159/94 *Commission v French Republic* [1997] ECR I-5815; Case C-158/94 *Commission v Italian Republic* [1997] ECR I-5789).

13. Case C-67/96, *Albany International BV v Stichting Bedrijfspensioenfonds Textielindustrie* [1999] ECR I-5751. The case is concerned with the legality, under European competition law, of a system of compulsory affiliation to supplementary pension funds. The issue was whether by granting the exclusive right to offer supplementary pension funds to selected companies the member state was in breach of European competition law.

14. As Edward and Hoskins point out, there is a danger of looking at each case in isolation (Edward and Hoskins 1995, 178). Although a single competing firm may not

threaten the financial viability of the privileged undertaking, the combined effect of all competing companies may do so. However, such complex analysis is extremely onerous for the Court, not to mention the national courts.

15. Case C-41/90 *Klaus Höfner and Fritz Elser v Macrotron GmbH* [1991] ECR I-1979.

16. To determine whether a dominant position has been created, the Court emphasizes the necessity of identifying the "relevant market" in which the privileged undertaking may abuse its dominant position. For this aim, it requires (Case 27/76 *United Brands v Commission* [1978] ECR 207, § 31), first, the evaluation of the particular features of the product or service; and second, the identification of the geographical area in which the product of service is marketed.

17. This interpretation is consistent with the fact that Article 82 (on the prohibition of the abuse of dominant position) is addressed to undertakings, rather than to member states.

18. Emphasis added.

19. This interpretation has also been upheld in the *Merci Convenzionali* case (Case C-170/90 *Merci convenzionali porto di Genova SpA v Siderurgica Gabrielli SpA* [1991] ECR I-5889).

20. Emphasis added.

21. European Commission 1999.

22. To the president of the *Bundeskartellamt*, in an early stage, competition policy was subordinated to the goal of market integration; it was not viewed as a complementary policy. Now that market integration has become a reality, "it is time for the emancipation of competition policy" (Wolf 1998).

23. These cases show that the fact that Article 86 is placed together with European competition rules does not prevent other juridical conflicts from arising, and in particular conflicts where rules on trade between member states are involved.

24. The *Manghera* case was concerned with the validity of a monopoly for importing manufactured tobacco, which was created by Italian law. The Court established that the conferral of exclusive rights to import manufactured products—and the related prohibition on importing those products by companies other than the privileged undertaking leads to a discrimination prohibited by Article 31(1) (§ 12).

25. Also, the case C-202/88 *France v Commission* [1991] ECR I-1223.

26. Trade restrictions, even if caused by discriminatory measures, are not contrary to European law if they can be justified by any of the grounds spelled out by Article 30, namely, public morality, public policy, or public security; the protection of the health and life of humans, animals, or plants; the protection of national treasures; or the protection of industrial and commercial property. These justificatory reasons have been strictly interpreted by the Court. The Court and Advocate General Cosmas disagreed as to whether the derogation clause of Article 30 should be applied to the *Gas and Electricity Monopolies* cases. To Advocate General Cosmas, once the breach of Article 31(1) was established, the following step was to evaluate the justification of such an infringement under Article 30. In particular, since Article 30 does not refer to the public interest (public mission task), the defendant states couldn't but argue that the exclusive rights in question are justified on the grounds of public security. However, Advocate General Cosmas dismissed such an argument: measures which do not have the particular, direct object of ensuring a minimum supply of electricity and natural gas cannot be deemed to contribute to safeguarding the public security for the purposes of Article 30 of the Treaty (§ 83). Then, his next question was whether exclusive import rights, which cannot be justified by mandatory requirements, are contrary to the Treaty. The answer is negative if the exclusive import rights could be justified by Article 86(2). Unlike the Commission,

Advocate General Cosmas and the Court agreed on evaluating the legality of exclusive rights for the provision of services of general economic interest within the framework of Article 86 rather than within the framework provided by Article 30. This raises a very interesting issue: a derogation clause for competition law, Article 86(2), can also be interpreted as a derogation clause of rules on trade.

27. This definition focused on the characteristics of the services, rather than on their category.

28. Moreover, a purely revenue-producing monopoly seems to be incompatible with Article 31 Treaty. See Buendía Sierra 1999, 228.

29. Case C-260/89 *Elliniki Radiophonia Tiléorassi AE and Panellinia Omospondia Syllogon Prossopikou v Dimotiki etairia Pliroforissis and Sotirios Kouvelas and Nicolaos Avdellas and others* [1991] ECR I-2925.

30. Case C-393/92 *Municipality of Almelo and others v NV Energiebedrijf IJsselmij* [1994] ECR I-1477.

31. Emphasis added.

32. The failure of the Commission could be appreciated during the proceedings before the Court and during the prelitigation procedure.

33. Case C-119/97 P *Ufex and others v Commission* [1999] ECR I-1341.

34. According to it, anticompetitive practices which affect trade between member states would be lawful ab initio if they met the conditions laid down in Article 81(3).

35. In the XXIXth Report on Competition policy, the Directorate-General for Competition spells out the consequences of this reform: (1) decentralized application of European competition rules; (2) more free resources which will allow the Commission to focus on broader policy questions; and (3) the Commission would coordinate (rather than monitor) the application of competition rules by a network of national authorities and national courts.

36. At present the effective application of Article 81(1) by national courts is undermined by the fact that the firms against which an action have been brought may notify the Commission of their agreement and block any court proceedings.

37. At least national courts may show a more sympathetic attitude than that held by the Court of Justice and the Court of First Instance.

38. Case C-234/89 *Stergios Delimitis v Henniger Brau* [1992] ECR I-935.

39. OJ 1993 C39/6. The cooperation between the Commission and the national courts, if taken seriously, will lead to the introduction in national law of procedures allowing such consultations.

40. For a further analysis of the role of national courts as Community courts in the interpretation and application of Community law, see Maher 1994.

41. Emphasis added.

References

Buendía Sierra, J. L. 1999. *Exclusive Rights and State Monopolies under EC Law*. Trans. A. Read. Oxford: Oxford University Press.

Edward, D., and M. Hoskins. 1995. Article 90: Deregulation and EC Law. Reflections Arising from the XVI FIDE Conference. *Common Market Law Review* 32: 157-86.

Ehrike, U. 1998. Zur Konzeption von Art. 37 I und Art. 90 II EGV. EuZW.

European Commission. 1999. Directorate-General for Competition. XXIXth Report on Competition Policy. Brussels: European Commission.

Flynn, L. 1995. Telecommunications and EU Integration. In *New Legal Dynamics of European Union*, ed. J. Shaw and G. Moore. Oxford: Clarendon Press.

Gardner, A. 1995. The Velvet Revolution: Article 90 and the Triumph of the Free Market in Europe's Regulated Sectors. *European Competition Law Review* 16: 78-86.

Maher, I. 1994. National Courts as Community Courts. *Legal Studies* 14: 226-43.

Pescatore, P. 1987. Public and Private Aspects of European Community Competiton Law. *Fordham International Law Journal* 10: 373-419.

Reich, N. 1992. Competition between Legal Orders: A New Paradigm of EC Law. *Common Market Law Review* 29: 861-96.

Ross, M. 2000. Article 16 E.C. and Services of General Interest: From Derogation to Obligation? *European Law Review* 25: 22-38.

Sauter, W. 1998. Universal Service Obligations and the Emergence of Citizens' Rights in European Telecommunications Liberalization. In *Public Services and Citizenship in European Law*, ed. M. Freeland and S. Sciarra. Oxford: Oxford University Press.

Slot, P. 1998. Case C-157/94 Commission v Netherlands. Comments. *Common Market Law Review* 34: 1183-1203.

Wolf, D. 1998. Communication to the Second Workshop on European Competition Law, European Competition Law Annual 1997: Objectives of Competition Policy. *European Competition Law, European Competition Law Annual 1997*: Objectives of Competition Policy, ed. C. D. Ehlermann and L. Laudati. Oxford: Hart.

List of Cases

Joined cases 56 & 58/64 *Consten SARL & Grundig v Commission* [1966] ECR 299.

Case 155/73 *Giuseppe Sacchi* [1974] ECR 409.

Case 59/75 Pubblico Ministero v Flavia Manghera and others [1976] ECR 91.

Case 13/77 *GB-INNO v ATAB* [1977] ECR 2115.

Case 27/76 United Brands v Commission [1978] ECR 207.

Case C-260/89 Elliniki Radiophonia Tiléorassi AE and Panellinia Omospondia Syllogon Prossopikou v Dimotiki etairia Pliroforissis and Sotirios Kouvelas and Nicolaos Avdellas and others [1991] ECR I-2925.

Case C-202/88 *France v Commission* [1991] ECR I-1223.

Case C-41/90 Klaus Höfner and Fritz Elser v Macrotron GmbH [1991] ECR I-1979.

Case C-170/90 Merci convenzionali porto di Genova SpA v Siderurgica Gabrielli SpA [1991] ECR I-5889.

Case C-234/89 Stergios Delimitis v Henniger Brau [1992] ECR I-935.

Case C-320/91 Criminal proceedings against Paul Corbeau [1993] ECR I-2533.

Case C-393/92 Municipality of Almelo and others v NV Energiebedrijf IJsselmij [1994] ECR I-1477.

Case C-157/94 Commission v Kingdom of the Netherlands [1997] ECR I-5699.

Case C-159/94 *Commission v French Republic* [1997] ECR I-5815.

Case C-158/94 *Commission v Italian Republic* [1997] ECR I-5789.

Case C-67/96, Albany International BV v Stichting Bedrijfspensioenfonds Textielindustrie [1999] ECR I-5751.

Case C-119/97 P *Ufex and others v Commission* [1999] ECR I-1341.

Part 2

Common Goods and the Role of Private Actors

National Level

10

The New Regulatory Regime: The Institutional Design of Telecommunications Regulation at the National Level

Dominik Böllhoff

Introduction

In recent years European Community member states have seen extensive changes in their utility and network industries. Instead of providing common goods, i.e., a network infrastructure or a service accessible to all, by themselves, states have opted for the liberalization of sectors and the privatization of network industries. Former state monopolies have been transformed into competitive markets with a shift from public to private actor provision of common goods (cf. sections 1 and 4). This development has mainly taken place in areas where the state had hitherto heavily invested in the infrastructure (Grande and Eberlein 1999) as in the cases of public utilities like telecommunications, energy, or transport (König and Benz 1997; Héritier 1998).

Up to now, the research interest of political scientists has mainly been concerned with the emergence of the "regulatory state" (Majone 1997), e.g., with a focus on regulative policies (Mayntz 1983; Czada, Lütz, and Mette 1999), changes of state functions (Grande 1993), or social regulatory and public interest issues (Wilson 1984; Héritier 1998).

One aspect which has not yet been well researched is the institutional design of state regulatory structures. The liberalization of utilities, with a change from public to private actor provision, causes an administrative reform of state structures and the transformation of traditional administrations (cf. Peters in this volume). A shift from centralized provision to the public regulation of market provision confronts the state with new tasks and competencies. States have to develop new administrative structures to "steer" the process of liberalization and privatization. This development results in the emergence of new "regulatory regimes."[1]

This contribution aims to analyze this process in reference to the case of telecommunications regulation in Britain and Germany.[2] The focus is on the core institution providing the day-to-day regulatory functions at the national level, and not on the whole regulatory regime in the multilevel governance system (cf. Ostrom in this volume). It aims to describe and explain why particular institutional solutions were chosen.

It starts out with the picture of regulatory designs in Britain's and Germany's utilities sectors. In Britain's central utility sectors, such as telecommunications, energy, or rail, one coherent regulatory agency model was chosen, and regulators were established for telecommunications (OFTEL— Office of Telecommunications), energy (OFGEM—Office of Gas and Electricity Markets), or rail (ORR—Office of Rail Regulation and SRA—Strategic Rail Authority). By contrast, there is still no cross-sector coherence in Germany. There are a range of regulatory designs. Whereas an administrative agency was set up in the rail sector with the *Eisenbahnbundesamt* (EBA), in the case of energy a self-regulatory model was institutionalized with associations' agreements. The only sector-specific regulatory agency presently in Germany was created for telecommunications regulation (*Regulierungsbehörde für Telekommunikation und Post*; RegTP).

This chapter aims to describe the designing process of the institutional designs in telecommunications regulation in Britain and Germany and to give initial explanations as to why the regulatory agency model was chosen. Diffusion theory and historical institutionalism are linked to explain the designing process as well as the institutional design. In contrast to earlier research on the topic (see e.g., Grande 1999; Schneider 2001), a two-level approach[3] on a *macro-organizational level* and a *micro-organizational level* is to achieve deeper insight into the new national regulatory regime. The macro-organizational level points to the framework and overall structure of regulatory institutions, i.e., for which general institutional structure to opt. The micro-organizational level refers to internal administrative structures: the goal is to "dive into the regulator" and to give an account on the internal institutional design, such as administrative structures or decision-making processes. Comparing regulatory designs on both a macro-organizational and a micro-organizational level shows important differences in the design and operation of regulators.

After introductory remarks on the role of the state in utility regulation, general explanations combining diffusion theory and historical institutionalism are outlined to guide the research on new regulatory regimes. The institutional path for setting up regulatory structures in telecommunications in Great Britain and Germany is then described and explained. Finally, concluding remarks are made regarding how the theoretical explanations fit with the empirical findings.

Utility Regulation and Institutional Design

The transformation from the positive to the regulatory state (Majone 1997), forced by developments like globalization, technical developments, or European pressures, is closely linked to institutional reform movements.[4] To enhance the state capacity for regulation requires the introduction of new administrative bodies with new administrative competencies. Administrations that formerly steered state monopolies have to be transformed into new structures.

In dealing with utility regulation, the overall development is described with catchwords like liberalization (Werle 1999), privatization (Hulsink 1999), or regulatory reform (OECD 1997). However, for the changes in utility regulation, three interrelated processes are combined: liberalization, privatization, and regulation, all of which include a dimension of institutional change. While liberalization leads to the opening of markets for new entrants, privatization changes the structure of former state monopolistic entities from the status of public law to private law in order to open them up to private investment. Regulatory reforms separate state functions and create new institutional solutions to maintain state influence in liberalized and privatized sectors. In the following, we examine more closely the new challenges for the state in utility regulation.

Challenges for the State in Utility Regulation

With the end of public monopolies in network and utility industries, the competencies of the state are changing. Instead of providing common goods defined as network infrastructure and network services, the new task is to supervise and monitor utility sectors. In the "regulatory state," state functions are shifted from "rowing to steering" (Osborne and Gabler 1992). States are keeping options open for intervening in liberalized sectors. On the basis of politically defined goals of service provision such as accessibility, security, continuity, and affordability, the state still has a hand in utility sectors (Héritier 1998, 3; Müller and Sturm 1999, 514ff.). The main challenge for states undergoing a transformation in the provision of public goods from monopolies to competition-based systems is to balance the interests between the already existing companies and the new entrants, and to do so on the basis of the defined law.

In the case of utility regulation, the state has to open markets to competition, regulate networks, and prevent market failures ("market making"). A core goal is to disempower former incumbents and create space for new entrants to the market. Furthermore, the state has to ensure social and redistributive goals ("market correction").

To cope with these demands, the key feature of utility regulation is continuous case-to-case intervention in single private companies (Noll 1985). To facilitate such intervention, utility regulation includes four steering functions: economic, social, technical, and administrative (see e.g., OECD 1997, 9ff.; Grande 1994, 148ff.). With economic regulation, the state defines "conditions under which firms may enter and exit the market, competitive practices, the size of economic units, or the price firms can charge" (Eisner, Worsham, and Ringquist 2000, 5). The goal is market creation. A variety of new steering instruments like price cap regulation, distribution of licenses, or net competition and third party access have to be introduced and developed. Social regulation "forces corporations to accept greater responsibility for the safety and health of workers and consumers" and deals with "negative by-products" (Eisner, Worsham, and Ringquist 2000, 5). Attention is paid to market correction with universal service and public service goals. Technical regulations include issues such as the maintenance of frequency management, net safety, numbering, and the standardization of utility networks. Additionally, administrative regulations focus on administrative principles and formalities, as well as decision-making procedures. These functions are used to "collect information and intervene in individual economic decisions" (OECD 1997, 11).

These functions can be found in every regulated sector. However, the institutional design of the key regulator depends on the definition of these functions and on how they are distributed between institutions within the regulatory regime. After making introductory comments on the challenges that utility regulation presents to the state, the following section gives some general insights into how institutions emerge and change their design.

Institutional Change and Design Theory

A starting point for the analysis of institutional changes in the regulatory structures is the institutional design theory.[5] In general, "design is the creation of an actionable form to promote valued outcomes in a particular context" (Bobrow and Dryzek 1987, 200). The central concern of this theory is on the shaping of institutions and the causes for institutional change, because it is often assumed that designing processes are random and guided by the principle of "anything goes" (Klages 1998, 51).

In general, institutional changes might be caused by accident, evolution, or intention (Goodin 1996, 24). Whereas in the case of accidental design, organizational changes just happen as "purely [a] matter of contingency," evolutionary design processes cause change via path-dependent selection processes and the choice of "some variants for survival" (Goodin 1996, 24ff.). Intentional changes are actions planned by individuals or groups to reach new institutional outcomes. Processes of institutional design are influenced by all three elements.

To avoid institutional determinism, institutional design theories point to the actors involved in the designing process. Theorists argue that designs are shaped by bargaining processes between a multiplicity of actors, such as politicians, bureaucrats, or interest groups (Moe 1990). Institutional design "arise[s] out of politics, and its design reflects the interests, strategies, and compromises of those who exercise political power"; that is why the administrative outcome is often a suboptimal polity solution (Moe 1989, 267).

For the analysis of new utility regulatory designs, institutional design theory gives us three insights. First, it highlights the need to analyze the designing process as well as the design of institutions (Pettit 1996, 54). Secondly, pointing to actors involved in the designing process, it reveals that there is neither a single design nor a single designer, and that the analysis should be focused on the "discursive design process" of different actors and their impact on the design (Dryzek 1990). Thirdly, design theories argue that the design is not purely contingent.[6] There are not just history-driven developments. The design is also shaped by external influences.

Theoretical Model: Diffusion Theory and Historical Institutionalism

From possible explanations for regulatory change (Dyson 1992; Levy and Spiller 1996), in the following, diffusion theory and historical institutionalism are presented as two core theories to explain the process of shaping the institutional design of regulatory structures. These theories are utilized to show that institutional designs can be shaped both by diffusion as well as by path dependency. Furthermore, we claim that these two developments vary between the macro-organizational and the micro-organizational level of regulatory institutions.

First, diffusion theory is introduced as a theoretical approach to explain the institutional design. Diffusion theory—in other contexts referred to as "policy transfer," "policy imitation," or "policy learning"—deals with "the borrowing of a policy from one political system for the use in another" (Wolman 1992, 27). Questioning what is transferred, different categories are defined, such as policies, institutions, ideologies, or attitudes (Dolowitz and Marsh 1996, 349f.). We predominantly point to the diffusion of institutions, i.e., administrative elements of polities.

Diffusion is of growing importance, particularly in state and administrative reform. The main reason is that in times of change it is seen as particularly useful to learn from the experience of countries which have already successfully developed solutions to similar problems. Diffusion mainly takes place when "policies are seen to address problems perceived in the country and to coincide with dominant or emerging ideas about the appropriate shape of policy" (Wolman 1992, 44). Diffusion does not only take place among countries within an international system, but three further diffusion mechanisms can be revealed (Halligan 1996, 291ff.):

  interactive effects among state institutions in a federal system,
  federal effects to which the states respond, and
  the impact of international organizations such as the OECD or the European Union.

When we introduce the distinction between the macro- and micro-organizational level, we claim that the impact of diffusion might differ when analyzing institutions and institutional change. It is argued that diffusion does not only explain the transfer of broad and general trends, but that it includes specific ideas and concepts "in fairly precise detail" (Halligan 1996, 290; 307f.). Diffusion can take place on a macro- as well as on a micro-organizational level. However, it is pointed out that "in many cases a specific policy idea . . . may be borrowed, but the specific design or structure through which this occurs in the original country may not be [identical]." (Wolman 1992, 41). An institutional design can be transferred; however, to implement it at home requires detailed adaptation. Since emulation in detail is rare, it is likely that overall concepts are set up; but on the micro-organizational level old concepts may persist.

A second approach which helps to explain how the institutional design of regulatory structures is shaped is historical institutionalism. Besides rational choice and sociological institutionalism (Hall and Taylor 1996), this theory is one variant of the "new institutionalism" (March and Olsen 1989). In "historical institutionalism" institutions are defined as "formal or informal procedures, routines, norms and conventions embedded in the organizational structure of the polity or political outcome" (Hall and Taylor 1996, 6). When referring to the topic of utility regulation, a more narrow and formal definition is utilized. We refer to organizations, i.e., public administrations with ministries and agencies or self-regulatory organizations supervised by the state.

The central concern of historical institutionalism is to stress the importance of historical processes when analyzing the structure and change of institutions. There are path dependencies which cause long-term effects on the future development of the institutional design. Path dependency often results in reform movements not developing the same outcome. Instead, solutions are shaped by "contextual features of a given situation often inherited from the past" (Hall and Taylor 1996, 9). As Loughlin and Peters argue, "[t]he historical context, and in particular the state tradition in which a reform occurs, to a large extent determines the outcome of the reform" (Loughlin and Peters 1997, 43).

However, how is the term path dependency to be defined? We distinguish between two approaches: researchers such as Mahoney criticize the often "vague notion" of the term and strive for a more narrow definition (Mahoney 2000). For a clearer operationalization, he argues that path dependency "occurs when a contingent historical event triggers a subsequent sequence that follows a relatively deterministic pattern" (Mahoney 2000, 535). Research on historical processes of change has to include the study of causal processes, and the outcomes of change have to be stochastically related to initial conditions. In contrast to this more rigid and deterministic approach, other researchers have a broader understanding. Thelen defines specific mechanisms of institutional change to explore how "history matters" (Thelen 2001). The mechanism of "institutional layering" points to changes, where new institutional structures are added to the existing ones without changing them. "Institutional conversion" refers to transitions which lead to "a change in the role the institutions perform and/or the function they serve" (Thelen 2001, 28).

For our research on the institutional design of telecommunications regulation at the national level, we refer to the broad understanding of path dependency.

Linking Diffusion Theory and Historical Institutionalism

First, to explain the development path towards regulatory institutions by exploring critical junctures, we argue that diffusion theory and historical institutionalism are linked. On the surface, the two approaches seem to contradict each other. Path dependent institutional changes exclude external influences caused by diffusions. However, in reality "policy ideas from abroad compete with other alternatives in . . . the 'policy primeval soup'" (Wolman 1992, 43). Here, diffusion theory can be linked with historical institutionalism in analyzing situations where established patterns are changing (Thelen and Steinmo 1992, 27). To explore "critical junctures," defined "as a period of significant change . . . which is hypothesized to produce distinct legacies" (Collier and Collier 1991, 29), helps to analyze radical breaks with the past that cause changes and caused the development of new institutional designs. Analyzing such turning points helps to find explanations for why "historical developments move onto a new path" (Hall and Taylor 1996, 10).

Secondly, we point out that the fact that these junctures and new paths are caused by diffusion does not mean that the old path has been fully exhausted. It can be expected that segments of the old path still exist. As this chapter will show, the design of regulatory institutions is shaped by path dependency as well as by diffusion. There are different developments on a macro-organizational and a micro-organizational level. In using a comparative approach, with case studies exploring the change of new institutional designs, we demonstrate that institutions show convergence on a macro-organizational level, due to diffusion processes and the establishment of new institutional designs. However, on the micro-organizational level divergence still exists because of the consistent, path dependent use of national administrative instruments.

Five Institutional Designs of Utility Regulation

At the national level, for the utility sector that provides services such as telecommunications, rail, electricity or gas, the process of liberalization requires that new regulatory regimes be put into place. For these regimes, institutional solutions have to be set up which are responsible for the day-to-day business of national, sector-specific regulation. Five institutional designs for utility regulation are distinguished, which range from formal state-centrist organized regulation to informal self-organized arrangements (Czada, Lütz, and Mette 1999, 13).[7]

In addition to this key institution, in the sectoral regulatory regime there are a variety of other bodies concerned with regulatory issues. In a multilevel governance system, regulatory competencies are distributed among different levels. There are supranational institutions, such as the World Trade Organization (WTO) or the International Telecommunications Union (ITU), which are mainly involved in defining overall principles on issues like liberalization and standardization.[8] At the European level, the European Commission and the European Court of Justice have not only paved the way for liberalization and regulatory reform (Schmidt 1998), but they have also supervised the implementation of European directives, and they are developing the regulatory framework to further increase European integration.[9] At the national level, ministries supervise the regulatory institution,[10] and parliamentary committees and advisory boards of the regulated institutions might be involved in the regulatory decision-making process. Furthermore, regulatory institutions are in close contact with competition authorities on issues of competition policy.

In the following, the five institutional designs that served as the central alternatives for the British and German cases are introduced.

Ministries

In the most centralized hierarchical organizational form of the state, headed by a minister, ministries are highly politicized bodies. They are responsible for supporting the government in policy planning and strategic issues. Insofar as they remain federal responsibilities, executive administrative tasks are delegated to subordinated agencies. In general, ministries are not directly involved in regulatory issues.[11] The main reasons are the continuous danger of ministerial interference, the goal of keeping regulatory issues out of party politics, the ministry's lack of expertise, and the need for efficiency in flexible regulatory decision-making (Baldwin and Cave 1999, 68f.).

Therefore, ministries are usually not the key regulatory institution used in utility regulation. Their task is only to supervise and guide subordinated units as a "parent department." However, depending on the institutional design and the functions shared by the regulatory institution, ministries might be heavily involved in utility regulation. Thus self-regulatory solutions often do not have the capacity for a full range of economic, social, technical, and administrative regulatory functions. Since private regulators are only specialized on a limited number of competencies, ministries might have to step in to provide functions. Additionally, the ministry takes over representation functions for the self-regulator. In the case of administrative and regulatory agencies, the ministry is often involved not only in strategic policy issues and the framing of regulations, but also in influencing the day-to-day decisions of agencies.

Administrative Agencies

Administrative agencies have been traditionally used as an administrative solution to set up executive units that deliver services for the government. These services are transferred to them by ministries, which is why administrative agencies remain in a hierarchical relationship with ministries which closely supervise them.[12]

Although there are agencies which have advisory functions for the ministries or peripheral agencies not linked to the main ministerial aims, we shall focus on administrative agencies which execute statutory functions derived from the core goals of their parent ministry.

Administrative agencies can take over regulatory functions; but when they do so they mainly take over social and technical regulatory ones. As far as economic regulation and the enhancing of competition are concerned, administrative agencies might not have the capacity to regulate a sector independently, e.g., there are no instruments for ex-ante regulation. Therefore, traditional administrative agencies supervise rather than regulate.

Competition Authorities

The function of competition authorities is to protect competition via ex-post regulation. The main objectives are to prevent anticompetitive behavior (cases of structural export and import cartels) and merger control (Baake and Perschau 1996, 149ff.). Apart from these classical competencies, competition authorities are involved in regulatory issues. In anticompetitive or discriminatory practice, competencies are separated between competition authorities and the sector-specific regulators. This might cause difficulties, because it is a complex task to clearly distinguish between competencies.

However, competition authorities can even become utility regulators. Competition authorities are seen as independent bodies with limited political interference and high regulatory capacities. Instead of creating new sector-specific regulatory bodies, these tasks could be carried out by the competition authority. A merger of competition and regulatory supervision might create "synergy effects" and coherent administrative regulatory procedures instead of the continuous fragmentation between two institutions. Regulation among the competition authorities could lead to "leaner regulation" and to phasing out regulation earlier (Knieps 1997, 18f.).

Self-Regulatory Institutions

With self-regulatory institutions, the regulated actors, not the state, are the core players in the regulatory process. The actors make decisions jointly on how to organize the regulatory process and on how to implement decisions (Héritier

1998a, 18). The state is not directly involved in the day-to-day regulatory process. Instead of the institutionalization of a regulatory body, market players define a regulatory framework which agrees upon the ministry responsible for the sector. However, self-regulation does not mean that the state is out of the regulatory game. Ministries have to supervise the functioning of the self-regulatory institution, and they might be involved in social, technical, and economic regulatory issues.

The main arguments in favor of self regulation are that they keep central governments small, produce rules more quickly, are more flexible in amending rules, and have an institution independent of political interference (Baldwin and Cave 1999, 64f.). Additionally, the direct involvement of private actors in designing, supervising, and changing their own regulatory model increases the acceptance of the regulatory approach (Mayntz 1983, 71). Ayres and Braithwaite point out that innovative regulatory designs that include "a mix of self-regulatory and governmental regulation—a mix that will cover the gaps left by one approach with the strength of another approach" (Ayres and Braithwaite 1992, 132).

However, there are misgivings about self-regulatory systems on account of the lack of rules, lack of regulatory functions, and lack of transparent decision-making; furthermore, it is also problematic that the interests of actors not directly involved in the decision-making process might not be taken into account (Baldwin and Cave 1999, 65). Here, state institutions such as ministries and competition authorities are often still involved, as described above.

Regulatory Agency Models

The implementation of the model of sector-specific regulatory agencies, known as "NRA" (new regulatory agencies) (Eyre and Sitter 1999) has become a fashion which has "multiplied in numbers through the last half-century" (Baldwin and Cave 1999, 69). Regulatory agencies are bodies supervised by a ministry, to whom functions of market creation and market correction are delegated. Their main regulatory approach is proactive and ex-ante. Regulatory agencies do not act in a purely executive capacity. They combine legislative, executive and judicial functions, i.e. they define and interpret rules, monitor and supervise them, and even introduce sanctions if necessary (Baldwin and Cave 1999, 70). The key arguments for introducing regulatory agencies are their—assumed—independence from both public and private interests and their continuity in making decisions beyond party politics and elections. Additionally, regulatory agencies can build up the expertise to decide on complex and technical matters and make decisions based on a great deal of knowledge (see Majone 1996, 15, 49).

Regulatory agencies are criticized on various grounds: they lack legitimacy; they are susceptible to political intervention in spite of formal independence; their functions are divided between competition and regulation; and they are known for bureaucratic and slow decision-making instead of "lean regulation" (Knieps 1997).

Links between the Five Models: Considerations with Respect to Britain and Germany

The fact that there are five different institutional designs makes it clear that there is no one best solution. There is not simply one answer and no "optimal design" which defines which model has to be institutionalized (Goodin 1996, 34ff.). In the following, it will be shown to what extent any of the five models described applies for utility regulatory issues in the British and German cases.

Ministries are closely related to party politics and politicization, and they were not originally designed for regulating utilities. However, they influence regulatory decision-making. This includes—as in the German case—"general directives" (allgemeine Weisungen), as well as informal daily involvement in regulatory issues that have political implications.[13]

Although the ministry model is not appropriate for day-to-day utility regulation, there is the "back-up" option of stepping in on special regulatory issues. In Britain, decision-making on licence agreements in telecommunications regulation shows that the Department of Trade and Industry (DTI) and OFTEL share competencies, i.e., the ministry is involved in day-to-day regulatory procedures. By contrast, in the case of German electricity regulation, instead of a regulatory agency, a self-regulatory approach based on the associations' agreements (AA) was chosen. Here, the German Federal Ministry of Economics (BMWi) not only influences the development of these agreements (e.g., on the contents or the interest groups who negotiate the agreements), but in addition the BMWi has to represent the "self-regulator" in electricity at the European level; ministries might take over some regulatory functions.

While administrative agencies are based on a traditional, hierarchical model, they can be set up for utility regulation. Originally only developed to execute administrative tasks, they can extend their competencies under certain conditions. While administrative agencies are most fit to focus on nonpolitical executive functions such as technical regulatory issues, they also have to develop new administrative decision-making procedures to steer markets; but they do not have ex-ante regulatory competence. An administrative agency may be transformed step by step into a regulatory agency, as can be seen in the case of the RegTP.[14]

A contrasting case is the "Radio Communications Agency" (RCA), which sticks to the agency model. In the case of telecommunications in Britain, besides OFTEL, the RCA was set up for technical regulatory issues (Knieps 1997, 7). Administrative agencies may be involved in utility regulation, too.

In the case of German rail regulation, the Federal Rail Authority (*Eisenbahnbundesamt*, EBA) was established as an independent higher federal administrative agency. The agency is predominantly involved in issues on technical regulation. Hence the EBA's core competencies do not lie in economical regulatory issues; the result is that there is little competition within the rail sector.[15] However, there are proposals to extend the competencies of the EBA, transforming it from a supervisory to a regulatory authority, for example, on net access and price regulation.[16]

Competition authorities are responsible for ex-post market-making regulation. For utility regulation, ex-post regulation had to be combined with competencies on ex-ante regulatory issues. As this may be too demanding, this particular solution has not yet been introduced in either Great Britain or Germany.

In Germany the main body is the Federal Cartel Office, while in Britain there is a more fragmented system with three institutions: the Office of Fair Trading (OFT), the Secretary of State, and the Competition Commission (former Monopolies and Mergers Commission) (see Wilks 1999a). In Germany there are discussions about increasing the competencies of the Cartel Office, especially in the sectors of rail and energy.[17] In contrast, in Britain there are no debates about enhancing the competencies of competition authorities on sector-specific regulation. Since a decision was made not to transfer regulatory competencies from the Post Office to the OFT,[18] with the 1998 Competition Act the competencies of the sector-specific regulator were increased and the power of the OFT reduced (Interview OFT, February 2001).[19]

Self-regulatory institutions are flexible bodies where the regulated actors, and not the state, are deeply involved. However, because of their formally limited decision-making capacity and lack of enforcement power, competencies are often shared with state bodies.

Up to now in German electricity and gas regulation, with the associations' agreements (AA) a self-regulatory model was opted for. While the AA is politically supported by former incumbents, net owners, and the Federal Ministry of Economics (BMWi), others, such as new entrants to the market, the European Commission, and consumer councils, criticize the AA for being discriminatory and lacking transparency. Calls for the establishment of a regulatory agency for energy are increasing.[20]

Regulatory agencies are an innovative model in both the British and the German administrative tradition. As newly established administrative bodies, which emerged from former administrative bodies, they may develop new administrative regulatory styles of "light regulation."

Whereas Britain was the first European country to set up regulatory agencies and to establish them for almost all utility sectors (see Hogwood 1990; Thatcher 1998), in Germany only one utility regulator has thus far been established with the Regulatory Authority for Telecommunications and Posts (RegTP) (Ulmen and Gump 1997; Müller-Terpitz 1997). However, as was outlined above, there are ongoing debates in the rail and electricity sector about establishing regulatory bodies, too.

To sum up, in the British and German contexts, the five models can be divided into two general groupings: traditional models, with a long administrative tradition, and new, innovative models. From a macro-organizational perspective, with respect to administrative traditions, the regulatory agency model is the only innovative model in both countries which might have led to a new design. The other four models have a longer tradition and have been used to fulfill state functions before. However, for these traditional models, analysis on the micro-organizational level could explore whether there are still traditional designs or whether new structures have been established, for example, via patching up or the transposition of new institutional solutions (Genschel 1995).

The following section describes and explains the establishment of the institutional design at both a micro-organizational and macro-organizational level in both British and German telecommunications regulation.

The Case of Telecommunications Regulation in Great Britain and Germany

Originally, telecommunications services were only a national issue, and they were provided by private or public monopolies. Operative and regulative functions—net, equipment, and service—were linked together in the post, telegraph, and telecommunications utilities (PTT). The net and services were vertically integrated and in the hands of a state monopoly (in Germany, the Deutsche Post; in Britain, the Post Office). These monopolies worked in close cooperation with producers of the equipment which had the status of private monopolies. The strong link between political, administrative, and private actors were "highly closed games" (Thatcher 1998, 123) and there was strong state intervention: tariffs were defined as "political prices" on the basis of social and macroeconomic criteria. However, a variety of factors, such as technical developments, the opening of the U.S. and Japanese telecommunications markets, paradigm changes in state economic policies, and the general financial constraints of nation states, brought about a transformation in the telecommunications sector, leading it to adopt market principles (Mette 1999, 184ff.).

With regard to regulatory reform, the key change was the transformation from the PTT to new regulatory agencies (NRA) (Eyre and Sitter 1999). Britain and Germany have chosen the regulatory agency model. However, regulatory reform in Britain and Germany has not been parallel, but sequential. Whereas Britain, as the European "forerunner," introduced its telecommunications' regulator, OFTEL, in 1984, Germany was a "latecomer," only establishing its RegTP in 1998.

The question which has to be answered is why the regulatory agency model was adopted instead of one of the other four designs outlined in section three. A comparative approach focuses on the institutional structure at both a macro-organizational and a micro-organizational level.

Great Britain as a "Forerunner": Designing Process and Design of OFTEL

Unlike all the other member states of the European Union, Britain began an extensive program of liberalization, privatization, and regulation in its telecommunications sector in the early 1980s. This was caused by the political structures: a unitary state, the strong position of the prime minister, and non-coalition governments. Administrative structures are mainly characterized by flexibility and informal procedures. Therefore, British administrative decision-making processes are traditionally described as an "art," with a high degree of discretion for the public service and a low supervision capacity by the courts (Ridley 1996).

Before regulatory reforms were initiated in the 1980s, the British PTT model included the Post Office, and was defined as a public corporation with postal as well as telecommunications services. General policy decisions were taken over by the Ministry for Post and Telecommunications, which was not an independent ministry, but part of the Department of Trade and Industry (DTI) (Thatcher 1999, 94ff.).

The transformation of the telecommunications sector started with the Telecommunications Act of 1981, whereby the Post Office was split into two public corporations, the Post Office and British Telecom. The separation prepared the ground for the second Telecommunications Act in 1984, where British Telecom was privatized and an independent regulatory body, the Office of Telecommunications (OFTEL), was created as a nonministerial department within the ambit of the DTI. OFTEL was the first network and utility regulatory body in Britain (DTI 1982).

While the privatization program provoked controversy among unions and politicians, the design of the telecommunications regulator was not regarded as a contestable issue (Moon, Richardson, and Smart 1986). A model was developed on the basis of a civil service proposal from the Department of Industry (DTI). The designing process for the regulatory agency was described as "hasty," and a design concept was "cobbled together in its formative stages mostly by hard-pressed civil servants under severe deadlines" (Foster 1992, 46).

At that stage, Britain did not have regulatory bodies for utility regulation. Either a traditional model had to be chosen, or a new model had to be introduced. The models of ministry, competition authority, and regulatory agency were under close consideration.

Because of the close link to politics, with the threat of constant politicization, the design of a ministry was rejected (Prosser 1997, 46). In contrast, there were debates about transferring the regulatory function to the Office of Fair Trading (OFT): "[A]nalogy suggested that the job should be done by the Director of Fair Trading, who was in fact pressed to take it on. However, he decided that he had enough to do, so a specialist look-alike was invented, the Director General of Telecommunications" (quoted in Prosser 1997, 46). The British competition authority was used to set up a new model, a sector-specific regulatory agency model.

OFT is considered to be a core model, which was transformed from a general ex-post regulator to a sector-specific regulator for the case of telecommunications (see Prosser 1997a, 46; Foster 1992, 124).[21] Others describe the regulatory-agency model as an example of "neglecting earlier history" (Helm 1994, 22) and view it as indicating a clear break with the previous regulatory regime (Thatcher 1998, 121).

The argument presented here is that after the OFT refused to take the job, the American influence was the core reason for opting for the regulatory agency model. Policy was frequently transferred between the United States and Great Britain in the 1980s (Wolman 1992). Since the United States telecommunications policy influenced the debate on how to liberalize and privatize the sector, it also guided the design of the regulatory body. Because of its long tradition of sector-specific regulatory bodies, the U.S. Federal Communications Commission (FCC), established in 1934, served as a model for the British regulatory agency (Thatcher 1999a, 95).

To sum up, on the macro-organizational level, after national options such as the takeover by the OFT were refused because of capacity problems, the decision to opt for the regulatory-agency model was mainly influenced by the American sector-specific regulatory agency model. However, OFTEL has close links to the British model of the OFT. This can be shown when analyzing the micro-organizational level with the institutional design of internal administrative structures.

To gain independence from the ministry, the model of a single Director General of Telecommunications (DGT) was diffused from the Director General of Fair Trading. Using this model, core regulatory functions were handed over to the DGT "as individuals and not to their office" (Thatcher 1998, 125f.). Regarding decisions, it is "left to the regulator to determine what their particular interpretation is" (Helm 1994, 27). Although the personalization and individual decision-making was later strongly criticized, it is a uniquely British feature and part of the above described state and administrative tradition.[22]

The internal administrative decision procedures of OFTEL reflect the strong position of the DGT. As OFTEL was established, it was separated into functional branches, each headed by a director, who had to report to the DGT as the key decision-maker. This structure was "partly inherited from the DTI and partly copied from the OFT" (Hall, Scott, and Hood 2000, 44).

In general, OFTEL is open to the introduction of new administrative practices under the headline of managerialism. Micro-organizational institutional change is mainly left to the DGT, and—depending on a new DGT coming into office—the institutional design changed. Reforms led to transforming traditional department structures into fashioned project structures, compliance procedures, and management plans.[23] As a consequence there are flexible regulatory decision-making procedures.

Summing up, on the basis of the preliminary findings it can be concluded that on a macro-organizational level the institutional design of the British Telecommunications regulator was mainly shaped by American influences, while on a micro-organizational level the design has been dominated by the British administrative tradition.

Germany as a "Latecomer": Designing Process and Design of RegTP

For a long time, Germany—like the majority of European states—was a strong opponent to reforms in its telecommunications sector, such as those carried out in the United States and Britain. Western Europe "adhered to the "old" PTT model well into the 1980's" (Grande 1994, 143).

However, parallel with the reform initiatives of the European Commission,[24] Germany started its own initiatives to liberalize, privatize, and regulate the telecommunications sector.[25] The reform process was not only enhanced by this interaction between policy-making at the European level and that at the level of the member states (Thatcher 1995, 265). The British regulatory reform showed that telecommunications services were able to be provided without monopolies (Schmidt 1998, 138). Additionally, the British government supported a European style of telecommunications reform; and it had an interest in "exporting" its own style of liberalization (Thatcher 1995, 245).

In Germany, radical reforms of the public sector are rare. The political system, with its particular institutional structure, such as the number of veto points in the intertwined federal system, coalition governments, or the corporatist structure with a strong orientation towards consensus, prevents such developments. Therefore, in Germany the model of the regulatory state emerged slowly. Instead of an ad hoc reform of the public sector, reforms show predominantly incremental developments that Ellwein describes as "adaptive administration" (Ellwein 1994).

While the reform of the German telecommunications sectors appears radical, the process was slow and adaptive. The transformation from the PTT to the NRA took place in three steps (see e.g., Mette 1999; Grande 1999): With the Post Reform 1 (1989/1990), three separate operational units for telecommunications, postal service, and post banking were established as public corporations. The Ministry for Postals and Telecommunications (BMPT) was responsible for steering competencies for the sector, including ownership and regulation.

In 1994, with the Post Reform 2, the intention was to separate ownership from regulatory competencies. While the competencies were left with the BMPT, a new administrative agency, the Agency for Postals and Telecommunications (BAPT), was institutionalized for ownership. The three public corporations were transformed into stock companies, one of which was the Deutsche Telekom AG (DTAG). With the Post Reform 3, in 1994, the decision was made to open telecommunications to full competition by 1 January 1998. With the new telecommunications law (TKG), sector-specific regulation was set up with a new telecommunications regulator, the Regulatory Authority for Telecommunications and Posts (RegTP), an institution under the supervision of the Federal Ministry of Economics (BMWi). The BMPT was disbanded and became part of the BMWi, and the responsibility for the ownership was transferred to the treasury (Bundesministerium für Finanzen, BMF). However, some civil servants of the BMPT moved to the newly created RegTP. Additionally, the BAPT was incorporated in the RegTP.

Up to that stage, Germany did not have regulatory bodies for utility regulation. The case of the RegTP shows that on the macro-organizational level, instead of a traditional model, a new institutional design was introduced. During the process of designing the RegTP, the models of administrative agency, competition authority, and regulatory agency were carefully scrutinized.

While the proposal for the German telecommunications law was formulated in the former BMPT, there were extensive discussions on which model to be opted for in the parliamentary committee for posts and telecommunications.[26] The Green Party favored an institution under public law (Anstalt des öffentlichen Rechts) as a special, more independent form of an administrative agency. However, for this institutional design a change in the Basic Law would have been necessary (Ulmen and Gump 1997, 398).

The monopoly commission, an advisory body to the BMWi, suggested transposing the regulatory functions to the Cartel Office (see Ortwein 1998, 207f.). However, although this proposal was strongly supported by the Cartel Office itself (Wolf 2000), it was rejected by the BMWi, mainly because, in 1994, with the BAPT, a body had been set up which had taken over central technical regulatory functions.

Having roughly described the development of the design, the question is why the "regulatory agency" model was chosen. First, it is important to state that the RegTP is named a "regulatory agency," but it has the status of an administrative agency (see TKG, § 66, 1). Therefore, from an administrative point of view, the setting fits well with the German administrative tradition. What is new is the title given to the administrative agency. As will be seen when analyzing the micro-organizational level, additional steering instruments have been established.

European Law is responsible for redefining the German telecommunications regulator as a "regulatory agency." Although the policy formulation was described as an interactive process between national and European levels (Thatcher 1995, 264), the strong "proactive course of action" of the European Commission has to be highlighted (Eliassen and Sjovaag 1999, 23). Although the member states have organizational sovereignty (*Organisationshoheit*) when implementing European Law on the national level (Schwarze 1996, 148ff), in some cases the European legislation gives clear directions on how to comply in the member states. In the case of telecommunications, the European Commission specified that a regulatory body for telecommunications had to be set up. The 1987 Green book on telecommunications reform (COM[87]290) proposed separating operational and regulatory competencies. Later directives, which put this in concrete form, such as the Council directive on open network provision (90/388/EEC), or the directive on open network provision to voice telephony (95/C122/04), gave more detailed instructions on which institutional designs should be set up on a national level. While the directive in 1990 proposed founding an "independent institution from service providers," the 1995 directive demanded the institutionalization of national regulatory agencies.[27] While the European Commission defined overall standards which pushed member states to set up the regulatory agency model, the Commission "did not specify the institutional arrangements" for the micro-organizational administrative designs, and it therefore allowed "institutional subsidiarity" (Thatcher 1995, 265).

Additionally, not only did European Law have an impact on the macro-organizational structure, but so did Britian. Britain utility regulatory agencies "have been pioneers of change and have served as an example . . . in other European countries" (Thatcher 1998, 121). In Germany, for example, the monopoly commission proposed the institutionalization of a telecommunications regulator, using the model of OFTEL (Ortwein 1998, 270).[28]

With respect to the micro-organizational level (internal administrative structures), the central component of jury-like decision chambers was set up in order to attain independence from the ministry. In these chambers, the decisions of the RegTP are made on the basis of the TKG.[29] The institutional design of this chamber system was diffused from the German Federal Cartel Office, which uses a comparable system. However, in addition to the decision chambers, the RegTP had a variety of traditional departments responsible for technical regulatory issues, which have now been taken over from the BAPT. Insofar as the RegTP combines traditional administrative departments and jury-like decision chambers, it is a unique institution.[30]

In conclusion, it has been shown that on the macro-organizational level the institutional design of the German sector-specific regulatory agency in telecommunications was mainly shaped by European and British influences, while the design on a micro-organizational level has been dominated by traditional German administrative solutions.

Comparison of Great Britain and Germany

A comparison of the regulatory agencies in Britain and Germany shows convergence on the macro-organizational level because they both opted for the same design; it also shows a convergence of the designing process, which was predominantly shaped by external influences in both countries. With a focus on the overall design (macro-organizational level), in both countries a sector-specific regulatory agency model was set up.[31] The designing process shows convergence insofar as no traditional design was used, but a new model was put in place instead. While there was a strong American influence in Britain, the German decision was influenced by Europe and the British experience.

The analysis of British and German regulatory agencies at the micro-organizational level shows convergence in the designing process, but divergence in the institutional design.[32] Convergence in the designing process could be revealed insofar as administrative designs have mainly been shaped by national administrative traditions on the micro level.

However, this has led to divergence in the institutional designs. In both regulatory agencies, to reach independence, different institutional structures have been developed. In Britain, a powerful DGT was put in place, linked to the British administrative tradition of individual and discretionary decision-making. In contrast, in Germany the model of decision chambers was employed because of the law-based administrative tradition. Additionally, while Britain has been open for administrative reforms and experiments, Germany has stuck to traditional department structures, taken over from the BAPT.

Concluding Remarks: Linking the Theoretical Model and Empirical Findings

This chapter has explored the designing process and the institutional design of telecommunications regulation at the national level in Britain and Germany. After having introduced some general explanations for the challenges of utility regulation, in a general explanation, diffusion theory and historical institutionalism were linked to account for the design and the designing process of regulatory institutions. Five existing institutional designs for utility regulation were outlined which could be set up in Britain and Germany as utility regulators. In an empirical section, in two case studies, preliminary findings for the British and German case on telecommunications regulation were presented and the reasons for choosing them were examined.

In the concluding remarks, the findings of the case study have to be related to the model developed in section two. Analyzing the implementation paths in Britain and Germany on both a macro- and micro-organizational level, the process cannot be interpreted as a path-dependent development. In contrast, the British and the German cases revealed that the shaping of the overall design of regulatory institutions (macro-organizational level) was influenced by a diffusion process. Designs were transferred from countries with a longer experience in utility regulation to countries with less sector-specific knowledge of these new demands. As a consequence of the liberalization and privatization of telecommunications, both Britain and Germany faced the challenge of introducing new regulatory institutions. While Britain gained knowledge of the U.S. model, Germany predominantly learned from the British example, and both introduced a sector-specific regulatory agency model. There is undoubtedly an "institutional download" and a "global chain reaction" to institutional designs on a macro-organizational level (Schneider 2001, 8, 20).

However, this argument of macro-organizational international diffusion becomes more relative, taking in consideration that—looking into the British case—the agency model was only the second-best option. International models were only diffused after the OFT refused to take over sector-specific regulatory functions in telecommunications. Additionally, opting for international diffusion is often not an autonomous decision. The German case reveals that European pressure forced a regulator to be set up. Both the British and the German case show that diffusion was caused less by voluntary emulation than by imposition and constraints.

Referring to the micro-organizational level, this diffusion process does not exclude the general claim of historical institutionalism, namely, that there are path dependencies which shape the institutional design. Analyzing the British and German regulatory design on the micro level, it has been shown that traditional institutional structures still exist. In Germany, the RegTP mainly took over the competencies and the departmental structure of the earlier existing BAPT. Additionally, in establishing the model of decision chambers for social and economic regulatory issues, it was diffused from the Federal Cartel Office. In Britain, the internal structure of OFTEL was largely designed from scratch, using predominantly the OFT as a model, e.g., in reference to the Director General.

Therefore, the overall finding of this comparison of the regulatory agencies in telecommunications in Britain and Germany reveals that the institutional design is shaped by both diffusion and by path dependency. The analysis has shown that diffusion among countries took place on the macro-organizational level. However, on the micro-organizational level the design has been shaped by sector-specific path dependency. Additionally, on the micro level well-established designs were diffused from institutions on the basis of administrative traditions within the countries, which demonstrated interactive effects among units in a federal system. While in general the concerns are with what best fits the optimal design, in a second step these ideal types are amended as the questions are addressed regarding what has worked well in the past and what we now know.

With the focus on the comparison between the British and German telecommunications cases, the overall finding is that in both countries, at the macro-organizational level with the regulatory agency model choices were made to institute convergent institutional designs; however, there has been divergence on the micro-organizational level in the regulatory agencies' internal administrative procedures.

Why are there different processes of change on the two organizational levels? Here, two considerations might provide preliminary answers: first, since the diffused concepts might not be defined in depth, the details of implementation are left to each country. General institutional designing concepts can be transferred; but in order to implement them, domestically detailed adaptation is necessary. General concepts are diffused, but on a micro-organizational level country-specific administrative traditions might survive without contradicting the macro-level design. Second, as the empirical account has shown, a variety of actors are involved in designing institutions. However, there is "bureaucratic politics" dominated by civil servants. If politicians make an effort in debates on institutional designs, they are mainly interested in overall design principles, but not in nitty-gritty micro-organizational details. Here, civil servants have strongly vested interests. Even if it is not possible to prevent change at the macro-organizational level, they might still strive to preserve stability on the micro-organizational level.

Notes

I would like to thank Tanja Börzel, Adrienne Héritier, Dieter Kerwer, Christoph Knill, and Dirk Lehmkuhl for their helpful advice on earlier versions of this chapter.

1. The term "regulatory regime" is often used for different purposes: e.g., Thatcher utilizes the term to describe the group of utility regulators, founded on the basis of the so-called "OF-type" model in the gas, energy, rail, or telecommunications sectors (Thatcher 1997). Hall, Scott, and Hood, with a focus on telecommunications regulation in Britain from 1982 up to 1992, explored a regulatory regime as a "ménage à trios" between ministry (DTI), the regulator, OFTEL, and the former incumbent, British Telecom (BT) (Hall, Scott, and Hood 2000, 17, 25ff.). In this section, the regulatory regime is defined as a system of state actors in a multilevel government system, which share regulatory competencies in order to steer markets.

2. Further research on "The European Regime: Private Actors Providing Public Service" aims to offer cross-country as well as cross-sectoral answers not just in the case of telecommunications, but also for rail and energy (gas and electricity).

3. A two-level approach refers to the problem of the "leveling of research" (Knill and Lenschow 2001). Most approaches on comparative administration focus only on macro-structural aspects. Peters points out that analyses on a micro level are all so important for understanding variations in bureaucratic performance, but they "occur at too low a level of generality" (Peters 1989, 3rd ed). Here, it is argued that only in comparing regulatory designs on a macro- and a micro-organizational level can valuable differentiation between regulatory approaches be made. Other research, such as Halligan's analysis of administrative diffusion, shares this view and focuses on administrative changes in broad directions, specific concepts, and precise detail (Halligan 1996, 307).

4. This trend is also discussed under the heading of New Public Management (NPM) (Hood 1991).

5. For an overview of the theory of institutional design see Goodin 1996; Weimer 1995; Olsen 1997.

6. Goodin writes that to explain the emergence of administrative outcomes, "we must refer essentially to intentions and the interaction among intentions. . . . Outcomes may be the product of evolutionary forces, but the selection mechanisms that guide that evolution might be intentionally altered. Design and redesign . . . still have some scope" (Goodin 1996, 28f.).

7. For further overviews see Baldwin and Cave 1999; Grande and Eberlein 1999.

8. For more details see Tegge 1994; Genschel 1995.

9. The analysis of institutional design at the European level is not dealt with in this chapter. It is covered by authors such as Coen and Doyle 1999; Kreher 1997; Dehousse 1997.

10. In contrast to the unitary state, in federal-intertwined systems even ministries on lower levels are concerned with the supervision of regulatory issues.

11. However, in the first half of this century, ministries had central regulatory functions (Prosser 1997, 35).

12. For a detailed overview of the institutional design of British and German agencies see Böllhoff 1998.

13. For the German and British case see Welz 1988; Greer 1994.

14. See the section on "Germany as a 'Latecomer': Designing Process and Design of RegTP."

15. In the case of the EBA, issues on discriminatory practices (e.g., on third-party access to the still vertically integrated rail net, owned by the Deutsche Bahn AG) are decided by the EBA only upon application for approval. The EBA is not actively involved in enhancing net competition, and there are only vague formal procedures or institutional structures on how these decisions are made (Interview EBA, March 2000).

16. See e.g., DPA 1 March 2000: "Bundesverkehrsminister Klimmt will den Wettbewerb im deutschen Bahnverkehr mit einer Regulierungsbehörde ankurbeln"; SZ 7 March 2001: "Koalition will offenbar Regulierungsbehörde für die Schiene."

17. For the discussions in Germany see e.g., Knieps 1997, 18f.; Ortwein 1998, 209.

18. See the section on "Great Britain as a 'Forerunner': Designing Process and Design of OFTEL."

19. OFTEL shares competencies with the Office of Fair Trading (OFT) in the area of competition policies ("concurrency rules," see Riley 2000); however, it is de facto the only institution to make decisions in telecommunications cases.

20. New entrants to the market founded the initiative "pro-competition" to lobby for fair competition and discrimination, free access to the net, and "real competition" in the electricity sector (http://www.pro-wettbewerb.de). They argue that the associations' agreement (AA) does not define clear rules for net access, and they therefore lobby for setting up a sector-specific regulatory institution with competencies for regulating prices and sanctioning. Additionally, the FEDV (Free Energy Supply Association) is in favor of a regulatory agency, too. See e.g., FR, 28 May 2000: "Verbraucherlobby fordert Regulierungsbehörde"; FTD 14 March 2001: "Brüssel will Regulierer für Deutschland."

21. A further reason for opting for the OFT model was that the history of the OFT showed an institution "not threatening to ministers" (Hall, Scott, and Hood 2000, 21).

22. The dominance of British administrative traditions on the micro-organizational level is further highlighted when comparing the American and the British decision-making structure. While the FCC has a multi-person regulatory commission structure, in contrast, for OFTEL, with the DGT a design with individual decision-making procedures was set up (Hall, Scott, and Hood 2000, 44).

23. For details on the period from 1993 to 1997, with Don Cruickshank as DGT, see Hall, Scott, and Hood 2000, 44.

24. The European telecommunications policies were mainly inspired by the single-market program, which is described as "deregulatory in nature" (Bulmer 1992, 60).

25. The Witte report was the main impetus for the German debate on telecommunications reform; see Werle 1999.

26. For a more detailed analysis of the actors involved and the decision-making processes, see Thorein 1997, esp. 295, 301ff.

27. For a more detailed analysis see Mette 1999, 231ff.

28. Additionally, Germany utilized the American experience and the FCC as a reference model.

29. The RegTP has five decision chambers, which are chaired by a president and two vice presidents, and which are responsible for decisions on specific regulatory tasks, such as licensing management or price regulation. For a detailed analysis of the decision-making chambers and their independence, see Oertel 2000.

30. While administrative agencies merely include departments, the Cartel Office only has a chamber system.

31. This view is shared by Schneider (Schneider 2001); however, see n. 32.

32. Schneider argues that "structural convergence does not mean that there is no variation in detail," and "convergence does not mean homogenization" (Schneider 2001, 71, 78). However, Schneider only analyzes developments on a macro level and he argues that "divergence is of minor importance." He points out that "[c]ompared to the enormous institutional shift from public monopoly to private competition, the concrete differences in . . . new regulatory procedures . . . are trivial," and "the variation in outcomes a matter of inches" (Schneider 2001, 71). This chapter argues that the analysis of micro level procedures is of importance because it shows the divergence between administrative patterns. Further research on the relation of institutional design and decision-making procedures might be less trivial than assumed.

References

Ayres, I., and J. Braithwaite. 1992. *Responsive Regulation: Transcending the Deregulation Debate.* Oxford: Oxford University Press.

Baake, P., and O. Perschau. 1996. The Law and Policy of Competition in Germany. In *Regulating Europe*, ed. G. Majone, 131-56. London: Routledge.

Baldwin, R., and M. Cave, eds. 1999. *Understanding Regulation: Theory, Strategy, and Practice.* Oxford: Oxford University Press.

Bobrow, D. B., and J. S. Dryzek. 1987. *Policy Analysis by Design.* Pittsburgh: University of Pittsburgh Press.

Böllhoff, D. 1998. Comparative Public Sector Reform in Britain and Germany— Implications of the Next Steps Initiative for a German Reform of Federal Executive Agencies. Thesis, Liverpool Institute of Public Administration and Management (LIPAM).

Bulmer, S. 1992. Completing the European Community's Internal Market: The Regulatory Implications for the Federal Republic of Germany. In *The Politics of German Regulation*, ed. K. Dyson, 53-78. Aldershot: Dartmouth.

Coen, D., and C. Doyle. 1999. Designing Economic Regulatory Institutions for European Network Industries. *Current Politics and Economics of the European Union* 9 (4): 83-112.

Collier, R. B., and D. Collier. 1991. *Shaping the Political Agenda: Critical Junctures, the Labor Movement, and Regime Dynamics in Latin America.* Pricetown: Pricetown University Press.

Czada, R., S. Lütz, and S. Mette. 1999. *Regulative Politik.* Hagen: FernUniversität - Gesamthochschule Hagen, Fachbereich Erziehungs-, Sozial- und Geisteswissenschaften.

Dehousse, R. 1997. Regulation by Networks in the European Community: The Role of European Agencies. *Journal of European Public Policy* 4: 246-61.

Dolowitz, D., and D. Marsh. 1996. Who Learns What from Whom: A Review of the Policy Transfer Literature. *Political Studies* 44: 343-57.

Dryzek, J. S. 1990. *Discursive Democracy.* Cambridge: Cambridge University Press.

DTI. 1982. The Future of Telecommunications in Britain. London: HMSO.

Dyson, K. 1992. Theories of Regulation and the Case of Germany: A Model of Regulatory Change. In *The Politics of German Regulation*, ed. K. Dyson, 1-28. Aldershot: Dartmouth.

Eisner, M. A., J. Worsham, and E. J. Ringquist. 2000. *Contemporary Regulatory Policy.* London: Boulder.

Eliassen, K. A., and M. Sjovaag, eds. 1999. *European Telecommunications Liberalization.* London: Routledge.

Ellwein, T. 1994. *Das Dilemma der Verwaltung: Verwaltungsstruktur und Verwaltungsreformen in Deutschland.* Mannheim: B.I.-Taschenbuchverlag.

Eyre, S., and N. Sitter. 1999. From PTT to NRA: Toward a New Regulatory Regime? In *European Telecommunications Liberalization*, ed. K. A. Eliassen and M. Sjovaag, 55-73. London: Routledge.

Foster, C. D. 1992. *Privatization, Public Ownership, and the Regulation of Natural Monopoly.* Oxford: Blackwell.

Genschel, P. 1995. The Dynamics of Inertia: Institutional Persistence and Institutional Change in Telecommunications and Health Care. MPIfG Discussion Paper 95/3, Cologne.

Goodin, R. E. 1996. Institutions and Their Design. In *The Theory of Institutional Design*, ed. R. E. Goodin, 1-53. Cambridge: Cambridge University Press.

Grande, E. 1993. Die Architektur des Staates. Aufbau und Transformation nationalstaatlicher Handlungskapazität - untersucht am Beispiel der Forschungs- und Technologiepolitik. In *Verhandlungsdemokratie, Interessenvermittlung, Regierbarkeit*, ed. R. Czada and M. G. Schmidt, 51-71. Opladen: Westdeutscher Verlag.

———. 1994. The New Role of the State in Telecommunications: An International Comparison. *West European Politics* 17 (3): 138-57.

———. 1999. The Regulation of Telecommunications in Germany. Paper read at Regulation Initiative Conference "Regulation in Europe," at London Business School, London, 4-5 November.

Grande, E., and B. Eberlein. 1999. Der Aufstieg des Regulierungsstaates im Infrastrukturbereich. Zur Transformation der politischen Ökonomie der Bundesrepublik Deutschland. München: Technische Universität München, Lehrstuhl für Politische Wissenschaften.

Greer, P. 1994. *Transferring Central Government—The Next Steps Initiative.* Buckingham: Open University.

Hall, C., C. Scott, and C. Hood, eds. 2000. *Telecommunications Regulation: Culture, Chaos, and Interdependence inside the Regulatory Process.* London: Routledge.

Hall, P. A., and R. C. R. Taylor. 1996. Political Science and the Three New Institutionalism. MPIfG-Discussion Paper 96/6.

Halligan, J. 1996. The Diffusion of Civil Service Reform. In *Civil Service Systems in Comparative Perspective*, ed. H. A. G. M. Bekke, J. L. Perry, and T. A. J. Toonen, 288-317. Bloomington: Indiana University Press.

Helm, D. 1994. British Utility Regulation: Theory, Practice, and Reform. *Oxford Review of Economic Policy* 10 (3): 17-39.

Héritier, A. 1998. After Liberalization: Public-Interest Services in the Utilities. Bonn: Max Planck Project Group. Common Goods: Law, Politics and Economics, Working Paper 1998/5.

———. 1998a. The Provision of Common Goods across Multiple Arenas: Political Science Research Perspective. Bonn: Max Planck Project Group. Common Goods: Law, Politics and Economics.

Hogwood, B. W. 1990. Developments in Regulatory Agencies in Britain. *International Review of Administrative Sciences* 56: 595-612.

Hood, C. 1991. A Public Management for All Seasons? *Public Management* 69: 1-19.

Hulsink, W. 1999. *Privatization and Liberalization in European Telecommunications: Comparing Britain, the Netherlands, and France.* London: Routledge.

Klages, H. 1998. Umbau ministerieller Strukturen: Kritische Beschreibung gegenwärtiger Strukturen. In *Verwaltungsmodernisierung: "Harte" und "Weiche" Aspekte II,* ed. H. Klages, 49-66. Speyer: Speyerer Forschungsberichte, No. 181.

Knieps, G. 1997. *Ansätze für eine "schlanke" Regulierungsbehörde für Post und Telekommunikation in Deutschland.* Freiburg: Institut für Verkehrswissenschaft und Regionalpolitik, No. 38.

Knill, C., and A. Lenschow. 2001. Seek and Ye Shall Find! Linking Different Perspectives on Institutional Change. *Comparative Political Studies* 41 (2): 187-215.

König, K., and A. Benz, eds. 1997. *Privatisierung und staatliche Regulierung—Bahn, Post und Telekommunikation, Rundfunk.* Baden-Baden: Nomos.

Kreher, A. 1997. Agencies in the European Community—A Step toward Administrative Integration in Europe. *Journal of European Public Policy* 4 (2): 225-45.

Levy, B., and P. T. Spiller, eds. 1996. *Regulations, Institutions, and Commitment: Comparative Studies of Telecommunications.* Cambridge: Cambridge University Press.

Loughlin, J., and B. G. Peters. 1997. State Traditions, Administrative Reform and Regionalization. In *The Political Economy of Regionalism,* ed. M. Keating and J. Loughlin, 41-62. London: Frank Cass.

Mahoney, J. ed. 1996. *Regulating Europe.* London: Routledge.

———. 2000. Path Dependency in Historical Sociology. *Theory and Society* 29 (4): 507-48.

Majone, G., ed. 1996. *Regulating Europe.* London: Routledge

Majone, G. 1997. From the Positive to the Regulatory State: Causes and Consequences of Changes in the Mode of Governance. *Journal of Public Policy* 17 (2): 139-67.

March, J. G., and J. P. Olsen. 1989. *Rediscovering Institutions: The Organizational Basis of Politics.* New York: Free Press.

Mayntz, R. 1983. Implementation von regulativer Politik. In *Implementation politischer Programme,* ed. R. Mayntz, 50-74. Opladen: Westdeutscher Verlag.

Mette, S. 1999. Telekommunikationsregulierung. Ein Überblick über die Entwicklung in der Europäischen Union und der Bundesrepublik Deutschland. In *Regulative Politik,* ed. R. Czada, S. Lütz, and S. Mette, 172-238. Hagen: FernUniversität - Gesamthochschule Hagen, Fachbereich Erziehungs-, Sozial- und Geisteswissenschaften.

Moe, T. M. 1989. The Politics of Bureaucratic Structures. In *Can Government Govern?* ed. J. E. Chubb and P. E. Peterson, 267-330. Washington, D.C.: Brookings Institution.

———. 1990. The Politics of Structural Choice: Toward a Theory of Public Bureaucracy. In *Organization Theory from Chester Barnard to the Present and Beyond,* ed. O. E. Williamson, 116-53. New York: Oxford University Press.

Moon, J., J. J. Richardson, and P. Smart. 1986. The Privatization of British Telecom: A Case Study of the Extended Process of Legislation. *European Journal of Political Research* 14: 339-55.

Müller, M. M., and R. Sturm. 1999. Ein neuer regulativer Staat in Deutschland? Die neuere Theory of the Regulatory State und ihre Anwendbarkeit in der deutschen Staatswissenschaft. *Staatswissenschaften und Staatspraxis* 8 (4): 507-34.

Müller-Terpitz, R. 1997. Die Regulierungsbehörde für den Telekommunikationsmarkt. *Zeitschrift für Gesetzgebung*: 257-74.

Noll, R. G. 1985. Government Regulatory Behavior: A Multidisciplinary Survey and Synthesis. In *Regulatory Policy and the Social Sciences*, ed. R. D. Noll, 9-63. Berkeley: University of California Press.

OECD. 1997. Regulatory Reform—Synthesis. Paris.

Oertel, K. 2000. *Die Unabhängigkeit der Regulierungsbehörde-Eine organisationsrechtliche Variable in der Privatisierung der Telekommunikation.* Berlin: Dunker & Humblot.

Olsen, J. P. 1997. Institutional Design in Democratic Contexts. *The Journal of Political Philosophy* 65: 203-29.

Ortwein, E. 1998. *Das Bundeskartellamt.* Baden-Baden: Nomos.

Osborne, D., and T. Gabler. 1992. *Reinventing Government: How the Entrepreneurial Spirit Is Transforming the Public Sector.* Reading, Mass.: Addison-Wesley.

Peters, B. G. 1989. *The Politics of Regulation.* New York: Longman.

Pettit, P. 1996. Institutional Design and Rational Choice. In *The Theory of Institutional Design*, ed. R. E. Goodin, 54-89. Cambridge: Cambridge University Press.

Prosser, T. 1997. *Law and the Regulators.* Oxford: Clarendon Press.

———. 1997a. The Development of British Regulatory Institutions. In *Law and the Regulators*, ed. T. Prosser, 32-57. Oxford: Clarendon Press.

Ridley, F. F. 1996. The New Public Management in Europe: Comparative Perspectives. *Public Policy and Administration* 11 (1): 16-29.

Riley, A. 2000. A Unique Antitrust Regulatory Problem: Coordinating Concurrent Competition Powers. *Utilities Law Journal* 11 (2): 36-40.

Schmidt, S. K. 1998. *Liberalisierung in Europa. Die Rolle der Europäischen Kommission.* Frankfurt am Main: Campus.

Schneider, V. 2001. Institutional Reform in Telecommunications: The European Union in Transnational Policy Diffusion. In *Transforming Europe. Europeanization, and Domestic Change*, ed. M. Green-Cowles, J. Carporaso, and T. Risse. Ithaca, N.Y.: Cornell University Press.

Schwarze, J., ed. 1996. *Das Verwaltungsrecht unter europäischem Einfluß. Zur Konvergenz der mitgliedsstaatlichen Verwaltungsordnungen in der Europäischen Union.* Baden-Baden: Nomos.

Tegge, A. 1994. *Die Internationale Telekommunikations-Union: Organisation und Funktion einer Weltorganisation im Wandel.* Baden-Baden: Nomos.

Thatcher, M. 1995. Regulatory Reform and Internationalization in Telecommunications. In *Industrial Enterprise and European Integration: From National to International Champion in Western Europe*, ed. J. Hayward, 239-69. Oxford: Oxford University Press.

———. 1997. Regulating the Regulators: The Regulatory Regime for the British Privatized Utilities. *Parliamentary Affairs* 51 (2): 209-16.

———. 1998. Institutions, Regulation, and Change: New Regulatory Agencies in the British Privatized Utilities. *West European Politics* 21 (1): 120-47.

———. 1999. *The Politics of Telecommunications—National Institutions, Convergence, and Change.* Oxford: Oxford University Press.

————. 1999a. Liberalization in Britain: From Monopoly to Regulation of Competition. In *European Telecommunications Liberalisation*, ed. K. A. Eliassen and M. Sjovaag, 93-109. London: Routledge.

Thelen, K. 2001. How Institutions Evolve: Insights from Comparative-Historical Analysis. In *Comparative-Historical Analysis: Innovations in Theory and Method*, ed. J. Mahoney and D. Rueschemeyer. Unpublished draft chapter.

Thelen, K., and S. Steinmo. 1992. Historical Institutionalism in Comparative Politics. In *Structuring Politics: Historical Institutionalism in Comparative Analysis*, ed. S. Steinmo, K. Thelen, and F. Longstreth, 1-32. Cambridge: Cambridge University Press.

Thorein, T. 1997. Liberalisierung und Re-Regulierung im Politikfeld Telekommunikation: Eine wissenschaftszentrierte Policy-Analyse des bundesdeutschen Telekommunikationsgesetzes. *Rundfunk und Fernsehen* 45 (3): 285-306.

Ulmen, W., and T. K. Gump. 1997. Die neue Regulierungsbehörde für Telekommunikation und Post. *Computer und Recht* 13 (7): 396-402.

Weimer, D. L., ed. 1995. *Institutional Design*. Boston: Kluwer Academic.

Welz, W. 1988. *Ressortverantwortung im Leistungsstaat. Zur Organisation, Koordination und Kontrolle selbständiger Bundesbehörden unter besonderer Berücksichtigung des Bundesamtes für Wirtschaft*. Baden-Baden: Nomos.

Werle, R. 1999. Liberalization of Telecommunications in Germany. In *European Telecommunications Liberalization*, ed. K. A. Eliassen and M. Sjovaag, 110-27. London: Routledge.

Wilks, S. 1999a. The Prolonged Reform of United Kingdom Competition Policy. In *Comparative Competition Policy: National Institutions in a Global Market*, ed. G. B. Doern and S. Wilks, 139-84. Oxford: Clarendon Press.

Wilson, G. K. 1984. Social Regulation and Explanations of Regulatory Failure. *Political Studies* 32: 203-25.

Wolf, D. 2000. Institutional Issues of Telecoms Regulation. In *European Competition Law Annual 1998: Regulating Communications Markets*, ed. C. D. Ehlermann and L. Gosling, 741-744. Oxford: Hart.

Wolman, H. 1992. Understanding Cross National Policy Transfer: The Case of Britain and the United States. *Governance* 5 (1): 27-45.

11

Contracts and Resource Allocation: Markets and Law as the Basis of Policy Instruments

B. Guy Peters

As the public sector has undergone continuous and large-scale reform during the past several decades, a number of fundamental assumptions about governing have been challenged (see Walsh and Stewart 1994; Pollitt and Bouckaert 2000; Hood 1999). As well as altering the nature of the public personnel management, the structures of government, and fundamental principles of accountability (see Peters 1996), these reforms have also addressed the manner in which public services are delivered. Phrased in terms of the overused phrase of Osborne and Gaebler, governments have been advised to "steer rather than row," meaning that government should focus its attention on making policy rather than on the actual delivery of the services. That service delivery function can be better performed, it is argued, by non-governmental actors whether they perform their activities on a for-profit or not-for-profit basis. As several chapters in this collection point out, the use of non-governmental actors will affect the outcomes of the policy process (Ostrom, this volume).

Contracting has become one of the more commonly used instruments of governments that seeks to fulfill public policy purposes while at the same time reducing direct public sector involvement in the provision of those public services. Some analysts of the changing nature of governing have argued that contractualism is a central, if not the central, feature of the emerging model of the state. Jonathan Boston, for example, has defined New Zealand—perhaps the most reformed of all the industrialized democracies—as the "State under Contract" (1995). Yvonne Fortin and Hugo Van Hassel (1999) and their colleagues have demonstrated the relevance of contracting in a range of industrialized democracies. The conservative Republicans in the United States chose to label their program for change "A Contract with America." This list of examples of the adoption of the concept of contracts as a central feature for reforming and reorganizing governance could easily be expanded.

Perspectives on Contracts

The basic point, however, remains that contractual thinking is motivating a good deal of change within wealthy countries, and many less wealthy countries as well. This increased utilization of contracts can be seen as fulfilling several different needs for public sector actors. One such need is political, and contracts are a means of producing public services while (perhaps) saving money and reducing the apparent degree of direct intrusion of government into the private sector. The public in most industrialized democracies has become extremely skeptical, and critical, of the capacity of the public sector to perform well, and therefore involving the private sector may legitimate the policies being delivered (see Nye, Zelikow, and King 1997).

In addition, even if the service being delivered remains in essence a public service the use of the private sector agent for delivery can make the state appear smaller to the less observant members of the political community. The assumption that Osborne and Gaebler (1992), and numerous other reformers and commentators, make is that private sector providers can deliver services less expensively and more efficiently than can providers within the public sector. The capability of reducing public expenditures may be especially evident when the contracting agent is a non-profit organization, but it may even be true for a commercial, for-profit, organization. Non-profit organizations enable the state to obtain the services of private sector organizations with substantially lower labor costs than most other organizations, public or private; they are also ideologically or professionally committed to the services provided.

Contracting may not, however, fulfill all those political objectives for government. The state may in some ways become even more intrusive by using contracting for delivering public services. If government begins to co-opt a significant number of private sector actors, and to impose its organizational and service template on society, then public sector values and priorities become pervasive for the society as a whole.[1] This can be seen in the social sector in the United States and other countries when private providers shape their services to the availability of public funds rather than set their own goals more autonomously. This increased influence of government may represent a marked divergence between the appearance of the retreat of government and the actual spread of its influence, albeit indirectly, throughout society.

Another significant political reason for the shift toward contracting as the preferred manner of service delivery is simply financial. It is believed by the advocates of contracting that the greater efficiency of those non-bureaucratic approaches to service delivery will make it possible for government to provide the same volume of services while spending less public money. In particular the ability to leverage non-profit organizations using volunteers or lower paid employees is an especially promising means of reducing the costs of service provision. That having been said, however, writing an effective contract may build in rigidities not dissimilar to those found in a bureaucracies. Further, as we will discuss at some length below, the most effective contracts for the provision of services may be just those that are least effective in controlling costs.

An alternative perspective, and the more commonly applied one, is that contracts are a more effective and efficient policy instrument than is the direct provision of services through bureaucratic means. Among other virtues, contracts are assumed to be able to solve some of the classic problems of agency involved in any method of delivering service. This faith in the efficacy of contracting may be misplaced but it has become a part of the dominant ideology about the public sector. To be effective in controlling agents, the principals in a contract must be able to specify the demands being made the agent, they must have the means to monitor those agents and also an effective means of controlling those agents. Those conditions are rarely met in the complex process of making and implementing public policies, especially the increasingly complex processes involved in social policy.

Another aspect of contracts, considered as an instrument, is that these tools can be useful mechanisms for specifying the nature of the services that government wants to deliver, or to have delivered, to the public. Governments have come to focus greater attention on performance and the quality of services provided to their citizens (Bouckaert 1995; Summa 1995). With this focus on quality contracts, whether with outside providers or with other actors within the state itself, or even with employees within individual organizations, government policy-makers are forced to specify what they want to do. To be effective, the contracts may also have to specify the logic of the policy being implemented so that the agent can have some sense of the anticipated consequences of their actions and the broad policy objective being pursued with the contract. The specification of services through contracts is more difficult for some aspects of government activity than it is for others. It is not particularly difficult to specify the contract elements required to build a highway, but it may be nearly impossible to specify performance for internal activities such as policy advice (Boston 1994), or perhaps for some social services that involve dealing with highly variable and unpredictable clientele. Although this specification may conventionally be thought of as "top down," contracting may actually be a means by which government collects needed information about the range of possibilities and for clarifying—through negotiation—the exact nature of the service to be delivered (see Krause 1999).

Following from the above discussion, contracts are means of specifying the relationships between principals and agents as they deliver public services (Fortin 2000; see also Krause 1999). As such, contracts become the operative mechanisms for controlling the agents who deliver services, given that such agents have all the familiar incentives to shirk responsibilities and pursue their own goals. Consequently, contracts become the means of identifying, if not always preventing the occurrence of, the standard litany of problems existing in relationships between principals and agents—whether operating in the public or the private sector. Thus, a well-written contract is the means of identifying when an agent may be shirking from what is expected, but which cannot be identified readily without some agreed on set of duties and requirements. The agreement of the actors is essential in this context, so that the agent cannot claim a lack of warning or understanding of the expectations, as might be true for the implementation by public organizations themselves.

This specification of service requirements is, however, a double-edged sword for principals in the public sector. Especially when the contract is made with a "for-profit" organization the specification of minimal requirements for fulfilling the contract very quickly becomes the specification of the maximum level of output that will be delivered by that contractor. This incentive for private sector actors to minimize services is in marked contrast to the traditional model of provision by a public organization imbued with at least some public service values and staffed by professionals with substantial personal commitment to their jobs.[2] In addition to personal commitments public organizations may have more tangible interests in the provision of high rates of service, using those as a means of developing political support. Thus, while the use of contracts may ensure that some level of services is delivered, and even that this something is delivered in a certain manner, it cannot readily provide for services that address the needs of particular groups of clients or, as we will discuss at greater length below, adapt to changing political and socioeconomic circumstances.

The remainder of this chapter will be concerned with a number of questions about contracting as an increasingly important instrument for public policy. The term "contract" has come to be used in a number of different ways, and to describe a number of different relationships between actors. This chapter will attempt to clarify some of the confusion about the use of contracts and especially to point to the implications of using one or another of the possible meanings of contracts when discussing the use of this "tool" for service delivery. I will focus on the nature of contracts as one of many policy instruments available to government for delivering services and for allocating resources within the public sector itself and also to the society. Such a focus requires asking if contracts are effective in reaching the policy goals, and can be as effective as other policy instruments.[3] Finally, I will examine the consequences of an emphasis on contracting on the accountability of government programs.

Issues in the Use of Contracts

Despite the increasingly common use of contracting as an instrument for achieving public purposes, there are a number of issues that continue to surround their use. Some of these issues are definitional, and it can be argued that relationships that are called contractual within government may lack some of the essential features of these interactions. If that is the case then the parties to the arrangements may be interacting under severe misunderstandings of their mutual obligations. Further, even when genuine contracts do exist they may be inappropriate for the tasks to which they are being applied. This is particularly true when we think about contracts in a formal sense, rather than considering the possibilities for "relational contracting," or using less formal arrangements to create stable patterns of interaction among participants in the policy process, a pattern not dissimilar to network thinking in service delivery (see Williamson 1985). The informal versions of contracting tend to focus on building trust among the participants in the process rather than on making specific allocations of obligations and rewards among the participants in the process.

Before we embark on that discussion, however, we should remember that contracting is not as novel in government as many students of "New Public Management" might have us believe. Most governments have a long history of contracting for goods, ranging from pencils and paper to complex weapons systems. While more tangible than contracting for services, that being an activity more characteristic of the New Public Management, many of the same problems arise when purchasing goods that arise in contracting for services. In particular, the governmental organization making the contract must be able to specify what it wants. That may be easy when procuring office supplies, but it becomes difficult when buying weapons, or environmental control systems, when the technology has yet to be fully developed.

Further, although we will emphasize some of the different meanings and interpretations of contracts in the public sector, there are also several central features that define the nature of this instrument, regardless of the variant of the instrument. The most important is that the use of contracts moves governments from thinking about hierarchy to thinking about greater equality among the participants (see below). Phrased somewhat differently, the emphasis on contracting shifts government from a hierarchical to the "enabling state" (Deakin and Walsh 1996; see also Perri 6 and Kendall, 1997). Contracts have some features of the market and some characteristics of law as the basis of the allocation, but depend little if any on hierarchical controls. Market reformers stress the use of contracts because they force the parties to reveal the true price of producing a public service and also tend to drive those prices down through competition. After the negotiations are completed, the legal character of this instrument comes into play and the justiciable element of enforcement is central to implementation.

Markets and Law

Following from the above discussion, we should also examine the nature of contracts, as one of numerous policy instruments available to government (see Salamon 2001; Linder and Peters 1998), each of which may have some utility in delivering public policies. Contracts are but one of many ways in which governments attempt to influence society and the economy, or to provide for their own needs, and they should be analyzed in that context. That is, although contracts have become a very popular means for governments to intervene in society, are they the most appropriate means, given a particular set of circumstances? As with many policy instruments, there can be an ideological or professional commitment to contracting that may drive policy-makers to accept this method even when it is not appropriate[4]. Indeed, one of the problems for any policy instrument is determining when it is appropriate and when it is not.

Policy instruments employ several of the generic resources held by the public sector. Hood (1986) typifies these resources as nodality, authority, treasure, and organization. Contracts combine some elements of authority, i.e., law, with some elements of treasure, i.e., the market and the economic resources of the public sector. That is, on the one hand, contracts are legal instruments and at the extreme depend upon legal procedures for enforcement. On the other hand, contracts tend to be the product of bargaining and exist as means of facilitating the use of market-type mechanisms for the delivery of services. Contracts assume that a market exists for the provision of services, rather than simply the hierarchy that has characterized traditional service delivery through the state itself.

Although contracts to some extent involve both markets and law in achieving their purposes, one of those two fundamental resources of the public sector may be emphasized more than the other in any one contractual relationship. For example, if governments emphasize the legal aspect they are likely to concentrate attention on enforcement and writing a binding, enforceable document that will constrain their agent. On the other hand, if government emphasizes the market element of a contract, it is likely to have greater concern with creating an effective exchange relationship between itself and the agent, and also with creating an arrangement that can endure and produce long-term benefits from the investment of time and energy in negotiating the relationship in the first instance.

To both of these considerations about contracting, we need match the several ways in which contracts are employed by public sector actors. The most common way of thinking about contracts has been in the sense of "contracting out," or taking a service that has been delivered to the public directly by government and replacing that mode of service provision with a private contractor (or perhaps with a contractor from another level of government, or from a quasi-governmental organization). Contracting out is also used to describe taking tangible services that governments have supplied for themselves and giving them to an outsider. A wide range of services is currently being delivered in this manner. Governments began by contracting out rather simple, repetitive operations, such as cleaning buildings or repairing streets, but the use of this instrument has spread: they now also contract out the management of numerous public facilities and the provision of social services and education.

Another way in which contracts have come to be used in government is contracting in, that is, buying services into government itself that might ordinarily be provided directly by public sector employees. For example, governments increasingly have come to use outsiders in policy advice roles that traditionally would have been the province of career public servants. This change represents not only the increasing use of contracts and a means of managing, but also the loss of expertise within the civil service, so that the advice that might at one time have been available is no more.[5] The loss of expertise may be a general problem for government, but it is here especially relevant for the manner in which certain basic internal functions of government are to be performed.

Yet another version of contracting in is to think about government as a provider of necessary services to the private sector, but as providing these on something other than the free basis, as it once might have. In many societies, privatization has been a major component of reform in the public sector, moving commercial activities offered by government into the private sector (Wright and Parotti 2000). At the same time the desire to make government more cost effective has led to creating a number of contracts through which governments provide specialized goods and services to the private sector. For example, although general weather forecasting is certainly a free good, more specialized weather forecasting is done on contracts, as is provision of some forms of data that once were provided free by government statistical organizations. In these cases, government is generally a monopolist, offering their product on a take-it-or-leave-it basis to actors in the private sector.

Finally, contracting may be a way of achieving legal ends without law. As Heritier (this volume) has pointed out, there are a number of ways of creating lawlike statements without having to invoke formal legislative powers. Contracts are yet another such means. The ability to write provisions into contractual arrangements permits governments to influence society in ways that perhaps have not been formally sanctioned.

Characteristics of Contracts

As already noted, a number of alternative meanings of contracts, and indeed many forms of contracting, operate within the public sector. Some relationships existing among parties that have their homes in the public and the private sectors have come to be characterized as contracts, but those arrangements may not fulfill the usual requirements for contracting. Sylvie Trosa (1997, 253-54) developed four criteria that help to define and describe contracts, especially those in operating within the public sector. These criteria are:

1. agreements on common rules of behavior;
2. specifications of the balance of rights and duties for the participants;
3. provisions for coping with changing circumstances; and
4. therefore contracts establish not only what but how the relationship is to be conducted.

These criteria for the existence of a viable contract appear rather fundamental, and also easy to achieve among reasonable participants in a bargaining process, and indeed they appear to be quite suitable mechanisms for allocating resources within the public sector. These criteria are not, however, quite as easy to obtain in practice as might be expected, and some examination of the difficulties in achieving working contractual relations in government can say a good deal about contemporary governing.

Although these criteria for the existence of a contract may appear clear, they still have sufficient ambiguity to provoke debate, and there is sufficient variance in the practice of creating contracting relationships in government to distinguish at least a "hard" and a "soft" version of contracting in the public sector (see Greve, 1999). The "hard" version of contracting assumes that the parties enter the arrangement as utility maximizers, each attempting to maximize his or her position vis-à-vis the other participants. This style of negotiating may also be characterized by an assumption on the part of the participants that the negotiations are "one-off" so that there is little reason to invest in building good will and comity that could sustain continuing patterns of interaction. Given the decidedly adversarial nature of bargaining in this conception of contracting settling upon the winners in a negotiation is likely to be a detailed process and perhaps will be determined by impersonal mechanisms such as sealed bids. Further, such contracts tend to be of limited duration, with multiple opportunities for monitoring.

In contrast, the softer conceptions of contracting involve some a priori agreement among the participants on goals and the means of achieving them, with a presumption that the necessary comity among the participants already exists. Some have described this as a Durkheimian approach to the question of contracting (Hodgson 1995). Given the common normative basis for reaching an agreement, that final agreement can itself be less precisely defined and more flexible, and may involve less formal monitoring of fulfillment. The standards used in the development of these relationships may be more based on policy and general administrative considerations than on formal legalism, and hence the participants in negotiations are also likely to be different.

These alternative versions of contracts also raise interesting questions about probity and accountability within the public sector. On the one hand, the softer version of contracting appears in the long run more efficient for government, providing as it does for the capacity to include a wider range of considerations in the bargain. The softer versions of contracting are also able to produce more enduring patterns of interaction between actors coming from the public and private sectors. On the other hand, the softer version of contracting appears to avoid, or even to undermine, many of the restraints on corruption and favoritism that have taken years to put into place in some political systems. Therefore, acceptance of the softer version of contracting must be considered carefully, and perhaps should only be considered when the administrative system has fully institutionalized a normative commitment to combat corruption. Paradoxically, these values are being stressed in many agendas for "good governance" at the same time that managerial reforms are reducing their viability.

The ethical questions that appear almost inherent in softer contracting are most identifiable when governments deal with for-profit organizations. The "sweetheart deals" that exist between governments and prominent defense contractors evidence the need to think about the accountability issues involved in long-term, relational contracting (see, for example, Hartley 1993). These same issues may arise, however, even for not-for-profit organizations, which may become dependent upon the state for their very existence. In either case, long-term relationships pose some of the same issues about capture that are raised in the literature on regulatory organizations. As the two sets of actors enter into symbiotic relationships, the capacity to monitor their behavior effectively is lessened and, with that, the capacity to ensure the pursuit of the public interest is also lessened.

Power and Policy Change in Contracting

In addition to the variations based upon the degree of "hardness" of the contracts being devised, there are a number of other general questions about the use of contracting in the public sector. In the first instance, these four characteristics of contracts above tend to imply relative equality between the actors, as might be expected in any private sector bargain. That is rarely the case, however, given that one of the parties to the contract is in essence the sovereign authority and may find it necessary to alter some elements of its bargains unilaterally. Of course, governments, no more than private actors, want to get into the business of abrogating contracts. That having been said, however, changes in the composition of government or changes in the overall legal framework governing a policy area may require changing the basis of contracts. Thus, there is no effective balance of rights and duties among the participants, and there are some rights that government will not be able to renounce readily.[6]

On the other hand, contracts may be means for private sector actors to attempt to achieve something closer to a parity of power with the sovereign when reaching agreements on partnerships. State and society interact in a variety of ways but the use of contract language is a means of regularizing that interaction and creating some reasonable expectation on the part of non-governmental actors. As already noted, this expectation may be created in formal "hard" contracting, but it may be even more evident in the "softer" versions of contracting (Greve 1999) that attempt to build stable relations and strategic alliances between the public and private sectors. There are, however, also dangers attendant in that strategy given that the political world is highly unstable and uncertain, and a change in government may generate an altered set of priorities and the end of a (presumably) stable relationship among actors.

A second issue is the capacity of contracts to cope with problems of change, and the different conditions that service providers may encounter when coping with public policies. We know that most public policies are written in rather imprecise, and even vague, terms, with the expectation that they can be changed subsequently. So long as the policies are to be delivered within the public sector itself, that vagueness is dealt with through writing secondary legislation (Kerwin 2000; Page 2000) within the bureaucracy itself. This development through secondary legislation permits a gradual evolution of the program in response to changes, and in response to the aggregation of experience during the course of implementation.

When policies are contracted out, on the other hand, the capacity for incremental elaboration of the policy is diminished substantially. Any elaboration of the legislative mandate generally must be considered in advance of implementation, so that the parties to any contract can know exactly what they are contracting for. This relative rigidity is in marked contrast to the possibilities of continual elaboration of policy when being administered within a government agency itself. Public organizations have some latitude in adjusting, whether through formal or informal means, the nature of the policies they administer and how they are administered (Kerwin 2000), a virtue that may be lost when a contract must specify just what expectations are for the policy area for some period of time.

This policy inflexibility is, of course, especially evident when the "hard" model of contracting is in operation. When a hard contract must be negotiated, then the terms and conditions of the program and its delivery must be decided upon prior to deciding on both the financial and substantive elements of the arrangement. The legal arrangement provides contractors strong incentives to conform to the letter of the law and not to seek more innovative solutions. This is especially so when contract monitoring is performed by people who are not themselves experts in the policy area. In most instances, then, relatively less adaptability can be expected from this style of decision-making than might be true for program delivery through government itself.

We should not, of course, overestimate the willingness of public organizations to alter their standard operating procedures, and hence the differences in adaptability may not be as great as they might appear at first glance. Public organizations have a number of well-known rigidities that may prevent their adaptation to changes in the environment. Further, as performance management and internal contracting become more central features of running public sector organizations, adaptive capacity may shrink further, for the same reasons encountered in contracts with the private sector. If the performance agreement specifies a certain type of output as the measure of adequate performance, then that will almost certainly be what the organization will produce.

The issue of adaptability, like so many other issues involved in using contracts as a means of defining relationships between the public and private sectors for the provision of goods and services, represents a clear trade-off of important values for the public sector. On the one hand, the pursuit of enhanced efficiency and effectiveness argues for pursuing highly adaptable contractual arrangements that can be tailored to changing needs, changing clienteles, and perhaps changing political priorities. On the other hand, the pursuit of accountability argues for making the most rigid and tightly defined contracts more desirable, assuming that government can persuade the prospective partner to agree to such strict arrangements. Such formality in a contract will permit governments to hold those parties accountable for their actions and to recapture some of the accountability that appears to have been lost as a result of moving toward a more businesslike and managerialist public sector (see Peters 2001a).

As well as coping with simple programmatic changes and changes in the relevant environment, contracting in the public sector also must address the question of "peak loads." That is, some types of services usually provided through the public sector have a high level of variance between their average demand for the service and their peak level of demand. For example, governments are prepared for disaster relief even though on an average day there are (mercifully) no disasters occurring, and all the emergency equipment and personnel can remain idle. Private sector organizations, in order to make a profit on a contract, have very strong incentives to prepare for less extensive peak loads than might be desirable, so that certain types of services are perhaps better maintained in the public sector rather than if they are farmed out to the private sector.

A final general concern about contracting is not contained neatly within Trosa's list of criteria, but rather with the more fundamental question of the ideology of managerialism and the propagation of contracts, seemingly without careful thought as to their real utility or appropriateness for the public management issue being addressed. The tendency to throw a popular, and presumably effective, "tool" in the general direction of any problem is far from unusual in the study of policy instruments (Peters 2001c), and contracts are but one of many "flavors of the month" that are components of the New Public Management (White and Wolf 1995). The ideologies involved in these choices are in part general acceptance of the market model as the exemplar of good management and policy, but also may represent more particular values concerning the use of law-based instruments.

As well as questioning the pursuit of contracts for general ideological reasons, we should question their pursuit for more specific reasons when those defy the usual criteria of logic and effectiveness. For example, contracting out is often seen as a means of controlling personnel costs and the number of people actually employed in the public sector. For some politicians the ability to say that government employs some N thousand fewer people at the end of their term than at the beginning is a powerful political argument. The careful citizen will want to know at what cost the reduction in the personnel was purchased, and whether this was really a superior way of approaching the problem of delivering the service.[7]

Conclusion

Contracts are a central feature of contemporary public policy and public management. Given the political, managerial, and even intellectual appeal of this form of service delivery, it is perhaps not surprising that the meaning and application of the term has been stretched significantly. In addition to maintaining simple conceptual tidiness it does matter how the term is used, and, more importantly, it does matter how contracts are implemented. On the one hand, if contracts emphasize the legal dimension of the instrument, then the "harder" characteristic of contracting will prevail, with some of the consequent strengths and weaknesses implied by that legalism and rigidity. On the other hand, adoption of the market-based considerations of bargaining and a dominant focus on policy implementation presses government toward a softer, and less confrontational, conception of contracting.

If there could be general agreement about the virtues of one form of contracting or another, even that agreement might not be applicable to all policies and in all situations. We have pointed out the important differences between contracting out—the usual way in which contracting has been used— and contracting in, which are crucial for understanding the true impact of the choice of this instrument on both government and on citizens. Likewise, different policy areas may be more or less amenable to contracting, given differential levels of specificity that may be possible with those different policy areas. In summary, contracting has become a widely accepted form of intervention for the state, and one that has become almost an ideology in itself. It is, however, one that requires careful consideration and matching with the conditions within which it will be applied.

Notes

1. It may be, as Bozeman (1987) argued, that all organizations are already public, but contracting will almost certainly accelerate the process of spreading public sector values. This discussion is especially relevant for the United States, given the drive from the Bush administration to provide greater support to "faith-based" organizations in providing social services. Opposition to this plan comes as much from religious organizations as it does from civil liberties organizations, the former fearing a loss of autonomy while the latter are fearing the imposition of religious values through nominally public programs.

2. Given the now common negative stereotypes of bureaucrats, this description may appear somewhat Pollyannaish. Still, there is good evidence from a number of sources that public sector workers, especially when delivering services directly to the public, have been committed and at times even altruistic. See Brehm and Gates (1997).

3. Given limitations of space, most of the comparison with other instruments will be implicit. For a more complete analysis of this instrument see Fortin and Van Hassel (1999).

4. For example, our earlier empirical research on the selection of policy instruments (Linder and Peters 1998) found that respondents with legal training tended to be more favorable to regulation and contracts as means of intervention than did respondents with other academic backgrounds.

5. In addition, the role ascribed to civil servants, even senior civil servants, has been shifting away from that of policy advocate to that of manager. Political leaders appear less interested in the dispassionate advice that might have been given by careerists and more interested in the politicized advice that can come from outsiders.

6. This disparity of power may be even more evident for actors all existing within the public sector itself. For example, bureaucratic agencies may enter into arrangements that approach being contracts with legislative bodies, but those bodies retain the latitude to revoke or modify contracts with little or no recourse for the agencies or for the executive branch (see Peters 2001b).

7. Hartley (1993) points out, for example, that the Ministry of Defense in Britain, in the height of enthusiasm over contracting, allowed contracts costing an additional £200,000 in order to save 52 civilian positions. This outcome hardly seems to reflect the ideological pursuit of cost-effectiveness through contracting even in the face of evidence that those savings may be illusory.

References

Boston, J. 1994. Purchasing Policy Advice: The Limits to Contracting Out. *Governance* 7: 1-30.
——. 1995. *The State under Contract*. Wellington: Bridget Williams.
Bouckaert, G. 1995. Improving Performance Measurement. In *The Enduring Challenges of Public Management*, ed. A. Halachmi and Bouckaert. San Francisco: Jossey-Bass.
Bozeman, B. 1987. *All Organizations Are Public: Bridging Public and Private Organizational Theory*. San Francisco: Jossey-Bass.
Brehm, J., and S. Gates. 1997. *Working, Shirking, and Sabotage: Bureaucratic Responses to a Democratic Public*. Ann Arbor: University of Michigan Press.
Deakin, N., and K. Walsh. 1996. The Enabling State: The Role of Markets and Contracts. *Public Administration* 74.
Fortin, Y., 2000. La contractualisation dans le secteur public des pays industrialisés depuis 1980: Hors du contrat point du salut? In *La contractualisation dans le secteur public des pays industrialisés depuis 1980*, ed. Y. Fortin. Paris: L'Harmattan.
Fortin, Y., and H. Van Hassel. 1999. *Contracting in the New Public Management*. Amsterdam: IOS Press.
Greve, C. 1999. Variations in Contracting in Public Organizations. Paper presented at European Group on Public Administration. Glasgow, Scotland.
Hartley, K. 1993. Defense. In *From Hierarchy to Contracts*, ed. A. Harrison. New Brunswick, N.J.: Transaction Books.
Hodgson, G. M. 1995. *The Economics of Institutions*. Cheltenham: Edward Elgar.
Hood, C. 1986. *The Tools of Government*. Chatham, N.J.: Chatham House.
——. 1999. *The Art of the State*. Oxford: Oxford University Press.
Kerwin, C. 2000. *Rule-Making*, 2d ed. Washington, D.C.: Brookings Institution.
Krause, G. A. 1999. *A Two-Way Street: The Institutional Dynamics of the Modern Administrative State*. Pittsburgh: University of Pittsburgh Press.
Linder, S. H., and B. G. Peters. 1998. The Study of Policy Instruments: Four Schools of Thought. In *Public Policy Instruments*, ed. B. G. Peters and F. K. M. Van Nispen. Cheltenham: Edward Elgar.
Nye, J. S., P. D. Zelikow, and D. C. King. 1997. *Why People Don't Trust Government*. Cambridge, Mass.: Harvard University Press.
Osborne, D., and T. Gaebler. 1992. *Reinventing Government*. Reading, Mass.: Addison-Wesley.
Page, E. C. 2000. *Secondary Legislation in British Government*. Oxford: Hart.
Perri 6, and J. Kendall. 1997. *The Contract Culture in Public Services*. Aldershot: Arena.
Peters, B. G. 1996. *The Future of Governing*. Lawrence: University Press of Kansas.
——. 2001a. *The Future of Governing*, 2d ed. Lawrence: University Press of Kansas.
——. 2001b. Implicit and Explicit Contracts: Contracts and Administrative Reform. In *Legislatures and Contractualization*, ed. Y. Fortin. Brussels: IIAS.
——. 2001c. The Politics of Policy Instruments. In *The Tools of Government: A Guide to the New Governance*, ed. L. M. Salamon. New York: Oxford University Press.
Pollitt, C., and G. Bouckaert. 2000. *Public Management Reform: A Comparative Analysis*. Oxford: Oxford University Press.
Salamon, L. M. 2001. *The Tools of Government: A Guide to the New Governance*. New York: Oxford University Press.
Summa, H. 1995. Old and New Techniques for Productivity Promotion: From the Cheese Slicing to a Quest for Quality. In *Public Productivity through Quality and Performance Management*, ed. A. Halachmi and G. Bouckaert. Amsterdam: IOS Press.

Trosa, S. 1997. The Era of Post-Managerialism. In *Managerialism: The Great Debate,* ed. M. Considine and M. Painter. Melbourne: University of Melbourne Press.

Walsh, K., and J. Stewart. 1992. Change in the Management of Public Services. *Public Administration* 70: 499-518.

White, O. F., and J. F. Wolf. 1995. Deming's Total Quality Management Movement and the Baskin Robbins Problem: Part 1: Is It Time to Go Back to Vanilla. *Administration and Society* 27: 203-25.

Williamson, O. E. 1985. *The Economic Institutions of Capitalism: Firms, Markets, Relational Contracting.* New York: Free Press.

Wright, V., and L. Parotti. 2000. *Privatization and Public Policy*, Vol. 13. Library of Comparative Public Policy. Cheltenham: Edward Elgar.

Part 2

Common Goods and the Role of Private Actors

Privatizing Governance in the Financial Markets

12

Private Makers of Public Policy: Bond Rating Agencies and the New Global Finance

Timothy J. Sinclair

Most political scientists spend their time studying obviously political phenomena like elections, political parties, and parliamentary debates.[1] Like the other authors in this collection, I offer a reinterpretation of what are traditionally thought of as mundane—even arcane—entities and processes.[2] In this chapter, I argue that the major debt rating agencies, Moody's Investors Service (Moody's) and Standard and Poor's (S&P), are what I have called embedded knowledge networks (EKNs), and that these (and related institutions) serve to privatize policy-making, narrowing the legitimate sphere of government intervention.

I argue that challenges to the legitimacy of private property relations have acted as a stimulant to the expansion and codification of EKNs, which in globalized conditions are increasingly substituted for public power in strategic areas. This narrowing of legitimate politics promises to reduce the contestation of property relations by confining what is understood as the legitimate sphere for future state-led public policy intervention.

EKNs are private institutions that possess authority as a result of a history of solving problems and acting as expert advisors in high-value transactions. Rating agencies are key EKNs. Their judgments influence the products we buy, the public services we use, and the scope of our democratic institutions. Their growth is increasingly a global concern as these agencies spread from their U.S. base to influence policy in Asia, Europe, and Latin America. Because of this influence, I argue we can view the rating agencies as de facto private makers of global public policy (Sinclair 1994a, 451).

I have organized this account in five parts. The characteristics of embedded knowledge networks as mechanisms of global public policy are considered in the first. In the second section, I examine the key dynamics of the new global finance and the characteristics of the rating agencies. Subsequently I consider the effectiveness of the rating agencies as mechanisms of governance. I then investigate some public-private linkages. The final section of the chapter ponders the political implications of these private makers of global public policy.

Authority of Embedded Knowledge Networks

What are embedded knowledge networks? EKNs are networks, but not in the usual sense of the term. The conventional usage implies "a set of objects tied together in a connective structure by links" (Batten et al. 1995, viii). My usage is indebted to Powell and Smith-Doerr (1994, 368), who suggest a network can be thought of an "organizing logic."[3] Scholars often analyze the organization of social life dichotomously, in either its market or state-centered dimensions (Strange 1994). Some scholars have sought to incorporate hybrid organizational forms, such as community or private associations (Streeck and Schmitter 1985). But these hybrid models still imply control on the part of the state, and put emphasis on the necessity for conscious coordination. We need an understanding of how authority has been reinvented via tools which investigate the *infrastructure* of contemporary commercial life (Cutler et al. 1999; Hewson and Sinclair 1999).

EKNs exercise power in two senses. First, they *control*, by limiting thinking to a range of possibilities, and as a consequence shape the behavior of market actors. On occasion, EKNs *rule*, that is, they exercise veto over certain options, leading to seismic changes in thinking and behavior in the financial markets (Scott 1993, 294). Rule is a less common and less important phenomenon than control, but rule is more visible and may stimulate political challenges to the role of EKNs.

Knowledge is key to understanding where the authority of EKNs is derived. Market actors in the new global finance are overwhelmed with data. EKNs supplement and organize readily available aggregate information through expert and local knowledge. Local knowledge—of "particular circumstances of time and place"—is vital to understanding processes of change and is as necessary as expert knowledge (Hayek 1949, 80-83). This combination of local and expert knowledge gives the agencies epistemic authority in the capital markets (Sinclair 2000, 495). A typical form of EKN knowledge output is some sort of recommendation or rating, which purports to condense these forms of knowledge. This output acts as a benchmark around which market players organize their affairs. Market actors depart from the benchmarks, but these still set the standard for the work of other actors, providing a measure of success or failure. In this way, EKN outputs play a crucial role in constructing markets in a context of less than perfect information.

Disintermediation and the Rating Agencies

The rating agencies operate in what I have called the New Global Finance (NGF). The NGF is a new form of social organization (Cohen 1996). Most of us are familiar with bank lending (Sinclair 1994a and 1994b). Banks traditionally acted as financial intermediaries, bringing together borrowers and lenders. They borrowed money, in the form of deposits, and lent money *at their own risk* to borrowers. However, in recent years disintermediation has occurred on both sides of the balance sheet. Borrowers have increasingly obtained money from non-bank sources. By the mid-1990s, mutual funds, which sweep depositors' money directly into financial markets, contained around $2 trillion in assets, not much less than the $2.7 trillion held in U.S. bank deposits (*Economist* 1994, 11). The reasons for this development lie in the heightened competitive pressures generated by globalization, and the high overhead costs of banks (*Economist* 1992). However, the degree of disintermediation varies greatly, with the universal banking system in Germany seemingly least affected (Mayer and Vives 1993, 7-8).

Disintermediation is the center of the NGF. It is changing banks and creating an information problem in the capital markets. In a bank-intermediated environment, lenders can depend on the prudential behavior of banks to maintain solvency. However, in a disintermediated environment there is an information problem because lenders must make judgments about the likelihood of repayment. Given the high costs of gathering suitable information with which to make an assessment, it is not surprising that institutions have developed to capture economies of scale and provide centralized judgments on creditworthiness.

Bond rating agencies are in the first instance a U.S. development, and we therefore should look at U.S. economic history in order to understand how they came into being. Three key features of American economic history initially impaired the quantity and quality of information flows between those with funds to invest and those seeking to utilize those flows. The first variable was space. Economic development in the western part of the United States occurred at great distances from the centers of population on the eastern seaboard. The second variable was the large number of middle-class people with savings, but who were not embedded in the sort of family-business ties that prosperous people might utilize to guide their investment in Europe. Taxes on consumption after the Civil War had raised the propensity to save rather than consume, greatly expanding the size of this group (Ratner et al. 1979, 369). The third variable was the poor economic and financial data the U.S. and state governments produced at this time compared with other rich countries (Kirkland 1961, 234).

Rating agencies are one product of a process of institutional innovation that has developed over many years. From around mid-nineteenth century until the First World War, American financial markets experienced considerable growth in information provision. *Poor's American Railroad Journal* appeared in the mid-nineteenth century. In 1868, Poor's produced the *Manual of the Railroads of the United States*. By the early 1880s this publication had 5,000 subscribers (Kirkland 1961, 233). John Moody first began publishing his *Manual of Industrial Statistics* in 1900. This publication proved to be a "gold mine" (Kirkland 1961, 234).

The transition between publishing data sets and actually making judgments about the creditworthiness of debtors occurs between the 1907 financial crisis and the Pujo hearings of 1912. This crisis—little known today—was as threatening as the 1990s Asian financial crisis. It changed attitudes toward financiers and expanded demand for bias-free information.

The emergence of what we can identify today as the rating system took place between the 1907 crash and the Second World War. During this period, with the experience of the market crash of 1929 as a further stimulus, information provision in capital markets radically changed. The Securities and Exchange Commission imposed standardization on information outputs to help make information comparable across corporations. Accounting firms flourished (Smith and Sylla 1993, 42). New rating firms appeared to compete with Moody's, and the rating processes themselves were codified and enhanced.

Rating entered a period of consolidation in the 1930s as rating became a standard requirement to sell any issue in the United States after many state governments incorporated rating standards into their prudential rules for investment by pension funds. A series of defaults by major sovereign borrowers, including Germany, narrowed the bond business to mainly U.S. firms and public agencies from the 1930s to the 1980s. This period was dominated by American blue chip industrial firms (Toffler 1990, 43-57). During this time, foreign corporate borrowers were largely excluded from U.S. securities markets.

The current phase of rating growth has a number of central features. Internationalization is the most obvious characteristic. As noted, cheaper, more efficient capital markets now challenge the commercial positions of banks in Europe and Asia. Ratings became a standard feature of any Eurobond offer by the mid-1990s. The New York-based agencies are now growing rapidly to meet their demand for their services in these newly disintermediating capital markets. Second, innovation in financial instruments is a major feature. Derivatives and structured financings, amongst other things, place a lot of stress on the existing analytical systems and outputs of the agencies, which are developing new rating scales and expertise in order to respond to these changes. The demand for timely information is greater than ever. Third, competition in the rating industry has started to accelerate for the first time in decades. The basis for this competition lies in niche specialization (for example, Fitch Ratings in municipals and financial institutions) and in the "better treatment" of issuers by smaller firms. The global rating agencies, especially Moody's, are sometimes characterized as high-handed, or in other ways deficient in surveys of both issuers and investors (Monroe 1995; United States Department of Justice 1998). While this has not yet produced any significant change in the institutionalization of markets, subsequent to the Asian financial crises of 1997-99 Moody's corporate culture became much less secretive.

The two major agencies dominate the market in ratings, listing around U.S. $30 trillion each (Moody's 2001). Both Moody's and S&P are headquartered in New York. Moody's was recently made a stand-alone corporation by parent Dun and Bradstreet, the information concern, while S&P is a subsidiary of McGraw-Hill, the publishing company. Both agencies have numerous branches in the United States, other OECD states, and in emerging markets. A distant third in the market is Fitch Ratings, which is the culmination of recent mergers between Fitch Investors Service (New York), IBCA (London), Euronotation (Paris), Duff & Phelps (Chicago), and Thomson BankWatch (New York).

An increasing number of domestically focused agencies in developed countries and especially emerging markets opened during the 1990s, including Japan, China, India, Malaysia, Indonesia, Thailand, France, Canada, Israel, Brazil, Mexico, Argentina, South Africa, and the Czech Republic (Greenberg 1993; www.everling.de).

The categories of issuers covered by the agencies have changed over time. Initially, the focus of rating activity were railroads, industrial corporations, and financial institutions in the United States. After the First World War, U.S. municipalities and foreign governments sought ratings. With the defaults of the 1930s and the creation of the Bretton Woods system, the rating firms retreated to higher-rated industrial firms in the United States in addition to U.S. municipalities. As noted, in this era of rating conservatism, sovereign rating coverage was reduced to a handful of the most creditworthy countries. With the end of the Bretton Woods system and the liberalization of financial regulation, the narrowness of the system that prevailed for half a century from the 1930s to the mid-1980s was challenged by the rise of a vibrant junk bond market in the United States. This enabled lower-rated companies to raise capital by selling debt on the bond markets for the first time. In this new market, rating helped to price debt rather than exclude it from the markets, as had been the case in the era of rating conservatism.

The outputs of the rating agencies are consumed by key capital market actors, including pension funds, investment banks, other financial institutions, and government agencies. Moody's have 4,000 clients for their publications and estimate around 30,000 people read their output regularly (Chmaj 2000). Annual fees range from $15,000 to $65,000 for heavier users, who also have the opportunity to talk to analysts directly. Increasingly, outputs are produced on-line. The "relationship-level clients" may also attend conferences and take part in other events related to credit quality. Moody's actively puts its analysts in front of journalists and, like Standard & Poor's, issues press statements on credit conditions regularly. Standard & Poor's produce a wider range of products in both traditional and digital format. Their core weekly publication, *CreditWeek*, has some 2,423 subscribers. *Global Sector Review* is bought by 2,988 clients (Bates 2000).

During the Bretton Woods era—the era of rating conservatism—the rating agencies did not dramatically change the way they did business. There were no competitors, and the rating institutions took on a gravitas in keeping with the nature of their task. Events like the unforeseen collapse in New York City's finances in the mid-1970s did not give rise to any fundamental change.

More recently, perceived rating miscalls are a significant issue for the agencies, as these potentially erode the reputational assets the agencies have built up since the 1930s. The 1990s saw more of these events as financial volatility grew in an increasingly liberalized world economy, including the Tequila crisis of 1994-95 and the Asian financial crises of 1997-99. At the same time, derivatives and other new financial technologies stimulated a number of corporate collapses in the United States.

Two main strategies characterized the responses of the agencies to these problems. Like other financial industry institutions, they ran to catch up with financial innovation, spending money on staff training and hiring. They pushed harder for analytical innovation in their own products. S&P created new symbols to indicate when, for example, ratings were based on public information only and did not reflect confidential data. Second, the agencies, especially Moody's, sought to change their cloistered, secretive image and became more transparent and willing to justify their ratings. This latter strategy may have more to do with reducing market and public expectations about rating than improving their product.

The Added-Value of Bond Rating

Why people are prepared to pay money for the work of the bond rating agencies is a matter of controversy. Bond traders and pension fund managers have paradoxical views on rating agencies.[4] On the one hand, they typically hold the rating agencies in high esteem. Indeed, market participants often treat the rating agencies and their views with reverence. In addition to respect for the reputation of the agencies, there is an awareness of the influence of the rating agencies in the markets. Even if a trader or issuer of bonds does not agree with a particular judgment of the rating agencies, the professional has to take account of others acting on that judgment in the market. Rating agency outputs therefore comprise an important part of the infrastructure of the capital markets—as facts of the marketplace—which form the basis for subsequent decision-making. Here, rating agencies are important not so much for any particular rating they produce as for the fact that they are a part of the market itself. So, traders commonly refer to a company as an "AA company" or some other rating category, as if this were a fact, an agreed and uncontroversial way of describing and distinguishing companies or countries.[5]

On the other hand, market traders certainly do express negative views of the agencies and their work. These criticisms can be voluble at times. A common idea is that the agencies are simply one source of information, whose views have to be considered alongside those of other sources. This view, which is often expressed by investment bankers, seems to be made most often when rating agencies make inconvenient judgments about an issue of bonds offered for sale, or when an issuer tries to deflect attention from a rating announcement just made about them. In these circumstances, ratings will be characterized as simply an opinion, one of the many sources of information used by financial market operatives to make their investment decisions.

During the junk bond era of the 1980s, some professionals took the view that the agencies were guilty of limiting access to the capital markets to blue chip corporations (Toffler 1990, 43-57). Others, including pension fund managers, have at times suggested that credit rating is not timely enough and is focused on applying the—presumably no longer relevant—lessons of the past to the future (Liu 1997). Of course, the most common cause for hostility is the view that the rating agencies have somehow made a "mistake" in issuing a rating lower than expected by the issuer of the debt (*Economist* 1997, 68). More recently, another cause of hostility has been the penetration of Europe and Asia by the major American rating agencies, with implications for established market practices in those places (Roberts 1991, 83; Appell and Goad 1998).

Academics cannot agree on the significance of the agencies. The most widely held view suggests rating agencies solve the problem in markets that occurs when banks no longer sit at the center of the lending process. Rating agencies solve this information problem efficiently, this view suggests, because they are able to gather information from many different issuers and issue comparable ratings. Rating agencies may also establish "rules of thumb" which make market decisions easier or less costly (Heisler 1994, 78). The agencies adopt various versions of these views at different times as justifications for their activities. Agency officials typically add the claim that they have access to confidential information not available to the markets. Their rating judgments are, they insist, more likely to be accurate as a consequence.

In the late 1960s and early 1970s, raters began to charge fees to bond issuers to issue ratings. Now 75 percent of the income of these agencies is obtained from fees charged to issuers.[6] In Canada, the Dominion Bond Rating Service gets more than 80 percent of its revenue from rating fees, while the Canadian Bond Rating Agency makes 50 percent of its revenue this way (Kilpatrick 1992). It has been suggested by a number of scholars that charging fees to bond issuers constitutes a conflict of interest (Fight 2001).[7] This may indeed be the case with some of the smaller, lower-profile firms, desperate for business. With Moody's and S&P this does not seem to be a significant issue. Both firms have fee incomes of several hundred million dollars a year, making it difficult for even the largest issuer to manipulate them through their revenues. Moreover, any hint of rating inflation would diminish the reputation of the major agencies, and this asset is the very basis of their franchise. In the case of rating agencies in Japan and the developing world, financing typically comes from some combination of ownership consortia, which often include financial institutions and government agencies. This casts real doubt on the independence of their work within the financial community.

Comparisons between the role of the Law Merchant (a form of private medieval commercial law) and bond rating agencies are useful. The Law Merchant developed as a way of enforcing contracts by making judgments on trade disputes and keeping records of these actions available for scrutiny by merchants engaging in intra-European trade. This mechanism backed up merchants when their names were not well-known to potential new trade partners in geographically distant places. Rating agencies share a number of characteristics with the Law Merchant. They too are responsible for keeping an eye on who is violating the norms of financial and commercial practice (Milgrom, North, and Weingast 1990; Cutler 1998).

Public-Private Dynamics

Rating agencies have close—sometimes difficult—relationships with governments.[8] The degree to which ratings have been subject to government utilization has grown since the late 1970s, as financial markets have become more sophisticated and extensive (Hawkins et al. 1983, 131-61). This has increased the importance of ratings by making the judgments of rating agencies more significant in the transactions of investors and traders. Government regulation in the United States has reinforced an oligopolistic ratings market and made it harder for new entrants to launch ratings businesses.

Public utilization of ratings goes back seventy years or so. The depression, the consequent sharp decline of credit quality, and the problems of domestic financial institutions it brought about led the U.S. Office of the Comptroller of the Currency (OCC) to rule that bank holdings of publicly rated bonds had to be "BBB" or better to be carried on bank balance sheets at their face value or book value. Otherwise the bonds were to be written down to market value, imposing losses on the banks (Cantor and Packer 1994, 6). Numerous state banking departments also adopted this rule. New OCC rules in 1936 prohibited banks from holding bonds not rated "BBB" by two agencies. This had far-reaching consequences because 891 of 1,975 listed bonds were rated below "BBB" at the time. This action effectively closed down the high yield bond market for the next forty years, until 1977. The bond business and bond rating became quiet predictable occupations.

The next important development was the adoption of Rule 15c3-1 by the SEC in 1975, the net-capital rule. Under this rule, brokers who underwrote bond issues had to keep a certain percentage of their financial capital in reserves—a haircut—of the market value of the securities they had on their books. However, the rule gave "preferential treatment if the instruments had been rated investment-grade by at least two 'nationally recognized statistical rating organizations' (NRSROs)," who would get a "shorter haircut" (Edwards 1994). The SEC did not define an NRSRO. Despite this, the NRSRO concept has subsequently been incorporated into many regulatory initiatives. Moreover, "state authorities, self-regulatory organizations and great swathes of the US mutual fund industry have adopted ratings to define, control and advertise risk" (Edwards 1994, 27). The NRSRO concept remains vague and unspecified in law but very significant in the market. The most explicit statements of the NRSRO criteria are contained in SEC "no action" letters given to Fitch Investors Service, Thomson Bankwatch, and IBCA. The criteria mentioned in these letters by the SEC are: conflict of interest scrutiny; appropriate institutional separations to avoid mixing investment advice and rating; adequate financial resources; adequate staff; and sufficient training (Rose interview). Moody's and S&P were simply deemed to be NRSROs. SEC control of NRSRO designation limits competition to those agencies that can demonstrate that they are "nationally recognized." This has been difficult for the two Canadian agencies, who have thus far been denied NRSRO status, even though harmonization of securities disclosure laws between the United States and Canada under NAFTA means that Canadian bonds can be sold in the United States without going through SEC procedures. However, this is contingent on the issue being rated by two NRSROs. Therefore, the Canadian agencies risk being uncompetitive in Canada because they are not NRSROs (Rose interview). While the SEC seems to be sympathetic to their plight, it has clear concerns about the credibility of the Canadian (and other foreign) agencies.[9] Interestingly, in early 2001 one of the two Canadian agencies (CBRS) was bought out by Standard & Poor's.

In August 1994, the SEC took the first steps towards changing the NRSRO system by issuing a "concept release," seeking comment on NRSRO ratings in SEC regulation, the process of becoming an NRSRO and the SEC regulation of NRSROs (SEC 1994). This release, which has now been transformed into a proposed rule, was made at the initiative of middle-level officials, who were trying to get the Commission to take a stand on the issue (Rose and SEC official interviews). Lobbying has been intense during the past seven years. This effort to establish formal procedures for designating and monitoring NRSROs has been attacked by the established rating agencies, which invoke the effectiveness of the market test of ratings as the most appropriate means for keeping rating accurate, and suggest that future extensions of the regulatory use of ratings should be carefully considered on a case-by-case basis (Standard & Poor's 1995). However, as Cantor and Packer observe, the current system "clearly favors incumbents," as new entrants to the rating business cannot become "nationally recognized" without NRSRO status (Cantor and Packer 1994, 8). As of late July 2001, there is no sign of any resolution of this issue.

The initiative to make the NRSRO status more transparent reflects the intensified competitive conditions of the global economy and its emphasis on removing barriers to entry, including the U.S. need to reciprocate where S&P and Moody's have been incorporated into foreign rating agency regulations (such as in Japan or Mexico). In these conditions, state intervention is becoming more codified, institutionalized, and juridified. Rules are more elaborate and made formal, with fewer tacit understandings (Moran 1991, 13). This tendency both devolves state activities onto nominally private institutions, like the rating agencies, which now find themselves increasingly part of disclosure rules, and sets the rules in which these networks operate (Moran 1991, 14). The latest example of this tendency is the Basle II capital adequacy proposals which invoke rating agency outputs for less sophisticated banks (BIS 2001). By invoking agency judgments in more and more regulation, and by codifying rules under which agencies can be established and operate, socially contestable public policy-making has been protected from the demands of the polity. Indeed, the agencies emerge in a strengthened position to apply their judgments to public agencies with the conviction that they are socially sanctioned judges of prudent economic and financial behavior.

Private Makers of Global Public Policy

How has the development of embedded knowledge networks in the new global finance—typified by bond rating agencies—changed the basis of effective policy-making? I suggest that rating agency activity does not just constrain policy, but that it also contributes to the generation of market actors themselves.

Coordination is an important consequence of the rise of the new global finance. Social networks which reduced the transactional uncertainty of markets in the past (such as banks and business ties) are now much reduced in effect by the increased social distance between market participants created by globalization. We can think of the new relations as at times consensual and at other times coercive. The process is consensual when it gives rise to wide agreement on a set of ideas amongst the relevant group about the basis for transactions (control). It is coercive when the EKN must use sanctions (such as rating downgrades) against firms and governments to bring behavior into line (rule).

As I have argued, rating agencies offer to solve the information problem between those with funds and those seeking them, to adjust the "ground rules" inside international capital markets, and thereby shape the internal organization and behavior of those institutions seeking funds. Their views on "the acceptable" shape the thoughts and actions of those dependent on the agencies. This anticipation process limits the scope of concrete policy initiatives. The coordination effect of EKNs, as exemplified by rating agencies, is therefore to narrow the expectations of creditors and debtors to a set of norms, shared amongst all parties.

The agencies see themselves as "quasi-regulatory institutions" (O'Neill interview). They are well placed to adjust government challenges to their prerogatives, as the hesitancy with which any new effort—including Basle II—to further pull them into regulation demonstrates. Nevertheless, a significant feature of their relationship with public authority is the tendency of government to use quasi-regulatory outputs as substitutes for their own action.

Conclusion

Global change makes the public-private distinction at the heart of traditional studies of public policy increasingly invalid. Public policy can also be made by "private" institutions or networks when the outputs of these private institutions shapes the basic norms which produce action in governments and business organizations.

Rating agencies were examined in this contribution as an example of the private making of public policy. Their specific structural power—and hence their influence on public policy—is derived first, from the disintermediation trend in global finance and the information problem it produces in capital markets, and second, from their internal construction (and outward behavior) as embedded knowledge networks, purveying judgments perceived as endogenous and therefore legitimate by other actors.

The key thing to understand about rating agencies from a political perspective is that their interpretive and judgmental function is not socially neutral. Unlike some of the contributors to this volume, I am critical of the idea that social and political mechanisms are ever neutral or universal and therefore can ever truly be said to be "common" goods. This notion implies an organic unity to communities which belies the cleavages and interest-based conflicts which are key characteristics of social life.

While the network discussed in this contribution offers greater understanding of markets (and is therefore attractive as a way of generating self-regulation in global finance, as evidenced by the Basle II capital adequacy proposals), EKNs lack two other resources we normally associate with public policy-making. First, non-elite societal legitimacy: endogeneity within the markets is not equivalent to wider social legitimacy. Second, an executive capacity to respond to crises: EKN rule capacity is less effective than their more diffuse control function. Without the ability to respond constructively in times of crisis, private makers of global public policy are likely to suffer from their own periodic crises of confidence.

Notes

1. This chapter builds on the ideas and concepts I developed in Sinclair (2000).
2. The author would like to thank Adrienne Héritier, Helmut Wilke, Dieter Kerwer, and the other workshop participants for helpful comments on this chapter.
3. One astute commentator at the workshop suggested I substitute "institution" for "network." Aside from the definition of network offered in the text, the problem with institution and the reason I prefer network is that institution is a synonym for organization.
4. Interview with Gary Jenkins, Managing Director, Barclays Capital, London, 13 February 2001.
5. Interview with Leo C. O'Neill, President, Standard & Poor's, New York, 18 August 1992.
6. Interview with Joanne Rose, Vice President and General Counsel, Standard & Poor's Ratings Group, New York, February 1993.
7. Edward Comor suggested this view to me.
8. This section is drawn from Sinclair (1995).
9. Interview with SEC official, Washington, D.C., 31 March 1994. Also see Kilpatrick (1992).

References

Appell, D., and G. P. Goad. 1998. APEC Leaders Question Sway of Rating Firms—Officials Seek a Review of Agencies' Practices but Few Expect Change. *Asian Wall Street Journal*. November 19, 1.

Bank for International Settlements. 2001. *Overview of the New Basel Capital Accord.* Basel, Switzerland, January.

Bates, A. 2000. Standard & Poor's Official, New York. E-mail communication to author. November 13.

Batten, D., J. L. Casti, and R. Thord. 1995. Introduction. In *Networks in Action: Communication, Economics, and Human Knowledge,* ed. D. Batten, J. L. Casti, and R. Thord. Berlin: Springer Verlag.

Cantor, R., and F. Packer. 1994. The Credit Rating Industry. *Federal Reserve Bank of New York Quarterly Review* 19 (2): 1-26.

Chmaj, A. 2000. Moody's Investors Service Official, London. E-mail communication to author. July 31.

Cohen, B. J. 1996. Phoenix Risen: The Resurrection of Global Finance. *World Politics* 48 (2): 268-96.

Cutler, A. C. 1998. Locating "Authority" in the Global Political Economy. *International Studies Quarterly* 43 (1): 59-81.

Cutler, A. C., V. Haufler, and T. Porter. 1999. Private Authority and International Affairs. In *Private Authority and International Affairs,* ed. A. C. Cutler, V. Haufler, and T. Porter. Albany: State University of New York Press.

Economist, The. 1992. Time to Leave: A Survey of World Banking. May 2.

———. 1994. Recalled to Life: A Survey of International Banking. April 30.

———. 1997. Risks beyond Measure. December 13, 68.

Edwards, B. 1994. Will the Agencies be SEC Puppets? *Euromoney.* November: 26-27.

Everling Advisory Services. 2001. List of Rating Agencies. www.everling.de. July.

Fight, A. 2001. *The Ratings Game.* London: Wiley.

Greenberg, S. 1993. New Rating Agency Causes a Stir. *The Guardian.* February 13.

Hawkins, D. F., B. A. Brown, and W. J. Campbell. 1983. *Rating Industrial Bonds.* Morristown, N.J.: Financial Executives Research Foundation.

Hayek, F. A. 1949. *Individualism and Economic Order.* London: Routledge.

Heisler, J. 1994. Recent Research in Behavioral Finance. *Financial Markets, Institutions, and Instruments* 3 (5). December.

Hewson, M., and T. J. Sinclair, eds. 1999. *Approaches to Global Governance Theory.* Albany: State University of New York Press.

Kilpatrick, L. 1992. Debt-Rating's Flaws. *The Financial Times of Canada*, March 30-April 5, 1.

Kirkland, E. C. 1961. *Industry Comes of Age: Busines, Labor, and Public Policy, 1860-1897.* New York: Holt, Reinhart and Winston.

Liu, B. W. 1997. Big Debt Downgrades in Asia Turn Harsh Spotlight on Ratings Firms. *Asian Wall Street Journal*, October 13, 27.

Mayer, C., and X. Vives. 1993. Introduction. In *Capital Markets and Financial Intermediation,* ed. C. Mayer and X. Vives. Cambridge: Cambridge University Press.

Milgrom, P. R., D. C. North, and B. R. Weingast. 1990. The Role of Institutions in the Revival of Trade: The Law Merchant, Private Judges, and the Champagne Fairs. *Economics and Politics* 2 (1): 1-23.

Monroe, A. 1995. Rating the Rating Agencies. *Treasury and Risk Management.* July.

Moody's Investors Service. 2001. About Moody's. www.moodys.com. July.

Moran, M. 1991. *The Politics of the Financial Services Revolution: The U.S., U.K., and Japan.* New York: St. Martin's.

Powell, W. W., and L. Smith-Doerr. 1994. Networks and Economic Life. In *The Handbook of Economic Sociology*, ed. N. J. Smelser and R. Swedberg. Princeton, N.J., and New York: Princeton University Press and the Russell Sage Foundation.

Ratner, S., J. H. Soltow, and R. Sylla. 1979. *The Evolution of the American Economy: Growth, Welfare, and Decision Making.* New York: Basic Books.

Roberts, J. 1991. Contesting the Ratings. *International Management* 46 (8): 83.

Scott, J. 1993. Corporate Groups and Network Structure. In *Corporate Control and Accountability: Changing Structures and the Dynamics of Regulation*, ed. J. McCahery, S. Picciotto, and C. Scott. Oxford: Oxford University Press.

Securities and Exchange Commission. 1994. Nationally Recognized Statistical Rating Organizations. Release Number 33-7085. Washington, D.C.: SEC, August 31.

Sinclair, T. J. 1994a. Between State and Market: Hegemony and Institutions of Collective Action under Conditions of International Capital Mobility. *Policy Sciences* 27 (4): 447-66.

———. 1994b. Passing Judgement: Credit Rating Processes as Regulatory Mechanisms of Governance in the Emerging World Order. *Review of International Political Economy* 1 (1): 133-59.

———. 1995. Guarding the Gates of Capital: Credit Rating Processes and the Global Political Economy. Unpublished doctoral dissertation. Department of Political Science, York University, Toronto.

———. 2000. Reinventing Authority: Embeddded Knowledge Networks and the New Global Finance. *Environment and Planning C: Government and Policy* 18 (4): 487-502.

Smelser, N. J., and R. Swedberg, eds. 1994. *The Handbook of Economic Sociology.* Princeton, N.J.: Princeton University Press and Russell Sage Foundation.

Smith, G.D., and R. Sylla. 1993. The Transformation of Financial Capitalism: An Essay on the History of American Capital Markets. *Financial Markets, Institutions and Instruments* 2 (2): 1-62.

Standard & Poor's Corporation. 1995. S&P Opposes Regulatory Intervention in Rating Activity. *Standard & Poor's Canadian Focus*, 6-7.

Strange, S. 1994. *States and Markets.* 2d ed. London: Pinter.

Streeck, W., and P. C. Schmitter. 1985. Community, Market, State—and Associations? The Prospective Contribution of Interest Governance to Social Order. In *Private Interest Government: Beyond State and Market*, ed. W. Streeck and P. C. Schmitter. London: Sage.

Toffler, A. 1990. *Powershift.* New York: Bantam.

United States Department of Justice. 1998. DOJ Urges SEC to Increase Competition for Securities Ratings Agencies. Press Release. Washington, D.C. March 6.

13

Standardizing as Governance: The Case of Credit Rating Agencies

Dieter Kerwer

Introduction

Undoubtedly, financial markets constitute a vital mechanism for allocating credit in advanced economies. Their undisputed benefits, however, are accompanied by significant externalities. In fact, the history of financial markets has often been told as an endless series of financial crises, which for their part have had severe effects on economic activities at large (Kindleberger 1996). No wonder that crisis prevention has become an important public policy-making goal. If this goal were attained, one would be able to reap the benefits of the market mechanism without having to live with its drawbacks. However, preventing financial crises has been a difficult task for many reasons. One of the most important challenges has been that the domain of the problem is incongruent with the jurisdiction. Whereas crisis prevention is usually organized at the national level, financial crises have an inherent tendency to spill over beyond national borders, even if merely in "psychological" affects, i.e., in the absence of credit relationships (Kindleberger 1996, 108). The globalization of financial markets over the last three decades has exacerbated this problem. Financial markets have transformed themselves from the numerous discrete infrastructures of their respective national economies into a single highly integrated autonomous global economic sector characterized by a vast volume of international financial flows (Held et al. 1999, chapter 4).

There has been an intensive debate on the political consequences resulting from the emergence of a global financial sector. The main hypothesis has been that it would lead to tight constraints on political action. Financial globalization has been viewed as bringing the postwar "embedded liberalism," which allowed national welfare states to domesticate modern capitalism, to an end (Cerny 1994). Furthermore, the regulation of financial markets itself has appeared to become much more problematic. Internationally mobile capital has exposed all national preventive regulation to regulatory competition and subsequently protective standards have experienced a "race to the bottom" (e.g., McKenzie and

Lee 1991). This process was supposedly accelerated as states tried to promote their country's financial sector through competitive deregulation (Helleiner 1994; Cerny 1997). More recently, doubts have emerged, especially with respect to the regulatory constraints resulting from financial globalization. This revised view starts out with the observation that the increasing integration of global financial markets did not sweep away financial service regulation (e.g. Coleman 1996; S. K. Vogel 1997). On the contrary, in many instances increasing global integration was accompanied by a process of "legalization" in which informal self-regulatory arrangements were recast in a formal legal mould (Lütz 1998). The collective action problems posed by regulatory competition have been overcome by the principle of "international coordination of home country control" (Kapstein 1994). At the international level, states coordinate their regulatory activities by minimum standards, which reduces the likelihood of a regulatory race to the bottom (T. Porter 1993; Dale 1996; Steil 1994). Subsequently, these standards are translated into national regulation, enforced at the national level; they thus facilitate compromise at the international level. The globalization of financial markets in the last three decades has given rise to a "multilevel system," which has even led to increasing levels of protection in some areas.

Research on the dynamics of financial market regulation has thus shown that the constraints resulting from financial globalization are less severe than initially expected. Still, this finding should not lead one to underestimate the transformation of governance provoked by globalization. In many global economic sectors and infrastructures the qualitative change in government has been so significant that it cannot be captured by a mere focus on regulatory dynamics. In many areas global governance is increasingly based on "private authorities," i.e., cooperating firms that can set binding rules for themselves or for others (Cutler, Haufler, and Porter 1999; see also introduction and Mayntz in this volume). This shift away from the state as a public authority, which was the only agent to legitimately make collectively binding decisions in the past, also involves a change in the nature of the rules used. Private authorities cannot resort to formal law; they typically coordinate via rules which rely on superior expertise in order to motivate others to follow them. The effectiveness and the broader consequences of this form of governance still have to be explored.

This chapter analyzes credit rating agencies as one example of a "private authority" involved in the governance of financial markets. Credit rating agencies such as Moody's, Standard & Poor's, or Fitch/IBCA are private financial service firms that estimate the creditworthiness of borrowers or financial instruments (Cantor and Packer 1994). By rating a wide range of different borrowers in accord with the same scale and publishing these risk assessments, they have established an important standard for credit risk. These risk assessments are widely used for making investment decisions in the marketplace. Furthermore, private credit ratings have been used to make the regulation of financial market risk sensitive, for example, by restricting the investment activities of banks to instruments of low credit risk. Both of these functions of credit ratings have become increasingly important in the last two decades as rating agencies have expanded geographically to cover the whole globe (Estrella et al. 2000, 14-54).

As a consequence of this development, a rating agency's negative judgment on a borrower's creditworthiness can significantly raise the cost of borrowing for both firms and sovereign states. In spite of the potential severity of the adverse effects of a downgrade, rating agencies will turn a deaf ear to borrowers' complaints about incorrect credit risk estimates, because negotiating with borrowers would risk tarnishing the rating agency's image of being a neutral information provider. As a consequence, despite the fact that rating agencies have become increasingly influential in global financial markets, it is very hard to hold them accountable for their action: rating agencies almost never have to justify their decisions, let alone provide compensation to others for the adverse consequences of their mistakes (see also Cutler in this volume). The breach between the magnitude of potential damages for borrowers and the possibilities of a remedy gives rise to an "accountability gap." The hypothesis of this chapter is that this accountability gap results from using credit ratings as risk measures in regulation designed to limit the risk taking of investors. Thus I argue that regulatory enforcement is the key to the rating agencies' power, and not their pivotal role in financial markets, as is commonly assumed. Public authority plays a crucial role in constituting private authority for credit rating agencies.

The chapter will proceed in the following manner. First, I will introduce a framework inspired by neo-institutionalist organization theory and then subsequently use that framework to analyze the empirical case of credit rating. It conceptualizes governance that is based on expertise as a form of organizational-standard setting, and identifies circumstances under which an accountability gap arises. Second, I will claim that rating agencies are setting organizational standards by defining models and practices conducive to high creditworthiness. Third, I will show that regulatory enforcement is the main reason for the dominance of the rating agencies' organizational standard. Fourth, I will present evidence supporting the claim that this leads to an accountability gap, which in turn has adverse consequences for the effectiveness and the legitimacy of this mode of governance. I will conclude by briefly sketching out a larger research agenda for comparatively exploring the preconditions and institutional remedies for the accountability problems of global governance arrangements.

Theory

In the following I shall survey the theoretical approaches to the phenomenon of credit rating by private firms. The lead question is: to what extent do they help to analyze the disconnection between power and accountability? Or in other words, to what extent do they help to analyze the accountability gap? According to the perspective of standard economic theory, there is no accountability gap since the agencies are adequately controlled by reputation. By contrast, critical political economy identifies the accountability problem as a major problem for analysis. This position is used as a starting point to mine neo-institutional organization theory for a more sophisticated explanation of the accountability gap based on the interaction of public and private authority.

Credit Rating as Information

Credit ratings provide investors with information on the creditworthiness of borrowers. For this reason, rating agencies are predominantly defined as information intermediaries. This view also forms the basis for the question that economists have tried to answer with respect to rating agencies: if and in what way does the information on the creditworthiness of borrowers expressed in the credit ratings enhance the efficiency of financial markets (Steiner and Heinke 1996)? Neo-classical finance holds that, as a rule, rating agencies reduce the efficiency of financial markets because their service is costly without producing tangible benefits. By contrast, neo-institutional finance theory suggests a more benign view. Rating agencies can enhance the efficiency of financial intermediation by reducing the lender's monitoring costs. In economics, the accountability of rating agencies is not a problem. Normally they are effectively policed by the market. Rating agencies have not been exploiting the informational asymmetry between themselves and their users. The reason is that information intermediaries are seen to be particularly vulnerable to a loss of reputation as credible sources of information (Mann 1999).

Credit Rating as Ideological Uncertainty Transformation

In political science it is less plausible that intermediaries in financial markets are neutral information providers. The work of Tim Sinclair challenges the conception that rating agencies are just firms selling a specific kind of information to the market (Sinclair 1994; Sinclair in this volume). The hypothesis guiding his analysis is that the risk assessment activities of rating agencies cannot remain external to the relation between the borrower and lender; they constitute the credit relationship. With their information on credit risk, credit rating agencies transform the uncertainties of credit relationships into calculable risks. By this they effectively shape the mutual expectations between the creditor and borrower. The validity of rating agencies is partly based on consensus, insofar as there is no alternative to credit ratings in credit relationships, but this knowledge is reinforced by the sanctioning power that the possibility of negative risk assessment (downgrades) confers on them. In this sense, rating agencies have epistemic authority (Sinclair 2000; see also Strulik 2000; Strulik this volume). Most importantly, this epistemic authority has a political dimension. It justifies financial markets as neutral and efficient means for allocating resources, even though they in fact favor the financial elite and disfavor redistribution. In other words, according to this perspective, and contrary to their self-projected image, rating agencies engage in what could be called "ideological uncertainty transformation." It is exactly because this uncertainty transformation is ideological that the lack of accountability is problematic.

The thesis of "ideological uncertainty transformation" highlights the existence and the nature of the power of rating agencies. However, this construction of the accountability problem is problematic for several reasons. First, the criticism of ideology-based uncertainty transformation raises a question that any critical theory needs to consider carefully: what are its evaluation criteria (Habermas 1981)? To make the criticism of intermediation by rating agencies more convincing, a comparison with other types of intermediation would be necessary. The most prominent alternative—bank-based intermediation—is characterized by a more coercive creditor-borrower relationship. In this perspective the subtle distribution consequences of a rating-based intermediation probably do not provide a strong case for increasing public accountability. Second, it is doubtful whether the power of the rating agencies can be explained solely by the fact that there is no alternative to their credit risk assessments. In fact, alternative sources of information on credit do exist, such as credit registers and export credit ratings (Estrella et al. 2000, 55-125). Beyond that, a wide range of sources exist that produce credit-related knowledge; for example, investment funds, banks, professional associations, and even academia. It would therefore be hard to demonstrate that in the face of these heterogeneous sources, rating agencies would be able to effectively monopolize the cognitive constitution of the credit relationship. Finally, the most problematic consequence of this analysis is that it does not open a perspective on how the negative effects of intermediation based on rating agencies can be mitigated or overcome. If they are the only source constituting a credit relationship in a disintermediated financial market, questions of institutional design cannot be asked. They have to be accepted as an inevitable fate. Public accountability appears necessary but at the same time utopian.

Credit Rating as Standardizing

In the following, I want to propose an alternative way of dealing with the phenomenon of rating agencies, one that builds on the insights of the international political economy. As will be shown, this allows a better account of the power of the rating agencies and makes it possible to conceive of the accountability problem in a way that does not preclude possibilities for an institutional remedy. For this purpose, I propose further pursuing a slightly different understanding of rating agencies as "coordination service firms" which function to "set standards of behavior for other firms" (Cutler, Haufler, and Porter 1999; Sinclair 1999). This comparison of the process of credit rating with standardizing seems a good lead: on the one hand, it preserves the insight that rating agencies are not merely neutral information intermediaries, but that they also establish a common understanding of what constitutes creditworthiness; on the other hand, "standardizing" avoids the connotation that there is an inevitable monopoly, since standards (as opposed to regulations) are not mandatory and often have to compete with other standards.

In order to gain insight into how standards coordinate behavior, this chapter closely follows neo-institutionalist organization theory. The starting point is a definition of a *standard* as *any rule based on expertise that can be adopted voluntarily*. In this sense standards are "advice given to many" (Brunsson 1999,

114). Examples of such standards are technical standards, the rules of international sports associations, or the OECD's recommendations of how to best run an economy, and many others. It is clear that such a definition aims at a vast area of rule-making in modern society. Standardizing in this sense is a mode of governance in its own right (Brunsson 2000). Standardizing is similar to hierarchical rule making in that it can only effectively coordinate action if the outcomes are seen to be desirable; it differs in the way this underlying legitimacy for rules is secured. In a world of autonomous actors, the legitimacy of hierarchical rules depends on the authority of the rule setter; and the validity of such rules is restricted to a limited range of actors, e.g., the members of an organization. But standards depend on the legitimacy of the underlying expertise. Since adopting them is voluntary, they do not have to be limited in application to be acceptable.

Standards, in the sense of expertise-based voluntary rules, not only differ from hierarchical rules, but also from the more conventional understanding of "standards." They are not technical standards specifying the desired properties of a technical artifact, nor are they just specifications of the minimum or maximum level of protection or risk defined in regulation, such as environmental emission standards. Rather, the underlying paradigm is that they are rules aimed at promoting certain organizational procedures or structures. Examples of such standards are the management rules developed by the International Standards Organization (ISO), the European Union's Environmental Management and Auditing System (EMAS), or the OECD's rules on corporate governance. In this chapter the term "standard" only refers to this subset of the whole universe of expertise-based rules. "Standard" is thus defined as an *expertise-based voluntary rule on organizational structures or procedures* (e.g., Kieser, Spindler, and Walgenbach).

Most importantly, seeing standardization as a mode of coordination which sets expertise-based, voluntary rules gives us access to systematic reasons for the accountability gap. Standards face an accountability problem whenever they are hierarchically enforced by a third party. This blurs the clear accountability criteria that usually apply in the pure cases. As a rule, in a hierarchy, the top of the pyramid, where the rules are set, is held accountable. In the case of standards, by contrast, the user of a standard is responsible, since per definition the adoption of a standard is voluntary. Whenever standards are made mandatory, the legitimacy pattern should shift to the hierarchical model. However, often this is not the case because third party enforcement is also justified by the legitimacy of expertise. In this case, the standard setter acquires power by third-party enforcement, which is not checked by corresponding accountability: "Even if standardizers bear relatively little responsibility, they may have great power. In such cases standardization may become a form of fairly strong organization, with concentrated power but diluted responsibility and little room for complaints" (Brunsson 1999, 124).

Two basic theoretical convictions that underpin this conceptualization of the accountability problem have to be mentioned. The first is that any type of governance structure can only coordinate insofar as it is seen to be legitimate

(Brunsson and Olsen 1998, 32). The second is the insight from organization theory that the discourse producing this legitimacy ("talk") and material decision-making ("action") are as a rule only loosely coupled in order to shield decision-making from the potentially crippling effects of the contradictory normative demands of the environment (Brunsson 1989). When this observation is applied to governance structures in general, it is possible to understand why there is a loose fit between the governance structure and its legitimation. Furthermore, it becomes plausible that a hybrid form of governance, with its inherently higher ambiguity about the nature of its coordination, allows an even greater degree of decoupling of the mode of legitimacy from the mode of action coordination.

The last important dimension of this approach to standardization is that it identifies a particular consequence of the accountability problem in standardizing. Since the major responsibility involved in using a standard rests with the user, when he is disappointed the user is less likely to complain to the standard setters and more likely to look for his own errors of judgment. In Hirschman's (1970) terminology, attributing blame to the user will make exit more likely than voice. As a rule, this will deprive standard setters of feedback, because standards are less sensitive to exit than markets (Jacobsson 2000). This drawback of standardization is even more pronounced whenever standards are hierarchically imposed by a third party. When this is done, the already feeble feedback mechanism of exit is further weakened, but no corresponding mechanism of voice is established. Thus, neo-institutionalist organization theory finds the accountability gap problematic for a different reason than critical political economy does. Whereas the latter points to the ideological bias underlying uncertainty transformation, the former points to a low likelihood that errors will be corrected.

Summing Up

The theoretical analysis presented has argued for a new approach to analyzing the power of private actors in the international economy. It has been demonstrated that, in identifying and explaining an accountability deficit, the neo-institutionalist approach, which sees standards as a form of governance, offers a genuine alternative to an approach based on epistemic authority. First, standardization is characterized by an accountability deficit because it is hard for standard users to hold standard setters accountable for errors. Second, in accord with this perspective the accountability gap is a problem because it prevents the correction of errors, not because of a hidden ideological agenda. However, it remains to be shown whether this theoretical perspective can be used to cast new light on credit rating agencies. In which ways is it possible for rating agencies to be conceived of as standard setters? This will be shown in the next section. Subsequently, the role of third-party enforcement in rating agencies will be analyzed. The argument here is that governmental third-party enforcement is an important reason for the pivotal role rating agencies play in global financial markets. In the next section the nature of the accountability gap will be analyzed with a view to the extent to which it is due to government third-party enforcement. The chapter will conclude with a consideration of possible remedies to the accountability gap and some theoretical lessons that this case suggests.

Defining a Standard of Creditworthiness

Rating agencies set a creditworthiness standard by publishing the criteria that guide them in the rating process. This standard is based on the in-depth expertise that they have accumulated over nearly one century of observing the determinants of credit risk. It is a highly influential organizational standard defining practices and processes conducive to high creditworthiness. Borrowers use it to assess the likely consequence of any event on its creditworthiness and investors use it as a model for their own credit risk assessment activities or to reflect on the validity of the analysis underlying a rating. The standard provides a set of criteria which defines, for a general audience, what credit quality is about and how it can be enhanced.

It is unusual to view rating agencies as being in the business of setting standards. Their most visible output—the rating—is a credit risk assessment of an individual borrower and not a general rule about what is desirable from the point of view of creditworthiness. Furthermore, rating analysts insist that they are not giving advice to individual customers, because they need to keep their judgments neutral (Interview Fitch/IBCA, New York, 12 November 1999). Without denying these obvious facts, in the following I want to present some empirical evidence in support of my claim that rating agencies are also standard setters. In the first section I shall show that the judgments rating agencies make depend on an elaborate set of criteria that define creditworthiness. In the second section I want to show that this definition is publicly available and acts as an influential, but by no means compulsory, expertise-based rule.

Assessing Creditworthiness

Rating agencies claim to rely on several criteria when assessing the "ability and willingness of an issuer to make timely payments on specific debt or related obligations" (McGuire 1991, 71). First, ratings depend on a consideration of the common economic environment of different borrowers. As a rule, the rating of a borrower will not be higher than the rating of the country of origin. Second, ratings depend on some properties of the borrower himself. For any type of firm, creditworthiness depends on the ratio of firm value to outstanding debt (Gordon 1991). The higher the value of a firm's assets, the higher the income flows, and the lower all debt obligations, the higher the credit rating is going to be. However, a credit rating goes beyond a selective reading of a firm's accounting statement in that there is an attempt to assess the stability over time and the likelihood of a declining performance under stress. In the process specific factors are more closely examined, for example, the stability of the revenue flows, which is likely to be higher in a public utility operating under the regime of a regional monopoly than in an ordinary commercial firm. These considerations vary in accordance with different types of borrowers such as banks, insurance and utilities companies, etc. The credit risk of public borrowers is another major important category for analysis. The rating of a "sovereign borrower" is the "measure of the ability and willingness of the country's central bank to make available foreign currency to service debt, including that of the central government itself" (Estebanez 1991, 157). This is seen to depend not only on economic factors such as the balance of payments, but also on a host of political factors such as the legitimacy of the political system and past records of crisis management. However, it is claimed that these factors are evaluated strictly according to the effects they have on creditworthiness, and not according to any political criteria (Estebanez 1991, 160). What distinguishes ratings from all other types of credit risk analysis is that they aim to give an estimate of the relative credit risk, no matter what type of instrument or borrower is rated (McGuire 1991, 85f.). The claim is thus that ratings allow a comparison of the creditworthiness of, for example, a Russian region with an Argentine electricity generator and a U.S. carmaker. And this comparability can only be achieved if rating agencies consistently use one set of assessment criteria.

Standardizing Creditworthiness

Even if it is accepted that rating decisions are based on a common set of criteria, it is not obvious how they could become organizational standards. These criteria are intertwined with the procedures of the credit rating process.[1] Each rating is established by a committee, in which analysts with different expertise are assembled in order to ensure that all the relevant knowledge is represented. Furthermore, all rating decisions are reviewed by a senior analyst from outside the committee who is likely to be especially careful if the ratings differ a lot from those of other agencies. Rating agencies continually monitor themselves by retrospectively comparing their creditworthiness estimates with statistical data. And finally, the agencies try to draw on local expertise by branching out into international webs. Thus, the expertise involved in a rating is closely linked to the organizational structure. What is more, rating decisions always have a qualitative side that is impossible to formalize (e.g., Hirsch 1996). This tacit dimension of the expertise of rating agencies is another indicator of the embeddedness of rating expertise. Surely then this type of expertise cannot be the basis of a standard.

No doubt, estimating credit risk involves knowledge that is deeply embedded in the organizational structure and cannot be disclosed. However, there can also be no doubt that rating agencies are engaged in wrapping some of the relevant knowledge into the standards of credit risk that become relevant in the capital markets. Along with every rating, the agencies publish a short comment giving reasons for the change. Periodically, they publish methodological outlines that disclose the criteria that are taken into consideration. This type of activity is an integral part of their business because this is important information for both type of users of credit ratings. In order to weigh the benefit against the risk, borrowers seeking access to the capital markets will want to know in advance the criteria used in evaluating them. Investors will want to be reassured that rating agencies have an adequate knowledge about what they are doing. To reach these goals it is not necessary to transfer all the knowledge relevant for the decision. But the fact that this is impossible anyway could be an important precondition for rating agencies active disclosure of some of it: they do not need to fear competitors copying them.

The standard of creditworthiness established by rating agencies—although sometimes contested—has an important orienting function for the decision-making of borrowers and investors alike. The influence on borrowers is more readily noted, since a rating determines the cost of borrowing. The nature of the influence is not straightforward, since there is no obligation to maximize the credit rating all the time. If, for example, by a bold investment, a firm achieves a lower credit rating, it might offset its increasing financing costs in the bond market by making use of a better possibility to raise capital in the equity market (Schmidt 1996, 270-71).[2] However, any borrower will have a strong incentive to monitor his decision-making in light of the rating agencies' standard of creditworthiness by asking how it will affect the credit rating. A distinct disciplining effect can be observed in management's decisions. This is especially visible in mergers and acquisitions, which can frequently lead to downgrades and are often interpreted as a negative judgment on the part of the market (Schnabel 1996, 321-22). The same disciplining effect of the creditworthiness standard can be observed among "sovereign borrowers" (Sinclair 1994). If municipalities, regions, or nation-states are downgraded by a rating agency, this can have detrimental effects on their capacity to provide public goods such as social welfare or a public infrastructure. The magnitude of the rating agency's influence on sovereign borrowers is shown by the protest from borrowers if the rating downgrade is seen to be unjustified. At times, government representatives even plead for mercy—at least according to the headlines of the financial press (*Financial Times Deutschland*, 6 June 2000, 19). That creditworthiness is a standard is also documented by the widespread skepticism among German borrowers about the U.S. rating agencies. German firms are reluctant to seek a rating, not because they fear that they will be treated unfairly, but because the same standards of creditworthiness will be applied as in the United States, which will not take into account the specificity of German corporate governance. If credit ratings did not serve as a standard, this concern would be meaningless.

Although the influence of the creditworthiness standard on borrowers seems to be more pronounced, investors might even be more heavily influenced by it. Today portfolio managers are confronted with an enormous range of choice among different financial products from different countries of origin. In the face of such complexity, portfolio managers have to rely on credit ratings for orientation (Behrenwaldt 1996, 294-96). For example, prior to the Asian crisis, institutional investors who only invested a small share of their assets in emerging markets often relied exclusively on credit ratings for information on the credit risk involved because it was too expensive for them to carry out a more sophisticated analysis (Adams et al. 1999). Another good example of the extent to which the rating agencies' standard of creditworthiness is accepted is provided by the fact that many institutional investors such as mutual funds or pension funds have internal rules that bar them from acquiring debt obligations rated below a certain threshold or not even rated at all (e.g., ten Brink 1996, 278). In this case, the credit rating agencies' standard of creditworthiness is built into the organizational routines in such a way that the influence might no longer even be acknowledged by the decision-makers. It is likely that the German banks' efforts to reorganize their creditworthiness-evaluation routines in line with the rating agencies' standards in order to comply with the revised Basel capital reserve requirements will be yet another example of the influence of the credit standard (*Frankfurter Allgemeine Zeitung*, November 29, 2000, 49).

Summing Up

So far my argument has been that the credit rating agencies set a standard of creditworthiness in accord with the major defining elements introduced in the preceding chapter: their expertise is based in their knowledge about creditworthiness. They provide organizational rules in that they define structures and practices conducive to a high creditworthiness. And finally, somewhat en passant, I have mentioned that firms can occasionally decide not to follow them, i.e., compliance is voluntary. However, rating agencies do not only standardize. No doubt, rating agencies also rate. So how can we bring rating back into the study of rating agencies? One way is to see rating as establishing the extent to which the standard of creditworthiness applies. Thus in the world of accounting, auditing would be the analogous activity to rating. This comparison with accounting also reveals an important institutional difference between the two institutions. Accounting and auditing standards are usually set by independent professional associations and drafted as rules, whereas the rating agencies themselves define the standard that they also audit. This lack of differentiation between rule setting and rule verification could possibly account for some of the peculiarities of the case. We will come back to this point in the conclusion.

Third-Party Enforcement

In financial markets the rating agencies' views of what constitutes creditworthiness matter. Usually their influence is viewed as resulting from the standard's importance in guiding the actors through the complexity of the market. However, this view cannot explain why rating agencies would be so influential, even though there are other sources of information on creditworthiness (see above). To understand the rating agencies' influential position, it is not enough to just look at what they do. My thesis is that the rating agencies' standard of creditworthiness counts because it has been adopted in financial market regulation. Third-party enforcement by public regulation makes it mandatory to observe the

standard in many instances, and it excludes the use of alternative views of creditworthiness as a substitute. In the following I want to show how and why credit
ratings are being used for regulatory purposes. Subsequently, I want to offer an
explanation for why they have become influential well beyond the United States,
where their use was pioneered in the 1930s. The expansion is not so much to be
attributed to the aggressive efforts of U.S. regulators to export the standard of
creditworthiness as to the investors' desire to access the U.S. capital market and
the emulation of regulators around the world for the use of that standard in
regulation.

Rating and Regulation

The financial market regulators in the United States were the first to use the
rating standard in regulation designed to mitigate excessive risk-taking in financial markets. Three types of regulatory requirements have been designed to vary
according to the magnitude of risk they address (Adams et al. 1999, 153). The
rating standard of creditworthiness was first used to increase the risk sensitivity
of investment restrictions for financial institutions (von Randow 1996). A second major use of the rating standard has been to adjust capital reserve requirements to the credit risk involved. The potential advantage is that such regulation
can better address the risks involved and at the same time avoid creating an
unnecessary burden for the financial industry involved. Finally, regulators have
defined disclosure requirements with reference to the rating standard. Since the
regulatory use of ratings seeks to curb excessive risk-taking, it targets the investors or borrowers. Thus, the immediate pressure of third-party enforcement
aims at convincing investors to observe the rating agencies' credit standard.
However, this obligation in turn creates constraints for lenders as well. If the
lenders' credit quality deteriorates below the threshold set by the regulator, the
investor is forced to withdraw (Interview International Monetary Fund, Washington, D.C. October 1999). As a consequence, lenders may find that, due to
their low creditworthiness, they cannot gain access to the funds of the big institutional investors, for example, pension funds. Thus, in order to avoid being
excluded from the credit market, lenders have a strong incentive to observe the
rating agencies standard of creditworthiness.

Towards Global Enforcement

In the last two decades rating agencies have started to influence capital
markets worldwide. The traditional U.S. rating agencies now boast a truly global
network of offices. Local rating agencies have been founded in several countries. This is not only true for highly industrialized countries; it can also be observed in the emerging economies (Adams et al. 1999, 189). Local rating agencies try to capitalize on the fact that they have a more detailed knowledge of the
industry than their international competitors. Newly founded rating agencies in

Germany, for example, try to exploit their knowledge of the famous *Mittelstand*, the dynamic sector of small- and medium-sized enterprises. Their claim to superior local knowledge makes them more attractive to these firms because they can expect to be evaluated in an appropriate manner; and many investors presumably feel that the analysis is superior. However, these local agencies have not challenged the position of the U.S. rating agencies. On the contrary, these local rating agencies often enter into joint ventures with one of the big U.S. rating agencies or are swallowed up by them, as happened in France, when Standard & Poor's took over the French rating agency, Agence d'Evaluation Financière (Raimbourg 1990, 31-33). Local rating agencies seem to be an attractive takeover target when they do not exclusively cater to the needs of local investors but also aim at providing international investors with information. Another indicator of their increasing importance is the number of sovereign ratings, i.e., ratings of foreign countries. These ratings are of pivotal importance because they place a ceiling on the credit quality that any other lender can achieve. Moody's reported an increase in the number of sovereign ratings from around ten in the 1980s to nearly seventy in 1999 (Adams et al. 1999, 196). In the same year Standard & Poor's listed seventy-nine sovereign ratings. Furthermore, they have become so active in the emerging economy that their role in this area has come within the purview of the critical inquiry into the causes of the Asian financial crisis.

There are two main reasons why the rating agencies' creditworthiness standard has become increasingly important beyond the parameters of the U.S. financial markets. The first explanation for the fact that firms all over the world have entered the rating game is that a rating has been a precondition for gaining access to U.S. investors. Since the big U.S. institutional investors are important players in the international capital markets and they can only acquire financial instruments that are rated, the de facto access to international capital markets depends on a rating. This is the most important reason for the rising demand for credit ratings in the Asian market (Adams et al. 1999), but it is also an important motivation in OECD countries (see e.g., ten Brink 1996, 278). The export of standards by a wealthy market is a mechanism that has been studied in international trade and has been termed the "California effect," since California—being an attractive market for cars—managed to impose its strict environmental standards on foreign producers (D. Vogel 1995).

The second explanation for the increasing influence of rating agencies worldwide is that national regulators have started emulating the use of the rating standard in regulation (Adams et al. 1999, 160f.). For example, in Japan, regulators started using ratings as access criteria for the bond market in the early 1980s. In the European Union this trend was promoted by the 1993 Capital Adequacy Directive, which specifies that companies should set aside more capital for their non-investment grade holding. By the end of the 1990s this directive had been implemented by most member states. Furthermore, the proposed amendment to the Basel capital adequacy standard refers to ratings as risk measurements. This is going to promote the use of ratings in the regulatory process in all countries with internationally active banks. Even regulators in emerging economies are increasingly using ratings in their liberalized markets.

The global diffusion of governmental third-party enforcement is another mechanism increasing the influence of rating agencies.

A common perspective in political economy would suggest that the increasing influence of rating agencies' in the rest of the world is due to the United States aggressively exporting its regulatory model in order to ensure the dominance of U.S. agencies, which are likely to rate domestic firms more favorably than foreign firms.[3] However, such an interest-based explanation is not entirely convincing. This is not to say that the United States never made an attempt to export its model of regulation based on the rating standard. In fact, the United States does support the use of a rating standard for creditworthiness in the reform of the international reserve-requirement standard. However, due to the opposition from countries that fear disadvantages, it is not going to be mandatory (*Financial Times Deutschland*, March 16, 2000, 30). Furthermore, even if it had been successful, the attempt to export the U.S. model to the international regulatory arena could not explain the influence that rating agencies have already had for some time.

Summing Up

There is substantial evidence to support the claim that governmental third-party enforcement is crucial for explaining the dominant position of rating agencies in financial markets. It is important to note the reasons that using a private standard of creditworthiness in financial regulation is attractive. Using ratings creates flexible rules that automatically adjust to different levels of risk: rules referring to ratings impose lower regulatory requirements if the rating signals a low level of credit risk, and vice versa. This flexibility is not just a matter of optional fine tuning—presumably with the goal of lowering the burden for investors—it is essential to avoid regulatory failure. A good example of the effects of inflexible regulation is the aforementioned capital adequacy rule of the Basel Banking Committee. By requiring expensive capital reserves for traditional lending activities, but not for the more recent activities off of the balance sheets, the regulation creates an incentive for banks to shift their business from the former to the latter. Banks have increasingly taken advantage of this possibility for regulatory arbitrage and by that have actually increased the riskiness of their operations (Basel Committee 1999, 26). In order to avoid such perverse effects, it is essential that rules be flexible. Using a private standard offers an excellent opportunity for this. Until other modes for this are found, rating agencies will probably be instrumentalized by regulators. However, solving the problem of regulatory inertia in this way has its own problematic consequences: the mandatory use of credit ratings makes them less flexible than they would be if they were only a voluntary market standard. This effect of using ratings in regulation shall be analyzed in the following section.

Compliance without Complaints

The neo-institutionalist theory of standardization on which this investigation is based holds that third-party enforcement can cause an accountability gap whenever voluntary expertise-based standards are converted into coercive rules. So far, I have argued that the private standard of creditworthiness defined by the credit rating agencies has become coercive due to the third-party enforcement of regulation. I now want to show that this has not been accompanied by a corresponding increase in accountability in the credit rating agencies. Although the standard of creditworthiness defined by rating agencies has become more consequential for more and different types of lenders, it has not become easier to challenge the rating agencies' decision. The reason for this is that public enforcement weakens the control exercised by competition in the market for credit risk assessment, but it does not offset this effect by establishing an effective supervisory mechanism. The problematic consequence of this is that lenders and borrowers have to live with the errors of rating agencies, while the rating agencies themselves miss out on information that could improve their performance.

The Accountability Gap

An accountability gap arises whenever there is a breach between the power of a rule maker and the possibility to attribute blame. Does an accountability gap exist with respect to the rating agencies? Certainly rating agencies decline any responsibility for their decisions: they maintain that their information on credit risks cannot preempt financial decision-making but only guide it (McGuire 1991, 83).[4] There are a number of good reasons for this stance. First, investment decisions always have to be related to the entire portfolio. A security with a low credit rating is not necessarily a bad investment, since it promises a higher yield. Second, investment decisions inevitably comprise other risks beyond the mere credit risk measured by the credit rating. Additional risks such as exchange-rate risks with foreign investments or liquidity risks are not included in a rating. For these reasons, rating agencies do not claim that their analysis is exhaustive in any way. To fend off liability claims, every rating and all information published is accompanied by a disclaimer to this effect. So far this has effectively shifted the blame to the user of credit ratings. However, in itself this is not enough to give rise to an accountability gap. In Hirschman's terminology, there are at least two possible ways of reacting to institutional decline: exit and voice. In this case the exit option would mean that lenders and borrowers would rely less on ratings. The other possibility would be to strengthen the voice mechanism, e.g., by establishing a strong supervisory structure or a strong liability regime. Neither of these options has yet been realized.

Limited Competition

Instrumentalizing the rating standard in regulation adversely affects the market mechanism. Since regulation forces investors and, as a consequence, also borrowers to observe credit ratings, there is no possibility to revert to other sources of information on credit risk. Thus, effective market supervision depends on vigorous competition between different rating agencies. However, competition is at best limited. The recent merger of Fitch/IBCA and Duff & Phelps has reduced the number of rating agencies on the global market from four to three. Given that most lenders need two ratings to gain access to capital markets, not much competition remains. Furthermore, market access for newcomers is difficult because of the ratings' positive network externalities.[5] Only a sufficiently large number of ratings allows investors to compare different types of investment opportunities and to rely on the competency of the rating agency. A new rating agency with few published ratings will find it hard to persuade a borrower of its usefulness, and thus to overcome the threshold of small numbers. As we shall see subsequently, the attempt of the U.S. Securities and Exchange Commission to supervise the rating agencies raises these entry barriers even more.

Limited Liability

In theory, liability law could offer a remedy for the limits of market control. However, up until now rating agencies have not been held legally accountable for the consequences of their actions. In the United States, credit rating agencies are protected by "freedom of speech" as enshrined in the First Amendment. From a legal point of view, published rating opinions are no different from newspaper editorials (Husisian 1990, 446-55). They are only liable in case of recklessness, not in case of negligence. The high level of protection this offers is demonstrated by the instances in which investors or borrowers have tried to challenge rating agencies in court (Bottini 1993, 493-95). For example, Orange County, California, has blamed the rating agencies for the unfortunate investment decisions that led to its spectacular financial difficulties (McGraw-Hill 1999). So far no liability suit has been successful. This insulation of the agencies from liability claims is not limited to the United States. In Germany the legal situation (although more uncertain) is similar (Ebenroth and Koos 1996). This points to more systematic reasons for the rather generous liability standards. One of the reasons could be that negligence is difficult to prove and/or that the introduction of the negligence standard could threaten the economic viability of the agencies (Husisian 1990, 434-44).

Limited Supervision

Besides holding rating agencies accountable with a liability law, rating agencies could be held accountable if the public supervision strengthened the voice mechanism. Since 1975 the principal financial market regulator in the United States, the Securities and Exchange Commission (SEC), has been supervising the agencies. However, so far this supervision has not been effective, because it is not truly independent of the market: "The single most important criterion is that the rating organization is nationally recognized, which means the rating organization is recognized in the United States as an issuer of credible and reliable ratings by the predominant users of securities ratings" (Securities and Exchange Commission 1997, 5). It is also unlikely that a presently ongoing reform will lead to real supervision, in spite of calls to this effect from lawyers (Bottini 1993) and even investors (Tyle 1998). On the contrary, the SEC's regulation has not only failed to establish an effective voice mechanism, but it has also weakened competition in the rating market (Molé 1994). Requiring that firms use rating agencies that have its stamp of approval raises the barriers to market access for new rating agencies. It is becoming more difficult to overcome the threshold to respectability because investors may not appeal to the new agencies to satisfy regulatory requirements. And because no investor uses the new agencies, they will not achieve NRSRO status. This is a regulatory catch-22.

Consequences of the Accountability Gap

The accountability gap arising from the unfettered mandatory enforcement of the rating agencies' standard of creditworthiness leads to problematic consequences. The approach chosen here predicts that expertise-based standards discourages "voice" on the part of the users as a reaction to a decline in performance. This is certainly true for rating agencies. In times of normal operation, investors using credit ratings rarely dispute them. Financial analysts or portfolio managers working for investors are indeed sometimes dissatisfied with ratings. For example, in the aftermath of the Asian crisis, the agencies' ratings of the "Asian Tigers" suffered a severe loss of credibility. However, they are more likely to ignore a rating they do not believe than to challenge rating agencies. The reason for this is that no institutionalized feed-back mechanism exists that could connect users and rating agencies. For example, there is no professional association of financial analysts which would serve as a permanent forum for a differentiated exchange of views between rating agencies and their various users (Interview Standard & Poor's, New York, 12 November 1999). The only option available to a dissatisfied investor is to call the responsible rating analyst to discuss a decision he or she believes to be wrong. Investors seem to be rather reluctant to do so (Interview American International Group, Washington, D.C. 10 January 2000). Borrowers, the other group using ratings, will even have a harder time voicing complaints to rating agencies when they feel that their rating does not adequately reflect their creditworthiness. Rating agencies will refuse to listen to them in order to avoid anything that could tarnish their image of neutrality. Furthermore, given the absence of effective supervision and the lenient liability regime, it is hardly surprising that borrowers and investors rarely challenge the rating agencies' work, even when they feel that the analysis was faulty. A weak voice mechanism does not necessarily mean that there is no incentive for correcting low institutional performance. Another highly effective mechanism associated with the market is "exit," i.e., the refusal to buy the products of a firm. However, in the case of the rating agencies' standard of creditworthiness, exit is not an option for users because the use of ratings is mandatory. Institutional investors such as pension funds cannot decide not to consider ratings for a while until they have become more reliable. They can only reduce the reliance on ratings for internal uses. At most one finds "hidden exit." Thus, unfettered mandatory enforcement deprives rating agencies of negative feedback and an external check on declining performance.

Strong negative feedback can only arise under exceptional circumstances. In times of a general crisis, communicating political risks can enhance the power of voice. This has been forcefully underlined in the recent debate on the future international financial architecture. Several international financial institutions have analyzed the role of rating agencies in financial markets and their share of the responsibility in the crisis (OECD, World Bank, IMF). A consensus seems to have emerged that the rating agencies on the whole have high professional standards and have performed no worse than the financial analyst community as a whole (Adams et al. 1999). However, they have not escaped unscathed. In times of crisis, changes of credit ratings seem to have a pro-cyclical effect on the dynamics of financial markets, and they thus aggravate rather than stabilize a crisis (Adams et al. 1999, 186). Furthermore, in times of crisis, control by reputation does not work either: rating agencies can intensify their mutual observations, thus producing similar ratings in order to avoid being the only one wrong (*Economist*, December 13, 1997, 87). Also, the use of ratings in regulation was called into question because of their low reliability in times when regulation is most necessary. Rating agencies have responded both by justifying their practices and publicly revising their rating methodology (Adams et al. 1999, 212; Interview Duff & Phelps, New York, November 10, 1999). If the dynamics of exit and voice presented here is correct, then drawing lessons cooperatively, as was done after the Asian crisis, is the exception, whereas quiet undisturbed operation is the rule. With their sense of the neutrality of expertise, as a rule rating agencies learn alone. The inferior adaptation capacity resulting from this is hardly likely to be adequate in a post-Fordist age characterized by a high rate of change (Piore and Sabel 1984).

In sum, neo-institutionalist organization theory suggests that rating agencies have to be observed with a dose of skepticism because their standard-setting activities largely go unchecked. Thus, the reason to be critical is not because they engage in "ideological uncertainty transformation," which provides legitimacy for organizing the financial world in a way that favors the interests of a capitalist class. It is because rating agencies may not adapt their standard of creditworthiness fast enough to avoid harm to borrowers and lenders. The risk of intermediation associated with the rating agencies makes it possible to appreciate the positive side of their activity. They enable transactions that otherwise would not be possible (and by so doing they may even have welfare enhancing effects). As such, they also merit a certain degree of protection. In the framework of the standardizing approach, the question following from the problematic aspects of rating agencies is: what possibilities are there for remedying the accountability gap? I shall specify this question of "institutional design" in the conclusion.

Conclusion

This chapter has proposed to understand rating agencies as standard setters for creditworthiness in international financial markets. This view is based on a specific concept of "standards" that highlights the normative character of the rating agencies' expertise for credit decision-making. I have argued that these standards are at the heart of a mode of governance that derives its peculiar characteristics from the fact that private nonbinding rules are enforced by government regulation. Given the potential of such a governance mode to enhance the flexibility of regulation, it seems to be an important mode of governance. That makes it even more important to acknowledge its systematic weaknesses, here identified as a systematic deficit in accountability which risks sacrificing the flexibility of the creditworthiness standard and thereby also jeopardizing the intended increase in regulatory flexibility.

The analysis in this chapter is based on the argument that insofar as the material criteria guiding the rating agencies are publicly available, they constitute a standard of creditworthiness. However, this is not to deny any difference between more common forms of standard setting and credit standardizing. Rather, the tension resulting from the comparison points to how this case could contribute to a theory of standardization as a mode of governance. So far, enforcement has only been attributed to third-party enforcement by government regulation. However, this neglects the "first-party enforcement" of the standard of creditworthiness by the rating agencies themselves. The process of assigning a rating can be seen as verifying their standard of creditworthiness. In this sense rating proper is similar to auditing, a form of control adapted to the increasing importance of self-regulation by the market (Power 1997). Thus, the case of credit rating raises the question: how could the theory of governance by standardization profit from the concept of "auditing"?

Another question for further research is the normative question of institutional design. This chapter has pointed to a weakly developed control mechanism for rating agencies—either through state supervision or liability law. What leeway is there for improving mechanisms that hold rating agencies accountable? In answering this question it could be helpful to compare rating agencies with similar intermediary organizations such as accounting firms or to the situation of rating agencies in different countries. The result of such a comparison is that there may simply be little institutional malleability. A comparison with international accountancy firms reveals a difference that could explain the difficulty in developing better mechanisms for holding rating agencies accountable. Whereas the standard of creditworthiness enforced by the rating agencies is drawn up by the very rating agencies themselves, in the field of accountancy these standards are set by independent national and international professional associations. This could be the reason why a well-developed supervisory regime exists in the area of accountancy. These external standards are useful as a supervisory standard because they contain explicit operating rules for the auditing firms (Gaa 1988, 5-7). The rating agency's creditworthiness standards do not contain explicit rules of behavior for credit rating agencies; as the frequent emphasis on the qualitative nature of the rating agencies' work indicates, such rules are tacit knowledge and thus stored away in an organizational black box. For this reason, should there be stronger public supervision of rating agencies, the public supervisors will have to develop their own material rules; and this is an extremely challenging task. A cross-national comparison reveals the difficulty in constructing a liability regime for credit rating agencies. In Germany a semi-public agency can be called upon to check on the creditworthiness of individuals and firms. Unlike the rating agencies, this agency is not exempt from liability. This may well be because, on request, the German credit information agency disseminates information on the past credit record of individuals and organizations, especially in cases of insolvency. Rating agencies' judgments do not refer to the past, but to the future likelihood of a default; and, on the basis of a past credit record, it is much easier to establish whether the information given was correct, and if not, who is to blame. For risk assessments that refer to the future, however, this question is much more difficult to settle (at least according to German civil law; see Lemke 2000, 32-33). Of course, no exhaustive list of speculative remarks on theoretical and institutional issues has been offered here. Those issues discussed here have been presented to outline the type of questions that are raised for future research once credit rating agencies are conceived of as standard setters.

Notes

For helpful comments on a first draft of this chapter, I would like to thank Adrienne Héritier, and the participants of the workshops "Common Goods and Governance across Multiple Arenas" at the Max Planck Project Group in Bonn and "Politik und Recht unter den Bedingungen der Globalisierung und Dezentralisierung" at the Max Planck Institute in Cologne. The chapter profited from presentations at the 12th Annual Meeting of the Society for the Advancement of Socio-Economics and at the meeting of the German Political Science Association (DVPW) in Halle/Saale. I conducted the empirical research during my stay at the German-American Center for Visiting Scholars in Washington, D.C. from October 1999 until January 2000. I would like to thank the center and especially Esther Holtermann for generous support. Conversations with other visiting scholars were highly stimulating, especially with Jens Beckert. Experts of the U.S. financial service industry and financial regulators contributed their time generously in spite of very busy work days. Also, I would like to thank Susanne Lütz, Tim Sinclair, and Torsten Strulik, who welcomed me on their turf with extensive written comments on the first version of this chapter. Darrell Arnold carefully revised my writing—except for this sentence. Remaining errors of fact or interpretation are my own.

1. The organizational features of rating agencies seem to be quite similar to the nonhierarchical "network organizations" found in investment banking (see Eccles and Crane 1988).

2. For a more recent example of firms violating the rating agency's standard of creditworthiness, see the decision by the European Telecom firms to invest heavily in the new UTMS licenses, despite the fact that this reduced their credit rating (*Financial Times*, 3 November 2000, 27).

3. I would like to thank Susanne Lütz for pointing this out to me.

4. Rating-agency analysts who I have spoken to have frequently stressed this point in personal conversations.

5. These arise when a good is more useful to a user if others use it, too. A good example is the telephone, which is useless for a single user and becomes increasingly attractive with the number of persons that can be reached (Furubotn and Richter 2000, 290).

References

Adams, C., D. J. Mathieson, and G. Schinasi. 1999. *International Capital Makets: Developments, Prospects, and Key Policy Issues*. Washington, D.C.: International Monetary Fund.

Basel Committee on Banking Supervision. 1999. *A New Capital Adequacy Framework*. Basel: Bank for International Settlements.

Behrenwaldt, U. 1996. Funktionen des Ratings für Anleger. In *Handbuch Rating*, ed. H. E. Büschgen and O. Everling, 291-304. Wiesbaden: Gabler.

Bottini, F. A. 1993. An Examination of the Current Status of Rating Agencies and Proposals for Limited Oversight of Such Agencies. *San Diego Law Review* 30 (3): 579-620.

Brunsson, N. 1989. *The Organization of Hypocrisy: Talk, Decisions, and Actions in Organizations*. Chichester: Wiley.

———. 1999. Standardization as Organization. In *Organizing Political Institutions: Essays for Johan P. Olsen*, ed. M. Egeberg and P. Laegreid, 109-28. Oslo: Scandinavian University Press.

———. 2000. Organizations, Markets, and Standardization. In *A World of Standards*, ed. N. Brunsson and B. Jacobsson, 21-39. Oxford: Oxford University Press.

Brunsson, N., and J. P. Olsen. 1998. Organization Theory: Thirty Years of Dismantling, and then . . . ? In *Organizing Organizations*, ed. N. Brunsson and J. P. Olsen, 13-43. Bergen: Fagbokforlaget.

Cantor, R., and F. Packer. 1994. The Credit Rating Industry: *Federal Reserve Bank of New York Quarterly Review* 19: 1-26.

Cerny, P. G. 1994. The Dynamics of Financial Globalization: Technology, Market Structure, and Policy Response. *Policy Sciences* 27: 319-42.

———. 1997. Paradoxes of the Competition State: The Dynamics of Political Globalization. *Government and Opposition* 32 (2): 251-74.

Coleman, W. C. 1996. *Financial Services, Globalization, and Domestic Policy Change: A Comparison of North America and the European Union*. Houndmills: Macmillan.

314 Dieter Kerwer

Cutler, A. C., V. Haufler, and T. Porter. 1999. Private Authority and International Affairs. In *Private Authority and International Affairs*, ed. A. C. Cutler, V. Haufler, and T. Porter, 3-28. Albany: State University of New York Press.

Dale, R. 1996. *Risk and Regulation in Global Securities Markets*. Chichester: Wiley.

Ebenroth, C., and S. Koos. 1996. Juristische Aspekte des Rating. In *Handbuch Rating*, ed. H. E. Büschgen and O. Everling, 483-519. Wiesbaden: Gabler.

Eccles, R. G., and D. B. Crane. 1988. *Doing Deals: Investment Banks at Work*. Boston: Harvard Business School Press.

Estebanez, G. 1999. Sovereign Nations. In *Global Credit Analysis*, ed. D. Stimpson, 157-68. New York: Moody's Investors Service.

Estrella, A. et al. 2000. Credit Ratings and Complementary Sources of Credit Quality Information. Basel Committee on Banking Supervision Working Papers no. 3.

Furubotn, E. G., and R. Richter. 2000. *Institutions and Economic Theory: The Contribution of the New Institutional Economics*. Ann Arbor: University of Michigan Press.

Gaa, J. C. 1988. *Methodological Foundations of Standard Setting for Corporate Financial Reporting*. n.d. American Accounting Association.

Gordon, S. 1991. Introduction to Moody's Rating System. In *Global Credit Analysis*, ed. D. Stimpson, 103-53. New York: Moody's Investors Service.

Habermas, J. 1981. *Theorie des kommunikativen Handelns*. Frankfurt am Main: Suhrkamp.

Held, D., A. McGrew, D. Goldblatt, and J. Perraton. 1999. *Global Transformations: Politics, Economics, and Culture*. Cambridge: Polity.

Helleiner, E. 1994. *States and the Reemergence of Global Finance. From Bretton Woods to the 1990s*. Ithaca, N.Y.: Cornell University Press.

Hirsch, U. 1996. Rating is objektiv subjektiv. In *Handbuch Rating*, ed. H. E. Büschgen and O. Everling, 657-72. Wiesbaden: Gabler.

Hirschman, A. O. 1970. *Exit, Voice, and Loyalty*. Cambridge, Mass.: Harvard University Press.

Husisian, G. 1990. What Standard of Care Should Govern the World's Shortest Editorials? An Analysis of Bond Rating Agency Liability. *Cornell Law Review* 75 (2): 411-61.

Jacobsson, B. 2000. Standardization and Expert Knowledge. In *A World of Standards*, ed. N. Brunsson and B. Jacobsson, 40-49. Oxford: Oxford University Press.

Kapstein, E. B. 1994. *Governing the Global Economy: International Finance and the State*. Cambridge, Mass.: Harvard University Press.

Kieser, A., G. Spindler, and P. Walgenbach. Recht und Organisationsnormung. Manuscript on file with the author.

Kindleberger, C., and P. Manias. 1996. *Panics and Crashes: A History of Financial Crisis*. New York: Wiley.

Lemke, R. 2000. *Haftungsrechtliche Fragen des Ratingwesens—ein Regulierungsproblem?* Frankfurt am Main: Lang.

Lütz, S. 1998. The Revival of the Nation-State? Stock Exchange Regulation in an Era of Globalized Financial Markets. *Journal of European Public Policy* 5 (1): 153-68.

Mann, R. J. 1999. Verification Institutions in Financing Transactions. *Georgetown Law Journal* 87 (7): 2225-72.

McGraw-Hill Companies, Inc. 10-K Report (March 26, 1999). Washington, D.C.: Securities and Exchange Commission.

McGuire, T. 1991. Introduction to Moody's Rating System. In *Global Credit Analysis*, ed. David Stimpson, 71-100. New York: Moody's Investors Service.

McKenzie, R. B., and D. R. Lee. 1991. *Quicksilver Capital: How the Rapid Movement of Wealth Has Changed the World*. New York: Free Press.

Molé, M. C. 1994. Concept Release Regarding Nationally Recognized Statistical Rating Organizations [letter submitted by Moody's Investors Service, Inc. in response to the request, as set forth in Release No. 33-7085 of the Securities and Exchange Commission]. New York: Moody's Investors Service.

Piore, M. J., and C. F. Sabel. 1984. *The Second Industrial Divide: Possibilities for Prosperity.* New York: Basic Books.

Porter, T. 1993. *States, Markets, and Regimes in Global Finance.* New York: St. Martin's.

Power, M. 1997. *The Audit Society: Rituals of Verification.* Oxford: Oxford University Press.

Raimbourg, P. 1990. *Les Agences de Rating.* Paris: Economica.

Randow, P. von. 1996. Rating und Regulierung. In *Handbuch Rating*, ed. H. E. Büschgen and O. Everling, 543-76. Wiesbaden: Gabler.

Schmidt, M. 1996. Zweck, Ziel und Ablauf des Ratings aus Emittentensicht. In *Handbuch Rating*, ed. H. E. Büschgen and O. Everling, 253-71. Wiesbaden: Gabler.

Schnabel, H. 1996. Die Funktionen des Rating für deutsche Industrieunternehmen und Emittenten. In *Handbuch Rating*, ed. H. E. Büschgen and O. Everling, 305-25. Wiesbaden: Gabler.

Securities and Exchange Commission. 1997. Capital Requirements for Brokers or Dealers under the Securities Exchange Act of 1934. Release No. 34-39457. Washington, D.C. <http://www.sec.gov/rules/proposed/34-39457.txt> (30 November 1999).

Sinclair, T. J. 1994. Between State and Market: Hegemony and Institutions of Collective Action under Conditions of International Capital Mobility. *Policy Sciences* 27 (4): 447-66.

―――. 1999. Bond-Rating Agencies and Coordination in the Global Political Economy. In *Private Authority and International Affairs*, ed. A. C. Cutler, V. Haufler, and T. Porter, 153-68. Albany: State University Press of New York.

―――. 2000. Reinventing Authority: Embedded Knowledge Networks and the New Global Finance. *Environment and Planning C: Government and Policy* 18: 487-502.

Steil, B., ed. 1994. *International Financial Market Regulation.* Chichester: Wiley.

Steiner, M., and V. G. Heinke. 1996. Rating aus Sicht der modernen Finanzierungstheorie. In *Handbuch Rating*, ed. H. E. Büschgen and O. Everling, 579-628. Wiesbaden: Gabler.

Strulik, T. 2000. Funktionen und Folgen privater Rating-Agenturen im Kontext der Regulierung globaler Finanzmärkte. *Soziale Welt* 51 (4): 443-62.

ten Brink, M. 1996. Ratingverfahren aus der Sicht der beurteilten Bank. In *Handbuch Rating*, ed. H. E. Büschgen and O. Everling, 273-87. Wiesbaden: Gabler.

Tyle, C. S. 1998. Proposed Definition of Nationally Recognized Statistical Rating Organization [letter to the Securities and Exchange Commission of March 2, 1998]. Washington, D.C.: Investment Company Institute.

Vogel, D. 1995. *Trading Up: Consumer and Environmental Regulation in a Global Economy.* Cambridge, Mass.: Harvard University Press.

Vogel, S. K. 1997. International Games with National Rules: How Regulation Shapes Competition in "Global" Markets. *Journal of Public Policy* 17 (2): 169-93.

14

Rating Agencies and Systemic Risk: Paradoxes of Governance

Torsten Strulik

Introduction

A close connection between the development of mixed public-private regulatory regimes and the limitations confronted by nation-states is discernible. Especially in the course of the ongoing integration of global financial markets, new modes of governance are characterized by the increasing involvement of private actors. Rating agencies are one significant example of private organizations which coordinate the decision-making of economic actors and contribute to the self-regulation of the financial system. The two market leaders, Standard & Poor's and Moody's, encompass more than 4,500 societies and bodies in more than forty nations. Their judgments are at the basis of liabilities at a value of over two billion U.S. dollars. Due to the fact that ratings are largely accepted in the market place and have proven to be reliable, they are also used for regulating financial markets and institutions (e.g., Cantor and Packer 1994). Rating agencies thus not only appear to contribute to the self-regulation of the global financial economy; beyond that, they also seem to expand the range of regulatory arrangements. As private authorities, they come into play where it is clear that public actors are not able to prepare the appropriate regulatory framework by themselves.

In considering the increasing involvement of private actors in governance and questions concerning the implications of these new modes of governance for the production of common goods (see Héritier's introduction in this volume), this chapter aims to analyze the consequences of instrumentalizing private ratings for regulatory purposes. The relevance of such a task is particularly underlined by the most recent developments in the area of banking regulation. Thus, according to the recommendations of the Basel Committee on Banking Supervision from June 1999, it is planned that the minimum capital requirements for bank credit be coupled with the borrower's credit standing (Basel Committee on Banking Supervision 1999, 26ff.). In other words, the greater the solvency of a borrower, the less capital the loan-offering bank has to set aside as "risk pad-

317

ding." Presently the main basis for the corresponding calculations are external credit-standing notes from the market-leading U.S. rating agencies, Standard & Poor's and Moody's. The idea behind the Committee's suggestion is that ratings are considerably better suited to determine both credit risks and the bank's risk situation. The expressed goal is to reduce the systemic risk of the global financial markets, i.e., the probability that the difficulties of an individual institution will affect the functional ability of the entire system.

Starting out with these expectations, there are questions concerning how well suited "regulation through rating" is to bring about the intended regulatory effects. For a detailed analysis, it is advisable to consider both the manifest and latent functions of rating agencies. For this purpose, it should be considered that the agencies do more than merely contribute to coordinating finance-market actors. From the perspective of the sociology of risk it will become clear that while the rating agencies are fulfilling their manifest functions, they also bring about new burdens of uncertainty. Precisely in increasing the capacity for complexity of a self-referentially operating financial economy, they follow the logic of a functionally differentiated society which concentrates on increasing options, and they thereby contribute to further forcing the intransparency of the financial markets. One can thus observe a paradox which has consequences for the problem-solving capacity of this new mode of governance: by producing "certainty equivalents" (Luhmann 1989, 54f.) rating agencies contribute both to absorbing and to (re)producing uncertainty.

In this chapter it is thus suggested that rating agencies are characterized by the *productive use of uncertainty*. The business of rating agencies consists in producing stable expectations, which serve to limit contingencies. On this basis it is possible for the actors in the global financial markets to make decisions, even when faced with unknown results. Besides that, the agencies' assessments and their use of these for regulatory purposes presupposes functions which are necessarily latent. These latent functions or "blind spots" not only lead to non-intended effects, but they are also a presupposition of the always risky absorption of uncertainty inherent to self-referential social systems (Luhmann 1984, 456ff.; Japp 1997a). Paradoxically, while using ratings for regulatory purposes aims to strategically and instrumentally produce security, it will inevitably contribute to expanding the potentials for uncertainty.

In order to develop this thesis, first the context which explains the increasing significance of ratings will be illustrated. To do this it will be helpful to explicate the current uncertainties under which the market agents and regulatory institutions of the global financial system are operating (section 2). In identifying their manifest and latent functions, it ought to be shown that rating agencies are able to be described as knowledge-based organizations which, on the basis of "authoritative expertise," reflexively take up these burdens of uncertainty, productively process them, and thereby inevitably produce results that lead to strains on themselves and on the environment (section 3). After that it will be demonstrated that, given the widespread acceptance and the recognized efficiency of ratings, private agencies seem to be attractive partners in a mixed private-public regime of banking regulation. As mentioned above, in the future, banks are to appeal to the assessments of rating agencies in calculating the regulatory required capital reserve. It is to be shown, on the one hand, that this form of "regulation through rating" increases the ability of the regulatory regime to process problems, but, on the other, inevitably entails problematic consequences (section 4). A short summary will recapitulate the findings (section 5).

The Intransparency of Global Financial Markets

Rating agencies are concerned with the risks of the financial economy. The increased importance of such risks can be appreciated if their functions are analyzed in the context of the global networking of financial transactions. It is significant that the increasing intransparency of the markets clearly shows itself in reference to the management of credit risks, those risks which rating agencies have traditionally concentrated on. According to definition, they are concerned with the possibility that a debtor does not meet his payment obligations at the agreed time point and/or that he does not pay enough. The growing importance of credit risks and the corresponding rating agency assessments can essentially be clarified in reference to two closely connected developmental lines: securitization and disintermediation. A substantial trigger for the securitization trend was the debt crisis in 1982 (Eichengreen and Lindert 1989). Because the credit standing of numerous third-world debtors had drastically decreased and many credit commitments were questionable, internationally operating banks increasingly began to give loans in the form of bonded claims or to accept bonded loans. Whereas there had been fixed obligation for bank loans, there was now a greater flexibility because of the negotiability of obligations. Loan holders and investors were able to fit transactions to individual circumstances and to liquidate capital more quickly. In this way the risks were able to be shared, and it was possible to expand the access to credit. Very clearly, this structural transformation in the banking sector reflects the increasing significance of the securities trade, which builds the basis for the global transaction of innovative and complex financial products. While the net amount of the securities issued in 1987 was at around 100 billion U.S. dollars, in 1999 it was at about 1,225 billion U.S. dollars (BIS 1995; 2000).

As a consequence of this development, which was reinforced by the increasing competitive pressure in the area of financial services and the investors' growing expectations for profit, it can be seen that a more direct relationship between the investors and the debtors is emerging. Banks are indeed still participating in this kind of business, but they have shifted their activity to organizing bonds and distributing securities. This process of disintermediation offers the investors an opportunity not available to them through their relationship with their house banks. At the same time, for the enterprises that are searching for capital there are new opportunities to gain financing directly through the capital markets, and thus to obtain more favorable conditions than they could get with a conventional loan from one of the house banks. While in the traditional credit operation, the banks largely carried the risk that a debtor would default on his payment obligation or not pay in full, and the investor could rely to a certain extent on the correct behavior of his bank and on the fact that they would be monitored by the supervisory board, the investor must now make a judgment for himself about the probability that a debtor will default on his payments.

The rating agencies come into play here. They react to the demand for the assessments of credit standing, and with their analysis they make corresponding judgments possible. On the basis of specialized and largely standardized procedures, they observe the markets and offer a context in which actors who are investing or seeking capital can orientate themselves. They transform the complexity of the financial markets into a form of expertise, which enables the participants in financial transactions to make productive use of the existing intransparency. The rating agencies do not only contribute to absorbing economic uncertainties, but they also create a stable basis from which risks can be approached and proportionate profits can be aimed at.

As the self-descriptions of agencies imply, rating is concerned with preparing risk analysis that offers information about the credit standing of certain financial-market actors or products. Among the objects suitable for assessments are companies, states, communities, or specific securities (Standard & Poor's 2000). In his work, Timothy Sinclair (1994; 1995; 1999; 2000) has impressively portrayed how the agencies perform in the context of the "new global finance." Here it is important to note that the rating agencies have emerged as specialized and global-oriented organizations that aim to interpret information relevant for determining credit standings. Their evolutionary advantage is recognizable in light of the interests of investors and borrowers. In providing capital, the latter essentially follow three goals: (1) securing unlimited access to national and global financial markets; (2) minimizing the costs of capital; and (3) maintaining financial security, judged on the basis of liquidity and the capital structure. A borrower's ability to realize these goals depends on his solvency or the appraisal of his solvency. The investor's interests counter those of the borrower. The investor's goal is to attain the highest possible return given the existing risk. Before he decides to invest, an investor must thus decide whether the profits he aims at are proportionate to the presumed risk. For this, he needs detailed information about the probability that the respective debtor will be unable to make his payments (Perridon and Steiner 1993, 8).

Against this background it is clear that the rating agencies position themselves as "financial consultants" between these two parties. From an economic point of view, they contribute to improving the transparency and the information efficiency of the markets. Their service seems to consist in observing markets on the basis of specialized and largely standardized processes, gathering information, and preparing risk assessments for investors. With quantitative and qualitative evaluatory processes and with the use of specific symbols, they offer communicative simplifications which help to make the intransparency of the markets manageable. From a sociological perspective, however, this evaluatory activity does not contribute to "solving" the existing information and knowledge problems. The rating agencies are not able to grasp the real complexity of their environment and produce "certain" knowledge. In spite of all the attempts to gain knowledge, every analysis leaves something unknown, a "blind spot," which will be reproduced in each further observation. However, with their assessments they transform an indeterminate complexity into a determinate "useful" one and enable the market actors to make "rational" decisions. In a functionally differentiated society designed to increase options, ratings are thus to be understood as effective instruments that react to the increasingly important requirement: the "control of intransparency" (Luhmann 1997a). At the same time, in respect to the consequences of ratings, it is important that—through their highly efficient activity of transformation—the agencies contribute to expanding contingency. The future is no longer indeterminable merely because it is dependent upon many unknown and known factors, but also because it is circularly connected with the decision-making context and thus dependent upon the assessments arrived at by the agencies—just take a look at the consequences of the agencies' downgradings of Indonesia, Korea, Malaysia, and Thailand during the Asian crisis, for example.

The Dynamics of Uncertainty Absorption and Risk Production

It is significant that one of the perceptible effects of the rating agencies' operations is that they contribute to deconstructing and constructing economic realities. On the one hand, the agencies attempt to look behind the complex scenes that are carefully erected by the businesses that are to be evaluated, for instance, the investor relation strategies and glossy business reports. On the other hand, in making certainty equivalents available through their analysis and the use of letter symbols, they create "facts" which are of great value in providing orientation to many market actors. Like school grades, which regulate access to career opportunities, ratings function as keys for opening future options. Without a rating or with a poor rating it is hardly possible for a capital-seeking company to gain access to the refinancing possibilities of the global financial economy. The agencies' importance and the fact that they are accepted as "private authorities" (Cutler, Haufler, and Porter 1999; see also Kerwer in this volume) is thus apparently based on the productive power with which non-knowledge is transformed into a form of expertise that makes it possible to use the intransparency of the markets economically. Accordingly, rating agencies do more than merely absorb uncertainty; they also take up the indeterminateness of the market, interpret it, and transform it into productive expectations, on the basis of which the market actors can "solve" decision-making problems and take profitable risks.

Following this consideration, the manifest functions of rating agencies can be further understood in respect to the production of stable expectations, and as a form of the operative use of the difference between unspecified and specified non-knowledge (Luhmann 1995, 151ff.; Japp 1997). While, on the one hand, unspecified non-knowledge appears to be an insolvable information problem (unlimited contingency), on the other hand, specified non-knowledge is a solvable information problem (limited contingency). On the basis of this difference it is clear that ratings serve to transfer indeterminate contingencies into structured (manageable) complexity. With their assessments of the probability of payment default, the agencies qualify the principal indeterminateness of the investment business. With their rating classification, which translates the result of the rating process into a letter combination (e.g., AAA or BB) (for extensive information see Standard & Poor's 2000), they make information available, which can be easily understood (and interpreted), and on the basis of which useful assumptions of risk can be made. In light of the uncertain future, the appeal to ratings makes it possible for financial actors (1) to decide with confidence, (2) to ground their decisions "rationally," and (3) to put themselves into a position to sufficiently deal with their risks in case of negative consequences.

It is clear that in specifying the factual, social, and temporal expectations, rating agencies contribute to dealing with the contingencies of the financial markets in a structured manner. And while they do not possess the ability to see into the future, they have developed techniques which—in a "destruction of the temporality of the future" (Kaufmann 1973, 16ff.) or "defuturization" (Luhmann 1990, 133)—serve to bridge the gap between present and future. On the basis of quantitative and qualitative analysis, they postulate and anticipate causal and statistical connections between future events in order to incorporate them into the present. From an economic point of view, it is clear that this activity of rating agencies is primarily valued because—in reference to the permanently increasing complexity and contingency of the financial markets—it not only makes risks calculable, but it also reacts to the possibility that favorable options will be closed if a decision is *not* made. The demand for corresponding mechanisms that make it possible to transform risks into opportunities further increases when there is economic competition and pressure to make profitable decisions.

If the mechanism of uncertainty absorption is viewed as aiming to temporarily integrate the certain past with the uncertain future, then, paradoxically, the rating agencies are seen simultaneously to contribute to new contingencies. On the one hand, their assessments and letter symbols serve to stabilize expectations. On the other hand, the interpretations they produce line up next to other interpretations, thus confronting the market actors with problems of choice and consequently with decision risk. Dirk Baecker portrays this with a view to the price formation on the stock exchange (Baecker 1999, 298): here every bit of information not only gives rise to more certainty, but also to more uncertainty—for instance, about how the price of stock will develop. For besides substantiating expectations, every bit of information also supports the possibility of counter developments, and thus creates uncertainty. For the rating agencies, changes in the environment are not the only reason that future events are becoming more difficult to predict. In addition, for example, every fine tuning of their analysis techniques also increases the number of disputable assumptions about future developments.

This notorious connection between uncertainty absorption and risk production is able to be explained if rating agencies are understood as self-referentially operating organizations (Luhmann 2000) whose continually risky decision-making simultaneously presupposes latent functions. Because it is risky for agencies to make profitable contributions to regulating the economy (with its central risk consisting in not reestablishing solvency), uncertain self-determinations are to be made. And these self-determinations, which are necessary in order for the agencies to make decisions, are accompanied by unobserved effects. So latency is not only demonstrated by the non-intentionality of the consequences of decisions, but it is also demonstrated by the fact that decisions are secured through functions which are not communicated and in this sense remain latent and protect the specific selections of a social system (Luhmann 1984, 456ff.; Japp 1997a). On the basis of these considerations, it is already clear that the world of financial markets cannot even be a possible object of knowledge for rating agencies. Their activities continually presuppose something ignored, which prevents holistic knowledge. From a theoretical perspective this matter can be explained if formal organizations are conceived of as social systems of great complexity. Given that the unlimited horizon of possibilities makes it impossible to produce perfect order in a system (on the basis of time limitations alone), complexity implies an obligation to relate the elements to one another selectively, and thus with risk. The pressure to select is not only due to the problem of system complexity, but it is also due to the relationship between the system and the environment. The grade of complexity between the system and the environment also forces appropriate selective mechanisms, because not everything from the environment can be relevant (Luhmann 1984, 46ff.). Against this theoretical background, ratings could be best understood as a way to reduce complexity. Even with the help of elaborated analytical techniques, rating agencies just produce risky organizational constructions, which are not able to reflect the real complexity of global financial affairs.

This examination of non-knowledge and of the connection between non-knowledge and risk is also relevant to the ways in which knowledge-based organizations operate. That an organization is knowledge based means that the activities of that organization are carried out on the basis of relevant knowledge which (1) is continually revised, (2) is always seen as able to be improved upon, (3) in principle is not viewed as truth, but as a context-dependent, productive resource, and (4) is inseparable from non-knowledge, such that it is connected with specific risks (Willke 1998, 21). If rating agencies are defined as knowledge-based organizations in this sense, then it is obvious that they burden themselves and their environment with new and different insecurities. This view is supported by the events occurring in the wake of the latest Asian crisis. Here it is extremely clear that rating agencies do not bring everything into view and that their judgments can lead to substantial problems. Moody's, one of the two market leaders, first added Thailand to what is known as the "watch list" in February 1997, long after the exchange rate of the Baht had already collapsed. And the agencies still considered South Korea's debt to be secure in October 1997. The depreciation of creditworthiness that followed the rating reassessments led to massive strains on the affected stock exchanges and to widespread consequences, which had effects far beyond the national economies of the region. At the same time, the reputation of the rating agencies was considerably damaged. They were criticized for having slept through the financial crisis and plainly and simply for having failed as financial consultants (Burgmaier and Reimer 1998, 56).

Despite such events, it can hardly be disputed that the leading rating agencies have a great deal of authority, in the sense that they are able to coordinate the actions and activities of the market actors. However, the basis of their key position and their authority is not clear. What is clear is that, given the developments in global financial affairs, investors, private customers, and even large institutional investors are increasingly finding it impossible to carry out the necessary credit analysis on borrowers by themselves. The emergence of a global financial system is being accompanied by decision-making problems which are due to a lack of information about the local conditions of the borrower (e.g., the legal system, the accounting) and which are made more dynamic by the new kinds of securities and financing instruments that are continually arising. In this context, unspecified non-knowledge is increasingly important in many areas: for example, in reference to the intransparency of the markets, to irresolvable information problems, and to the delimitation of contingencies. However, in order to be able to make acceptable decisions, the actors need reference points which they can use to calculate the consequences of their actions. As already shown with regard to the manifest functions of rating agencies, in specifying non-knowledge the rating agencies react precisely to this demand. In preparing a rating, or calculating the probability that a debtor will default, the agencies contribute to solving decision-making problems by specifying non-knowledge and thereby limiting contingencies.

An analysis of the procedures of rating agencies shows that sophisticated methods of assessment are employed to specify non-knowledge. In producing a rating a "top-down approach" is used, in which first the country risk, then the branch risk, and finally the specific company risk is considered. While considering the country risk, the agency analyzes the danger of political or economic instability in the country in which a debtor is based; the emphasis in evaluating the branch risk is on the future prospects for the industrial branch as well as the state of competition; finally, in establishing the company risk, the business risk (e.g., the quality of the management, the applied technology) and the financial risk (e.g., the financing policies, the capital structure) are measured on the basis of quantitative and qualitative methods (Steiner 1992, 511ff.). In the intensive analysis line, the rating agencies then express their opinion of the credit risk connected with the rating object with symbols. Standard & Poor's rating scaling differentiates between thirteen levels in all, beginning with "AAA," which indicates that the ability of a debtor to meet his financial obligation is exceptionally good, to "SD" (Selective Default). This latter signifies that the debtor has defaulted on one or more debts, but at the same time duly met other debts or obligations.

The preceding theoretical considerations already illustrate that even with the most complex analysis procedures, rating agencies only specify non-knowledge; they are not able to generate "certain" knowledge. However, the trust in the corresponding symbols spares one the search for further information, and allows sound assumptions of risk. In assessing the solvency of a debtor, rating agencies supply probabilities which can be understood as representations of complexity and used to make decisions under conditions of uncertainty. Ratings serve to generate trust in the system and help to make complex decision-making situations manageable (Luhmann 1989, 23). At the same time, the authority of rating agencies appears to be derived from the knowledge-based generation of certainty equivalents. Authority can be understood as representing complexity that is not spelled out in detail (Luhmann 1989, 57). The trusting agent—that is, in the present case the market participant, especially the investor—makes concession in advance: he trustingly utilizes information generated by others, in this case the rating agencies. Remarkably, the certainty factor, or the authority of suitable ratings, does not merely appear to be determined by the trust in the expertise and the agencies' construction of reality alone; beyond that, it obviously relies on the reflexive "trust in the trust" that others will use the assessments of the rating agencies for orientation in the same way. Authoritative expertise thus designates a specific phenomenon: on the basis of a reflexive trust in their knowledge-based observations, rating agencies exercise influence on the decisions of economic actors. As "intermediaries in trust" (Coleman 1982, 287f.), they make "profitable" information available, which possesses such a high value for guiding action that the market actors will regard it as especially relevant.

It is possible to understand the authoritative expertise's "indirect" power to exercise influence if the economy is seen as a system which is set up on the basis of payments, which are its final, non-dissolvable elements (Luhmann 1988, 13ff.). From this point of view, the economy is not merely an aggregate of actors or actions, but a communication system which consists of payments that lack a temporal duration. Given the problem of generally reproducing these payments, the economic system must continually provide for new payments if it is not to cease to exist. It thus requires concrete motivation, which is insured by internally determining payment operations. And ratings seem to be suited precisely for this. In supplying information about the money payments that are to be expected and thus contributing to forming prices, ratings solidify the operations of the economic system. They not only regulate payments that ensue, but also the payments which do not ensue. Additionally, on the basis of ratings, the economic system can draw up self-descriptions, on the basis of which it specifies that and how it will react to itself with its self-produced sensibilities. Ratings can be described as important mechanisms for the self-regulation of the economy. The authority which rating agencies require for this obviously results from their cognitive orientation and their productive intercourse with non-knowledge. Rating agencies do not simply adjust to changed environments and contribute to limiting contingencies; they also use the existent uncertainty in decision-making and construct viable, practicable economic realities.

Instrumentalizing Ratings for Regulatory Purposes

In the face of the manifest functions of the authoritative expertise described above, it is hardly surprising that rating agencies are viewed as "private regulating instruments" (Sassen 1998, 350), as "private makers of global public policy" (see Sinclair in this volume), or as "private standard setters" (see Kerwer in this volume), which make an important contribution to the self-regulation of the global financial economy. Beyond that, their assessments have long been used for regulatory purposes, above all in the United States of America. There, rating-related specifications of considerable scope have existed since the thirties of the last century. They aim, for instance, at determining the appropriate capital reserves to be demanded of banks or at limiting the spectrum of investment. It is not possible to describe the presently existing forms of "regulation through rating" in detail here (see Cantor and Packer 1994). For the given formulation of the question, the matter discussed at the outset is important: namely, a paper published by the Basel Committee on Banking Supervision. That discussion paper, published in June 1999, deals in detail with banks' capital adequacy. In view of the obviously increased systemic risk, one of the primary goals of the Committee has been to improve the assessment of credit risks as well as to guarantee solid "risk padding," which the individual bank can use to cushion the possible loss in credit operations. Therefore it is proposed that the banks be able to use external credit assessments for determining their required capital resources. The solvency notes of the market-leading rating agencies should serve as a basis for this (Basel Committee on Banking Supervision 1999, 26ff.). In order to understand the range of this new approach to banking supervision, it seems appropriate to more precisely examine the regulatory regime, which is characterized as a public-private mix. What do the current initiatives in the area of banking regulation aim at, and what problems turn up again in the further development of the existing approaches?

A short review of the development of the Basel Accord in 1988 will make it easier to answer both questions. It is important that the accord represents the first standardized and internationally recognized approach in banking supervision (for details see Strulik 2000, 215ff.). Those earlier efforts of the national legislature and supervisory boards were advanced after the outbreak of the debt crisis in 1982. This crisis not only drew attention to the precarious relationship between the industrial nations and the developing countries, but above all also to the need for banks to keep a sufficient capital reserve, which would enable them to compensate for possible defaults. The results of a working group showed that, despite the increasing risks connected with both the access to new markets and the development of innovative financing instruments, the amount of the capital resources of the banks diminished. This was the context in which the Basel Committee strove to spread an understanding of the standardized formula for measuring and securing bank operations. After long and hard negotiations (for details see Genschel and Plümper 1996), an international supervisory-legal approach was finally agreed upon, the essence of which was that the banks were to secure their credit risks in the suitable amounts through their own capital so that, should a crisis occur, they would be robust enough to support the trust of investors. Referring to this, the members of the Committee agreed to a rate of at least 8 percent of the risk assets. In addition, they agreed to a formula for categorizing the risks and for weighting them in percentage points; they also agreed to groups of components of the capital resource that could be used to pad risks (Basel Committee on Banking Supervision 1988).

And it is precisely this agreement that is to be revised in the future. For despite the structural transformation of financial operations, which is demonstrated—not the least of all—in the importance of innovative products (Strulik 2000), the traditional credit risks are still the most common cause of existence-threatening difficulties for banks and entire banking systems. As the most recent banking and financial crises in Japan and Korea illustrate, the intensifying competition between the banks and the corresponding sinking margins leads both to an increasing willingness to take risks in credit transactions and to a neglect of the complex and thus costly processes of risk supervision. In order to counter these problems as well as the possible eruption of crises and to limit the public costs of corresponding attempts to bail the banks out, the current recommendations of the Basel Committee aim at limiting the systemic risk. In consideration of the conceivable effects of a corresponding chain reaction, the goal of the supervisory board consists in immunizing the global financial system from the breakdown of individual financial institutions. For this purpose, in the future, credit risks should be more precisely recorded, and the banking regulations for capital resources ought to be improved. In this respect "Basel II" indeed requires a capital risk cushion of at least 8 percent for credit operations. However, in contrast to the previous arrangement, the capital resource charge for loans is no longer supposed to be calculated on the basis of four standard classes (0 percent for claims on countries of the OECD, 20 percent for claims on banks, 50 percent on securities, and 100 percent for claims on corporates); instead, it is to be calculated with more differentiation—corresponding to the specific borrower's solvency (Basel Committee on Banking Supervision 1999).

The Basel Committee (Basel Committee 1999, 26ff.) thus suggests that external ratings be used in the future to calculate the banks' capital reserve. It considers the methods of analysis and the judgments of agencies to be exemplary for recording credit risks. The recourse to rating is supposed to take into account the demand that banks "more realistically" manage their risks. If, for example, an external credit rating of a company is particularly strong (e.g., at least AA- in accordance with Standard & Poor's gradation), allowance is no longer to be made for the full amount (100 percent) of the loan. Banks are then only liable for 20 percent of the loan amount, and they must put aside the corresponding capital reserves. If the solvency is worse, however (e.g., under a B- in accordance with Standard & Poor's gradation), then the loan should show in the books at 150 percent (Basel Committee 1999, 26ff.). At the same time, this larger range of risk classification is accompanied by a dynamic adaptation of risk assessments, which did not previously exist. Because rating agencies regularly scrutinize their judgments and revise them if necessary, it seems certain that the planned approach will make it possible to more quickly record, evaluate, and supervise risks. The recommendations of the Committee fit closely with theoretical approaches that emphasize the necessity for "reflexive" or "procedural" forms of regulation and the need to improve the synchronization of the different time horizons of the legal system and the economy (e.g., Teubner and Willke 1984; Hiller 1993; Ladeur 1995).

In view of this new orientation in the area of banking regulation, it is clear that the initiative of the Basel Committee aims to counter the increasingly dynamic complexity and intransparency of banking operations with a suitably built governance structure. By integrating private rating agencies into the process of regulation, the regulatory regime has attempted to adjust to the growing credit risks. A form of "regulation through rating"—as a public-private mixed institutional arrangement—ought to contribute to limiting systemic risk. The public actors' reliance on the self-regulating potential of the economy is clearly accompanied by an increase in reflexivity or self-sensibility. The banking supervisors appear to recognize that the previous regulatory approach, which was both coarse and static, was not able to cope with the growing demands to manage risks in the area of banking regulation; indeed, it was not even capable of generating stable expectations, as is necessary if markets are to operate efficiently. Given these facts, one chance for dynamic and process-related regulation is available through recourse to the cognitive orientation of agencies—that is, an orientation showing the readiness and willingness to learn. It appears quite clear that, in considering private ratings, public actors have recourse to a form of "organizational intelligence" (Willke 1996, 396), which is to some extent compatible with their own observations and goals. They increasingly rely on the self-regulation or the "self-coercion" of the economy in order to limit the costs resulting from the self-dynamic and riskiness of financial markets which are not able to be controlled externally.

On the one hand, this supervisory-legal use of ratings suggests that there is an improved fit between the organized complexity of the regulatory regime described and the complexity of its environment; yet, on the other hand, against the background of the preceding theoretical considerations about the manifest and latent functions of authoritative expertise, it can be expected that new insecurities will emerge as the Basel recommendations are realized. What—quite concretely—might these consist in? It is possible that the recommendations of the Basel Committee in fact aim at decreasing the systemic risk, but that in pursuing this goal they paradoxically contribute to further increasing the risk. Above, we have already intimated that rating agencies function as "gate keepers" for the global financial markets in which a development occurs in the form of "regulation through rating" being sought, which essentially quickens market integration and burdens the national financial arenas with an extreme pressure to adapt.

Corresponding problems arising as a consequence are able to be clarified if rating agencies are viewed as influential actors on a "deep infrastructure of contemporary commercial life" (Sinclair 2000, 489) through which certain social interests are channeled. In this way, the large agencies do not merely appear to be the product of the Anglo-Saxon model of a market- and globally oriented form of capitalism, in which the stock exchange represents the dominant financial source for companies in search of capital; they are also seen as the motor of this form of capitalism. With a view to this issue and to the *Finanzplatz Deutschland*, numerous observers point out that the instrumentalization of rating has sped up the propagation of the Anglo-Saxon model and possibly led to a disadvantage for the Continental European "house-banking-system," which is marked by a close connection between the companies and the banks. As a consequence of the implementation of the Basel proposals, in particular it is expected that small- and middle-sized credit institutes—whose customers normally do not have a rating, or at best have a low one—will fall behind in the competition with large banks, because they will have to lay comparatively more costly capital resources aside. As a whole, this could contribute to further aggravating the currently ongoing process of concentration in the banking system, and in so doing it could simultaneously increase the systemic risk. It is thus presumed that, in comparison to a more decentralized and diversified banking system structure, the difficulties of large banks will spread to other market participants much more quickly. Besides that, some observers wonder what effects there will be when banks presume that they have reached the status of being "too big to fail" and in a sense of "moral hazard" take exaggerated risks with the expectation that the public will step in if there are difficulties in making payments (Interview 11 January 2000, Deutsche Sparkassen- und Giroverband, Bonn; Interview 26 November 1999, Landesbank Hessen-Thüringen, Frankfurt am Main).

A closer look at the Basel proposals shows that such considerations are not unfounded, and that by coercing the concentration processes in the banking system, regulation through rating can paradoxically lead to an increase in systemic risk. As already mentioned, the risk cushion that the banks have to set aside for every loan ought to be identified with considerably more refinement. For this reason, among others, it is planned that claims on corporates no longer be flatly fixed at 100 percent and cushioned with 8 percent capital resources; instead, they will be weighted according to the solvency of the borrowing corporation (see table 14.1).

Concretely: If a company's rating turns out to be very good (e.g., AAA), the loan will no longer be considered for the full amount (100 percent). Banks then will only have to guarantee 20 percent of the loan amount with capital resources. If the solvency is poor, by contrast, the loan is to be weighted at 150 percent. In the first case, as a rule it would primarily be the highly rated "global players" who would benefit. For them, the share for which the banks would be liable would shrink from 8 percent to 1.6 percent (8 percent capital-resource coefficient x 20 percent risk weight). As a consequence, the interest rates on loans would decrease for many large corporations. However, for companies receiving a poorer assessment, or those without a rating, the banks would have to set aside more capital resources. For one thing, that could lead to an increase in financing costs, especially for small- and middle-sized companies, because the banks would attempt to shift the costs arising from the regulation to the customers.

Table 14.1. Minimum Capital Requirements for Claims on Corporates.

Ratings	Bank Supervisory Weight for Claims on Corporates (in %)	
e.g., Standard & Poor's	Basel Accord 1988	Proposals from June 1999
AAA, AA+ AA, AA-	100 %	20 %
A+, A, A- BBB+, BBB BBB- BB+ BB BB- B+ B B-		100 %
CCC – C SD		150 %
without a rating		100 %

Source: EuroRatings 2000; prepared by the author.

The second point—and one relevant in view of a possible increase in the systemic risk—is that it is above all middle-sized banks and credit unions, which have traditionally been strongly involved in the credit business with medium-sized companies, which—in comparison to large companies—would have to develop capital resource reserves. For a loan on a middle-sized company, which normally has no credit rating, a bank would have to have five times the capital resources available as would be necessary for a company which had the best rating note, AAA. Beyond that, those banks which themselves have only been given a weak rating would have to adjust to increasing refinancing costs. As a result, there would be increased danger that they would fall behind in competition with large banks and be taken over by them. It thus seems that one can fully expect the proposals of the Basel Committee to contribute to speeding up the concentration process in the banking sector and, paradoxically, to increasing systemic risk to the global financial system.

With a view to the obviously existing problems that accompany the Basel Committee's consideration of ratings, the proposals are already being amended. The hidden motive for this, however, does not seem to be fear about system stability so much as concrete competitive political interests. Given the particularity of the "house-banking-system," the German banks are thus insisting upon giving equal entitlement to the use of "internal ratings." For the German banks, which have traditionally given priority to credit operations, have their own procedures which they use to help assess customers' solvency. However, because these procedures have not been adequately developed in all the banks, the Basel Committee has only planned to take the internal rating of "sophisticated banks" into consideration, and for the time being they have indicated the need for testing (Basel Committee on Banking Supervision 1999, 13). Further, the initiatives of the newly established German rating agencies are being supported by the Deutsche Bundesbank. In view of the relatively low number of company ratings in Germany in comparison to the United States of America, it is hoped that the new agencies will contribute to closing the gap in ratings, and especially improve the latitude for action or for the financing of middle-sized companies; for while around 8,000 companies in the United States of America presently possess a rating, in Germany less than 100 do. Ultimately, proposals are being sought that lead to a refined graduation of risks. With reference to middle-sized banks, the present trend primarily appears to be to provide those companies which have rates between A+ and BBB- with a lower risk load and consequently to increase their ability to compete with the highly rated large companies (EuroRatings 2000, 3). As a whole, the efforts at the national level locally cushion the adaptation pressure created by regulation through rating so that the structures of the German financial system are not overburdened with learning requirements which are too strong.

Conclusion

It can hardly be denied that rating agencies make an important contribution to the self-regulation of the global financial system. That they are organizations specializing in assessing solvency shows that the globally netted and primarily issue-oriented economy also forms globally oriented organizations which—in a reflexive manner—contribute to concentrating economic decisions and also regulate the contingency of corresponding transactions. At the same time, against the background of the findings described here, it is clear that the activities of the agencies and their use for banking supervision can best be understood as management of *and* by complexity (Baecker 1997), accompanied by inevitable new uncertainties. With their assessments, rating agencies do not merely supply simplifications that make financial occurrences clearer; instead, they are themselves part of a network of observations of economic risk, and they contribute to increasing the organized complexity of the economic system. With their authoritative expertise, they make *profitable* information available which is considered relevant by market actors and which those actors use to relate their action and decisions. What is central is that agencies actively grasp the indeterminateness of the markets, interpret it, and transfer it into practicable expectations on the basis of which the market actors can take risks and make appropriate profits. In the production of certainty equivalents, the rating agencies thus do not merely function to absorb uncertainties; at the same time, they contribute to increasing the options for economic transactions, which inevitably gives rise to new burdens of contingency. For regulation through rating, on the one hand, it is important that the instrumentalization of ratings contributes to increasing the internal complexity of the regulatory regime described; on the other, however, it is important that new problems also result from it. As is able to be detected from the Basel proposal, the latent functions of a supervisory-legal appeal to ratings are putting pressure on the German banks to deal with the problems and stimulating them to develop strategies to bring their own procedures into accordance with solvency assessments and to insist upon the equally valid use of their own internal ratings. But this is obviously not a matter of creating "more security," but of reacting to competitive pressure with quite particular, insecure outcomes.

It is significant that, on the one hand, the public-private interplay portrayed here creates new problems which might increase the systemic risk of the global financial system. On the other hand, the new regulatory setting is characterized by a more adequate fit between the regulatory problem and the governance structure. The proposed use of private ratings for regulatory purposes marks not only a change in the form of the state; above all, it indicates the instrumentalization of a more refined and dynamic form of private expertise, which is obviously superior to a public approach alone. So when attempting to determine credit risks as precisely as possible, it makes a considerable difference whether only four categories of borrowers are formed and these are provided with a corresponding solvency weight, as was done according to the Basel Accord of 1998, or whether the judgments of the rating agencies are referred to, which assess their objects on the basis of twenty-two levels of solvency. In being able to quickly register risks, ratings have another advantage: namely, when there is a change in the conditions of solvency, the ratings can be checked and, if necessary, revised. Consequently, it can be presumed that the "public" recourse to ratings actually increases the possibilities for managing risks. These conditions, however, should not be interpreted as generally increasing the level of security of the global financial system. Above all, in light of the highly competitive character of finance operations, it is rather to be expected that regulating through rating not only subjects local structures to the pressure to adapt, but that it generally leads to a higher degree of trust in the system, and in so doing simultaneously increases the tendency to take higher risks. Paradoxically, it is precisely the ability to register risks more exactly and quickly which increases both the scope of possibilities and the readiness for riskier strategies.

On the basis of this appraisal, the concluding question arises: namely, how can the management of *and* by complexity be controlled? If it is presumed that the main problem of our knowledge society consists in the speed at which non-knowledge is progressively (re)produced, then it is a matter of directing more attention to non-knowledge (Willke 2001). And precisely here lies the important and precarious demand to which alternative views of regulation must adapt. The demand is important because only by discussing non-knowledge is the system able to recognize its structural blindnesses, to anticipate the negative repercussions of its manifest functions, and to integrate these into its decision-making calculations if necessary. It is at the same time precarious, because by observing non-knowledge, the trust in the system—which is necessary for decision-making—becomes fragile, and the expectations cease to be stable. Controlling the corresponding processes of change thus seems to be a matter of making a useful interplay between trust in the system and reflection on the results possible. Regarding the most wide-ranging analysis of the way that rating agencies and regulation through rating function, one would thus have to investigate whether and to what extent "functional observational complementarities" (Japp

1996) are able to be identified and developed that not only create trust in the system, as in the case of the relationship of financing and rating agencies, but that also provide for a useful degree of reflection on the consequences.

In this respect, the most recent concentrated initiatives of German banks, associations, and supervisory institutions suggest that the described regulatory regime has institutional equipment available that is pervious for formulating thoughts or articulating consequential scenarios. The currently running consultation process gives the organizations concerned the opportunity to scrutinize the recommendations of the Basel Committee and to develop their own proposals. Along these lines, and driven by the anticipation of competitive disadvantages, the initiatives have led the German actors to unveil the latent functions of the supervisory-legal instrumentalization of ratings, which, as already described, may provide the impetus for a further, more refined approach to managing credit risk. It is thus to be kept in mind that the existing regulatory regime obviously has a cognitive orientation and can reflect on consequences. This allows incongruent, but complementary observational perspectives to be formed and moderated.

From this diagnosis, however, one should not conclude that the risks of the global financial markets can be limited or reduced—as always is (or has to be) pretended, especially by the public actors involved in regulation (e.g., Meister 1999). The case test treated here substantiates the sociological research on risks, which refers to the self-reference of risk (e.g., Baecker 1991; Luhmann 1991; Japp 1996) and the relationship between potentials for shaping society and potentials for uncertainty, which increase reciprocally (e.g., Krohn and Krücken 1993; Bonß 1995; Japp 1996; Nassehi 1997). However, in respect to effective forms of managing risks, it appears possible to establish procedures and institutional arrangements which expand the options of regulation and increase the ability to adapt to emergent conditions of risk. On the basis of a more refined and dynamic institutional arrangement, the planned "regulation through rating" indicates a more adequate fit between the regulatory problem and the governance structures.

Note

This chapter presents preliminary results from the project "Rating agencies as institutions of 'second modernity'?" financed by the Volkswagen Foundation. For helpful comments and stimulating discussions, I would like to thank Stephan Hessler, Dieter Kerwer, Konstanze Piel, Timothy Sinclair, and Helmut Willke.

References

Baecker, D. 1991. *Womit handeln Banken? Eine Untersuchung zur Risikoverarbeitung in der Wirtschaft*. Frankfurt am Main: Suhrkamp.

————. 1997. Einfache Komplexität. In *Komplexität managen. Strategien, Konzepte und Fallbeispiele*, ed. H. W. Ahlemeyer and R. Königswieser, 21-50. Wiesbaden: Gabler.

————. 1999. Die Preisbildung an der Börse. *Soziale Systeme* 5 (2): 287-312.

Basel Committee on Banking Supervision. 1988. *International Convergence of Capital Measurements and Capital Standards*. Basel.

————. 1999. A New Capital Adequacy Framework. Consultative Paper Issued by the Basel Committee on Banking Supervision. <http://www.bis.org> (June 5, 1999).

BIS, Bank for International Settlements. 1995. *65th Annual Report*. Basel.

————. 2000. *70th Annual Report*. Basel.

Bonß, W. 1995. *Vom Risiko. Unsicherheit und Gewißheit in der Moderne*. Hamburg: Hamburger Ed.

Burgmaier, S., and H. Reimer. 1998. Rating-Agenturen schlicht versagt. *Wirtschaftswoche* 52 (7): 56.

Cantor, R., and F. Packer. 1994. The Credit Rating Industry. *Federal Reserve Bank of New York Quarterly Review* 19: 1-26.

Coleman, J. S. 1982. Systems of Trust: A Rough Theoretical Framework. *Angewandte Sozialforschung* 10 (3): 277-99.

Cutler, C. A., V. Haufler, and T. Porter, eds. 1999. *Private Authority and International Affairs*. Albany: State University of New York Press.

Eichengreen, B., and P. H. Lindert, eds. 1989. *The International Debt Crisis in Historical Perspective*. Cambridge, Mass.: MIT Press.

EuroRatings. 2000. *EuroRatings—Europäische Rating-Agentur für den Mittelstand*. Frankfurt am Main.

Genschel, P, and T. Plümper. 1996. Wenn Reden Silber und Handeln Gold ist. Kooperation und Kommunikation in der internationalen Bankenregulierung. *Zeitschrift für Internationale Beziehungen* 3 (2): 225-53.

Helaba (Landesbank Hessen-Thüringen Girozentrale). 1999. Bankenmärkte in Euroland: Stärkere Konzentration—latente Fragilitäten—mehr Regulierung? <http://www.helaba.de> (November 4, 1999).

Hiller, P. 1993. *Der Zeitkonflikt in der Risikogesellschaft. Risiko und Zeitorientierung in rechtsförmigen Verwaltungsentscheidungen*. Berlin: Duncker & Humblot.

Japp, K. P. 1996. *Soziologische Risikotheorie. Funktionale Differenzierung, Politisierung und Reflexion*. Weinheim, München: Juventa.

————. 1997. Die Beobachtung von Nichtwissen. *Soziale Systeme* 3 (2): 289-312.

————. 1997a. Die Ausdifferenzierung regulativer Politik. In *Risiko und Regulierung. Soziologische Beiträge zu Technikkontrolle und präventiver Umweltpolitik*, ed. P. Hiller and G. Krücken, 222-52. Frankfurt am Main: Suhrkamp.

Kaufmann, F.-X. 1973. *Sicherheit als soziologisches und sozialpolitisches Problem. Untersuchung zu einer Wertidee hochdifferenzierter Gesellschaften*. 2d ed. Stuttgart: Enke.

Kerwer, D. 2000. Governance by Standardization: The Case of Credit Rating Agencies. Bonn: Max Planck Project Group. Common Goods: Law, Politics and Economics, unpublished paper.

Krohn, W., and G. Krücken. 1993. Risiko als Konstruktion und Wirklichkeit. Eine Einführung in die sozialwissenschaftliche Risikoforschung. In *Riskante Technologien: Reflexion und Regulation*, ed. W. Krohn and G. Krücken, 9-44. Frankfurt am Main: Suhrkamp.

Ladeur, K.-H. 1995. *Das Umweltrecht der Wissensgesellschaft. Von der Gefahrenabwehr zum Risikomanagement*. Berlin: Duncker & Humblot.

Luhmann, N. 1984. *Soziale Systeme. Grundriß einer allgemeinen Theorie*. Frankfurt am Main: Suhrkamp.

———. 1988. *Die Wirtschaft der Gesellschaft.* Frankfurt am Main: Suhrkamp.
———. 1989. *Vertrauen. Ein Mechanismus zur Reduktion sozialer Komplexität.* 3d ed. Stuttgart: Enke.
———. 1990. Die Zukunft kann nicht beginnen: Temporalstrukturen der Modernen Gesellschaft. In *Vor der Jahrtausendwende: Berichte zur Lage der Zukunft,* ed. P. Sloterdijk, 119-50. Frankfurt am Main: Suhrkamp.
———. 1991. *Soziologie des Risikos.* Berlin: de Gruyter.
———. 1995. *Gesellschaftsstruktur und Semantik. Studien zur Wissenssoziologie der modernen Gesellschaft,* Vol. 4. Frankfurt am Main: Suhrkamp.
———. 1997. *Die Gesellschaft der Gesellschaft.* Frankfurt am Main: Suhrkamp.
———. 1997a. The Control of Intransparency. *Systems Research and Behavioral Science* 14 (6): 359-71.
———. 2000. *Organisation und Entscheidung.* Opladen: Westdeutscher Verlag.
Meister, E. 1999. Neue Finanzarchitektur und Stabilität der Finanzmärkte. *Deutsche Bundesbank, Auszüge aus Presseartikeln.* October 12: 1-5.
Nassehi, A. 1997. Das Problem der Optionssteigerung. Überlegungen zur Risikostruktur der Moderne. *Berliner Journal für Soziologie* 7: 21-36.
Perridon, L., and M. Steiner. 1993. *Finanzwirtschaft der Unternehmung,* 3d ed. München: Vahlen.
Sassen, S. 1998. Zur Einbettung des Globalisierungsprozesses: Der Nationalstaat vor neuen Aufgaben. *Berliner Journal für Soziologie* 8: 345-57.
Sinclair, T. J. 1994. Passing Judgment: Credit Rating Processes as Regulatory Mechanisms of Governance in the Emerging World Order. *Review of International Political Economy* 1: 133-59.
———. 1995. Guarding the Gates of Capital: Credit Rating Processes and the Global Political Economy. Toronto: unpublished doctoral dissertation.
———. 1999. Bond-Rating Agencies and Coordination in the Global Political Economy. In *Private Authority and International Affairs,* ed. C. A. Cutler, V. Haufler, and T. Porter, 153-67. Albany: State University of New York Press.
———. 2000. Reinventing Authority: Embedded Knowledge Networks and the New Global Finance. *Environment and Planning C: Government and Policy* 18: 487-502.
Standard & Poor's. 2000. Ratings Definitions. <http://www.standard-poors.com/ResourceCenter/RatingsDefinitions.html> (May 1).
Steiner, M. 1992. Rating. Risikobeurteilung von Emittenten durch Rating-Agenturen. *Wirtschaftswissenschaftliches Studium* 21 (1): 509-15.
Strulik, T. 2000. *Risikomanagement globaler Finanzmärkte. Herausforderungen und Initiativen im Kontext der Bankenregulierung.* Frankfurt am Main: Campus.
Teubner, G., and H. Willke. 1984. Kontext und Autonomie: Gesellschaftliche Selbststeuerung durch reflexives Recht. *Zeitschrift für Rechtssoziologie* 5: 4-35.
Willke, H. 1996. *Ironie des Staates. Grundriß einer Systemtheorie polyzentrischer Gesellschaft.* Frankfurt am Main: Suhrkamp.
———. 1997. *Supervision des Staates.* Frankfurt am Main: Suhrkamp.
———. 1998. *Systemisches Wissensmanagement.* Stuttgart: Lucius & Lucius.
———. 2001. Die Krisis des Wissens. *Österreichische Zeitschrift für Soziologie 26:* 3-26.

Conclusion

Adrienne Héritier

What answers do the contributions in this volume offer to the central questions raised here: what are common goods and by which institutional means are they provided across arenas? Which role do private actors play in this context? What are the implications for traditional forms of governing within the nation-state? The concept of common goods used in this volume essentially follows the economic definition characterizing collective goods: public goods are defined in terms of accessibility and non-rivalry of consumption, common pool resources accordingly as subject to rival consumption and accessibility, and toll/club goods as subject to rival consumption and restricted accessibility. However, these attributes are not thought to derive exclusively from the physical features of the goods in question; rather, it is assumed that their accessibility may just as well depend on a political decision to safeguard the accessibility of particular goods or services. In accord with this, the contribution of Leonor Moral Soriano, for instance, analyzes the role of the ECJ in defining the extent to which accessibility to universal network services—as a politically defined goal—is compatible with the conflicting politically defined goal of free competition. Here, clearly the mode of the institutional provision of the good and the nature of the good cannot be separated.

All contributors in this volume employ the notion of governance when they talk about modes of providing common goods across arenas. However, the concept of governance is used in two different ways. A wider and more restricted notion of governance comes to bear in this volume and the literature in general. The wider notion, as used by Knill and Lehmkuhl, denotes any type of political steering, including the hierarchical guidance of public bodies with respect to citizens; that is, it includes the classic notion of government. It thus becomes an umbrella concept for any type of political guidance. The narrower notion, as used by Mayntz and myself, defines governance as the use of non-hierarchical forms of political guidance and/or the involvement of private actors in policy formulation. The wider notion, while being useful in bundling different meanings, runs the danger of lacking analytical bite. In the subsequent analytical conclusions, I will therefore focus on the narrower sense of governance.

Notwithstanding this difference in the use of the concept of governance, all the contributions here agree that, while there are a variety of the institutional modes in which common goods are produced and allocated across arenas, an increasing number of modes of political guidance rely on soft modes of steering and the active involvement of private actors in policy formulation; that is, there has been an increase in governance as defined in a stricter sense. This shift is thought to be due to the fact that many problems arising from internationalization increasingly extend across existing political boundaries. This means that traditional national modes of hierarchical steering within nation-states are more difficult to employ and that policy solutions have to be negotiated with other sovereign political actors or relatively independent private actors. In view of this, Christoph Knill and Dirk Lehmkuhl argue that economic and political internationalization has brought about a change: the traditional form of interventionist regulation is increasingly being replaced by regulated self-regulation, private self-regulation, and interfering regulation, as they illustrate in reference to different cases of regulation in information technology communications. In response to problem interdependence with actors who are simultaneously independent, Henry Farrell, in his contribution on the negotiation of an agreement on data protection and privacy between the United States and the EU, shows how an interesting new mode of political steering has been developed by private actors in the United States. This is largely based on the voluntary action of companies that commit themselves to certain quality standards in data collection and transfer so as to inform individuals about data collection practices. They offer them a right to opt out of collection and transfer practices; they offer them protection from misuse, etc. These voluntary practices—to which firms can sign up—are backed up by various enforcement mechanisms; for example, they provide users with the possibility of signing up to third-party dispute-resolution bodies in case of conflict. In the United States signing this commitment is considered a public commitment, and firms failing to abide by such commitments can be penalized. Under certain circumstances the European data protection authorities can still unilaterally suspend the data flow.

This reveals a pattern which seems to be quite typical—as other contributions show as well—namely, that the soft modes of governance are still linked to some form of hierarchy: if they do not work, a decision or sanction can be imposed hierarchically (that is, through a majority decision or through a court ruling). As I show in my analysis, in a deeply institutionalized political context such as the European Union, where there is a political arena for deciding interdependence problems on a majoritarian basis, the soft modes of governance are used to save the political costs of coming to an agreement. Such costs are high among member states in the Council of Ministers. Hence in order to speed up the policy-making process in areas that are particularly resistant to communitization, these new avenues of decision-making are chosen—for example, the open coordination method and voluntary accords. But here too, as is shown in these studies, the link to hierarchy is frequently just around the corner: legislation is envisaged should there be non-agreement or non-compliance; or the soft mode of governance is simply presumed to be the predecessor to legislation. The same features emerge in Claire Cutler's description of the private dispute-settlement authorities in international trade law. The rulings of dispute-settlement authorities are enforced through the offices of public authorities under domestic public law. Still another example is discussed in this volume by Dieter Kerwer, Timothy Sinclair, and Torsten Strulik: they show how public regulatory authorities in the United States seek to use the risk rating activities of companies to intervene in the operations of financial markets. In brief, while there seems to be an increase across political arenas in soft modes of governance in the institutional provision of common goods, all the empirical policy areas in which new modes of governance are employed that have been examined in this volume indicate that these institutional modes of provision are hybrids, still relying on some form of hierarchical support.

The way that institutional solutions are shaped—as Elinor Ostrom and Katharina Holzinger as well as Christoph Knill and Dirk Lehmkuhl argue in their contributions—significantly depends on the problem of interdependence being dealt with. Katharina Holzinger, in her contribution, systematically shows how different cost and benefit structures lead to different strategic constellations, which, in turn, make different opportunities available for institutional solutions to collective-action problems. Mere coordination problems of a "win-win" nature may emerge spontaneously without hierarchical guidance or negotiations among actors with diverse interests. Correspondingly, private authorities of third-party dispute resolutions in international commerce have emerged spontaneously because a mere coordinative problem is at stake. All stand to win from such an institutional solution. A different path to the provision of common goods in a win-win situation is revealed by studying the private rating firms in financial markets, as is shown by Dieter Kerwer, Timothy Sinclair, and Torsten Strulik. Here the institutional provision derives from a positive externality of market operation: the public good produced is a positive external effect of the profit-oriented service production of a private actor.

However, the political costs of bringing a solution about are high in a prisoner's dilemma situation. Negotiations take place among actors—public or private—in which each actor involved has an interest in shirking implementation. This is found in the data protection example discussed in this volume: the United States was free riding on the (European) data protection regulation, and there were no possibilities for governmental sanctioning. In this particular case it was only possible to threaten to impose private sanctions; that is, it was possible to threaten to stop exporting data to the United States. This facilitated the subsequent negotiations. An even more difficult case regarding the political costs of negotiation is presented by the problem of redistribution, where the loss for one involved party constitutes the gain for another. In my chapter it is shown that the European voluntary coordination methods for social policy issues with redistributional implications are difficult to bring about. If redistributional issues are at stake, policy targets can only be very vaguely formulated.

An important point that emerges from the various contributions is that the dynamics of common goods provision across multiple arenas makes a difference —regardless of whether those dynamics are in the vertical or horizontal dimension. Governance across arenas—with governance understood in the narrower sense—logically comes in two different guises: as planned cooperation, or as spontaneous coordination. The first, i.e., cooperation, implies that public and private actors at various levels act together intentionally in order to provide a common good. They depend on each other for their decision-making. If there is no cooperation, i.e., one of the involved actors refuses to agree, the common goods are not provided. The multi-arena aspect makes a difference in policy outcomes because it offers new opportunities for political coalition formation as well as additional arenas where decisions can be made should a previous decision-making process end up in gridlock. Hence, interlinked political arenas engaged in joint decision-making trigger a certain dynamics, which offers domestic actors new political opportunities. As Henry Farrell shows in his chapter, U.S. data protection groups gained more domestic political clout because the EU put the United States under pressure to come up with some data protection regulation. A similar effect is noted by myself: I argue that the soft modes of policy-making at the European level may help some national actors overcome domestic policy-making gridlocks, such as in domestic pension reform.

In the second case, i.e., of spontaneous coordination, actors at various horizontal levels act independently from each other in providing common goods. There is no intentional cooperation or communication. Indeed, actors not only act independently from each other, but they may even compete with each other in providing solutions for common goods provision. The existence of a plurality of institutional solutions or multiple arenas has important consequences: one institutional form may be substituted for another in the process of regulatory competition. The competing solutions mean that—under specific conditions, such as when the good is portable—the consumers have more choice in a multiple/competing authority setting. In accord with this, Claire Cutler points out that multiple forms of private law for regulating international commercial conflicts presently compete with each other.

While the role of private actors in providing common goods is at the center of many of the contributions in this volume, the functions those actors have in securing a particular type of good vary extensively. Elinor Ostrom argues that, in the implementation of collective action solutions, it is by no means sufficient to crudely distinguish between public and private actors. Rather, to understand the complicated division and intertwining of activities between public and private actors in the production of a common good and to understand how the benefits of a common good are produced and allocated, a refined notion of property rights is needed. Property rights, defined as "actions that individuals can take in relation to other individuals regarding some 'thing'"(Ostrom, 39), may be differentiated as entitling "access to a thing," "withdrawal from a thing," "management of a thing," "exclusion of others from a thing," and "the alienation (right to sell) of a thing." Private and public actors may hold property rights in any of these different ways, and these ways of holding property rights may be linked in a large variety of ways. Accordingly, the privatization of the network industries in different countries, as analyzed in the articles of Dominik Böllhoff and Leonor Moral Soriano, reveals very different ways of distributing different property rights between public and private actors. So, for example, in the case of German railways, public actors still have the right to "alienate" the network and rolling stock while management rights are in the hands of private actors. Or: the right to exclude access to the energy network is defined by public actors in Britain, while it is negotiated among private actors in Germany.

Finally, several important consequences of cross-boundary governance and their impact on the operation of nation-states in the provision of common goods are pointed out in the various contributions. An increase in the use of new modes of governance, which relies on the incorporation of private actors and the use of soft modes of steering, has made an impact on the functioning of the nation-state. At a structural level, the nation-state has probably not lost its functions, but in the wake of the increasing cross-boundary negotiations, it is assuming different functions. As has been pointed out, this is reflected in the fact that the new soft modes of governance are frequently hybrids, in which public actors to some degree still hierarchically steer the activities of private actors. Hence, an increase in the activities of private actors is not necessarily linked to diminished activity on the part of public actors. Rather, as Knill and Lehmkuhl emphasize in their chapter, we are faced with a synergetic relationship, with public and private activities reinforcing each other. And at the level of European legislative implementation, as the contribution of Tanja Börzel argues, member state governments remain of great importance. Moreover, as Guy Peters indicates in his analysis of the outsourcing of public services to private actors, they mutually change each other. The private providers tend to adjust their services to the conditions of public funding.

While most contributions in this volume contend, and indeed show, that public actors will continue to bear weight under conditions in which common goods are provided by private institutions that hold particular property rights, Tim Sinclair and Claire Cutler clearly disagree with this view and point to an increasing imbalance in policy formation to the detriment of public actors and the favor of private actors (rating agencies—Sinclair; the modern law merchant—Cutler). They critically point to the implications of the new modes of governance for democratic accountability: a shift in rendering accountability can be noticed, if not a dwindling of accountability. This holds for the new modes of governance at the European level: there the European Parliament does not play a role (my chapter in this volume). It is even much more pronounced in the case of the regulatory function of rating agencies. Dieter Kerwer clearly shows that by rating creditworthiness these agencies assume a standard setting function, essentially offering a regulatory decision. But they do so without taking on responsibility for the consequences of this decision. In general, the creation of new regulatory structures in the privatized sectors, as described by Dominik Böllhoff, has far-reaching implications for governing. The new regulatory structures lead to a fragmentation of political decision-making, impingement upon coherent political leadership and, indeed, impingement upon the democratic legitimation of political decisions in the polity as such.

The new modes of governance are the only viable forms of governance across boundaries in situations in which other autonomous public and private actors are involved, and they are expected to guarantee substantively efficient policy outcomes. With respect to their distributional impacts, as Cutler and Sinclair argue, they favor the haves over the have-nots. However, other accounts in this volume indicate that there are also countervailing powers. Leonor Moral Soriano shows that public authorities monitor private actors who have been empowered by the introduction of market mechanisms. In the privatized network industries the distributional impacts of liberalization are contained by the rulings of the European Court of Justice. In view of the tension between free competition and public interest services, the Court has upheld the discretionary powers of member states to grant special or exclusive rights to undertakings that provide common goods.

Index

Information Center (EPIC)
ERT case, 219
ETUC. *See* European Trade Union
   Confederation (ETUC)
European Court of Justice (ECJ): and
   Commission, 221–22; and
   liberalization, 341–42; messages
   on Article 86(2), 223–26; and
   public mission exception, 207–31
European Parliament, 186; and data
   protection, 113–14, 121–22
European Trade Union Confederation
   (ETUC), 197
European Union: political issues
   within, 113–14; and privacy
   problems, 109–12, 121–22; ratings
   standard in, 305; Safe Harbor
   discussions with United States,
   105–26
exclusion: and collective-action
   problems, 30–31; as property
   right, 39; resource attributes and,
   48–50
exclusive public goods, 31. *See also*
   common pool resources
exclusive rights: versus abuse of
   dominant position, 214–15;
   compatibility with EC law, 211–
   17; and competition rules, 212–14;
   and free trade, 216–17
exit: and Internet privacy problems,
   107; and rating standards, 310

Farrell, Henry, 105–26
Fear outcome, 34
Federal Cartel Office, 246
Federal Ministry of Economics
   (BMWi), 245–46, 250–51
Federal Rail Authority (EBA), 245–46
Federal Trade Commission (FTC), 108
financial crises: 1907, 281; 1982, 319;
   Asian, 309, 323, 327
financial services. *See* rating agencies
fishing rights, 49
Fitch Ratings, 282, 286
flexible accumulation, 142
Flynn, L., 225
forerunner, Britain as, 247–50
Fortin, Yvonne, 263
France v Commission, 211
free riding, 62, 107

free trade: versus exclusive rights, 216–
   17; production standards and, 74;
   product standards and, 73–74, 73*t*
FTC. *See* Federal Trade Commission
   (FTC)

Gardner, A., 213
Gas and Electricity Monopolies cases,
   213, 216–17, 221–23, 227
GB-INNO v ATAB, 211, 225
General Agreement on Tariffs and
   Trade (GATT), 142
General Agreement on Trade in
   Services (GATS), 116
genetic structures, 23; scope of, 23–24
Germany: banking system in, 329–30;
   models of utility regulation in,
   245–47; telecommunications
   regulation in, 236, 247, 250–53;
   urban melioration program in, 24–
   25
Gill, Stephen, 137
global finance: intransparency of, 319–
   21; rating agencies and, 279–91
global governance, 21; definition of,
   128–29; privatization of, 127–57,
   288
globalization: and common goods
   problems, 105; and governance,
   85–104
goal attainment, 18
goods: attributes of, and provision, 62;
   classification of, 29–30, 30*f;*
   properties of, 59
Gordon, Scott, 34
governance: broad versus narrow
   concepts of, 3, 21, 86, 337;
   common goods and, 15–27; and
   communal property-rights
   systems, 45, 50; as coping
   structure, 25; globalization and,
   85–104; rating agencies and, 293–
   315, 317–35; without government,
   90. *See also* new governance
governance capacity, factors affecting,
   86–92
government, definition of, 3
Greed outcome, 34
Green Party, Germany, 251
group characteristics: and common
   goods provision, 62–63; and

About the Contributors

Dominik Böllhoff is a junior researcher at the Max Planck Project Group "Common Goods: Law, Politics and Economics" in Bonn. He received master's degrees in public policy and management at the Universities of Potsdam and Liverpool. His current work for a Ph.D. is on comparative administrative research on telecommunications regulation in Britain and Germany.

Tanja A. Börzel is a senior researcher at the Max Planck Project Group "Common Goods: Law, Politics and Economics" in Bonn. Her teaching and research interests include comparative politics with a specialization on Europe, comparative federalism, and the implementation of European policies. Her current research project is on member state compliance with Community Law.

A. Claire Cutler is an associate professor of international law and relations in the political science department at the University of Victoria, Victoria, British Columbia, Canada, where she teaches international law and organization and international relations theory. Her publications focus on private authority and international affairs.

Henry Farrell is a senior researcher at the Max Planck Project Group "Common Goods: Law, Politics and Economics" in Bonn. His current research examines the Safe Harbor arrangement reached between the EU and the United States in the field of data privacy as an example of new "hybrid" forms of governance in the international arena.

Adrienne Héritier is a professor of political science and codirector of the Max Planck Project Group "Common Goods: Law, Politics and Economics" in Bonn. Her research focuses on policy research, European policy-making, and the comparative analysis of member state policy-making under the impact of European policies.

Katharina Holzinger is a senior researcher at the Max Planck Project Group "Common Goods: Law, Politics and Economics" in Bonn. Her main research interests include rational choice theory, political decision-making procedures, the European Union and multilevel governance, environmental policy, and global financial markets.

Dieter Kerwer is a senior researcher at the Max Planck Project Group "Common Goods: Law, Politics and Economics" in Bonn and a former researcher at the European University Institute in Florence. His current interests include governance and organization theory, European integration, and financial markets.

Christoph Knill is professor of political science at the University of Jena, Germany. His research interests include governance in multilevel systems, European integration, comparative politics and public administration, and environmental policy-making and implementation.

Dirk Lehmkuhl is a senior researcher at the Max Planck Project Group "Common Goods: Law, Politics and Economics" in Bonn. His work concentrates on governance in a multilevel system and public and private adjudication.

Renate Mayntz is professor of sociology and founding director of the Max Planck Institute for the Study of Societies, which she directed together with Fritz W. Scharpf until her retirement from this position in 1997. She continues to work at the institute. Major fields of interest include governance, research and technology, and the methodology of macro-social analysis.

Leonor Moral Soriano holds a Ph.D. from the European University Institute, Florence. She was awarded an EU Marie Curie Postdoctoral Fellowship to undertake research at the Center for Law and Society, University of Edinburgh. Currently she is senior researcher at the Max Planck Project Group "Common Goods: Law, Politics and Economics" in Bonn, and lecturer in public law at the University of Granada. She has extensively published in the areas of judicial reasoning, especially on the legal reasoning of the European Court of Justice, competition law and public services, and environmental protection.

Elinor Ostrom is Arthur F. Bentley Professor of Political Science and co-director of the Workshop in Political Theory and Policy Analysis and the Center for the Study of Institutions, Population, and Environmental Change (CIPEC), Indiana University, Bloomington.

B. Guy Peters is Maurice Falk Professor of American Government at the University of Pittsburgh and Honorary Professor at the City University of Hong Kong. He has published extensively in the areas of comparative public administration and comparative public policy.

Timothy J. Sinclair is visiting scholar at the Weatherhead Center for International Affairs, Harvard University (2001-2002), and lecturer in international political economy at the University of Warwick in England. His research focuses on global governance theory and international capital mobility. Timothy Sinclair is currently completing a book on bond rating and the global economy.

Torsten Strulik is research associate at the University of Bielefeld, Faculty of Sociology. After receiving his diploma in economics at the University of Applied Sciences in Mönchengladbach in 1989, he worked as a marketing assistant in the fields of financial services and consumer goods. From 1993 to 1997, he studied sociology in Düsseldorf and Bielefeld. In 1999, he received his doctorate in social sciences at the University of Bielefeld. His current research focuses on the regulation of financial markets and the Internet.